The Sworn Book of Honorius
Liber Iuratus Honorii

The Sworn Book of Honorius

Liber Iuratus Honorii

by

Honorius of Thebes

With Text, Translation, and Commentary by

Joseph Peterson

Original Sourcebook of Medieval Magic

Ibis Press
Lake Worth, FL

Permission is hereby granted to make one handwritten copy for personal use, provided the master bind his executors by a strong oath (*juramentum*) to bury it with him in his grave. Beyond this, whoever copies this sacred text without permission from the editor will be damned.

Published in 2016 by Ibis Press
A division of Nicolas-Hays, Inc.
P. O. Box 540206
Lake Worth, FL 33454-0206
www.ibispress.net

Distributed to the trade by
Red Wheel/Weiser, LLC
65 Parker St. • Ste. 7
Newburyport, MA 01950
www.redwheelweiser.com

Copyright © 2016 by Joseph H. Peterson

All rights reserved. No part of this publication may be reproduced or transmitted in any form or by any means, electronic or mechanical, including photocopying, recording, or by any information storage and retrieval system, without permission in writing from Nicolas-Hays, Inc. Reviewers may quote brief passages.

ISBN 978-0-89254-215-4
EBOOK ISBN 978-0-89254-630-5

Library of Congress Cataloging-in-Publication Data
Available upon request

Book design and production by STUDIO 31
www.studio31.com

Printed in the United States of America
[MV]

Table of Contents

Introduction	7
Abbreviations	45
Text and Translation	47
Prologue	49
The oath	51
Book I. Preparing the seal of God, and the Divine vision	53
Composition of the Seal of God	65
Beatific vision	77
First purification	127
Second purification	173
Placating the Divine Majesty	175
Separation	177
Names of the living God	181
Completion of the work	183
Book II. Angels	197
Natures and offices of planetary angels	199
Construction of the circle and rituals for invoking and binding them	207
Book III. Spirits of the air	223
Nature of spirits of the air	227
Manner of working with them	239
Raising up the winds and constructing the circle	245
Preparation and raising up the spirits	259
Seals and bonds	269
Placating the spirits	273
Book IV. Spirits of the Earth	277
Manner of working with them	279
Calling them forth	281

BOOK V. General exposition	283
Consecration of the ink	287
Details on the masses	291
Beginning of undertaking the work	295
Instructions for making the magic whistle	297
APPENDIX I. Corrections and Addenda to Hedegård 2002	303
APPENDIX II. Variants of some of the figures	304
Bibliography	306
Index of Spirit names	313
Index of Divine names	321
General Index	324

Introduction

EUROPEAN HISTORY IS PEPPERED with accounts of a mysterious book of magic called the *Sworn Book of Honorius*. It was so-called because its owners were sworn to secrecy by one of the most severe oaths ever recorded. They evidently took the oath quite seriously, for only a few manuscripts are known to survive, and only one is complete. Its actual contents have remained almost completely unknown, and no complete translation has been published until the present.

It is not surprising then that scholars and historians have only recently started to recognize its exceptional importance. In fact it is now recognized as one of the oldest and most important texts of Medieval magic. The text teaches a highly religious magic, or magic religion, but acutely at odds with the established church authorities. Religious historian Claire Fanger called it a "key text, in the sense that it stands at a crossroads for many areas and disciplines."[1] Robert Mathiesen notes that it provides important evidence for the flow of esoteric teachings between through Europe, and between Christian, Jewish, and Arab communities.[2] University of Hertfordshire historian Owen Davis lists it as one of the "top ten grimoires," stating the writings of Honorius were "second only to those of Solomon in notoriety in the medieval period."[3]

Although little known today, this text must have been widely known in Medieval times and beyond. References to it appear in notices and legal proceedings throughout the period. Jean-Patrice Boudet provides details of the major references, which I will only list:

- –(circa 1230) Possible mention by William of Auvergne condemning the text;
- –(circa 1347) clear description in a trial record of Olivier Pépin from Mende France;

---

1 Fanger 2006 p. 180.
2 Mathiesen 1998 p. 143.
3 *The Guardian*, April 8, 2009, http://www.theguardian.com/books/2009/apr/08/history, retrieved Sep 12, 2015. Skemer 2006 p. 118 also describes it as "one of the leading texts of ritual and ceremonial magic."

- –(late 14th century) inventory of the library of the Augustinian friars of York;
- –(1376) a reference in Eymerich's *Directorium inquisitorum*;
- –(1389) possible mention by Mézières in his *Dream of the Old Pilgrim*;
- –(1398) various condemnations by the Faculty of Theology of the University of Paris likely referred to the text;
- –(1397) reference by John Gower in *Confessio Amantis*;
- –(1400) Jean d'Astarac possessing a copy of *Liber sacratus*, which seems very likely that of Honorius;
- –(circa 1494) the colophon in Italian magic manuscript Florence, Laurent., Plut. 89 sup. 38;
- –(1518) Trithemius references the magic of Honorius of Thebes in *Polygraphia*;
- –(1582) references in the secret writings of John Dee;
- –(1583–1585) possible allusion by Giordano Bruno in his *Cabala of Pegasus*.[4]

To this can be added

- –(1623) a condemned sorcerer, Jean Michel Menuisier used a book titled *Philippus Attinius onorius*, likely *Liber Iuratus Honorii* to judge by the details of its contents.[5]

In spite of its importance, these references reveal almost nothing of its actual contents. Better known than the text is the Sigil or Seal of God – a central component of Honorius's magic. It was apparently part of "a magical tradition that must have spread from the Mediterranean region across Europe."[6] Besides examples on metal, it can be found in manuscripts and at least one printed edition of the *Key of Solomon*. The later examples exhibit consider-

---

4 Jean-Patrice Boudet 2002 p. 853-855, 869–870. On the Pepin case, see also Bulman 2005 p. 4 ff. For details on Jean d'Astarac, see Jan Veenstra 1998 p. 84. For details of the library of the Augustinian friars of York, see Klaassen 1998 p. 29, and more detail in Klaassen 2013, pp. 69, 73, and 76. For Plut. 89 sup. 38 (Firenze, Biblioteca Medicea Laurenziana), see also Véronèse 2012, p. 98. Most of these notices were also given by Mathiesen 1998 p. 158.
5 Davies 2009 pp. 64–65.
6 Chardonnens and Veenstra 2014 p. 130.

Seal of God from La Véritable Magie Noire *(1750) p. 69.*

able divergence from the earliest ones, and its barely recognizable state in *La Véritable Magie Noire* (1750)[7] testifies to a long and elaborate transmission.

The title *"Sworn book of Honorius"* came to be adopted in English literature based on the catalog entry for the 16th century English translation in London, brought to a wider audience's attention by influential occultist A. E. Waite (1898).[8] Waite judged the text important, but "unaccountably overlooked by writers on ceremonial magic."[9] Ironically, he himself didn't go into details on the contents of the text, only describing the prologue, which gives the text's own account of its origin. Waite was aware of two manuscripts, only one of which he identified—Sloane 313 in the British Library.

---

7 "Iroé-Grego" 1750
8 British Library Royal MS 17 A XLII (on which see below). The catalog entry actually reads "THE SWORNE BOOKE of Honoryus," even though the manuscript itself uses the spelling "Honorius."
9 Waite 1911 p. 20. He mentions it again in his translation of Levi's *History of Magic*, 1913.

The great pioneer on the history of magic, Lynn Thorndike, refers to the text as *Liber Sacratus* in his 1923–1958 monumental survey of magic literature. He translated the entire prologue, and went on to briefly survey the contents of the text, identifying five manuscripts.[10]

Butler mentions it only briefly in her 1949 *Ritual Magic*, apparently based solely on Waite's references. Shah also mentions it in his 1956 *Oriental Magic*, but again showed no knowledge of its actual contents, almost certainly having seen the references only in Waite's books.

Intrigued by these references, I took a summer in the Seventies to examine the manuscripts firsthand, and order microfilms for further study. It proved to be every bit as fascinating as hoped. The other purpose of my visit was to study the manuscripts and magic artifacts of Elizabethan polymath John Dee, and I was surprised to discover his connection to the *Sworn Book* (on which see below).

In 1977, Daniel Driscoll published a hybrid version of the text, based on the two manuscripts described by Waite. This was limited to only 450 signed and hand-numbered copies, beautifully printed in red, blue, and black ink. Although it was missing much of the text found in other manuscripts, it provided a fuller account of the contents than Waite and Thorndike, and has come to be a valuable collectible.[11]

In spite of the taboo, the *Sworn Book* was one of the first texts I published on the Internet in 1998, on what was later to become esotericarchives.com.[12] That version was based largely on the English manuscript, Royal 17 A XLII, which omits much of the later material, but it finally made the bulk of the text accessible to a wider audience.[13]

Since then, scholarly interest has exploded. Recent detailed studies have been published by Mathiesen, Kieckhefer, Klaassen, Boudet, Jan Veenstra, Mesler, and Chardonnens, as well as abundant references in literature.[14] A critical edition of the Latin text was published by Göste Hedegård in 2002,

---

10 Thorndike 1923, p. 284.
11 Driscoll's audience was contemporary magicians. His text was uncritical, with much tampering and insertions to best serve that intended audience. In spite of this, it is still relatively unnoticed by modern practitioners.
12 It was in fact only the second text on the website, after Bruno's *Umbris Idearum*.
13 As an example, a copy of my text was printed and displayed at the Museum of Witchcraft in Boscastle, UK.
14 See references.

and another critical edition of much of the text was published by Boudet in the same year. An alternate version of the text has recently been recognized from extensive passages in Berengar Ganell's *Summa Sacre Magice*, virtually revolutionizing our understanding of this text.[15] In particular, some of Ganell's Honorius material appears to be older than that of the better-known northern European manuscripts. For more on this topic, see below.

Title

The title in the Latin manuscripts is variously given as *Liber sacer sive iuratus* ("the Sacred or Sworn Book" I.18), *Liber Sacer* ("the Sacred Book", CIII.1), and *"liber sacer vel liber angelorum vel liber iuratus ... quem fecit Honorius, magister Thebarum"* ("the Sacred Book, or the Book of the Angels, or the Sworn Book, which was made by Honorius, the master of Thebes," CXLI.1).

The title *Liber sacratus* ("consecrated book"), in the possible references by William of Auverne, is not actually found in the text, although the word *sacratus* is used descriptively in chapter I.19, saying it is called *"Sacred*, as it acts through the sacred, or because sacred things emerge from it, or because it is *consecrated* through the angels, and because the angel Hocrohel called it *consecrated before the Lord*." Note too that Ganell does in fact refer to it as *Liber Sacratus*.[16]

Date

Hedegård has established a date of between 1100-1350 A.D. for the text. Varying attempts have been made to narrow it further. In 1998, Mathiesen proposed a date of the first half of the 13th century, while Kieckhefer proposed a date a century later.[17] The main argument for the earlier date is that the brief references to a *Liber Sacratus* by William of Auvergne (circa 1230) are temptingly close to our text. On the other hand, he may be referring to some other magic text.

---

15 Gilly, 2002. Damaris Gehr produced a critical edition for her Doctoral Thesis, and a forthcoming edition is in press.
16 L.1.f.23.
17 Matheisen 1998 pp. 145–147; Kieckhefer 1998 pp. 253–254; Hedegård 2002 pp. 11–12.

Thorndike favored the earlier date on the basis of William's statements. Lawrence-Mathers and Escobar-Vargas also favor the identification of William's text with the *Sworn Book*.[18]

The main argument for the latter date is the observation that the prologue most likely refers to the actions of John XXII, pope from 1316-1334, to persecute heretics. In fact the wording in the prologue comes very close to some of his sermons. Both Kieckhefer and Hedegård thus favor the early 14th century. Of course the persecution passage could be a later insertion, as we now know the text has been redacted. It could also refer to another, less notorious papal action. This view is supported by the fact that this persecution/origin myth is missing from Ganell's text, as noted by Veenstra.[19]

The possibility that these were later insertions also fits nicely with a theory raised by Boudet, that an earlier version circulated in the time of William, and was known as *Liber Sacratus*. This would also explain the use of the title *Liber Sacratus* by Ganell, and not by the northern manuscripts. It would also explain the absence of persecution statements in the *Summa Sacre Magice*. Let me point out that there is also a logical inconsistency in the persecution story, which a late insertion might explain: If the magic was revealed to Honorius by the angel Hocroel, there would be no reason to assemble experts from all over to preserve their traditions from such Church actions.

Another problem with the fourteenth century date, is that the oldest manuscript, Sloane 3854, dates to then. This would not allow much time to develop such a complicated manuscript tradition and stemma as demonstrated by Hedegård and others.[20]

One further argument for the fourteenth century date is the inclusion of prayers from the "glossed version" of *Ars Notoria*, which has been dated to the fourteenth century.[21] The importance of this as evidence is lessened however by the discovery that Ganell's Honorius does not include that material, but rather demonstrates that the text underwent a later revision.[22]

---

18 2014, pp. 38-39, 78.
19 Veenstra 2012 p. 155.
20 Hedegård 2002, especially p. 25.
21 Véronèse 2007 pp. 135 ff.
22 Actually, for the record, Ganell does include the *Ars Notoria* prayers, but later in his compilation.

Author

As mentioned, the prologue gives an intriguing account of the text's origin, which smacks of fiction: A council of eighty-nine magicians assembled, choosing one of their own, Honorius, to preserve the sacred magic from the attacks of the church. The experts were assembled from Naples, Athens, and Toledo. Honorius was said to be from Thebes—in this case probably not Egypt,[23] but Thebes Greece was intended. This may be pure fiction of course, but that city did in fact have a large Jewish population, and saw much turmoil during medieval times between the Eastern and Western Christian churches. In many ways Thebes was at the crossroads. Interestingly, Thebes Greece (now called Thiva) was referred to as "Thebes of the seven gates" to distinguish it from the city in Egypt. These seven city gates were associated with the seven planets—might these have inspired Honorius to design his magic circle with a sword for each planet, stationed at seven directions around the perimeter?

The name Honorius, son of Euclid, has been largely dismissed as a pseudonym. Aside from *Liber Iuratus*, the only independent reference to Honorius of Thebes is possibly Trithemius (1462–1516), who attributes a magic alphabet to him: "Here follows another alphabet of Honorius surnamed the Theban, and the use thereof is for hiding the foolishness of his magic, such as Petrus de Abano testifies in his greater fourth book."[24] I have not been able to identify any such passage in the many voluminous works of De Abano (c. 1257–1316). Since pseudo-de Abano writings are not unknown, the evidence this provides for a historical Honorius is shaky at best. The only manuscript of Honorius which actually includes the alphabet is Sloane 3853, where it is clearly identified as having been taken from Trithemius's student Agrippa,[25] thus making a remarkable round-trip back to Honorius. This so-called Theban alphabet is clearly based on the Latin alphabet, not Greek. This magical alphabet

---

23 Idries Shah, *Oriental Magic,* London: Octagon, 1992, p. 192, pronounced the work of Egyptian origin on the basis of this name.

24 "Sequitur aliud alphabetum Honorii cognomento Thebani, cuius ministerio suas in magicis fatuitates abscondit, sicut Petrus de Apono testatur in suo maiore libro quarto" Johannes Trithemius, *Polygraphia 6,* 1508, p. 579.

25 Fol. 49v: "De characteribus predict. ... in liber tercius Henr[icus] Cornelius" i.e. Agrippa, *de Occulta Philosophia* Liber III.29. The passage in question is not in the 1510 manuscript, but new to the 1533 edition. Agrippa does not actually identify his source, but it is certainly that of his old mentor Trithemius.

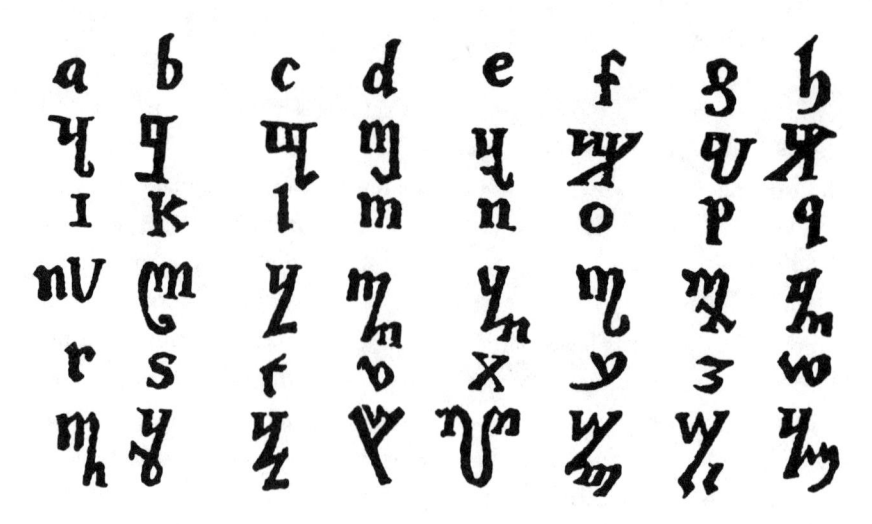

Magic alphabet of Honorius

incidentally has seen widespread popularity by modern practitioners of magic, Wicca, and other forms of witchcraft.

Contents

I will not recount the contents in depth, since the translation makes that redundant, but only make a few observations. Seemingly the work of a single author, the *Sworn Book* has an internal coherence based on medieval science and theology. In short, it is a comprehensive method of magical attainment, not a collection of unrelated spells like most magic texts that have come down to us.

The centerpiece of the text is the ritual to attain nothing less than the beatific vision. Subsequent rituals use the same framework for both spiritual and material benefits, using prayers, conjurations, seals, swords, a wand, circles, and names of God, as well as names of angels and demons. A long list of various practical uses that can be obtained appears at the beginning of the book. It seems this was copied from material later in the text, making it appear to be a list of chapters or table of contents. This is unfortunately not the case, and a source of some confusion.[26]

---

26 GH p. 27, Veenstra 2012 p. 174.

Although the method of Honorius is distinctly Christian, it directly attacks church authorities of the time, and teaches direct knowledge as opposed to relying on the Church. It has Jewish elements as well as we will see.

Origins and parallels i:
Jewish and "Solomonic" magic

The *Sworn Book* shares some common concepts with medieval Jewish Byzantine magic texts from Spain, France, and Byzantium. These include conjunction with God by magical means (*devequt*), whereupon the angels and demons will bring one anything. Other key concepts are the powers of the seven planets, and the magical uses of names of God—the 72-letter name in particular.[27] One of the earliest Kabbalists, R. Abraham Abulafia, was known to have composed and disseminated his teachings in the 1270's in Greece, including Thebes.[28] Abulafia composed a treatise on the 72-letter divine name, although the details are different in Honorius and Abulafia. The similarities suggest possible influence or fertilization in the development of Honorius's Christian art of magic.

Interestingly, *Hekalot Rabbati* (8th or 9th century), a core text of Jewish mystical literature, has a similar origin narrative: "when R. Nehunia ben ha-Kana heard that Rome was planning to destroy the sages, he gathered a company of rabbis together to 'reveal the nature (*midda*) of the secret of the world.'"[29]

Honorius claims his magic as coming from Solomon. The great seal is called the Seal of Solomon (as well as the Seal of God), famous from antiquity for controlling demons. Some of the prayers and magical essentials are also labeled with the name of that Jewish king. Honorius clearly saw himself as following in the tradition, and endowed with the authority of Solomon. Some elements of the method of Honorius indeed show familiarity with that tradition: The use of magic circles protected by sacred names, suffumigations and ink with familiar ingredients, and use of virgin parchment. Of the names of God and those of spirits, there is a mixture of Hebrew, Greek, Latin, and others not identifiable. Some are well known in magical literature, and others

---

27 Schwartz 2003 pp. 196, 202–203.
28 Idel 2012 p. 663.
29 Michael D. Schwartz 2006, p. 404.

otherwise unknown. One example, Corniger, sounds like it could be from some medieval popular drama.

Kieckhefer identifies sleep visions as an essentially Jewish element.[30] Another connection with Jewish mysticism may be found in chapter XCVIII, where the text refers to seeing the heavenly palace; this definitely is a concept found primarily in Hekaloth literature and Merkabah mysticism.

Honorius also recognizes the traditional Jewish concept of *Shem ha-Meforash*, but again differs in the details from Kabbalistic tradition. The use of this term, the planetary classification of spirits, and the concept of the heavenly throne, all suggest Jewish influence akin to *Sepher Raziel*. Some prayers, such as CXV.25, are very reminiscent of those found in *Raziel*, but don't match exactly. In at least one small instance, however, Honorius seems to have drawn on this mystical text more or less directly.[31] The text also uses the term *Shamayim*, which is the Hebrew word for heaven. In medieval Jewish Merkabah literature, it is the name of the First Heaven, found in *Raziel* and other sources.[32] Of the prayers, only one is labeled Hebrew (LXIII), though it doesn't seem to have any Hebrew content.

Besides these slender connections with *Liber Razielis* and *Liber Semiphoras*, very little of the method of Honorius appears to be directly related to other treatises on Solomonic magic, such as *Clavicula Salomonis, Ars Almadel, De officiis spirituum, De novem candariis*, or *De quattuor annulis*. The concept of angels and daemons associated with the days and hours is also found in the *Clavicula*, but details again differ. The use of prayers from *Ars Notoria* is the exception, but again these were evidently added later.

Origins and parallels II:

Western/Latin Christianity

A major influence on the magic of Honorius is traditional devout Christian practice, with its common prayers (adapted in some cases), observance of liturgical hours, abstinence, use of the hair shirt, and enlisting the help

---

30 Kieckhefer 1998 p. 256. See also Veenstra 2012 p. 186 n. 27.
31 Namely, seven divine names used in the Seal of God (IV.14–47, CXXVII.15): Layaly, etc. See below.
32 See Raziel and *Liber Semiphoras*, 6/7Moses in Peterson 2008 p. 265.

of a priest. Honorius includes both the Apostle's Creed and the Athanasian Creed, both of which point to the influence of the Western or Latin (Catholic) church. Similarly, near the very end, the text quotes the blessing of salt, which is a traditional part of Western or Roman ritual. In this form it is not part of Byzantine or Orthodox tradition.

The text also recognizes the traditional Christian classification of angels, as codified by Pseudo-Dionysius (5th–6th century A.D.) and Gregory the Great (circa 540–604 A.D). Honorius differs however in the order, placing the Cherubim before Seraphim, and Principalities before Powers: Cherubim, Seraphim, Thrones, Dominations, Virtues, Principalities, Powers, Archangels, and Angels.[33]

Many of the prayers are reminiscent of medieval Benedictine spiritual exercises, such as those of German mystic Saint Gertrude of Helfta (1256–ca. 1302). Gertrude also had special sympathy towards the souls in purgatory, a subject which is alluded to a couple of times in the *Sworn Book*.

Origins and parallels III:

Eastern Christianity and Byzantium

As Mathiesen pointed out, the author of the *Sworn* Book clearly had "some knowledge of the liturgy of the Greek Orthodox Church."[34] In his edition of the Latin text, Hedegård suggested the planetary spirits chapters of the *Sworn Book* might be based on a Greek source.[35] Boudet too raised the possibility that the classification of aerial daemons might be of Byzantine origin. This is supported by the fact that many of them are found in a Byzantine manual of exorcism, published by Delatte. This manuscript was dated by the catalogers as 1735. The names of the demons and their controlling angels correspond closely with Honorius chapters CV–CXI. According to Delatte, "Each group of air demons and wind demons is under the authority of three angels who, under the direction of an archangel, impose his authority through a special seal." There are also parallels in Petrus de Abano's *Heptameron seu Elementa*

---

33 Boudet 2002 p. 863.
34 Mathiesen 1998 p. 161 n34.
35 Hedegård 2002 p. 50.

MICHAËL

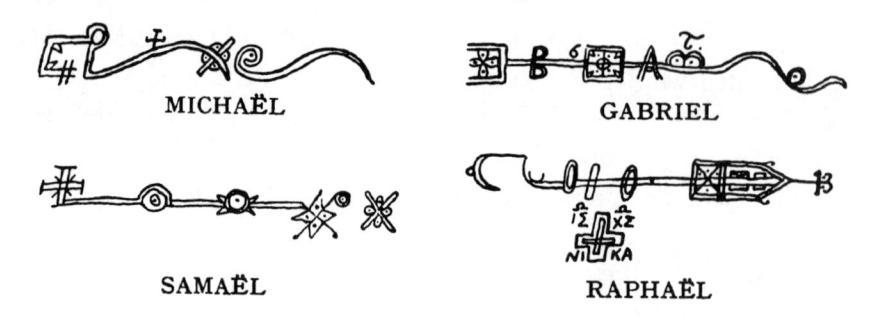

GABRIEL

SAMAËL

RAPHAËL

Seals of the archangels from Byzantine exorcism manual / Delatte 1957 p. 98

Magica,[36] as well as the fifteenth-century *Book of Angels*,[37] and in the fifteenth-century necromancer's manual published by Richard Kieckhefer.[38]

The spirits associated with the Moon also occur in the *Astromagia* of Alfonso X (written circa 1280). This treatise is primarily about constructing astrological talismans; many of these are taken from *Picatrix*, but this one is attributed to Raziel. The text reads:

> Engrave on the sigil the name of the angel and the wind serving the Moon, and commanding over its sign (which is Cancer), with his aides. The angel is Gabriel and his aides are Michael and Samiel. These are the names of the winds that command over Cancer: Hebetel and Halmitab [later spelled Almutab]; and their aides who are Bylol [later spelled Bibol], Milalu, and Abuzoba.[39]

---

36 The earliest edition of this concise handbook of ritual magic appears to be Venice, 1496 (Lynn Thorndike, *Magic and Experimental Science*, vol. II, p. 925.) The attribution of the text to the famous physician Petrus de Abano (1250–1316) "seems quite certainly spurious" according to Thorndike (*op. cit.*, p. 912). His reputation as a magician developed quite early however.

37 Boudet 2002 p. 867: "L. Delatte, *Un office byzantin d'exorcisme*. [Bruxelles]: [Palais des académies], 1957, p. 121–122, points out, among others, Arcan, called king of aerial spirits, then king of Zephyr (the West) and his servants Bileth, Misabou, and Abouzaba. They can be found with names distorted in § 23 (of the spirits of the Moon) and 28 (on Western spirits). But the same names also appear in the *Astromagia* of Alfonso X (see Alfonso el Sabio, cit., pp. 138–139 and 144–145) and in the *Liber de angelis* of Pseudo-Messahala, published by J.G. Lidaka, *The Book of angels*, cit., p. 64–65." (translation mine). The *Book of Angels* was published in Lidaka 1998.

38 Kieckhefer 1998 pp. 181, 303–305.

39 Alfonso X 1992 pp. 138–139 (my translation).

Introduction

Un office byzantin d'exorcisme f 15, 27, 36-36v, f99v	Heptameron	Honorius	Book of Angels
King: Maimon (Μαϋμὸν) Servants: Aboumaleth, Asaïbi, Balidet (Ἀβουμαλήθ, Ἀσαϊβί, Βαλιδέτ) Ruling Angels: Kasiel, Machotan, Ourouel (Κασιήλ, Μαχωτάν, Οὐρουήλ)	K: Maymon S: Abumalith, Assaibi, Balidet RA: Cassiel, Machatan, Vriel (Saturn)	K: Maymon S: Albunalich, Assaibi, Haibalidech, Yasfla RA: Bohel, Cafziel, Michrathon, Saterquiel (CV/ Saturn)	K: Mayrion "the Black One will create the voids" Cassael, Maxtarcop, Stanalcon
K South (Σούθ) S: Magouth, Goutriz (Μαγούθ, Γουτρίζ) RA: Sakiel, Kastiel, Asasiel (Σακιήλ, Καστιήλ, Ἀσασιήλ)	K: Suth S: Maguth, Gutriz RA: Sachiel, Castiel, Asasiel (Jupiter)	K: Formione S: Guth, Maguth, Guthryn RA: Satquiel, Raphael, Pahamcocihel, Asassaiel (CVI/ Jupiter)	K: Marastac S: Aycolaytoum, Lord of Torments RA: Sariel, Staus, Iucuciel [or Cricios, Faccas, Casfeel]
K: Samax (Σαμάξ) S: Carmax, Ismoli, Pafran (Καρμάξ, Ἰσμολί, Παφράν) RA: Samael, Satael, Amabiel (Σαμαήλ, Σαταήλ, Ἀμαβιήλ)	K: Samax S: Carmax, Ismoli, Paffran RA: Samael, Satael, Amabiel (Mars)	K: Iammax S: Carmox, Ycanohl, Pasfran RA: Samahel, Satihel, Yturahihel, Amabiel (CVII/Mars)	Rubeus Pugnator ("Red Fighter")* S: Karmal, Iobial, Yfasue Saliciel [aka Salatiel], Ycaachel [aka Taxael], Harmanel [aka Harnariel]
K: Barcan (Βαρκαν) S: Tous, Adas, Cunabal (Τούς, Ἀδάς, Κυναβάλ) RA: Michael, Dardiel, Khourataphel (Μιχαήλ, Δαρδιήλ, Χουραταφήλ)	K: Varcan S: Tus, Andas, Cynabal RA: Michael, Dardiel, Huratapel	K: Barthan S: Thaadas, Chaudas, Ialchal RA: Raphael, Cafhael, Dardihel, Hurathaphel (CVIII/ Sun)	Barchan Chatas, Hycandas, Yaciatal RA: Raphael, Dardaci [aka Daniel], Talanasiel [aka Caualasyel]
K: Sarabotres (Σαραβότρες) S: Amabiel, Aba, Abalidoth, Phlaeph (Ἀμαβιήλ, Ἀβά, Ἀβαλιδώθ, Φλαέ) RA: Anael, Rakhiel, Sakhiel (ἀναήλ, ῥαχιήλ, Σαχιήλ)	K: Sarabrotres S: Amabiel, Aba, Abalidoth, Flaëf RA: Anael, Rachiel, Sachiel (Venus)	K: Sarabocres S: Nassar, Cynassa RA: Hanahel, Raquiel, Salguyel (CIX/Venus)	

* On these seven kings addressed by colors, see Scholem 1965 p. 2.

Un office byzantin d'exorcisme f 15, 27, 36-36v, f99v	Heptameron	Honorius	Book of Angels
K: Modiath (or Mediath) (Μοδιαθ or Μεδιάθ) S: Soukinos, Sallales (Σουκίνος, Σαλλάλες) RA: Raphael, Miel, Saraphiel (ῥαφαήλ, Μιήλ, Σαραφιήλ)	K: Modiat S: Suquinos, Sallales RA: Raphael, Miel, Saraphiel (Mercury)	K: Habaa S: <u>Hyyci, Quyron,</u> Zach, Eladeb RA: <u>Mychael</u>, Myhel, Sarapiel (CX/Mercury)	K: Zombar S: Darial, Faccas RA: Michael, Sariel, Miriel†
K: Arcan (Ἀρκαν) S: Bileth (Βιλέθ), Misabou (Μισσαβού), Abouzaba (or Abuzampa) (Ἀβουζαβα) RA: Gabriel, Michael, Samael (Γαβριήλ, Μιχαήλ, Σαμαήλ)	K: Arcan S: Bilet, Missabu, Abuzaha RA: Gabriel, Michael, Samael (Moon)	K: Harthan S: Bileth, Misabou, Abouzaba RA: Michael, Gabriel, Samyel, <u>Atithael</u>. (Moon) (CXI/Moon)	K: Abdalaa S: Baysul, Maylalu, Ebuzoba RA: Gabriel, Samayel, Michael

† Planet is not identified, so correspondence is uncertain.

Another passage shows even more variations on these names:

> The angels who have power over (the Moon) are Gabriel, Szamahel [later spelled Esmahel], and Michael.... The king who rules over this image is the honored Abdala, and his servants are Baylul, Maylalu, and Ebuzoba. Over this talisman recite the following invocation: "I beseech you, angels in charge of the character of the Moon, by the name of Ilamos, Namoz, Heyeyl, Caffaa, Bassal, Nacha, Cana, swift Calta, Cahala."[40]

It seems therefore that by 1280, the names had already been known long enough for significant variations to develop, and that some unknown Raziel text was the source.[41] Given how far these differ from Honorius, it seems

---

40 Alfonso X 1992 pp. 144–145.
41 The editor likewise comments (p. 383): "This talisman must derive from the *Book of Raziel*, but I have not tracked in ms. Reg. Lat. 1300." Since Damaris Gehr is working on these texts, hopefully she will shed more light on it in the future.

unlikely that Honorius was informed by Alfonso's Greek and Arabic translation activities.

We can also see from the above that Honorius is sometimes closer to the Byzantine text than are the other texts. For example, "H" in Harthan, "th" in Bileth, and "ou" in Abouzaba and Misabou reflect the Greek spellings more closely than the other texts. Incorporation of Byzantine material would also explain the puzzling variety of spellings by Honorius, for example, the seemingly arbitrary insertion of the letter "h." This could reflect indecision on how to transliterate the Greek: A few examples should illustrate: Miel vs. Mihel (Gk. Μιήλ), Dardiel vs. Dardihel (Gk. Δαρδιήλ), and Harkan vs. Arcan (Gk. Ἀρκάν).

In other cases, Honorius differs where Petrus and the Greek agree. Honorius generally includes more names than the others. The ruling angel of Mercury is also interesting. In Petrus (similarly Cardanus and Michael Scotus), the ruling archangel is identified as Raphael, while *Liber Semiphoras* and Agrippa identify him as Michael.[42] Hence Honorius is closer to *Liber Semiphoras*.

In the great exorcism in the Byzantine manual only seals of four archangels are preserved, owing to damage at the bottom of folio 102. These four are similar to those in *Heptameron*, which has all seven. It has generally been assumed that the seals of the archangels found in the Royal manuscript are an insertion directly from *Heptameron*, but perhaps they were actually present in the original *Sworn Book* after all. *Heptameron* clearly labels the archangels associated with each seal, but the Royal manuscript just associates them with the planet, which is odd if the scribe took them directly from de Abano. Nothing resembling these appear in Ganell however.[43]

Another part of the Byzantine exorcism manual has parallels in Honorius: The "great exorcism" (f36v), parallels Honorius CXXXIII.38: "πάντα τὰ πονηρὰ δαιμόνια Βεραλανεῦσις, Βαλδακιόνσης, Πανμαχιά, Ἀπολογίου καθέδραι, δοῦλοι τῆς ταρταρέας καθέδρας, Πριμάκ, Βαρκάν, Τούς...." ("the ever-evil demons Beralanysis, Baldakionsis, Panmachia, Apologias cathedrai, slaves of Tartar cathedra, Primak, Barkan, Tous...")[44]

---

42 Peterson 2008 pp. 156, 165.
43 See also parallel seals in Kieckhefer 1998 pp. 303-305.
44 The "Exorcism of the Spirits of the Air" (f. 11–14v, 102v–104v) also closely parallels *Heptameron* "Exorcismus Spirituum Aereorum," pp. 112–120..

The concept of angels and daemons associated with the days, hours, and cardinal directions is also found in Byzantine sources, although the details differ.[45] Likewise with the use of magic circles with sacred names, and features aligned to the compass, gloves and other apparel,[46] as well as incenses (*aromata*) used to attract and placate the daemons.[47]

Another puzzle is found in CXL.11 where we read the following: "Casziel, Satquiel, and so on. Furthermore, there are seven superiors, namely Barachiel, Uriel, and the rest." This is the only place that Barachiel is mentioned, so it is apparent the original reference has gotten lost, or was expected to be well known. Unfortunately, this doesn't help identify the provenance, since Uriel and Barachiel are both known as archangels from a variety of traditions, including Orthodox, Latin, the Sibylline Oracles, and ancient Jewish magic.[48]

In summary, it seems likely that all these sources descended from a common ancestor, likely a Byzantine one, and none of them are directly dependent on another.

Evolution of the text

As Frank Klaassen has pointed out, the literature of ritual magic often encourages the process of personalizing or transforming the text.[49] The Elizabethan magi John Dee and Edward Kelly clearly do this with Honorius material in their experiments with spirit communication.[50]

Although many minor differences occur in the manuscripts, only one (Sloane 3854) appears to contain the complete text. Moreover, recent studies

---

45 Greenfield 1988 pp. 338 ff. Marathakis 2011 pp. 55–74, pp. 101–106, pp. 285–291.
46 Greenfield 1995 p. 136; Marathakis p. 94–95.
47 Greenfield 1995 p. 135.
48 For Sibylline Oracles, see Charlesworth 1983 p. 350. For examples from Jewish magic see Bohak 2008 pp. 315, 318, and Casanowicz 1976 p. 162. Barachiel (also spelled Baruchiel, Barakiel, or Baraqiel) is one of the seven archangels in orthodox tradition (along with Michael, Gabriel, Raphael, Uriel, Salathiel, Jegudiel) See St. Nikolai Velimirovic, *The Prologue of Ohrid—Volume One*. The Synaxis icon includes Jegudiel, Gabriel, Selaphiel, Michael, Uriel, Raphael, and Barachiel. Images on the Basilica of St. Mary of the Angels and the Martyrs (16th century) testify to the Western tradition. (Mark Bredin, *Studies in the Book of Tobit: A Multidisciplinary Approach*, London [u.a.]: T & T Clark, 2006, p. 121.)
49 Klaassen 2014 p. 4.
50 Peterson 2008.

have deduced some evolution of the text. This can be shown from the fact that large portions of the text are quoted in Ganell's *Summa Sacre Magice* (SSM), including apparently some original "Honorius" material which is not found in the other manuscripts. Ganell's text also shows differences in the order of the material. Analyzing these differences, researchers have found evidence that the better-known group of manuscripts has been redacted at some point. Thus scholars have started referring to this better-known material as the "London Honorius" or "Northwestern European" tradition. (The use of "London" is somewhat of a misnomer, since a German manuscript also exists.[51])

Veenstra has demonstrated that the "London Honorius" has adapted the text somewhat, such as likely moving the instructions on consecrating the Seal of God to the beginning.[52] Further evidence of this change is that the German manuscript preserves the presumed original order: PART 1: To behold the face of the Deity; PART 2: Knowledge of the angels; PART 3: Knowledge of the spirits of the air, their binding and which spirits are under them; PART 4: Knowledge of the spirits of the earth; PART 5: Knowledge of the great name of God, in Hebrew *Shem ha-Meforash*, with instructions for constructing the Seal of God.

More evidence of the editorial process may be the unusual variation of the Tetragrammaton, "Ioth He Vau *Deleth*," found in two places in the text: CXXXIII.39 and CXXXVII.5. These may be mistakes, evidence of the compiler's unfamiliarity with Hebrew, a possibility suggested by both Mesler and Veenstra.[53] However this seems unlikely to me given the fact that the "mistake" recurs. Moreover, the form also occurs in other texts, such as *Vinculum Salomonis*, a text which does not appear to derive from Honorius.[54] The substitution of Deleth could also have been intentional to avoid writing the

---

51 Leipzig Cod. Mag. 16.
52 Veenstra 2012 pp. 151 ff, and especially pp. 167–168.
53 Mesler 2012 p. 118, Veenstra 2012 pp. 172–173. There is a parallel passage to CXXXIII.39 in de Abano's text, *Heptameron* (H) pp. 120–122, which reads "per hoc nomen ineffabile, Tetragrammaton IHVH Iehouah," but this may easily be a later editorial correction. Similarly SSM L.3.f.37.
54 For example, Wellcome 110 fol. 36r. This manuscript has been dated late 16th century: "et quod ex quatuor literis constat scilicet **Ioth he vahu deleth** et per novem celestia candelabra [sic], et per eorum virtutes quatenus etc."

correct name (maybe clued by *deleth* = he deletes?).⁵⁵ However, since the text abounds in sacred names of God, that explanation seems unlikely to me too. A third possibility is that the compiler was simply preserving the form found in his source material, which had itself conservatively censored the correct form of the name. This is consistent with the eclectic nature of the text.

A comparison of the manuscripts shows other evidence of *transformations* aside from introducing minor errors. For example, the Royal manuscript in some instances preserves earlier readings; however, it also seems to have excised material on demons, leaving only the angels (which it also expanded upon). Some of the manuscripts altered the magic circle to have seven equal segments. To judge by comparison with Ganell's Honorius material, the northern European redactor may have removed material about the four demon kings (Amaymon, Oriens or Orienens, Paymon, and Egyn), seals of the spirits, and further instructions about ritual instruments.⁵⁶

The psalter is another interesting case. These core prayers are essential to the magic of Honorius, yet they differ in the northern Honorius and in the Honorius quoted by Ganell. Perhaps they were originally a separate detached text, or possibly they got omitted at some point. In the northern European recension, the want was supplied by prayers taken from *Ars Notoria*. In Ganell's text, the core prayers are taken from a book called the *Liber Trium Animarum* (LTA). It now seems certain that the use of *Ars Notoria* is a departure from the hypothetical Ur text, based on the dating of the specific variations of *Ars Notoria* used. The original version of Honorius may have included the LTA prayers, but it is of course possible the LTA was a different attempt to fill the gap left from the missing prayers. Curiously, Ganell's *Summa* also includes prayers from the *Ars Notoria*, which he refers to as the "old art."⁵⁷

In conclusion, it seems likely that the compiler had some knowledge of Jewish Kabbalah and Merkabah traditions, and wanted to incorporate the

---

55 Suggested by Mesler, p. 139.
56 Ganell goes into details of 4 kings of the N/S/E/W. In some cases he specifically states that Honorius does not provide instructions, so he will supplement the information, for example his chapter on the vestments. Ganell's text shows clear signs of redaction in some cases, such as crossing out words which are found in other manuscripts. There are many example where he uses th and t interchangeably, e.g. *thetragramaton* but elsewhere *tetragramathon*.
57 For example, L.4.f.9 "oracio quartus artis veretis: Helyscemath, hazaram, hemel" = Honorius chapter XVI = Ars Not. 7, JV p. 146.

concepts into his own system, based more on Christian elements, such as names of Christ, and traditional prayers. He also likely incorporated material from some Byzantine source, resulting in a method that was truly at the crossroads of various traditions.

Elements of magic as taught by Honorius

Vision of God, or the Beatific Vision

The key to the entire of system of magic taught by Honorius is the magical means for achieving the vision of God, even as the saints and prophets themselves knew God. This section of the text was probably the first part originally. Mathiesen singles out this as the most interesting and important historically, without parallel in magical literature.[58]

As mentioned above, this was a key element of Jewish Merkabah mysticism,[59] as well as various Christian authors such as Pseudo-Dionysius. Theodoric of Freiberg (ca. 1240–ca. 1320), a German Dominican theologian, wrote an influential treatise on the subject, called *Tractatus de visione beatifica*. The writings of Christian mystics, such as Saint Gertrude of Helfta, abound in visions of Jesus and Mary, so this may be a logical extension of those too.

Honorius professes to provide a practical way to achieve this, going far beyond anything the conventional church rituals could offer.

Seals of angels

The term seal (*sigilla*) is used in two different senses in the magic of Honorius. The first designates specific texts to be recited to bind the spirits.[60] It can also mean physical seals or sigils of angels or spirits that can be held in the hand.[61] Unfortunately, no examples of the second type are represented in the manuscripts.[62] Chapter CXXV.4 states these seals may be engraved on silver, and possibly tin or other metals. Ganell, who has a tendency to supplement

---

58 Mathiesen, 1998 pp. 150 ff.
59 Michael D. Schwartz 2006, pp. 415.
60 See Veenstra 2012 p. 190 n 79.
61 CXXXI: magister habens signum Dei et sigilla in manu sua dextra. See also CXXXIX.2.
62 The exception is R, which may be an accretion derived from *Heptameron*.

Seal of Amaymon, from Ganell

Seals of the archangels from Royal MS 17 Axlii fols. 67v–70r

Honorius, in some cases simply uses the written names of the spirits, sometimes in Hebrew.[63] One rare exception is the "seal of Amaymon" found in the *Summa* on L.3.f.22.

Given the parallel texts, perhaps something close to the seals found in the Royal manuscript were originally present in the lost Ur-text.

Other variations of these same seals are included in the fifteenth-century Munich handbook.[64]

---

63 For example, L.5.f.63.
64 Kieckhefer 1998 pp. 367–368.

Seal of God or Seal of Solomon: Signum Dei, Sigillum Dei

The concept of a great seal, commonly called the Seal of Solomon, is central to Solomonic magic. Early references can be found in the Greek Magical Papyri.[65] Duling mentions a second to third century metal-foil amulet which mentions it.[66] One of the oldest examples is found in the Testament of Solomon (1st to 3th CE), described as engraved on a precious stone, which some manuscripts expand on as being a pentalpha, or five-pointed star.[67] Many versions of the seal of Solomon can be found in magical literature, from the simple pentalpha to the extremely elaborate.[68] Many versions, including that in the *Sworn Book* contain the pentalpha as a central or key element.

The great seal as described by Honorius is likewise central to his magic. He refers to it variously as the Seal of the True and Living God, the Seal of the Eternal, Living, and True God, the Sign (or Seal) of God, the Sacrosanct Seal, the Seal of the Sacred Names of God, the Sacred (or Holy) Seal; the Sign of Solomon, the Seal of Solomon, the Sign (or Seal) of the Lord, the Sacred Seal, the Sacred [Seal] of God; the Sign of Solomon given by the Lord, or simply the Sign.[69] Ganell also refers to it at times as the Divine Sign.[70] Note, it is never referred to as the Seal of Truth (Heb. *Aemeth*), which John Dee uses.[71]

---

65 PGM IV.3041. Betz, Hans Dieter. *The Greek Magical Papyri in Translation, Including the Demotic Spells*. Chicago: University of Chicago Press, 1986, p. 96.
66 Duling 1983, p. 948.
67 For a recent translation, see Duling 1983 pp. 935 ff. On the seal, see p. 962 and note k. On later treatment of the *Testament*, see Sarah Iles Johnston, "The Testament of Solomon from Late Antiquity to the Renaissance" in Bremmer and Veenstra 2002. For bibliography, see also G. Fitzer, *Theological Dictionary of the New Testament* 7 (1971): 947, n. 72.
68 The version in *Grimorium Verum* (Peterson 2007, p. 80) is fairly simple. Jean-Patrice Boudet 2006 planche XIV shows a particularly elaborate example from an Italian edition of the *Key of Solomon* (1446). Paris, BnF, ms. Ital. 1524, fol. 186.
69 Sigillum Dei, III.7, IV.51, CXXXVII.15, 18, 21, CXL.5; Sigillum Dei vivi et veri, IV.1; Sigillum Dei eterni, vivi, et veri, CXXXVII.1; Signum Dei, CXV.7, CXXXI.1, CXXXIX.2. Signum Domini, CXV.2, CXXIX.4, CXXXIII.46, CXXXVII.22. Sigillum Domini CXXXIX.3; Sacrosanctum Sigillum IV.65; Sigillum sanctorum nominum Dei, CXV.14; Sacrum Sigillum, CXXXIII.13, CXXXVII.7; Sacrum Sigillum Dei, CXXXII.12; Sanctum Sigillum, CXXXIII.53, CXXXVII.12; Sigillum Salomonis, CXXXIII.37; Signum Salomonis, CXXVI.14, CXXXIII.30, 51; Signum Salomonis a Domino datum, CXXXIII.30; Signum, CXV.45, CXXXIII.37.
70 *Signum diuino*, e.g. SSM L.3.f.6.
71 Peterson 2003, especially pp. 22, 79.

Jan Veenstra has shown that the example found in London manuscript Sloane 313 (see appendix II) does not actually agree with the description in the text, but the drawing in SSM is much closer.[72] For example, a passage in LIH IV.12 matches the drawing in SSM, but not Sloane 313.[73] For this edition, I have reconstructed the Seal based on the elaborate description in the text, as well as Ganell's drawing.

According to Veenstra, this seal was also "known independently as an amulet in Spain." This is based on Athanasius Kircher's observations, as detailed by Gilly.[74] Chardonnens and Veensstra published details on other exemplars from the Netherlands and Italy, both found in the walls of buildings.[75] The Dutch seal dates from the 15th or early 16th century, making it the earliest such artifact known.[76]

Chardonnens and Veenstra suggest the creator of the Dutch seal must have had access to the descriptive text. Another possibility is that they had access only to a similar seal, perhaps that of a practicing magician, which may have been properly prepared. This seems more likely to me than the possibility that it had been re-purposed or retired by its text-informed originator.

Many variants of this Seal of God occur, including many outside Honorius-related texts, exhibiting various states of divergence from the earliest exemplars. Some texts of the *Key of Solomon* contain versions of the Honorius seal. That in Aubrey 24 describes it as effective against a long list of physical dangers, as well as protection from ghosts or phantasms.[77] This might account for its use in protecting buildings. MS. Mich. 276, fol 13r describes its use similarly. A version found in *La véritable magie noire*[78] is barely recognizable, testifying to a long and complex transmission. This is further attested by the apparent mixture of lineages apparent in the Dutch seal.[79]

---

72 Veenstra 2012 pp. 151 ff, especially p. 165.
73 See Veenstra 2012 p. 161, 186 n34.
74 Veenstra 2012 p. 161. Gilly 2002 p. 291.
75 Chardonnens and Veensstra 2014 p. 127, p. 137. See also Gilly 2002 p. 280.
76 Chardonnens and Veensstra 2014 p. 139.
77 Oxford, Bodleian Library MS. Aubrey 24, dated 1674 60r-v.
78 "Iroé-Grego," "1750."
79 As detailed so aptly by Chardonnens and Veensstra 2014, especially pp. 150–155. Perhaps future building demolitions will help clarify the picture.

The magic circle and the magical seven-fold universe

The magic of Honorius is heavily structured around a seven-fold classification, including the seven classical planets (or "wandering stars"), cardinal directions and their associated winds, and the four elements and humors of the ancients. A representation of this "map of the universe" is the basis for the magic circle used for invoking spirits. This is not described in the text, but illustrated graphically. Variations exist in the manuscripts: The oldest

Region	Humors	Element	Tetrabiblos ch 4	Planet	Angel	Name of God
East	warm and moist, [masculine]		Hot & dry, masculine	The Sun	Boon	Ysicres
Consol (Southeast)	hot, mixed moist dry [NOT DRY]		Hot & moist, masculine	Jupiter	Uriel	Zebedey
South	hot and dry	Fire	Very hot & dry, masculine	Mars	Karathiel	Eloy
Nogahel (Southwest)	warm, and feminine	Air	Warm & moist (similar to Mars, but not as hot or dry), feminine*	Venus	Uriel	Ienomei
West	cold and moist / feminine	Water	Cold & moist, feminine	The Moon	Hocroel	Theos
Frigicap (Northwest)	cold and damp, masculine		Sometimes dry, sometimes moist, uncertain gender†	Mercury	Vihel	Sother
Northern part	cold and dry	Earth	Very cold & dry, masculine	Saturn	Lanael	Christ
(Northeast is not included)						

* Note: "The Greeks considered Venus to be slightly warm and moist (fertile qualities); however, from the Arabic era onward, Venus is always called cold and moist." (The Well-Tempered Astrologer, by Dorian Gieseler Greenbaum, https://www.scribd.com/doc/182979617/welltemperedastrologer-pdf retrieved Oct 10, 2015.

† According to Grosseteste: cold & dry. See Matt Dowd, PhD Dissertation, Astronomy and Compotus at Oxford University in the Early Thirteenth Century: The Works of Robert Grosseteste, 2003, p. 120, http://www3.nd.edu/~mdowd1/disschapters/FullDiss.pdf, retrieved Oct 10, 2015.

manuscripts (Sloane 3854 133v and Sloane 313 24r) both show North as occupying 90 degrees of the compass. Leip. Cod. Mag. 16 (pp. 98 and 112, circa 1750) shows the West as occupying 90 degrees. Other manuscripts show the circle divided into seven *equal* segments (SSM L.3.f.29, Sloane 3853 fol. 150v). See appendix II.

The correspondence of the planets with the elements and humors seems to be based ultimately on the Ptolomaic model of the universe, as found in chapter 4 of *Tetrabiblos*. This explains the influences of the planets through their associations with the humors, namely the productive qualities of warmth and moisture, and the reductive qualities of cold and dryness.[80]

The magic circle is required for calling spirits, and is described as providing the "greatest fortification" against the spirits. This seems to be mainly precautionary, because certain of them could potentially respond with malice (CXXVII.10).

In the manuscripts, the magic circle diagram is surrounded by descriptive passages, such as "East, warm and moist, where the angels of the Sun dominate." These passages are probably not intended to be part of the magic circle itself. In Sloane 3854, the descriptions are outside the three concentric circles. In Sloane 3853, SSM, and some of the others, the circles extend outside the descriptive material, likely in deviation from the original.

To call forth the planetary and aerial spirits, the text describes a second (double) circle, drawn a ways from the main circle. Around this second circle should be written "the names of the angels of the hour, day, month, time, and aspect" (CXIV.8, CXXVII.7). This is reminiscent of de Abano, but unfortunately, the text does not identify the corresponding names.

Names of God

The use of the names of God is central to the method of Honorius, as well as Solomonic and Jewish magic in general. Honorius uses prayers constructed around the hundred names of God listed in chapter CI. The names themselves are an eclectic mixture of Greek, Hebrew, Latin, and others of undetermined origin.

---

80 Ptolomy and Robbins 1980 pp. 35 ff. The correspondence of the planets and elements is also recounted in the eleventh century Arabic magic text now generally known as *Picatrix*; see I.4, Greer and Warnock 2011 p. 31.

The text also uses the Hebrew term *Shem ha-Meforash*, probably meaning something like "explicit name" of God. Honorius uses the term to refer to the seventy-two letter name of God given in several places in the text, including the border of the Seal of God. Although the use of this term might lead us to suppose a Jewish connection, the name itself turns out to be derived from the initial letters of seventy-two names of God, a subset of the longer list.[81] They are as follows:

Seventy-two names comprising the Name of God – Shem ha-Meforash.[82]

Ha; 1. Theos; 2. Onay; 3. El; 4. Xρς;[83] 5. On; 6. Raby; 7. Alpha ω; 8. Baruch; 9. AGLA; 10. Letamynyn; 11. Adon, 12. Ioth, 13. Quyesteron, 14. Tunayon, 15. Yalgal, 16. Ysyston, 17. Sampsoyny, 18. Thetebar, 19. Athyonodabazar, 20. Lauaquyryn, 21. Geuer, 22. Athedyon, 23. Onoytheon, 24. Nomyx, 25. Oristyon, 26. Sanathyel, 27. Vabalganarytyn, 28. Lauagelaguyn, 29. Araton, 30. Radix, 31. Yaua, 32. Capkyb, 33. Ely, 34. Kyryos, 35. Suparyas, 36. Pantheon, 37. Flemoyon, 38. Yuestre, 39. Onella, 40. Maniyas,[84] 41. Elgybor, 42. Maney, 43. Asmamyas, 44. Nathanathoy, 45. Abracalabrah,[85] 46. Romolyon, 47. Epafgricus, 48. Narach, 49. Vagalnarytyn, 50. Gofgamel, 51. Alla, 52. Rabur, 53. Eloon, 54. Lauazyryn, 55. Abracaleus, 56. Tantalatysten, 57. Eye, 58. Delectycon, 59. Ay, 60. Tunayon, 61. Occynomeryon, 62. Nomygon, 63. Oryona, 64. Nosulaseps, 65. Abryon, 66. Orlon, 67. Ye, 68. Layafalasyn, 69. Eye assereye, 70. Ydardycon, 71. Ocleyste, 72. Tucheon.[86]

This list is not found in the *Sworn Book*; although most of the names appear in CI.2-8, the order varies. The resulting series of seventy-two letters is divided into eight groups of nine letters:[87]

---

81 Veenstra 2012 pp. 168 ff. The more traditional Jewish name is based on Ex. 14:19-21.
82 SSM L.2.f.25 ll 5-26, which Ganell attributes to Tot Grecus. This important identification was made by Veenstra 2012 p. 172, and later corrected in Chardonnens and Veenstra 2014 pp. 142–143. With the availability of better photographs of the manuscript, I can propose two minor corrections to their transcript.
83 = Christus.
84 JV: Mamyas.
85 Skemer 2006 p. 120 notes the use of this name in thirteen century manuscript Sloane 1717.
86 JV: Tutheon.
87 SSM L.4.f.20. See Chardonnens and Veenstra 2014 p. 144 for variants.

¶Toexoraba ¶Layqtiyst ¶Algaonosu ¶Laryceksp ¶Fyomemana ¶Renugarel ¶Atedatono ¶Naoyleyot

The result is not only an abbreviation, but in fact an acronym, pronounceable in its own right. This may be the motive for rearranging the list as found in CI.2.

In addition to the Seal of God, this 72-letter name is used on the bed of ashes, and according to Ganell, should be written on the swords as well.

An additional list of seven divine names are used in the Seal of God (IV.14-47, CXXVII.15): Layaly, Lialg, Veham, Yalgal, Narath, Libarre, Lybares.[88] These seem to derive from *Sepher Raziel*, fifth Semaforas: Lyaham, Lyalgana, Lyafar, Viahirab, lelara, lebaron, Laasasalos.[89] These seven names are also to be used in conjunction with the magic circle, as described in chapter CXXVII.15, where they are written on small pieces of parchment set around outside the circle, but later removed. Wellcome 110 (late 16th CE,) has a very similar procedure, instructing the operator to make an incense offering to the spirit, then write the seven [sic] sacred names around the circle, "hay + byalg + vehem + yasgal + Narath + libaree, but you must remove them when you wish to operate, for no spirit is able to operate while they are there, so they must be erased."[90] Sloane 3885 32r (in a 17th ce section of the manuscript giving a version of the *Thesaurus Spirituum*) is almost identical, but the names read: "Hay + Lealge + Vehe + Valgah + Narach + Libarroe + Libaroes."

This process of writing these sacred names on pieces of parchment, and later erasing them is reminiscent of the changes against the Byzantine sorcerers Kappadokes and Tzerentzes, "for the former was said to have left his amulet lying beneath the stars all night, while the latter was alleged to have written, and then erased and trampled on, 'God's holy name.'"[91]

---

88 SSM: Layaly, lyalg, <u>vehem</u>, yalgal, <u>narach</u>, lybarre, lybares.
89 *Book of Oberon* manuscript p. 44: uses a similar list in a conjuration to bind spirits: "by these seven names of God: Largia + Gaaghum + Levalogni lavafarim + Vbalgana + Haia + Layazogin + Layarosin + Layaschesyn + by which all things are bound." Compare also Bodleian Rawlinson D252 51r: lyalth, lyalg, vehem, thalgal, narath, libarre, libares. Leipzig Cod. Mag, 16 p. 113: Lagaly, Vellim, Narach, Lyaeh, Yalgal, Librare, Librares.
90 45v: "scribantur ista septem nomina dei hay + byalg + vehem + yasgal + Narath + libaree+ et ponantur in septem mundi partibus iuxta circulum, et cum operari volueris, remove, quia in istorum presentia nullus spiritus potest operari, et ideo deleantur."
91 Greenfield 1995 pp. 134–135.

Names of Saints

Various saints are commemorated in the prayers. Most interestingly, the operator is instructed to use whichever saints resonate most for him or her (LII.7).

Spirits, Angels, and Demons in LIH

Honorius or his informants have categorized supernatural beings into logical categories, of which the traditional hierarchy of angels of Pseudo-Dionysius is only a part:

> There are three types of angels, the celestial, the aerial, and the earthly. There are two types of celestials, those who only serve God, and those are the nine orders of angels, namely, the Cherubim, Seraphim, Thrones, Dominations, Virtues, Principalities, Powers, Archangels, and Angels, concerning whom it is spoken among mortals neither by forced power nor by artificial force, and therefore in nowise should they be invoked, because they always stand praising the divine majesty, and never separated from his presence. (III.9)

Thus the spirits are divided into four categories—celestial or higher angels, planetary or lower angels, aerial spirits or daemons, and terrestrial spirits (or daemons). The aerial spirits are also listed alongside with the planetary spirits, with the explanation that the planetary angels are used to control them.[92] The list is repeated later (with some variations) in the catalog of aerial spirits. According to Honorius, "whenever good angels are called, you must not have the whistle, wand, nor the swords."

The table of topics or contents also refers to elemental spirits, namely those of the fire, water, air, and the earthly or infernal spirits. In the text, these are included in the sevenfold scheme, such that fire spirits are identified with those of Mars, and the South for example. See above discussion on the magic circle.

---

92 e.g. "veniatis ... per istos sanctos angelos, Boel, caphzyel, mycraton, satryquiel, mychael, myel, sarypyel." (SSM L.3.f.59).

The text gives detailed signs that the spirits are there, such as the magicians breaking into a sweat, or the sound of thunder. These signs perhaps have an even more ancient origin.

Only a few of the spirits listed are well known in the literature. Asmodeus (CXXXV.10) is of course well known from Tobit, the Testament of Solomon, and the Babylonian Talmud. Bileth is another name well-known in the literature. Scholem has traced his origin to Bilar in apocryphal literature and the Dead Sea scrolls.[93]

The concept of seven demon kings is also found in Arabic demonology, but "undoubtedly shows a connection with the much older ideas of planetary divinities."[94]

The Winds

Air, being invisible, can act as a bridge between the physical and spiritual world, and can be influenced by the magician to bring about physical changes in the world.[95] Winds and unexplained movements of vegetation are seen as evidence of the presence of spirits.

There is much wind lore going back to ancient times, and names assigned such as zephyr, "blowing from the west." The Greek *anemoi* are four wind gods ascribed to each cardinal direction, with lesser (minor) gods identified with the northeast, southeast, northwest, and southwest winds.[96] In the system of Honorius, these are syncretized with the seven-fold classifications based on the seven classical "planets." The result either drops one sector, or expands the remaining sectors as seen above.

Ganell's *Summa* includes both seven-fold and eight-fold classifications of the winds. In the latter the Northeast wind is given the well-known name Aquilo.[97]

---

93 Dan Ben-Amos "On Demons" in Dan 2005 p. 31.
94 Scholem 1965 p. 2.
95 See in particular, LIH CXVII.4. For discussion, see McGraw, 2013, pp. 51–52.
96 See for example, McCartney, 1930.
97 SSM L.2.f.15 has a diagram with the eight winds. SSM L5.f.11 has yet another *seven*-fold scheme: De ventis. Ventus qui flat ab Oriente dicitur Eurus. Et qui flat a meridie Auster. Et qui ab occidente zephyrus. Et qui a septentrione, Boreas. Et qui ab aquilone, Aquilo. Et qui a cosole, subsolanus. Et qui afrigicap, fauonius, vel circius. ("Concerning

Spirits associated with the Winds from Robert Fludd, Medicina, *1629*

The names of the diagonals in Honorius, Frigicap, Consol, and Nogahem, are of uncertain etymology, and otherwise unknown. Nogahem may be compared with Nogah, Hebrew for Venus, but none of the other winds show any resemblance to Hebrew words. In two places (CXXXII.11, CXL.4), the Nogahem sword is referred to as the Nogahel sword, which Agrippa (OP3.28) identifies as the spirit of Venus/Nogah. Consol (SSM: cosol), the southeast wind, may be compared with *subsolanus*, (literally "beneath the Sun" a com-

---

the winds. The wind which blows from the east is called Eurus, and that which blows from the south Auster, and which blows from the west the Zephyr, and which blows from the north, Boreas, and from the north, Aquilo, and that which blows from cosole, Subsolanus/eastern, and that which blows from Afrigicap, Favonius = the west wind, or Circius = the WNW wind.")

mon name for the east wind); *co-* and *con-* are common enclitics, both meaning "with," or "alongside." Frigicap (the northwest wind) may be compared with Africus, a common name for the southwest wind. The winds and their associated humors play an important part in medicine from ancient times up to early modern times, as seen from the writings of Robert Fludd.[98]

Preparations

The preparations taught by Honorius are not arduous compared with the rituals themselves. They include a special diet, shaving the hair from your body, sexual abstinence, confession and contrition, observing physical and spiritual purity, giving alms to three poor persons, and especially frequent prayer. During the first purification, fasting on bread and water is required. In other cases meat, fish, water, and wine are acceptable under some circumstances. On the third day of preparation, an angel will reveal in a dream if the operator is worthy. If so, the ritual proper can commence, lasting 72 days.

Ritual implements

While it has been suggested that expensive ingredients are sometimes used as part of the sacrifice needed for magical achievement,[99] quite the contrary is the case according to Honorius.[100] Intentional destruction of wealth in the form of expensive ingredients, or use of expensive ritual garments, etc. is rejected "because neither God nor the blessed angel care anything about material things. From this it is seen that the poor labor more quickly and truly (in this art) than the rich." (Chapter V.4)

Requisites include:[101]

- Candle of virgin wax. It should be noted that wax was more expensive than tallow candles, but provided a much cleaner flame. (CXXIX.1, CXXXIX.2)
- Censer for burning incense, with charcoal. (CXXIX.1)

---

98 Fludd 1629, p. 113.
99 McGraw, 2013, p. 28.
100 On which, see discussion in Gehr 2015.
101 Listed in CXXXIX.2.

- Charcoal. Used in the censer for burning incense. Also used to write (on tiles) the petition or requests being made to the spirits.
- Circles. The rites are performed both inside and outside the main ritual circle. In addition, circles are constructed where the spirits appear. For aerial spirits, it is elevated, while for earth spirits, a pit is dug.
- Clay or earth: See stones.
- Garments of clean white hemp. For the divine vision the garments should be black (CI.20), but for calling forth spirits, they should be white (CXV.1).[102] They should be new, or *virtutes* ("of worth"), or at least very newly washed, and in no event should they be foul smelling.
- Gloves, new, made without whitening chalk.
- Incense: the Seal of God consecration specifies a mixture of amber, musk, aloe, white and red labdanum, mastic, frankincense, pearls, and "incense" (CXXIX.1).[103]
- Knife (new) (Lat. *cultello*) Ganell reads *culter* (knife), while Honorius reads *cultellus* ("small knife"). This is used for drawing the magic circles in the earth.
- Paper (*cedula*), Small pieces of paper with divine names are used in conjunction with the magic circle,
- Parchment, of calf, foal, or deer. Used for the Seal of God.
- Seal of God
- Seals of angels, not given in most manuscripts, but perhaps similar to those given above.
- Shirt, hair-, also known as a cilice. Because these are so uncomfortable, their use is associated with denial of the flesh, and a reminder of the suffering of Christ.
- Stole (*stolla*). From the instructions that it is worn around the neck (CXXXVII.22), it is clear that a priestly stole is intended. This is typically between two and four inches wide and around eighty inches long. Silk is commonly used by priests. A cross is generally embroidered mid way, and often at the ends as well.

---

102 Compare SSM L.2.f.2.
103 *Ambra, musco, aloe, lapdano albo et rubeo, mastice, olibano, margaritis et thure* (IV.57). The last word, *tus*, can be either generic for incense, or frankincense specifically, but since the more specific word for frankincense, *olibanum* (from the Hebrew הנבלח) is already listed, it is not clear what ninth ingredient is intended.

- Stones (or tiles) and mortar. These are needed to prepare a flat surface on which to construct the magic circle. In cases of poverty, clay or even clean earth can be substituted.
- Stools: Wooden stools may be used to sit on during the rituals.
- Swords (called *gladius* or *ensis*). Seven are needed when calling forth spirits, but not the higher angels. The swords should all be equal in length, and if possible they should be lustrous or brightly polished (CXXIX.1, CXXXIX.2). Nothing is said about their consecration or decoration, but Ganell includes instructions which he attributes to Honorius (L.2.f.13): On the haft should be attached a small clean piece of paper on which is written the "fourth ineffable name" of God "which is of seventy-two letters, namely H.t.oexoraba, ..."[104]
- Tiles, on which should be written the petition or requests being made to the spirits. Tiles can also be used to make a more uniform surface for the magic circle.
- Wand of laurel or hazel.[105] This is needed when calling forth spirits, but not the good angels. The text uses the terms *baculus* ("a stick or staff") and *virgula* ("small wand, rod, twig") synonymously. Ganell additionally uses the word *virga* ("a slender green branch or switch"). He further states the the hazel rod/switch (*virga avellane*) should be the length of the master's arm, extended (L.3.f.25). The wand cannot be too slender, as is clear from the instruction that it should have four sides on which are written figures and sacred names (CXXXIX.6–7). I thus have to interpret the phrase "from that year"[106] as meaning it should be cut fresh each year, not that it should be of the same year's growth, as the latter would be too small to meet the other requirements.
- Whistle: It is sounded and struck at various points in the ritual to call the spirits. It is not used with the higher angels. Its construction is detailed in chapter CXL. According to Honorius, it can be made of copper, silver, gold, or hazel wood. Ganell (L.2.f.9) states that Solomon in his "fifth

---

104 Which name of course is found in IV.4 and on the Seal of God. SSM L.2.f.13: *habere gladium vel ensem, in cuius manubrio in sedula munda sit in castratum quartum nomen ineffabile quod est 72 literarum, Que sunt iste, H.t.oexoraba ....*
105 *Baculum lauri vel coruli*, (CXXXII.2); *virgula coruli*, (CXXXIX.2).
106 *Illius anni* (CXXXII.2).

book" commanded that it should be made. He adds that it can be made of copper, silver, or hazel (*"ere, argento, vel avellane"*).

- Wine: Choice or "the finest" wine may be consumed during the ritual of calling forth the spirits, to help calm the nerves.[107]

Spirit thrones

The text refers to the thrones or seats (*sedes*) of the supernatural beings, such as the seat of Samaym, and the seats of Primachia and Apologia (CXXIII.38). According to Ganell (L.3.f.3), this is the second circle, placed next to the circle of the operator.[108]

The Rituals

The core ritual takes seventy-two days in the London Honorius, but forty days in SSM. Since the Seal of God (also called the Seal of Solomon) is needed in the other rituals, its preparation is described in great detail (LII, XCVIII-CI). Ganell's description is much simpler, but the accompanying diagram makes the details redundant anyway.

A twenty-day purification comes next, involving attending mass, and reciting certain prayers both before and during the service. This is followed by twelve days of fasting and prayer; for this stage of the operation, a discreet priest is enlisted to help with prayers and services. Near the end of the ritual, you prepare a bed surrounded by ashes with divine names written therein. This is the stage for critical sleep visions.

The process for calling the spirits commences similarly, followed by a four-part ritual: the "invocation," the "seal and binding," the "conjuration," and the "placation."[109] Placating involves offering the spirits a "small gift."[110] This is evidently the pleasing suffumigation offered.[111]

Note much of the work is performed outside the magic circle, including the excitations.[112]

---

107 CXXIX.1, CXXXIX.2.
108 On this see also Veenstra 2012 p. 173–175.
109 Mesler 2012 p. 122.
110 *Munusculum*, (CXIV.7, CXV.16–17, 35, 41).
111 *Placatum suffumigium*, CXVIII.24.
112 Veenstra 2012 p. 176.

Influence

As mentioned above, examples of the Seal of God and its variants are much more frequent and widespread than the text itself. The actual text of the *Sworn Book* seems to be little noticed by practitioners. The main legacy seems to have come to us in the form of the so-called Heptarchic and Enochian systems of magic which originated with John Dee and Edward Kelly.

In 1582, John Dee, one of the leading scientists and occultists of his age, undertook a series of "Mystical Experiments."[113] He quickly became convinced that he was communicating with supernatural creatures. One of the first instructions he received was to construct a Seal of God, based on one "already perfected" in his books. Dee consulted several manuscripts, one of which was apparently Sloane 313.[114] Another of his sources was Ganell's *Summa*, which contains annotations in his hand. With his shrewd eye he noticed discrepancies, and consulted the angels to help resolve them. This prompted them to reveal an almost totally new version of the *Sigillum Dei*, but with elements from both manuscripts. The design is now widely known, with examples on coffee mugs and tee-shirts available.

As one last example of its influence, I think it quite likely that the name and reputation of Honorius "of Thebes" led to the creation of an unrelated text, the so-called *Grimoire of Pope Honorius*. Boudet noted the "huge success of the *Grimoire of Pope Honorius*, whose first edition dates from 1629 and is still republished regularly to the present, for the use of contemporary magicians." More than a few times that text has been confused the *Sworn Book*, including individuals making such uninformed assertions as the *Grimoire of Honorius* or even the *Grand Grimoire* being derived from it.[115]

---

113 Peterson 2002, pp. 12, 70.

114 Roberts and Watson, in their 1990 *John Dee's Library Catalogue*, pg. 168, identify Sloane 313 as being one of Dee's manuscripts. They give it catalog number DM70, and note, "On fol.9 (originally the first leaf, fol.1–8 having been misbound) is [Dee's ladder symbol] and, very faint, 'Fragmentum Magicum', which may be in Dee's hand. At the foot is 'Sum Ben: Jonsonij liber.'"

115 Boudet 2002 p. 870. Owen Davies 2009 pp. 34–35 discusses these later texts.

Problems with the text

Here is a summary of some of the problems with the text as it has reached us:

- Names frequently have multiple spellings.
- Seals of angels, of the type that can be held in the hand during the rituals, are mentioned in the instructions, but never given.
- There are thirteen topics listed in chapter II, but never covered in the text, not counting 92 and 93, which are described as intentionally omitted: 36, 38, 39, 59–62, 76–78, 82, 86, and 87.
- Names of the angels of the months, hours, and decans are never identified.
- *Penatur, penantur*. In the descriptions of the daemons of the winds, the text says these spirits *penantur vel requiescunt* ("they ??? or they rest") The first word, *penantur*, (*pennor*) is uncommon, and generally means "they may have feathers (or wings)." This is perhaps not a very satisfactory reading of the text however, as Hedegård 2002 p. 50 points out. Manuscript C reads *ponantur* on two occasions ("they may be placed"), and *paenantur* twice, also not a convincing reading. Hedegård with much hesitation proposes a Latinized form of Greek πένομαι ("toil") on the theory that it might be based on a Greek source. Another possibility is that it is a unique verbal (subjunctive) form of *penator* ("one who carries provisions") meaning "they may carry provisions." A slightly more satisfactory reading is suggested by the legal maxim *Clerici non penantur in officiia* "The clergy cannot be compelled to serve temporal offices," which is what I have based by translation on.[116]

Relation to other Solomonic manuscripts

In his prologue, Honorius states that the work is an arrangement of the "works of Solomon," and records the teachings of Solomon with "as much

---

116 From Coke, *The First Part of the Institutes of the Lawes of England. Or, a Commentarie upon Littleton* , 1628, 96b, quoted in Peloubet, S. S. *A Collection of Legal Maxims in Law and Equity, with English Translations*. Littleton, Colo: F.B. Rothmann, 1985, pp. 29-30. https://books.google.com/books?id=4x5HAQAAMAAJ&pg=PA29&lpg=PA29&dq =penantur&source=bl&ots=KUr2RvLpWF&sig=bNbj3VD6L2UtYM746S_pT0NiHn s&hl=en&sa=X&ved=0CE4Q6AEwCG0VChMIt-_uu-TJyAIVk_WAChouwgSq#v= onepage&q=penantur&f=false retrieved 10/17/2015.

exactness as possible." Solomon is mentioned repeatedly in the text, and is quoted repeatedly. In some cases the quotes are otherwise unknown.[117]

Nevertheless, Honorius has only a few elements in common with other Solomonic magic texts. Aside from the prayers drawn from *Ars Notoria*, these include ink made from blood, a Seal of Solomon, names of God and angels (only some well known in Solomonic literature), hazel wand, seals of spirits, incense offerings, magic circles, swords, and whistle.

Many elements in Honorius are unknown in other texts: most of the names of angels and God are otherwise not known, as are specific design details of the wand, swords, whistle, and magic circle. As far as I know, the spirit throne being elevated or a depression according to the type of spirit is also otherwise unknown.

As mentioned above, another handbook of ritual magic popular in the Middle Ages, *Thesaurus Spirituum* (14th century or older),[118] makes use of the same seven sacred names as Honorius (IV.14–47, CXXVII.15). These appear to derive from *Razielis* (different sections ascribed to different Biblical authors, including Solomon.)

There are direct parallels between the *Sworn Book* and pseudo-Agrippa and pseudo-de Abano, but whether they drew on Honorius or some common ancestor is unclear.

Other magic texts have detailed instructions for specific practical benefits only briefly mentioned in the text. For example, operations to secure a magically-fast horse, or making a banquet appear, are frequent, including the Munich handbook published by Kieckhefer.[119] This may indicate some level of an awareness of these other texts.

Editions

Latin. A critical edition of the Latin text was published in 2002 by Gösta Hedegård. Hedegård's text was largely based on Sloane 3854, which is the most complete, most senior, and "least tampered with." Unfortunately, he did not make use of Sloane 3853, which is an important second witness to por-

---

117 III.3, IV.54, on which see Mesler 2012 p. 119 and 139 n 48.
118 Klaassen 2013 pp. 234–235 n 21.
119 E.g. Kieckhefer 1989 pp. 54, 208; Wellcome MS 110 87v; Rawlinson D 252 73r; Sloane 3885.

tions of the text. Also, as Claire Fanger noted in her 2006 review, some of his findings have been superseded due to the considerable amount of scholarly activity on the subject. His careful comparison of the text with *Ars Notoria*, for example, has been obsoleted by Véronèse's 2007 edition of that text.[120] In another review, Juris Lidaka checked thirteen samples from Hedegård's edition, and found "very few major errors." The only concrete example he gives is that 4.1 "diameter" should be "diametrus"—on which I disagree: The manuscript supports GH's reading, and the usage is not unknown.[121]

Boudet also provided a critical edition of much of the text in his 2002 article "Magie théurgique" etc. His readings vary slightly with Hedegård's, and his critical apparatus is conveniently placed with the text rather than as an appendix.

English. Driscoll 1977. The only attempt at publishing any significant portion of the English translation was Daniel Driscoll's *The Sworn Book of Honourius* (sic) *the Magician*, Heptangle Books, 1977. Unfortunately, Driscoll did not make use of the best manuscripts, omitted large portions, misread and misplaced angelic names and words from the prayers, and otherwise took serious liberties with the text.

Peterson 1998/2009. Edition on CD Rom and http://esotericarchives.com/juratus/juratus.htm. The earliest version of this covered only the chapters included in the Royal manuscript, but with alternate readings from the other manuscripts. This was later supplemented with the rest of the text, and has incorporated corrections pretty much continually to this date.

Blanchard, Robert. The supposed translation published by Blanchard proves to be entirely dependent on Driscoll, altered superficially to disguise the fact, but perpetuating all of his Driscoll's errors and his artwork.[122]

This edition

Publishing a new edition is a daunting task, given that "so much of interest hangs in the balance around this work."[123] My intent has not been to sum-

---

120 Fanger 2006 pp. 180–183.
121 Lidaka 2004. Boudet 2002 p. 876 also supports the reading of *diameter*.
122 Ironically, in promoting his publications, Blanchard wrote "Bad translations taken from bad sources mean failure for the practitioner."
123 Fanger 2006 p. 180.

marize all of the recent literature, but to provide a modern translation for those unwilling to tackle the difficult medieval Latin. I also wanted to offer some corrections and observations suggested by the literature, or by my own research.

Editorial principles

I have not tried to reproduce the critical apparatuses of Hedegård 2002 or Boudet 2002, but in some cases I supplement those in my footnotes. In the case of the magic circle, the text arranged around the diagram was not transcribed, or critical apparatus provided, by either of those publications, so I have taken the opportunity of providing it in this edition.

In order to facilitate reference to Hedegård's critical apparatus, I have included his paragraph numbers. For other corrections to his text, see Appendix I.

Hedegård used italics, and the notations |ᵃ⁻ᵃ|, and ||ᵃ⁻ᵃ|| to indicate where LIH and *Ars Notoria* coincided; since this has been obsoleted by the critical edition of Julien Véronèse 2007, I have not tried to maintain the use of those notations. Instead, I have indicated the paragraphs of Ars Not. from that edition, abbreviated JV.

Abbreviations: Abbreviations in the manuscript have generally been expanded.

Chi Rho: The manuscripts generally uses this common practice of abbreviating the name Iesus Christus with Greek letters IHS XP (Iηs Xρ); these have been expanded to "Iesus Christus." Note particularly the frequent use of Greek "XP" or "χρ" for "Christ." In textual studies this is commonly referred to as "chi rho." Thus "XPus" (abbreviation for "Christus") looks like Latin "Xpus," Similarly the Greek "IHS" or "ιης," standing for the Latin "Iesus" ("Jesus") is found throughout the text.[124]

---

124 GH expanded this as Ihesus Christus.

Acknowedgments

I owe thanks to many for their roles in making this book possible. First to John Dee for collecting and preserving old manuscripts, the curators of the British Library manuscripts department for allowing me access to those manuscripts, Universität Kassel Bibliothek for digitizing the Ganell manuscript, Carlos Gilly for bringing it to our attention, Damaris Gehr for her pioneering work, Leipzig University for digitizing their amazing magical manuscripts; the officers of the Societas Magica for their many important contributions, and Ioannis Marathakis for his insights and suggestions. Finally I owe great thanks once again to Jim Wasserman for his many years of support and encouragement.

Abbreviations

_ I use underlining in the footnotes to highlight differences the readings between source texts.

++ = text seems to be corrupt

<> = text that should be deleted

[] = text that should be added

[*] Corrected readings are indicated by * in front of the correct form.

{} = Text cannot be read because of physical damage.

A: MS Sloane 3854

B: MS Sloane 313

BoO: *Book of Oberon,* Harms, Clark, Peterson 2015

C: MS Sloane 3885

D: MS Sloane 3853

GH: Gösta Hedegård, also his critical edition (2002)

H: *Heptameron,* Petrus de Abano 1565

JV: Julien Véronèse 2007 critical edition of *Ars Notoria*

L: Leipzig Cod. Mag. 16

LIH: *Liber Iuratus Honorii*

LTA: *Liber Trium Animarum,* i.e. SSM IV.2.3

R: British Library MS Royal 17 Axlii

Sl. London, British Library, Sloane manuscript collection

SSM: Ganell, *Summa Sacre Magice,* Kassel, Ms. 4° astron. 3.

Summa: Ganell, *Summa Sacre Magice,* Kassel, Ms. 4° astron. 3.

The Sworn Book of Honorius

Liber Iuratus Honorii

Liber Iuratus Honorii
Text

[Prologus]

Cum convenissent maligni spiritus demonia in cordibus hominum intonantes, cogitantes utilitatem fragilitatis humane +posse suo corrumpere et+ totam mundi machinam volentes suis viribus superare, (2) ypocrisim cum invidia seminantes, pontifices et prelatos in superbia radicantes, dominum papam cum cardinalibus in unum venire fecerunt, dicentes adinvicem que secuntur:

(3) "Salus, quam dedit Dominus plebi sue, modo per magos et nigromanticos in dampnacionem convertitur cuiuscumque. (4) Nam et ipsi magi potu diabolico inebriati et eciam excecati contra statuta sancte matris ecclesie procedentes ac preceptum Dominicum transgredientes, sic dicens: (5) 'Non temptabis Dominum Deum tuum' set 'ei soli servies,' ipsi Deo sacrificium abnegando et temptando nomina creatoris, demones invocando et eis sacrificia tribuendo, quod est contra baptismatis sacri preceptum, (6) nam ibi dicitur:

'Abrenuncio Sathane et omnibus pompis eius;' qui non tantum pompas et opera Sathane prosecuntur set universum populum in suis erroribus provocaverunt, (7) cum suis mirificis illusionibus attrahentes ignorantes pro huiusmodi anime et corporis dampnacionem optinere, et cum hoc nullum propositum aliud cogitantes, propter quod oportet omnes alias sciencias deperire.

(8) Dignum est ergo radicem mortis huius stipitis penitus exstirpare cum cultoribus seminum huius artis."

(9) Ipsi vero Diabolo inspirante moti invidia et cupiditate sub similitudine veritatis falsitatem publicantes, quod falsum est dicere et absurdum, quia virum iniquum et immundum impossibile est per artem veraciter operari, (10) nec spiritibus aliquibus homo obligatur, set ipsi inviti coguntur mundatis hominibus respondere et sua beneplacita penitus adimplere. (11) Tamen nullo nostrum volente eis artis principia nec causam ostendere veritatis, ob hoc nos et artem magicam morti suo iudicio tradiderunt.

The Sworn Book of Honorius Translation

[Prologue]

When evil spirits had convened, intending to invoke demons into the hearts of men, thinking it possible to use human frailty <wishing> to spoil <their> and overcome the whole world order by force, (2) planting the seeds of hypocrisy and hatred, so that arrogance takes root in the bishops and prelates, they caused the Pope and cardinals to gather together, who said to each other as follows:

(3) "The salvation which the Lord has given to his people, has now been turned to their damnation, through magic and nigromancy. (4) For even the magicians themselves have intoxicated themselves with the devilish drink, and even blinded against the holy statutes of the mother Church, and transgressed against the Lord's teachings which say: (5) 'You shall not test the Lord your God';[1] but 'you shall serve him alone,'[2] thus they deny the sacrifice due to God himself, and testing the names of the Creator, invoking demons, and giving them sacrifices, contrary to their baptismal vows, (6) for there it is said: 'I renounce Satan and all his pomp;' whereby not only do these (magicians) pursue the pomp and works of Satan, but they also draw all people into his errors (7) with their amazing illusions, thereby attracting the ignorant to the damnation of their bodies and souls, and they thinking this for no other reason, than that they ought to obliterate all other knowledge.

(8) It is therefore appropriate to root out this root of death, along with those who cultivate the seeds of this art."

(9) So they, inspired by the Devil, and moved by hatred and greed, published falsehood disguised as truth, saying things which are false and absurd, because it is impossible that a wicked and impure man can operate truly in this art, (10) nor is a person bound to any spirits, but spirits are forced against their wills to answer pure men, and to thoroughly fulfill their good pleasures. (11) Nevertheless, none of us was willing to reveal the principles nor causes of this truth, because they had handed down a judgment of death to us and this art of magic.

---

1 Deut. 6:16
2 Deut. 6:13

(12) Nos autem permissione divina illud iudicium prescientes, scientes eciam, quod inde possent accidere multa mala, (13) quoniam impossibile erat nos congregacionis populi corporis viribus manus evadere, nisi a spiritibus cepissemus auxilium, dubitantes inde maius periculum evenire, (14) quoniam hostilis demonum potencia per precepta nostra sola hora eos integre destruxisset, ob hoc unum consilium fecimus magistrorum generale, (15) in quo ex 89 magistris a Neapoli, Athenis et Tholeto congregatis elegimus unum nomine Honorium, filium Euclidis, magistrum Thebarum, ubi ars illa tunc legebatur, ut deberet super predictis pro nobis omnibus operari.

(16) Qui consulente angelo Hocrohel nomine 7 volumina artis magice deffloravit nobis florem accipiens et aliis cortices dimittendo. (17) De quibus voluminibus subtraxit 93 capitula cum omnibus virtutibus huius artis, que sub verbis brevibus continentur, (18) de quibus libellum composuit, quem sacrum sive iuratum vocamus hac de causa, quoniam 100 sacra Dei nomina sunt materia huius libri; (19) et ideo sacrum, quasi actus ex sacris, vel quod per istum exeunt sacra, vel quod ab angelis est sacratus, et quia cum hoc angelus Hocrohel eum sacratum a Domino appellavit.

(20) Tunc placatis principibus et prelatis contentis de combustione fabularum et destruccione scolarum—et credebant hanc artem penitus destruxisse—nos moti furore et iracundia ista fecimus iuramenta:

(21) Primo, quod nulli dabitur iste liber, donec magister fuerit in extremis; et quod nisi tribus tantum copietur; et quod nulli dabitur mulieri nec homini nisi maturo actu tantum et probissimo ac fideli, (22) et qui cognoverit per annum mores et condiciones; et quod de cetero non destruetur sed danti restituetur aut eius successoribus;

(23) et quod, si non inveniatur homo sufficiens, cui liber dari debeat, quod magister secum faciat in tumulo sepeliri executores per iuramenta fortissima constringendo (24) vel ipsum alicubi in vita sua sepeliat munde

(12) But we with divine permission, knowing about that judgment beforehand, knowing also that it would be the cause of great evils, (13) because it was impossible for us to evade the hands of a large body of people, except through the help of spirits we had captured, and fearing that a greater danger would result, (14) because the hostile force of the demons at our command would have destroyed them entirely in only an hour, on account of this we convened a general council of masters, (15) from which out of 89 masters gathered from Naples, Athens, and Toledo, we selected one named Honorius, son of Euclid, master of Thebes, where that art at the time was established, in order that he would labor on our behalf to this end.

(16) And he, with the consulting angel Hocrohel, named seven books of the magic art, plucking for us the flower and dismissing all the rest as bark. (17) From those books he extracted ninety-three chapters with all the worth of this art, which are succinctly captured, (18) from which he composed the short book which we call "Sacred" or "Sworn," so-called because the hundred sacred names of God are included in this book; (19) and therefore "Sacred" as it acts through the sacred, or because sacred things emerge from it, or because it is consecrated through the angels, and because the angel Hocrohel called it consecrated before the Lord.

[The Oath]

(20) Then the princes and prelates (secular and church authorities), contented with the burning of fables and the destruction of schools, believed this art to be utterly destroyed. We, being moved by their madness and rage, have made these oaths:

✠ (21) First, that nobody should be given this book, unless the master is at the point of death;

✠ [2] And that he should provide himself no more than three;

✠ [3] And that it will be given to no woman, nor to a man unless he is mature, and most upright and faithful, (22) both of which should be assessed by observing his mannerisms throughout an entire year;

✠ [4] And that otherwise it should not be destroyed, but returned to him or to his successors;

✠ (23) [5] And that, if no one sufficient is found to whom the book might be given, that the master must bind his executors with the strongest oaths to

et honeste nec locum alicui per aliquas circumstancias revelabit; (25) et si magister ex discipulis aliquam necessitatem habeat aut velit eos aliqualiter probare, quod pro preceptis suis complendis mortem pati, si necesse fuerit, non timebunt; (26) et quod habens non inquiret de dictis vel factis magistri sui, nec ipsum magistrum suum talia scire alicui revelabit, nec dabit ad hoc circumstancias declarantes; (27) et quod sicut pater alligat filios suos, ita magister discipulos suos alligabit in concordia et amore, (28) ita quod unus detrimentum alterius pacietur nec unus secretum alterius revelabit, sed erunt fideles, unanimes et concordes. (29) Nono iurabit recipiens—et post istud transsibit iuramentum—hec omnia predicta observare, et ob hanc causam librum hunc vocitamus iuratum.

II Incipit liber.

In nomine igitur omnipotentis Domini nostri Iesu Christi, vivi et veri Dei, ego Honorius opera Salomonis in libro meo taliter ordinavi, quod premisi capitula, ut pateant clarius que secuntur.

(2) Capitula primi operis

Primum capitulum de composicione magni nominis Dei, quod apud Hebreos dicitur Semenphoras et est 72 literarum, quod est principium in hac arte.

(3) 2um de visione divina.

3um de cognicione potestatis divine.

4um de absolucione peccatorum.

5um ne homo incidat in peccatum mortale.

6um de redempcione trium animarum de purgatorio.

bury it in his tomb, (24) or he himself while living should bury it in some clean and honorable place, and not reveal the place under any circumstances;

✠ (25) [6] And if the master has a need for some students, or otherwise wishes to test them, that they promise they will not fear to suffer death, if necessary, for the sake of his teachings

✠ (26) [7] And that he will not investigate the teachings or doings of their master, nor will he reveal to anyone that his master himself knows such things, nor will he allow the circumstances for declaring it.

✠ (27) [8] And as a father binds his sons, so the master will bind his disciples in harmony and love, (28) so that each will bear the suffering of the others, nor will one reveal the secrets of another, but they will be faithful, harmonious, and in agreement.

✠ (29) [9] With the ninth he will swear on receiving the oath that he will pass on all of the preceding in turn, and for this reason we call this the *Sworn Book*.

II. Beginning of the Book.

Therefore, in the name of our almighty Lord Jesus Christ, the living and true God, I Honorius have laid out the works of Solomon in such a manner in my book, which topics I have listed in advance, in order to more clearly show what follows.

(2) The Topics of the First Work.

1. The first topic, concerning the composition of the great name of God, which the Hebrews call "Shem Ha-Meforash," and is of 72 letters, which is the beginning of this art.

(3) 2. Concerning the Divine vision.

3. Concerning the knowledge of Divine power.

4. Concerning the absolution of sins.

5. Lest one falls into mortal sin.

6. Concerning the redemption of three souls from Purgatory.

(4) Capitula secundi operis

Septimum de cognicione celorum.

8um de cognicione angelorum cuiuslibet celi.

9um de cognicione cuiuslibet angeli et nominis et potestatis eius.

(5) 10um de cognicione sigillorum cuiuslibet angeli et virtutis eorum.

11um de cognicione superiorum cuiuslibet angeli.

12um de cognicione officii cuiuslibet angeli.

(6) 13um de invocacione et associacione cuiuslibet angeli.

14um de impetracione voluntatis per quemlibet angelum.

15um de impetracione omnium scienciarum.

16um de hora mortis sienda.

(7) 17um de omnibus presentibus, preteritis et futuris sciendis.

18um de cognicione planetarum et stellarum.

19um de cognicione virtutum planetarum et stellarum et quid habent influere.

(8) 20um de influenciis planetarum et stellarum mutandis.

21um de mutacione diei in noctem et noctis in diem.

22um de cognicione spirituum et animalium aereorum.

(9) 23um de cognicione spirituum ignis et eorum nominum et superiorum et sigillorum et potestatum et virtutum eorum.

24um de cognicione nominum et virtutum superiorum spirituum.

(10) 25um de cognicione sigillorum et virtutum eorum.

26um de cognicione permixtionis et permutacionis elementorum et corporum ex hiis mixtorum.

(11) 27um de cognicione omnium herbarum, plantarum et omnium animalium existencium super terram et virtutum eorum.

(12) 28um de cognicione humane nature et omnium factorum hominis, que sunt cogitata et que sunt abscondita et ignota in ipsa.

(13) 29um de cognicione aquaticorum spirituum et virtutum [et] superiorum ipsorum.

30um de cognicione terrenorum et infernorum spirituum.

(14) 31um de visione purgatorii et inferni et animarum ibidem existencium.

32um de obligacione corporis et anime ad revertendum.

33um de sacracione huius libri.

(4) The Topics of the Second Work.

7. Concerning the knowledge of the Heavens.
8. Concerning the knowledge of the angels of each of the Heavens.
9. Concerning the knowledge of each angel's name and powers
(5) 10. Concerning the knowledge of the seals of each angel, and their virtues.
11. Concerning the knowledge of the superiors of each angel
12. To know the office of any angel.
(6) 13. Regarding the invocation of any angel, and associating with them.
14. To obtain your wishes through any angel.
15. To obtain all knowledge.
16. To know the hour of death.
(7) 17. To know all things past, present, and future.
18. To know the planets and stars.
19. To know the virtues of the planets and stars and their influences.
(8) 20. To change the influences of the planets and stars.
21. To change day into night, and night into day.
22. To know the spirits and creatures of the air.
(9) 23. To know the spirits of the fire, their names, superiors, seals, powers, and virtues.
24. To know the names and virtues of the higher spirits.
(10) 25. To know their seals and virtues.
26. To know the mixing and changing of elements, and of the bodies mixed from them.
(11) 27. To know all herbs, plants, and all animals which exist on the earth, and their virtues.
(12) 28. To understand human nature and all human achievements, and what are his hidden and unknown intentions.
(13) 29. To know the aquatic spirits, and their virtues and superiors.
30. To know all terrestrial and infernal spirits.
(14) 31. Concerning the vision of purgatory and hell, and of the souls abiding there.
32. Concerning the promise that the body and soul will be reunited.
33. Concerning the consecration of this book.

(15) Capitula tercii operis

Tricesimum quartum de constriccione spirituum per verba.
35um de constriccione spirituum per sigilla.
36um de constriccione spirituum per tabulas.
37um de forma cuilibet spiritui imponenda.
(16) 38um de inclusione spirituum.
39um de incluso spiritu ut respondeat vel non.
40um de fulgure et tonitruo provocando.
41um de combustione facienda.
42um de purificacione aeris.
(17) 43um de corrupcione aeris.
44um de nive et gelu facienda.
45um de rore et pluvia facienda.
46um de floribus et fructibus provocandis.
47um de invisibilitate.
48um de equo.
(18) 49um de absente quod veniat in hora sanus.
50um de re, que deferatur in momento ubicumque volueris.
51um de abstraccione rei.
52um de revocacione rei.
53um de transfiguracione cuiuscumque.
(19) 54um de flumine provocando in terra sicca.
55um de commocione regni contra dominum.
56um de regno vel imperio destruendo.
57um de habendo potestatem super quemlibet.
58um de mille militibus armatis habendis.
(20) 59um de formacione castri indestructibilis.
60um de speculo perverso componendo.
61um de destruccione loci vel inimici per speculum perversum.
62um de speculo aparicionis mundi.
(21) 63um de fure et furto revocando.

(15) The Topics of the Third Work.

34. Concerning the binding of spirits through words.
35. Concerning the binding of spirits through seals.
36. Concerning the binding of spirits through tables.
37. Concerning imposing a form to any spirit.
(16) 38. The confinement of spirits.
39. In order that a confined spirit will answer or not.
40. To call forth lightning and thunder.
41. Concerning suffumigations that must be made.
42. Concerning the purification of the air.
(17) 43. Concerning the corruption of the air.
44. To make snow and frost.
45. To make dew and rain.
46. To call forth flowers and fruit.
47. For invisibility.
48. Concerning a horse.[3]
(18) 49. To bring a missing person back safely in an hour.
50. To transport something wherever you wish, in a moment.
51. To have something removed.
52. To recall something.
53. To transfigure anything.
(19) 54. To cause a river on dry land.
55. To incite a kingdom against its ruler.
56. To destroy a kingdom or state.
57. To have power over anyone.
58. To have 1 thousand armed soldiers.
(20) 59. To form an indestructible fortress.
60. How to make a mirror of destruction.
61. How to destroy a place or an enemy using the mirror of destruction.
62. The apparition of the world in a mirror (or glass).
(21) 63. To return anything which a thief has stolen.

---

3 CXVI reiterates the topics with more detail: "Concerning a horse, which will carry you anywhere you wish in a single night." CXX specifies that the spirits of the West can make horses fast. Sl. 3853 fol. 38v has a chapter on how to magically have a fast horse, "which can carry you from England to Jerusalem in under an hour." Compare Kieckhefer, *Forbidden Rites*, p. 54.

64um de seraturis aperiendis.
65um de discordia facienda.
66um de concordia provocanda.
67um de habenda gracia et benivolencia omnium personarum.
(22) [68um de mulieribus habendis ad libitum.]
69um de diviciis habendis.
70um de curacione cuiuslibet infirmitatis.
71um de dando infirmitatem cuilibet et qualemcumque placuerit operanti.
72um de interficiendo quemcumque.
(23) 73um de tempestate et periculo terre et maris faciendo.
74um de nave retenta in mari per adamantem vel aliter retrahenda.
75um de omni periculo evitando.
76um de congregacione et capcione avium.
(24) 77um de piscibus congregandis et capiendis.
78um de animalibus silvestribus congregandis et capiendis.
79um de bello faciendo inter aves vel pisces vel animalia.
(25) 80um de apparencia combustionis.
81um de apparencia ioculatorum et puellarum psallencium.
82um de apparencia gardinorum vel castrorum.
83um de apparencia militum pugnancium.
(26) 84um de apparencia griphonum et drachonum.
85um de apparencia omnium ferarum.
86um de apparencia venatoris et canum in venacione.
87um de apparencia hominis quod sit alibi quam est.
88um de apparencia tocius voluptatis.

(27) Capitula quarti operis

Octagesimum nonum de incarceratis habendis.
90um de seris et carceribus reserandis.
91um de thesauris, metallis et lapidibus preciosis et omnibus rebus absconditis in terra habendis.

64. To open locks.
65. To cause discord.
66. To cause agreement.
67. To have the good will and favor of all persons.
(22) [68. To have the desire of women.]⁴
69. To have wealth.
70. To cure any sickness.
71. To make anyone sick, whenever you wish.
72. To kill anyone.
(23) 73. To hold back storms and dangers of the earth and sea.
74. To hold back a ship at sea using the adamant stone, or otherwise to bring it back again.
75. To avoid all danger.
76. To flock birds together, and collect them.
(24) 77. To cause fish to gather and be caught.
78. To cause woodland animals to gather and be caught.
79. To cause war between the birds, or fish, or animals.
(25) 80. To make burning appear.
81. To make appear jesters and girls singing Psalms.⁵
82. To make gardens or fortresses appear.
83. To make appear soldiers fighting.
(26) 84. To make griffins and dragons appear.
85. To make all wild beasts appear.
86. To make hunters and dogs appear hunting.
87. To make someone appear as if they were somewhere other than where they actually are.
88. To make all pleasures appear.

(27) The Topics of the Fourth Work.

89. To release someone who is imprisoned.
90. To unlock bars and prisons.
91. To obtain treasure, metals, and precious stones, and all things that are hidden in the earth.

---

4 See chapter CXVI which recounts the topics.
5 Chapter CXVI: balancium ("babbling"). SSM: ballancium ("dancing").

(28) 92um de apparencia corporum mortuorum quod loquantur et resuscitata appareant.

93um ut animalia de terra creari appareant.

Set ista duo capitula subtraximus, quoniam erant contra Domini voluntatem.

III Incipit libero

Nos igitur cum divino adiutorio precepta Salomonis et vestigia sequi volentes tanteque subtilitatis vires recipere unum principium necessarium esse profitemur. (2) Nota, quod primum principium est divina maiestas, et est invocacio vera a fide cordis procedens et est opera iusta efficaciam ostendens. (3) Dixit Salomon: "Unus est et solus Deus, sola virtus, sola fides," a quo unum opus, unum principium. Una perfeccio in arte consistit, quamvis in membris dividatur multiplicibus. (4) Et sicut partes integrales capiunt suum totum, licet fuerit imperfectum, similiter ex hiis nascitur tota virtus.

(5) In nomine igitur illius Dei vivi et veri, qui est Alpha et Ω, principium et finis, qui est Pater et Filius et Spiritus sanctus, tres persone, unus deus, vite dator, mortis destructor, (6) unde dicitur: " ... qui mortem nostram moriendo destruxit et vitam resurgendo reparavit, qui Novum condidit Testamentum,"

(7) de composicione sigilli Dei ad noticiam prime partis, de visione divina ad noticiam secunde partis, de visione angelorum ad noticiam tercie partis, (8) de constriccione spirituum ad noticiam 4^e partis et de ligacione infernorum ad noticiam 5^e partis vere operantibus per hunc modum.

(9) Angelorum tres sunt modi, celestes, aerei, terrestres. Celestium duo sunt modi, quorum quidam serviunt Deo soli, (10) et isti sunt 9 ordines angelorum, videlicet cherubyn, seraphin, troni, dominaciones, virtutes, principatus, potestates, archangeli et angeli, (11) de quibus nec ex coacta virtute nec ex artificiali potencia inter mortales est loquendum, et isti nullatenus invocantur, (12) quia magestati divine continue laudantes assistunt et nuncquam ab eius presencia separantur.

(28) 92. Concerning the appearing of dead bodies which appear to rise again and speak.

93. In order that animals of the earth appear to be created.

But we have removed those two topics, because they were against the Lord's will.

III. Here begins the book.

We therefore, with divine help, wishing to record the teachings of Solomon, and to follow his footsteps with as much exactness as possible, we declare there to be one principle necessity. (2) Note, that the first principle is the Divine Majesty, and it is the true invocation proceeding from faith of the heart and just works, showing the effectiveness.

(3) Solomon said: "There is only one God, one power, one faith," from which a single work, a single beginning. Perfection in the art consists of one, although it can be divided into multiple parts. (4) And just as the integral parts make up the whole, although it had been incomplete, similarly from these the whole power is born.

(5) Therefore, in the name of that living and true God, who is Alpha and Omega, the beginning and the end, who is Father, Son, and Holy Spirit, three persons, one God, the giver of life, and the destroyer of death, (6) of whom it is said: "... Who by dying has destroyed our death, and renewed our life with his resurrection, establishing a New Covenant."[6]

(7) The First Part concerns the composition of the Seal of God; Part Two concerns the Divine Vision; Part Three concerns the vision of angels; (8) Part Four concerns the binding of spirits; and Part Five concerns binding the inhabitants of the underworld.

(9) There are three types of angels, the celestial, the aerial, and the earthly. There are two types of celestials, those who only serve God, (10) and those are the nine orders of angels, namely, the Cherubim, Seraphim, Thrones, Dominations, Virtues, Principalities, Powers, Archangels, and Angels, (11) concerning whom it is spoken among mortals neither by forced power nor by artificial force, and therefore in nowise should they be invoked, (12) because they always stand praising the divine majesty, and never separated from his presence.

---

6 From the mass.

(13) Tamen quia humani generis anima cum ipsis formata, expectans cum ipsis feliciter coronari per donum et graciam Salvatoris, (14) potest suo vivente corpore eos presencialiter cum summa maiestate veraciter aspicere et cum ipsis Deum laudare et suum cognoscere creatorem. (15) Et ista cognicio non est cognoscere Deum in maiestate et potencia nisi illo modo, quo Adam et prophete cognoverunt.

(16) Set istud est principaliter notandum, quod operancium tres sunt modi, pagani, Iudei, Christiani. Pagani sacrificant spiritibus aereis et terreis et eos non constringunt, (17) set fingunt spiritus se constringi per verba legis eorum, ut ydolis fidem adhibeant et ad veram fidem nullatenus convertantur. (18) Et quia fidem malam habent;opera eorum nulla. Et qui per talia experimenta operari voluerit, Dominum Deum suum dimittat et derelinquat et spiritibus sacrificet et ydolis fidem adhibeat, (19) quia fides operatur in homine, sive bona fuerit sive mala, unde in Evangelio: "Fides tua te salvam fecit."

(20) Iudei in hac visione nullatenus operantur, quia per adventum Christi donum amiserunt, nec possunt in celis collocari testante Domino, (21) qui dicit: "Qui baptizatus non fuerit condempnabitur," et sic in omnibus angelis operantur imperfecte. (22) Nec per invocaciones suas veniunt ad effectum, nisi Christo fidem adhibeant, quia dictum est eis per prophetam: (23) "Quando venit rex regum et dominus dominancium, cessabit uncio vestra," que nuncquam cessaret, si per hanc artem haberet efficaciam veram, et sic opera eorum nulla. (24) Et quamvis Iudei, in quantum Iudei, a Deo sunt condempnati, tamen summum adorant creatorem set indebito modo. (25) Tamen virtute sanctorum Dei nominum coguntur venire spiritus, set quia Iudei non signantur signo Domini, scilicet crucis et fidei, nolunt spiritus veraciter eis respondere.

(13) Yet because the soul of man was formed with the angels, awaiting with them to be happily rewarded by the gift and grace of the Saviour, (14) he is able to truly look at the most high Majesty face to face while alive and to praise God along with them (the angels), and recognize his Creator. (15) And that knowledge is not to recognize God in his greatness and might, except in that manner by which Adam and the prophets recognized him.

(16) But this should principally be observed, that there are three types of people who perform this art: pagans, Jews, and Christians.

The pagans sacrifice to the aerial and earthly spirits, and do not bind them, (17) but the spirits pretend themselves to be confined by the words of their law, in order that they have faith in idols, and never be converted to the true faith. (18) And because they adhere to a false faith, their works are invalid. And he that wishes to perform such experiments must abandon and forsake the Lord their God and sacrifice to the spirits and put faith in idols, (19) because faith works in man, whether good or evil, from which the Gospel says: "Your faith has made you well."[7]

(20) Jews can in nowise work to obtain this vision, because with the arrival of Christ they have lost the gift, nor can they be stationed in heaven as the Lord testified when he said: "Whomever has been baptized will not be condemned,"[8] and so they work imperfectly with all angels. (22) Nor will their invocations be effective, unless they put their faith in Christ, because it was said through the prophet: (23) "When the king of kings and lord of lords comes, your anointing will cease,"[9] which should never have ceased, if they could have true effectiveness through this art, and thus their works are null. (24) And although the Jews, as they are Jews, have been condemned by God, yet they honor the most high Creator, but in an improper manner. (25) Yet with the power of the holy names of God, the spirits are compelled to come, but because the Jews are marked not with the Sign of the Lord, namely of the cross and of the faith, the spirits are unwilling to answer them truly.

---

7 Luke 17:19. In the parallel text in SSM L.4.f.49, the main target of derision is Islam. See Veenstra 2012 pp. 188–189 n62.

8 Compare Mark 16:16: "He who believes and is baptised shall be saved, but he who believes not shall be condemned."

9 Widely cited by church writers, and attributed to Daniel, the actual source of this quotation seems to be the pseudo-Augustinian sermon "Against the Jews, Pagans, and Arians." See Fanger 2012 pp. 203–204, p. 215 n29. See also Mesler, 2012, p. 118, 139 notes 42–46.

(26) Solus igitur Christianus potest in hac visione et in omnibus aliis veraciter operari. (27) Et quamvis per hanc artem magicam trium hominum genera operentur, non credendum est, quod in hoc nomine "magus" debeat malum includi. (28) Nam magus per se philosophus Grece, Hebraice scriba, Latine sapiens dicitur. Sic ars magica a "magos" dicitur, quod est "sapiens," et "-ycos," quod est "sciencia," (29) quasi "sciencia sapientum," cum in ipsa efficiatur homo sapiens, et per hanc sciuntur omnia presencia, preterita et futura.

Primum opus vel tractatus.

IV De composicione sigilli Dei vivi et veri.

Primo fac unum circulum, cuius diameter sit trium digitorum propter tres clavos Domini vel 5 propter quinque plagas vel 7 propter 7 sacramenta vel 9 propter 9 ordines angelorum; set communiter 5 digitorum fieri solet.

(2) Deinde infra illum circulum fac alium circulum a primo distantem duobus granis ordei propter duas tabulas Moysi vel distantem a primo tribus granis propter trinitatem personarum.

(3) Deinde infra illos duos circulos in superiori parte, que dicitur angulus meridiei, fac unam crucem, cuius tibia aliquantulum intret circulum interiorem.

(4) Deinde a parte dextra crucis scribe h—aspiracionem—deinde t, deinde o, deinde e. x. o. r. a. b. a. l. a. y. q. c. i. y. s. t. a. l. g. a. <a>. o. n. o. s. u. l. a. r. i. t. e. k. s. p. f. y. o. m. o. m. a. n. a. r. e. m. i. a. r. e. l. a. t. e. d. a. c. o. n. o. n. a. o. y. l. e. y. o. t.

(5) Et iste litere sint eque distantes et circumdent circulum. eo ordine, quo sunt prenominate, et sic magnum nomen Domini "Semenphoras" lxxii literarum erit completum.

(6) Hoc facto in medio circulorum, scilicet in centro, fac unum pentagonum talem: ★, in cuius medio sit signum "tau" tale: ⊤, et supra illud signum scribe nomen Dei "El" et sub nomen aliud Dei, scilicet "Ely," isto modo:

(26) Therefore only Christians are able to attain this vision, and in all other things operate truly. (27) And although three types of people operate in this art of magic, it should not be thought that, in this name "magus" should be implied any evil. (28) For in Greek "magus" signifies a philosopher, in Hebrew a scribe, and in Latin a wise man. Thus the "magic art" is the art of the magi, which is to say the "wise men," and "-ycos," which is "knowledge," (29) thus "the knowledge of the wise men," since in it a man is made wise, and through this art all the past, present, and future are known.

The First Work or Treatise.

IV. Concerning the composition of the Seal of the True and Living God.

First make a single circle, whose diameter is three fingers (on account of the three nails of the Lord), or else 5 (for the five plagues), or 7 (for the 7 sacraments), or even 9 (for the 9 orders of angels); but generally it is made of 5 fingers.

(2) Then, below that circle make another circle, distant from the first by two grains of the barley-corn (on account of the two tablets of Moses, else the distant from the first can be three grains on account of the three persons in the Trinity.

(3) Then below those two circles in the uppermost part, which is called the southern angle, make a single cross, the leg of which may slightly enter the more interior circle.

(4) Then from right part of the cross, write 'h'—the exhalation—then t. o. e. x. o. r. a. b. a. l. a. y. q. c. i. y. s. t. a. l. g. a. <a>. o. n. o. s. u. l. a. r. i. t. e. k. s. p. f. y. o. m. o. m. a. n. a. r. e. m. i. a. r. e. l. a. t. e. d. a. c. o. n. o. n. a. o. y. l. e. y. o. t.

(5) And these letters should be made an equal distance apart, and should surround the circle. That series, which were previously named, and thus it will be filled with the great name of the Lord "Shem Ha-Meforash" of seventy-two letters.

(6) This finished, in the middle of the circles, namely in the center, make a pentagonal thus: ★, in the middle of which should be the sign 'tau', thus: ✝ and above that sign write the name of God "El" and underneath this other name of God, namely "Ely," in this fashion:

(7) Deinde infra angulum superiorem pentagoni scribe istas duas literas: "l," "x" et infra alium angulum dextrum istas duas: "a," "l" et in alio post istum istas duas: "l," "a" et in alio post istum: "l," "c" et in alio post istum "u," "m."

(8) Deinde circa pentagonum fac unum eptagonum, cuius latus superius + secundum sui +[1] medium contingat angulum superiorem pentagoni, ubi "l," "x" scribebatur,

(9) et in eodem latere eptagoni scribe hoc nomen sancti angeli, quod est "Casziel,"

et in alio latere a dextris istud nomen alterius sancti angeli, (10) quod est "Satquiel,"

deinde in alio "Samael" et in alio "Raphael," postea "Anael," postea "Michael," postea "Gabriel,"

et sic septem latera eptagoni erunt adimpleta.

(11) Deinde circa istum eptagonum predictum fac alium eptagonum non quomodo primus factum set taliter, quod unum latus ipsius intercedet alterum latus eiusdem.

(12) Deinde fac alium eptagonum talem, qualis primus fuit, cuius anguli 7 contingant angulos 7 eptagoni secundi, qui binus esse videtur. + Hic tamen eptagonus infra predictum secundum concludetur +. (13) Unum latus secundi eptagoni supereundo et aliud subeundo set latus primo angulo succedens subeundo ibit, et que secuntur serie supereuntis et subeuntis alterutrim[2] se habebunt.

---

1 ++ = *turbata* ("out of order")

2 So Sl. 3854 115r. Other ms: *Altrutrum* ("one to another"). GH p. 156 cites Habel—Gröbel, *Mittellateinisches Glossar* (Paderborn, s.d.) [elsewhere, wechselseitig, gegenseitig: mutually, reciprocally (Adv.).]

(7) Then, below the uppermost angle of the pentagon, write these two letters: 'l', 'x'

and below the other in the right angle, these two: 'a', 'l'

and in the next after those, these two: 'l', 'a'

and in the next after that: 'l', 'c'

and in that following: 'u', 'm'.

(8) Then around the pentagon make a heptagon, it should touch the uppermost side of the pentagon, <its second> which is after the middlemost above angle, where are written 'l', 'x'.

(9) And in the same side of the heptagon write this name of the holy angel, which is 'Casziel.'

And in the next side from the right-most the name of the holy angel, (10) which is 'Satquiel'.

'Then in the next 'Samael', and in the next 'Raphael', afterwards 'Anael', afterwards 'Michael,' afterwards 'Gabriel.'

And thus the seven sides of the heptagon will be completed.

(11) Then around that preceding heptagon make another heptagon, not made like the first, but in such a manner that the one side of it will intersect the previous side of the same.

(12) Then make another such heptagon, like the first, whose seven angles touch the seven angles of the second heptagon, and the which should be shown doubled. + Yet this heptagon will be contained within the preceding second one +.[10] (13) The one side of the second heptagon going over, and the other going under, but the first side should go under the following angle, and that which follows in sequence should go over and under each other.

---

10 This passage matches the drawing in SSM, but not Sl. 313, demonstrating that the drawing in SSM is closer to the original. See Veenstra 2012 p. 161, 186 n34. GH p. 67, 155–156 marks this as *turbata*.

(14) Deinde in quolibet angulo secundi eptagoni una crux depingatur. (15) Deinde in illo latere secundi eptagoni, quod transit ab ultimo angulo eiusdem ad secundum angulum eiusdem, in eadem parte, que est supra "Casziel," sillabe cuiusdam sancti Dei nominis scribantur, (16) ita quod hec sillaba: "la" scribatur in illo loco lateris predicti, qui est supra primam sillabam de "Casziel," (17) et hec sillaba: "ya" in illo loco eiusdem lateris, qui est supra ultimam sillabam eiusdem "Casziel," (18) et hec sillaba: "ly" in illo loco eiusdem lateris, qui est [inter] latus intersecans predictum latus et crucem secundi anguli eiusdem.

(19) Deinde in latere illo, quod tendit ab angulo primo eiusdem secundi eptagoni ad tercium angulum eiusdem, scribatur hoc nomen sanctum Dei: "Narath," (20) ita quod hec sillaba: "na" scribatur in illo loco eiusdem lateris, qui est supra primam sillabam de "Satquiel," (21) et hec sillaba: "ra" in illo loco, qui est supra ultimam eiusdem, et hec due litere: "t," "h" in illo loco, qui est in eodem latere inter latus intersecans ipsum et crucem terciam.

(22) Deinde in illo latere eiusdem secundi eptagoni, quod tendit a tercio angulo eiusdem ad quintum eiusdem, scribatur hoc creatoris nomen sanctum, quod dicitur "Libarre," (23) ita quod hec sillaba: "ly" scribatur supra primam sillabam de "Raphael" et hec sillaba: "bar" supra ultimam sillabam eiusdem (24) et hec sillaba "re" in illo loco eiusdem lateris, qui est inter latus intersecans ipsum et quintum angulum eiusdem secundi eptagoni.

(25) Deinde in illo latere eiusdem secundi eptagoni, quod est a quinta cruce usque ad ultimam, scribatur hoc aliud sacrum creatoris nomen: "Libares," (26) ita quod hec sillaba: "ly" scribatur in illo loco lateris, qui est supra primam sillabam ipsius "Michael," (27) et hec sillaba: "ba" in illo loco lateris, qui est supra ultimam sillabam eiusdem, (28) et hec sillaba: "res" in illo loco eiusdem lateris, qui est inter latus intersecans ipsum et ultimam crucem.

(29) Deinde in illo latere eiusdem secundi eptagoni, quod vadit a secundo angulo eiusdem secundi eptagoni ad quartum, scribatur hoc aliud sanctum nomen: "Lialg" cum coniunctiva, (30) ita quod coniunctiva in illo loco eiusdem lateris scribatur, qui est supra primam sillabam de "Samael," (31) et hec sillaba: "ly" in illo loco eiusdem lateris, qui est supra ultimam eiusdem, (32) et hec sillaba: "alg" in illo loco eiusdem lateris, qui est inter latus intersecans ipsum et quartam crucem.

(14) Then in each of the angles of the second heptagon make a cross. (15) Then in that side (of the second heptagon) which crosses from the last angle of the same to after the angle of the same, in the same part which is above "Casziel," should be written this syllable from a certain sacred name of God, (16) thus: "la" it should be written in that place of the preceding side, which is above the first syllable of "Casziel," (17) and this syllable: 'ya' in that place of same side, which is above the most far syllable of same "Casziel," and this syllable: "ly" in that place of the same side, (18) which is [between] the side intersecting the preceding side and the cross of the following same angle.

(19) Then in that side, which stretches from the first angle of the same heptagon and continues towards the third angle of same, this holy name of God should be written: "Narath," (20) with this syllable: "na" written in that place of the same side, which is above the first syllable of "Satquiel," (21) and this syllable: "ra" in that place, which is above the farthest syllable of same, and these two letters 't,' 'h' made in that place, which is in the same side between the side intersecting itself and the third cross.

(22) Then in that side (of the same second heptagon) which stretches from the third angle of same towards the fifth of same, should be written this holy name of the Creator, which is called "Libarre," (23) thus with this syllable: "ly" written above the first syllable of "Raphael," and this syllable: "bar" above the last syllable of the same, (24) and this syllable "re" in that place of the same side, which is between the side intersecting itself and the fifth angle of same second heptagon.

(25) Then in that side (of the same second heptagon) which is farthest from the fifth cross, this other sacred name of the Creator should be written: 'Libares', (26) with this syllable: "ly" written in that place of the side, which is above the first syllable of "Michael," (27) and this syllable: "ba" in that place of the side, which is above the farthest syllable of same, (28) and this syllable: "res" in that place of same side, which is between the side intersecting itself and the last cross.

(29) Then in that side of the same second heptagon, which goes from the second angle of the same second heptagon towards the fourth, this other holy name should be written: "Lialg" with the connective. (30) Therefore the connective should be written in that place of the same side, which is above the first syllable of "Samael," and this syllable: "ly" in that place of the same side, which is above the farthest of the same, and this syllable: "alg" in that place of the same side, which is between the side intersecting itself and the fourth cross.

(33) Set cave, quod coniunctiva sic debet scribi: ⨒ cum titulo intersecante propter timorem Dei malum volitum dividentem.

(34) Deinde in illo latere eiusdem eptagoni tendente a quarta cruce ad sextam scribatur hoc aliud sacrum Dei nomen: "Ueham," (35) ita quod hec sillaba: "ue" scribatur in illo loco eiusdem lateris, qui est supra primam sillabam de "Anael," et hec litera: "h" supra ultimam sillabam (36) et hec sillaba: "am" in illo loco eiusdem lateris, qui est inter latus [inter]secans ipsum et sextam crucem.

(37) Deinde in illo latere, quod tendit a sexto angulo eiusdem secundi eptagoni ad primum angulum, scribatur hoc aliud sacrum Dei nomen: "Yalgal," (38) ita quod hec litera: "y" scribatur in illo loco eiusdem lateris, qui est supra primam sillabam de "Gabriel," (39) et hec sillaba: "al" supra ultimam et hec sillaba: "gal" in illo loco eiusdem lateris, qui est inter latus intersecans ipsum et primam crucem.

(40) Deinde in medio lateris primi <et> tercii eptagoni a dextris scribatur "Vos" et in sequenti latere eiusdem tercii eptagoni a dextris hoc nomen: "Duynas" (41) et in alio "Gyram" et in alio "Gram" et in alio "Aysaram" et in alio "Alpha" et in alio "Ω."

(42) Deinde in illo spaciolo, quod est sub secundi et tercii angulo primo eptagonorum, scribatur hoc nomen Dei: "El"

(43) et in illo spaciolo, quod est a dextris sub angulis secundi et tercii eptagonorum sub secunda cruce, hoc nomen: "On"

et in illo alio spaciolo sub tercia cruce iterum hoc nomen: "El"

(44) et in alio sub quarta cruce iterum "On" et in alio sub quinta cruce iterum "El"

et in alio sub sexta cruce iterum "On" et in alio sub septima cruce "Ω.'"

(45) Deinde in illo spaciolo, quod clauditur inter angulum primum secundi eptagoni et secundum angulum eiusdem et primum latus tercii eptagoni et porcionem circuli contingentem illos angulos, depingatur una crux in medio, scilicet spacii illius.

(33) But beware, that the connective should be written thus: ☩ with the inscription intersecting, because of the fear of God, separating evil is willed.

(34) Then, on that side (of the same heptagon) that goes from the fourth cross to the sixth, write this other sacred name of God: "Ueham," (35) such that the syllable: "ue" is written above the first syllable of "Anael," and the letter "h" is above the last syllable of the same, (36) and the syllable "am" is in the space of the same side which is [inter]secting the side itself and the sixth cross.

(37) Then, on that side which goes from the sixth angle (of the same second heptagon) to the first angle, this other sacred name of God should be written: "Yalgal," (38) such that the letter "y" is written in the space of the same side which is above the first syllable of "Gabriel," (39) and the syllable "al" is above the last, and the syllable "gal" should be in the space of the same side which is between the intersection and the first cross.

(40) Then in the middle of the first side and the third heptagon on the right should be written "Vos" and in the next side to the right of the same third heptagon this name: "Duynas" (41) and in the next "Gyra" and in the next "Gram" and in the next "Aysaram" and in the next "Alpha" and in the next "Ω."

(42) Then in that small space which is under the second and the third angle of the first heptagon, should be written this name of God: "El"

(43) and in that small space which is to the right under the second and third angles of the heptagons under the following cross, this name: "On"

and in space-small that one elsewhere under the third cross again this name: "El"

(44) and in the other under the fourth cross again "On"
and in the other under the fifth cross again "El"
and in the other under the sixth cross again "On"
and in the other under the seventh cross " Ω"

(45) Then in that small space which is closed between the first angle of the second heptagon and the second angle of same, and the first side of the third heptagon, and the part touching those angles of the circle, draw a single cross in the middle.

(46) Et in bucca superiori a leva crucis scribatur hec litera: "a" et super buccam crucis secundam a dextris hec litera: "g" (47) et sub bucca inferiori a dextris scribatur hec alia litera: "a" et sub quarta bucca hec alia litera: "1."

(48) Deinde in alio spaciolo sequenti a dextris in medio scribatur hoc nomen: "Ely" et in alio hoc nomen: "Eloy" et in alio "Χρς"[3] et in alio "Sother" et in alio "Adonay" et in alio "Saday."

(49) Deinde scias, quod in exemplaribus communiter pentagonus fit de rubeo cum croceo in spaciis tincto, et primus eptagonus de azurio, secundus de croceo, tertius de purpureo, et circuli de nigro. (50) Et spacium inter circulos, ubi est nomen "Semenphoras," tingitur croceo. Omnia alia spacia viridi habent tingi. (51) Set in operacionibus aliter fieri debet, quia de sanguine aut talpe aut turturis aut upupe aut vespertilionis aut omnium horum figuratur et in pergameno virgineo vitulino vel equino vel cervino, et sic completur Dei sigillum. (52) Et per hoc sanctum et sacrum sigillum, quando erit sacratum, poteris facere operaciones, que postea dicentur in hoc libro sacro. (53) Modus autem sacrandi hoc sacrum sigillum talis, sicut sequitur, debet esse.

---

3 = Christus. GH simply expands the "Chi-Rho" to its Latin equivalent, "Christus."

(46) And in top left space of the cross write the letter: "a"
and in the top right space of the cross this letter: "g"
(47) and in the lower right space write another letter: "a"
and under the fourth space below this other letter: "l."
(48) Then in the middle of the next small space on the right, write this name: "Ely"
and in the next this name: "Eloy"
and in the next "Χρς"
and in the next "Sother"
and in the next "Adonay"
and in the next "Saday."

(49) Know then, that in the exemplars generally the pentagon is made from red, with the space tinted yellow, and the first heptagon of azure, the second from yellow, the third from purple, and the circle from black.

(50) And the space between the circles, where the name Shem Ha-Meforash is, is tinted yellow.

All other spaces must be tinted green.

(51) But in the operations it must be done otherwise, because it should be written with the blood either of a mole, a turtledove, or hoopoe, or of a bat, or of all of these. Also, it is should be formed on virgin parchment, either from a calf, foal, or deer. And thus the Seal of God is completed.

(52) And through this holy and sacred seal, once consecrated, you will be able to perform the operations, which afterwards will be revealed in this sacred book.

(53) But the manner consecrating this sacred seal must be done as follows.

Seal of God, reconstructed based on Summa and text of Honorius

(54) Inspirante Domino dixit Salomon: "Vnus est [et] solus Deus, sola fides, sola virtus," quam Dominus hominibus voluit revelari et distribui tali modo. (55) Dixit angelus Samael Salomoni: "Hoc dabis populo Israel, qui et aliis similiter tribuent." Sic placuit creatori, et iubet ipsum Dominus taliter consecrari. (56) Primo sit mundus operans, non pollutus, et cum devocione faciat, non astute. Non comedat neque bibat, donec perfecerit opus, et sanguis, quo scriptum fuerit, primo sit benedictus, sicut postea dicetur. (57) Deinde suffumigetur hoc sigillum ambra, musco, aloe, lapdano albo et rubeo, mastice, olibano, margaritis et thure invocando et orando Domi-

Seal of God, reconstructed based on Summa and text of Honorius

(54) With the Lord's inspiration, Solomon said: "There is only one God, one faith, one power," which the Lord wished to be shown and disseminated to men in such a manner. (55) The angel Samael said to Solomon: "This you will give to the people of Israel, which they will similarly bestow to others." Thus it has pleased the Creator, and the Lord himself orders it to be consecrated in such a manner. (56) First, the worker must be clean, not impure, and should do so with devotion, not cunningly. He must not eat or drink until the work is completed, and the blood, with which the writing will be done, must first be blessed, as will be declared afterward.[11] (57) Then this seal should be suffumigated with amber, musk, aloe, white and red labdanum, mastic, frankincense, pearls, and incense, calling upon and begging the Lord, as will be

---

11 See chap. CXXXVII.

num, sicut postea de visione divina erudietur. (58) Post in vocando angelos, sicut infra eciam dicetur, mutabitur tamen peticio tali modo.

(59) "Vt tu, Domine, per annunciacionem, concepcionem" et cetera "hoc sacratissimum nomen ac sigillum tuum benedicere et consecrare digneris, (60) ut per ipsum te mediante possim vel possit talis N celestes convincere potestates, aereas et terreas cum infernalibus subiugare, invocare, transmutare, coniurare, constringere, excitare, congregare, dispergere, ligare ac ipsos innocuos reddere, (61) homines placare et ab eis suas peticiones graciosius habere, inimicos pacificare, pacificatos disiungere, sanos in sanitate custodire vel infirmare, infirmos curare, (62) homines bonos a malis custodire et distinguere et cognoscere, omne corporale periculum evadere, iudices in placito placatos reddere, victoriam in omnibus optinere, (63) peccata carnalia mortificare et spiritualia fugare, vincere et evitare, divicias in bonis augmentare, et dum in die iudicii apparebit a dextris tuis cum sanctis et electis tuis, tuam possit cognoscere maiestatem."

(64) Et tunc illa nocte sub aere sereno extra domum dimittat. Tunc habeas cirothecas novas sine creta factas, in quas quis nuncquam manum posuerit, in quibus signum +glutetur+. (65) Et sic complebitur hoc sacrosanctum sigillum, cuius primus eptagonus 7 ordines, secundus 7 articulos duplos, tercius 7 sacramenta designat.

V *Viso de composicione sigilli Dei vivi videndum est de visione divina, ad quam habendam sic est procedendum.*

Primo sit operans vere penitens et confessus. Sit a mulieribus et ab earum aspectibus sequestratus. (2) Nam ut Salomon ait: "Tucius est cum ursa et leone in cavernis morari quam cum muliere nequam." Ab hominibus malis

taught afterwards concerning the divine vision. (58) After calling the angels, you should also say as follows, but you should modify the petition in such a manner.

[Prayer.]

(59) "That you, O Lord, through the annunciation, the conception" etc.[12] "that you would deign to bless and consecrate this most holy name and your seal, (60) so that through it with your mediation, I or such person N, will be able to conquer such heavenly powers, of the air or earth, with the infernal ones, to subjugate, invoke, transmute, conjure, constrain, raise up, congregate, disperse, bind and render them harmless. (61) To appease people and favorably obtain from them their petitions, to pacify enemies, to disunite those pacified, to protect the health of those who are healthy, or to sicken them, and to cure the sick. (62) To guard good people from evil, and to distinguish and recognized them, to evade all physical danger, to make favorable judges be favorably disposed again, to have victory in all things, (63) to destroy carnal sins, and rout, conquer, and avoid spiritual ones, to increase wealth in good things, and on the Day of Judgment that I may appear on your right hand with your saints and elect, and be able to recognize your majesty."

(64) And then that night, he should set it outside the house, under clear skies.

Then you should have new gloves, made without whitening chalk, into which no one should have placed a hand, in which the seal must be <glued> [*held]. (65) And thus is completed this sacrosanct seal, whose first heptagon designates the 7 orders, whose second designates the seven twofold events, and whose third designates the seven sacraments.

V. Having considered the composition of the Seal of the living God, which is necessary for seeing the divine vision, we will now proceed to that topic.

First he must perform true penance and confession. He must separate himself from women, and from seeing them. (2) For as Solomon said: "It is safer to dwell with a she-bear and a lion in its den than to abide with a wicked

---

12 See chap. XCIX.2 for full text.

et infirmis separetur. Nam dicitur in Psalmo: "Cum sancto sanctus eris, et cum viro iniquo iniqus eris."

(3) Vitam suam munde deducat, quia dicitur: "Beati immaculati in via, qui ambulant in lege Domini." Vestimenta eius non sint fetida, immo nova vel mundissime lota. (4) Et intendit Salomon vestimenta nova virtutes esse, quia Deus nec beati angeli de mundanis curant. Ex hoc patet, quod pauperes cicius et verius operantur quam divites. (5) Set in operacione subsequenti istorum angelorum istud convenit, quia habitant cum hominibus et sunt mundi. Ideo mundas vestes appetunt, et ideo Salomon generaliter loquebatur.

(6) Nuncquam aliquis, dum hoc facere voluerit, sit ociosus, ne cicius decidat cor suum ad peccatum. Nam dicitur: "Semper aliquid agite, ne ociosi inveniamini." (7) Semper et continue roget Deum per has sanctissimas oraciones, que secuntur, quia dicitur: "Beatus servus, quem, cum venerit Dominus, invenerit vigilantem."

VI Prima oracio

Acciones nostras, quesumus, Domine, aspirando preveni et adiuvando prosequere, ut cuncta nostra operacio a te semper incipiat, et per te incepta finiatur, qui vivis et regnas per omnia secula seculorum. Amen.

woman."[13] He must also separate himself from evil and sick men. For he said in the Psalm: "With the holy you will be holy, and with the unjust you will be unjust."[14]

(3) He must lead a clean life, because it is said: "Blessed are those whose ways are undefiled, who walk in the law of the Lord."[15] His garments must not be foul-smelling, but rather they must be new or very cleanly washed. (4) And by "new garments" Solomon means "of worth," because neither God nor the blessed angel care anything about material things. From this it is seen, that the poor labor more quickly and truly (in this art) than the rich. (5) But in the following operation the same angels, who are pure, are assembled together with men. Therefore they greatly desire clean garments, and therefore Solomon was speaking generally.

(6) He who wishes to accomplish this work must never let himself be idle, lest his heart more quickly falls towards sin. For it is said: "Always strive for something, lest you are found idle."[16] (7) So you should continually pray to God through these most holy prayers which follow, because it is said: "Blessed is that servant, whom his lord when he comes, shall be found vigilant."[17]

VI. Prayer 1.

"Direct, we beg you, O Lord, our actions by your holy inspirations, and carry them on by your gracious assistance, that every prayer and work of ours may begin always with you, and through you be happily ended, who lives and reigns through all the ages of the ages. Amen."[18]

---

13 Paraphrasing Ecclesiasticus 25:16.
14 Ps. 18:26.
15 Ps. 119:1.
16 Paraphrased from Jerome, *Epistolae*, letter 125. See Mesler, 2012, p. 118 and p 139 n 41.
17 "Blessed is that servant....": Matt. 24:46. R inserts a section on suffumigations and names of angels, largely drawn from Agrippa.
18 This prayer appears in the *Liturgia Horarum (Liturgy of the Hours)* and other medieval collections of prayers. A slightly different version is found in the *Rituale Romanum (Roman Ritual)*. Other magic texts incorporate it as well, including the *Book of Oberon*, p. 51; Sloane 3851, fol. 21; and Kieckhefer, *Forbidden Rites*, p. 252.

VII 2ᴬ ORACIO

Ave, Maria, gracia plena. Dominus tecum. Benedicta tu in mulieribus, et benedictus fructus ventris tui. Mater Dei, ora pro nobis. Amen.

VIII 3ᴬ ORACIO

Salve, regina, mater misericordie,
vita, dulcedo et spes nostra, salve.
Ad te clamamus exules filii Eve. Ad te suspiramus gementes et flentes in hac lacrimarum valle. Eya!
(2) Ergo, advocata nostra,
illos tuos misericordes oculos ad nos converte,
et Iesum, benedictum fructum ventris tui,
nobis post hoc exilium ostende,
o clemens, o pia, o dulcis Maria.

(3) Ora pro nobis, sancta Dei genitrix, ut digni efficiamur promissionibus Christi.

IX 4ᴬ ORACIO

O gloriosa virgo semper Maria, mater glorie, mater ecclesie, mater pietatis et indulgencie, ave, carissima domina, semper virgo Maria, mater luminis, honor eternus, signum serenitatis. (2) Ave, piissima domina Maria, aula Dei, porta celi, sacrarium Spiritus sancti. Ave, piissima domina Maria, urna aurea, templum divinitatis, reclinatorium eterne pietatis. (3) Ave, clementissima domina Maria, decus virginum, domina gencium, regina angelorum. Ave, amantissima domina Maria, fons ortorum, ablucio peccatorum, lavacrum animarum. (4) Ave, desideratissima domina Maria, mater orphanorum, mamilla parvulorum, consolàcio miserorum. Salve, sancta parens. Salve, sancta et immaculata virginitas assistens vultui Dei, memor esto nostre fragilitatis.

VII. Prayer 2.

Hail Mary, full of grace, the Lord is with thee. Blessed art thou amongst women and blessed is the fruit of thy womb, [Jesus. Holy Mary,] Mother of God, pray for us. Amen.

VIII. Prayer 3.

Hail holy queen, mother of mercy,
Hail our life, our sweetness, and our hope.
To you do we cry, poor banished children of Eve. To you do we send up our sighs, mourning, and weeping
in this valley of tears.
(2) Turn then, most gracious advocate
your eyes of mercy toward us.
And after this, our exile,
Show us the fruit of your womb, Jesus.
O clement, O loving, O sweet [virgin] Mary.
(3) Pray for us, Holy Mother of God
That we may be made worthy of the promises of Christ.[19]

IX. Prayer 4.

O glorious Mary, eternal virgin, glorious mother, mother of the church, mother of piety and leniency, hail, O dearest lady, Mary, eternal virgin, mother of light, the eternal honor, the image of serenity. (2) Hail, most pious lady Mary, the court of God, the gate of heaven, the shrine of the Holy Spirit. (3) Hail, most pious lady Mary, that vessel of gold, that temple of the divinity, cushion of eternal piety. Hail, most merciful lady Mary, the glory of maidens, the ruler of nations, the queen of the angels. Hail most loving lady Mary, overflowing fountain, the washing of sins, the refreshment of souls. (4) Hail, most desired lady Mary, mother of orphans, the breast of infants, comforter of the wretched. Hail, holy parent. Hail, holy and immaculate virgin, who stands near the face of God, mindful of our frailty.

---

19 This is the well-known Salve Regina prayer (up to "O Sweet [virgin] Mary") along with the standard response.

(5) Salve, benignissima, salve, suavissima, salve, misericordissima. Propiciaberis, semper virgo benedicta et gloriosa semper virgo Maria, que virga sacratissima et Dei mater es piissima, maris stella clarissima.

(6) Salve, semper gloriosa, margarita preciosa, ficus [*sicut], lilium, formosa, olens velut rosa. Alleluia! Dirige me in visione beata.

(7) Obsecro te, regina perhennis, sancta Maria, per amorem Patris et Filii et Spiritus sancti et per commendatum tibi celeste sacrarium et per multas miseraciones, quas fecit super me et super genus humanum, (8) et per virtutes et per misteria sancte crucis et per sanctos clavos fixos in suas preciosas manus et pedes et per sancta 5 vulnera sui preciosi corporis et per precium sancti corporis sui, quo nos redemit in sancta cruce, (9) ut ores pro me et pro omnibus peccatis meis et necessitatibus anime et corporis mei ad dilectum filium tuum, *ut me vivente ipsum videre et collaudare merear*. Amen.

X

Gaude, virgo immaculata, Dei genitrix. Gaudium michi dona. Gaude, que gaudium ab angelo suscepisti, et gaudium visionis divine michi dona. Gaude, que genuisti eterni luminis claritatem. (2) Gaude, Dei genitrix, et gaudium visionis divine michi dona, ut sublever de omnibus angustiis et tribulacionibus et viciis meis, que sunt in corde meo, et quero amplius, ut tecum sim a latere constans ad videndum me vivente Deum eternum. (3) Adoro te, sancta mater Domini nostri Iesu Christi, et laudo et magnifico te. Adoro altitudinem tuam.

Adoro castitatem et virginitatem tuam. Adoro pietatem et misericordiam tuam. (4) Adoro viscera beata tua, que portaverunt deum et hominem. Adoro beatum uterum tuum, qui portavit Iesum Dominum. Adoro beata ubera tua, que lactaverunt salvatorem mundi. (5) Precor te, carissima semper virgo Maria, per amorem filii tui, Domini nostri Iesu Christi, ut

(5) Hail, most kind, hail, most agreeable, hail, most merciful. You will be propitiated, eternal virgin, blessed and glorious, ever chaste Mary, you who are the most hallowed virgin and blessed mother of God, brightest star of the sea.

(6) Hail, ever glorious, precious pearl, beautiful as the lily, fragrant as the rose.[20] Hallelujah! Direct me in this blessed vision.

(7) I entreat you, eternal queen, holy Mary, through the love of the Father, Son, and Holy Spirit, and through your trusted heavenly shrine, and through the great pities which you have made over me and over the human race, (8) and through the virtues and through the solemn mysteries of the cross, and through the holy nails fastened to his precious hands and feet, and through the five sacred wounds to his precious body, where he redeemed us on the holy cross, (9) in order that you may plead to your beloved son on my behalf, and on behalf of all my sins, and for the needs of my soul and of my body, *in order that I, while yet living, may be worthy to see and praise you.* Amen.

X.

Rejoice,[21] O immaculate virgin, mother of God. Give me joy. Rejoice, you who received the tidings of joy from the angel, and give me the joy of the vision of God. Rejoice, you who brought forth the clarity of eternal light. (2) Rejoice, mother of God, and give me the joy of the vision of God, that I may be raised up from all my difficulties and tribulations and the faults which are in my heart, and I ask further, that I may be firmly by your side, for seeing the living and eternal God. (3) I adore you, O holy mother of our Lord Jesus Christ, and I praise and glorify you. I adore your exaltation.

I adore your chastity and virginity. I adore your piety and your mercy. (4) I adore your blessed innermost parts, which have born God and Man. I adore your blessed womb, which has born Lord Jesus. I adore your blessed breasts, which have nursed the savior of the world. (5) I beg of you, dearest Mary ever virgin, through the love of your son our Lord Jesus Christ, to intervene for me, a sinner, that I may have the vision of the eternal God while yet alive, and

---

20 Compare Francisco Guerrero's (1528–1599) most famous work: "Ave virgo santissima, Dei mater piissima, maris stella clarissima / Salve semper gloriosa, margarita pretiosa, sicut lilium formosa, nitens, olens velut rosa." It was evidently based on an older text.

21 This is an adaptation of the popular eighth century *Anthem of the Blessed Virgin*, also known as the *Five Gaude antiphon*.

intercedas pro me peccatore ad visionem Dei eterni me vivente habendam et succurras michi in omnibus angustiis et necessitatibus meis et ne derelinquas me, (6) neque sim sine adiutorio in hac visione beata neque in illo tremendo die, cum exierit anima mea de corpore meo, aut in illa mirabili hora, cum rapta fuerit ad videndum me vivente Deum eternum.

(7) Postulo, graciosa, me ad portas paradisi facere venire, ut merear videre ibi filium tuum et merear habere leticiam sempiternam visionis divine cum ipso filio tuo gloriosissimo, qui vivit et regnat per omnia secula seculorum. Amen.

XI 5ᴬ ORACIO

Ego peccator indignus ad laudem et honorem gloriosissime semperque virginis Marie, genitricis Domini nostri Iesu Christi, eius sacra nomina, cum sim indignus, iuxta meum exiguum sensum Spiritu sancto dictante nominare curo.

(2) O gloriosa Dei genitrix, semper virgo Maria, ne indigneris contra me nequissimum et innumerabili iniquitate plenum set accipe propicia misericorditer quod indignus ad honorem tuum offero et affecto. (3) Etenim, piissima, sacra tua nomina corde, ore, opere distinte nominare et exaltare volo.

Nominaris namque Maria, Genitrix, Mater, Sponsa, Filia, Theotan, Virga, Vas, Balsamus, Nubes, Ros, (4) Pacifica, Princeps, Regina, Aurora, Imperatrix, Domina, Ancilla, Ortus, Fons, Puteus, Via, Vita, Semita, Splendor, Stella aurea, Lumen, Luna, Fenestra vitrea, Ianua, Porta, Velum, Cella, (5) Domus, Hospicium, Capsa, Templum, Aula, Tabernaculum, Manna, Civitas, Liber, Stola, Flumen, Pons, Uva, Malogranatum, Femina, Nutrix, Mulier, Turris, Navis, Redemptrix, Liberatrix, Amica, (6) Thalamus, Vallis, Cinamomum, Turtur, Columba, Lilium, Rosa, Consolacio, Portus, Spes, Salus, Gloria, Fundamentum, vera peccatorum Medicina, Sacrarium Spiritus sancti, Radix Iesse, Antitodum, Recreatrix, Syon, Puella, Miseratrix.

assist me in all my difficulties and needs, and do not abandon me,[22] (6) so I may not be without help in this blessed vision nor on that terrible day when my soul departs from my body, or in that wonderful hour, when it will be dragged away, for seeing the living eternal God.

(7) I graciously ask you to make me come to the gates of Paradise, that I may be worthy to see your son there, and that I may be worthy to have the wondrous eternal divine vision, with your most glorious son himself, who lives and reigns world without end. Amen.

XI. Prayer 5.

I, an unworthy sinner, for the praise and honor of the most glorious and eternal virgin Mary, mother of our Lord Jesus Christ, of his sacred names, since I am unworthy, because of my meager perception I take care to name with the Holy Spirit's command.

(2) O glorious mother of God, O eternal virgin Mary, do not deem me unworthy because of my great wickedness and innumerable iniquities, but mercifully and favorably accepting that which I, although unworthy, offer and desire for your honor. (3) And so I wish to clearly name and exalt your holy names most conscientiously, with my heart, with my mouth, and with my labor.

So you are named Mary, Creator, Mother, Bride, Daughter, Theotan, Rod, Vessel, Balsamus, Cloud, Dew, (4) Peace Maker, the First, Queen, Dawn, Empress, Lady, Handmaiden, Risen, the Spring, the Well, the Way, the Life, the Path, the Brilliance, the Golden Star, the Light, the Moon, Glass Window, the Doorway, the Gate, the Curtain, the Chamber, (5) the Home, Guest Room, the Receptacle, the Temple, the Hall, the Tabernacle, the Manna, Community, Free, the Stole, the River, the Bridge, the Grape, the Pomegranate, Female, Nurse, Woman, Tower, Ship, Redemptress, Liberator, Friend, (6) the Bedroom, the Vally, Cinnamon, the Turtle-dove, the Dove, the Lily, the Rose, the Consolation, the Refuge, the Hope, the Salvation, the Glory, the Foundation, the True Medicine of Sinners, the Shrine of the Holy Spirit, the Root of Jesse, the Antidote, the Recreatrix, Sion, the Girl, She who is Compassionate.

---

22 Compare Ps. 37:22–23; BoO, p. 100.

(7) Tuam deprecor sanctissimam misericordiam, ut per hec divina tua nomina, que ego nunc tibi plenus immundicia coram altari tuo de te presumendo optuli, (8) ut in hac hora me audias et insaciabiliter digneris me facere videre atque laudare te et tuum filium gloriosum corpusculo meo vivente.

(9) Teque interpello, gloriosa, per tuum filium, quem concepisti, quem genuisti, quem peperisti, quem in carne lactasti, quem in balneo misisti, quem pannis involvisti, quem in templo presentasti, (10) quem predicantem audisti, quem in cruce pro nobis suspensum vidisti, quem mortuum et sepultum inspexisti, quem surgentem a mortuis scivisti, quem ad celum ascendentem ad Patrem vidisti, (11) et inde venturus est iudicare vivos et mortuos et seculum per ignem, per ipsum quoque pollutus labiis, pollutus carne, pollutus corpore, pollutus mente [te] ausus nominare imploro, (12) quatinus in hoc opere te et sanctam trinitatem cum sanctis angelis tuis facias me aspicere et videre et in extremo magno iudicio ab eternali pena eripias per Christum, Dominum nostrum. Amen.

XII 6[A] ORACIO

Credo in Deum, Patrem omnipotentem, creatorem celi et terre, et in Iesum Christum, filium eius unicum, Dominum nostrum, qui conceptus est de Spiritu sancto, natus ex Maria virgine, passus sub Poncio Pilato, crucifixus, mortuus et sepultus. (2) Descendit ad inferna, tercia die resurrexit a mortuis, ascendit ad celos, sedet ad dexteram Dei Patris omnipotentis, inde venturus est iudicare vivos et mortuos. (3) Credo in Spiritum sanctum, sanctam ecclesiam catholicam, sanctorum communionem, remissionem peccatorum, carnis resurreccionem et vitam eternam. Amen.

XIII 7ᴬ ORACIO

Quicumque vult salvus esse *et visionem Dei habere*, ante omnia opus est, ut teneat catholicam fidem, quam nisi quisque integram inviolatamque

(7) I beg for your most holy compassion, that through these divine names of yours, which I, though full of filth, have now dared to offer before your altar, (8) that you hear me in this hour, and deign to make me insatiably worthy to see and praise you and your glorious son, while my insignificant body is still living.

(9) And I address you, O glorious one, through your son, whom you conceived, whom you begat, whom you have borne, whose body you nursed, whom you bathed, whom you wrapped in cloths, whom you presented at the temple, (10) whose preaching you heard, whose suspension from the cross on our behalf you saw, whose death and burial you witnessed, whose rising from the dead you observed, whose ascension to the Father in heaven you saw, (11) and who will soon return from there to judge the living and the dead and the world by fire, likewise through him I dare to name [you] and beg for help, with impure lips, with impure flesh, with impure body, with impure mind, (12) that through this work you will enable me to look at and see yourself, and the holy Trinity, with your holy angels, and in the end at the Great Judgement you will snatch me away from eternal punishment, through Christ our Lord. Amen.

XII. Prayer 6. [The Creed].[23]

I believe in God, the Father Almighty, Creator of heaven and earth, and in Jesus Christ, his only Son, our Lord: who was conceived by the Holy Spirit, born of the Virgin Mary, suffered under Pontius Pilate, was crucified, died, and was buried; (2) he descended into hell; the third day he rose again from the dead; he ascended into heaven; sits at the right hand of God the Father Almighty; from thence he shall come to judge the living and the dead. (3) I believe in the Holy Spirit, the holy Catholic Church, the communion of Saints, the forgiveness of sins, the resurrection of the body, and life everlasting. Amen.

XIII. Prayer 7.[24]

"Whoever wishes to be saved *and have the vision of God*, should above all things hold to the Catholic faith. Whoever fails to keep it whole and unde-

---

23 The Apostles' Creed—Roman Ritual.
24 This prayer is based on the well-known Athanasian Creed (*Symbolum Athanasianum*.)

servaverit, absque dubio visionem divinam non habebit. (2) Fides autem catholica hec est, ut unum deum in trinitate et trinitatem in unitate veneremur neque confundentes personas, neque substanciam separantes. (3) Alia est enim persona Patris, alia Filii, ali a Spiritus sancti. Set Patris et Filii et Spiritus sancti una est divinitas, equalis gloria, coeterna maiestas. (4) Qualis Pater, talis Filius, talis Spiritus sanctus. Increatus Pater, increatus Filius, increatus Spiritus sanctus. Inmensus Pater, inmensus Filius, inmensus Spiritus sanctus. (5) Eternus Pater, eternus Filius, eternus Spiritus sanctus, et tamen non tres eterni set unus eternus, sicut non tres increati nec tres inmensi set unus increatus et unus inmensus. (6) Similiter omnipotens Pater, omnipotens Filius, omnipotens Spiritus sanctus, et tamen non tres omnipotentes set unus omnipotens. (7) Ha Deus Pater, Deus Filius, Deus Spiritus sanctus, et tamen non tres dii set unus est Deus. (8) Ha Dominus Pater, Dominus Filius, Dominus Spiritus sanctus, et tamen non tres domini set unus est Dominus, qui a sicut singillatim unamquamque personam Deum ac Dominum confiteri Christiana veritate compellimur, ita tres deos aut dominos dicere catholica religione prohibemur. (9) Pater a nullo est factus nec creatus nec genitus. Filius a Patre solo non factus nec creatus set genitus. Spiritus sanctus a Patre et Filio non factus nec creatus nec genitus set procedens. (10) Unus ergo Pater, non tres patres, unus Filius, non tres filii, unus Spiritus sanctus, non tres spiritus sancti. (11) Et in hac trinitate nichil prius aut posterius, nichil maius aut minus, set tote tres persone coeterne sibi sunt et coequales, ita ut per omnia, sicut iam supra dictum est, et unitas in trinitate et trinitas in unitate veneranda sit. (12) Qui vult ergo salvus esse *et visionem divinam habere*, ita de trinitate senciat.

(13) Set necessarium est ad eternam salutem et divinam visionem, ut incarnacionem quoque Domini nostri Iesu Christi fideliter credat. (14) Est ergo fides recta, ut credamus et confiteamur, quia Dominus noster Iesus Christus, Dei filius, deus et homo est. (15) Deus est ex substancia Patris ante secula genitus, et homo est ex substancia matris in seculo natus. (16) Perfectus deus, perfectus homo ex anima racionali et humana carne subsistens, equalis Patri secundum divinitatem, minor Patre secundum humanitatem. (17) Qui licet deus sit et homo, non duo tamen set unus est

filed, without doubt shall perish everlastingly. (2) And the Catholic faith is this: That we worship one God in Trinity, and Trinity in Unity, neither confounding the persons, nor dividing the substance. (3) For there is one person of the Father, another of the Son, and another of the Holy Spirit. But the Godhead of the Father, of the Son, and of the Holy Spirit is all one, the glory equal, the majesty co-eternal. (4) As is the Father, so is the Son, and so is the Holy Spirit. The Father uncreated, the Son uncreated, and the Holy Spirit uncreated. The Father incomprehensible, the Son incomprehensible, and the Holy Spirit incomprehensible. (5) The Father eternal, the Son eternal, and the Holy Spirit eternal. And yet they are not three eternals, but one eternal. As also there are not three uncreated, nor three incomprehensibles, but one uncreated and one incomprehensible. (6) So likewise the Father is almighty, the Son almighty, and the Holy Spirit almighty. And yet they are not three almighties, but one almighty. (7) So the Father is God, the Son is God, and the Holy Spirit is God, and yet they are not three Gods, but one God. (8) So likewise the Father is Lord, the Son is Lord, and the Holy Spirit is Lord, and yet they are not three Lords, but one Lord. For even though we are compelled by Christian truthfulness to acknowledge each person by himself to be God and Lord, we are forbidden by the Catholic religion to say that there are three Gods or Lords. (9) The Father is made of none, neither created, nor begotten. The Son is of the Father alone, not made nor created, but begotten. The Holy Spirit is of the Father and of the Son, neither made, nor created, nor begotten, but proceeding. (10) So there is one Father, not three Fathers; one Son, not three Sons; one Holy Spirit, not three Holy Spirits. (11) And in this Trinity none is before or after another, none is greater or less than another. But the whole three Persons are co-eternal together, and co-equal. So that in all things, as is aforesaid, the Unity in Trinity and the Trinity in Unity is to be worshiped. (12) He therefore that will be saved, *and have the divine vision*, must thus think of the Trinity.

(13) Furthermore, it is necessary to everlasting salvation that he also believe rightly the incarnation of our Lord Jesus Christ. (14) For the right faith is, that we believe and confess that our Lord Jesus Christ, the Son of God, is God and Man. (15) God, of the substance of the Father, begotten before the worlds; and Man, of the substance of his mother, born in the world. (16) Perfect God, and perfect Man, of a reasonable soul and human flesh subsisting. Equal to the Father as touching his Godhead, and inferior to the Father as touching his human nature. (17) Who, although he be God and

Christus, unus autem non conversione divinitatis in camem sed assumpcione humanitatis in Deum, unus omnino non confusione substancie sed unitate persone. (18) Nam sicut anima racionalis et caro unus est homo, ita deus et homo unus est Christus, qui passus est pro salute nostra, descendit ad inferos, tercia die resurrexit a mortuis, ascendit ad celos, sedet ad dexteram Dei Patris omnipotentis, inde venturus est iudicare vivos et mortuos. (19) Ad cuius adventum omnes homines resurgere habent cum corporibus suis et reddituri sunt de factis propriis racionem. (20) Et qui bona egerunt, ibunt in vitam eternam *et visionem divinam*, quam nunc petimus, qui vero mala, in ignem eternum, cui nunc abrenunciare postulamus.

(21) Hec est fides catholica, quam nisi quisque fideliter firmiterque crediderit, salvus esse non poterit *nec hanc divinam visionem optinere quibit*.

XIV 8ᴬ ORACIO

Ego divina institucione formatus et preceptis salutaribus +imprecatus+ audebo dicere:

Pater noster, qui es in celis, sanctificetur nomen tuum. Adveniat regnum tuum. (2) Fiat voluntas tua sicut in celo et in terra. Panem nostrum supersubstancialem da nobis hodie. (3) Et dimitte nobis debita nostra, sicut et nos dimittimus debitoribus nostris. Et ne nos inducas in temptacionem set libera nos a malo. Amen.

XV 9ᴬ ORACIO

Alpha et Ω, Deus omnipotens, principium omnium rerum sine principio, finis sine fine, exaudi hodie preces meas, piissime, (2) neque secundum iniquitates meas neque secundum peccata mea retribuas michi, Domine, Deus meus, set secundum misericordiam tuam, que est maior rebus omnibus visibilibus et invisibilibus, miserere mei, (3) sapiencia Patris, Christe, lux angelorum, gloria sanctorum, spes et portus et refugium peccatorum,

Man, yet he is not two, but one Christ. One; not by conversion of the Godhead into flesh, but by taking of the human nature into God. One altogether, not by confusion of Substance, but by unity of Person. (18) For as the rational soul and body together constitute one man, so God and Man constitute one Christ, who suffered for our salvation, descended into hell, rose again the third day from the dead. He ascended into heaven, and sits on the right hand of the Father, God, Almighty; from whence he shall come to judge the living and the dead. (19) At whose coming, all humanity shall rise again with their bodies, and give an accounting for all their deeds. (20) And those who have done good shall go into eternal life, *and the divine vision*, while those that have done evil shall go into the eternal fire.

(21) This is the Catholic faith, which unless a man believe faithfully, he cannot be saved, *nor will he be able to achieve this divine vision.*[25]

XIV. Prayer 8.

Following divine instruction, and the teachings of the Saviour +called down+ I dare to say:[26]

Our Father, who art in heaven, hallowed be Thy name; Thy kingdom come; (2) Thy will be done on earth as it is in heaven; give us this day our daily bread; (3) and forgive us our trespasses, as we forgive those who trespass against us; and lead us not into temptation; but deliver us from evil. Amen.

XV. Prayer 9.[27]

Alpha and Omega, O almighty God, the beginning of all things, without beginning, the ending without an end, hear today my prayers, O most holy one, (2) neither repay me according my iniquity nor my sins, O Lord, my God, but according to your mercy, which is greater than all things visible and invisible. Have mercy on me, (3) the wisdom of the Father, O Christ, the light of the angels, the glory of the saints, the hope and haven and refuge of sinners,

---

25 The traditional ending is, "*salvus esse non poterit*" ("he cannot be saved").
26 The mass introduces the Lord's Prayer with nearly identical wording: "Praeceptis salutaribus moniti, et divina institutione formati, audemus dicere:" GH indicates "imprecatus" (called down, prayed for, uttered curses or blessings) as *turbata* ("disturbed"), i.e. out of place.
27 Ars. Not. Glose de la version B, Var. 1—glose, JV p. 141.

cunctarum rerum conditor et humane fragilitatis redemptor, qui celum et terram mareque totum ac moncium pondera palmo concludis. (4) Te, piissime, deprecor et exoro, ut una cum Patre illustres animam meam radio sanctissimi Spiritus tui, (5) quatinus in hac sacrosancta arte taliter possim proficere, ut valeam ad facialem tui, Deus eterne, visionem virtute tui sanctissimi Spiritus et tui nominis pervenire. (6) Et tu, qui es Deus meus, qui in principio creasti celum et terram et omnia ex nichilo, qui in Spiritu tuo sancto omnia reformas, comple, instaura, sana animam meam, ut glorificem te per omnia opera cogitacionum mearum et verborum meorum. (7) Deus Pater, oracionem meam confirma et intellectum meum auge et memoriam meam ad suscipiendum beatam visionem tuam meo vivente corpusculo et ad cognoscendum superexcelsam et supereternam facialiter tuam essenciam, qui vivis et regnas per infinita secula seculorum. Amen.

XVI Oracio

Helysemath. hazaram. hemel. saduch. Theon. Heloy. zamaram. zoma. ietromaym. Theos. Deus pie et fortis, hamathamal. ietronamayhala. zanay. hacronaaz. zay. (2) colnaphan. salmazaiz. ayhal. geromelam. haymasa. Ramay. genzi. zamath. heliemath. semay. selmar. iecrosamay. iachat. lemar. harana. hamany. memothemath. Hemelamp. (3) et tu, sancte Pater, pie Deus et incomprehensibilis in omnibus operibus tuis, que sunt sancta et iusta et bona. (4) Megalhamethor. semassaer. zamathamar. geogremai. megus. monorail. hamezeaza. hillebata. maraama. iehenas. iehemia. malamai. sephormay. zemonoma. Melas. hemay. hemesua. iecormay. (5) lemesey. senosecari. zemaher. helcamay. calion. tharathos. tronios. nebay. tharathos. vsyon. gezsethon. semynathemas. zezahas. thamam. helomany. hamel. Amen.

XVII

Theos. megale. Patir. ymos. hebrel. habobel. hecoy. haley. helihot. hety. hebeot. letiel. iezei. sadam. salaseey. salatial. salatelli. samel. sadamiel. (2) Saday. helgion. helliel. lemegos. micron. megos. myheon. legmes. muthon. mychohyn. heel. hesely. iecor. graual. semhel. semobzhat. semeltha. samai. geth. (3) gehel. rasahanay. gelgemana. semana. harasymihon. salepatir.

the originator of all things and redeemer of human frailties, who holds the weight of heaven and earth, and the seas and mountains in the palm of your hand. (4) I beg and entreat you, O most holy one, that you, being one with the Father, will illuminate my soul with the ray of your most Holy Spirit, (5) that I may be able to progress in this most sacred art, so that I might be worthy to achieve the vision of your face, O God eternal, through the virtue of your most Holy Spirit and of your name. (6) And you, who are are my God, who in the beginning created the heaven and the earth, and all things out of nothing, who through your holy Spirit you restore, fill, and renew all things, heal my soul, that I may glorify you through all my thoughts, and words, and deeds. (7) O God the Father, strengthen my prayer, and increase both my comprehension and my memory, for undertaking your blessed vision while my mortal body is yet living, and for seeing your most high and eternal essence face to face, you who live and reign through the infinite ages of the ages. Amen.

XVI. Prayer.[28]

Helysemath. hazaram. hemel. saduch. Theon. Heloy. zamaram. zoma. ietromaym. Theos. O God, pious and strong, hamathamal. ietronamayhala. zanay. hacronaaz. zay. (2) colnaphan. salmazaiz. ayhal. geromelam. haymasa. Ramay. genzi. zamath. heliemath. semay. selmar. iecrosamay. iachat. lemar. harana. hamany. memothemath. hemelamp. (3) And you, O holy Father, pious God, and incomprehensible in all your works, which are holy, just, and good. (4) Megalhamethor. semassaer. zamathamar. geogremai. megus. monorail. hamezeaza. hillebata. maraama. iehenas. iehemia. malamai. sephormay. zemonoma. Melas. hemay. hemesua. iecormay. (5) lemesey. senosecari. zemaher. helcamay. calion. tharathos. tronios. nebay. tharathos. vsyon. gezsethon. semynathemas. zezahas. thamam. helomany. hamel. Amen.

XVII.[29]

Theos. megale. Patir. ymos. hebrel. habobel. hecoy. haley. helihot. hety. hebeot. letiel. iezei. sadam. salaseey. salatial. salatelli. samel. sadamiel. (2) Saday. helgion. helliel. lemegos. micron. megos. myheon. legmes. muthon. mychohyn. heel. hesely. iecor. graual. semhel. semobzhat. semeltha. samai. geth. (3) gehel.

---

28 Ars. Not. 7, JV p. 146.
29 Ars. Not. 10, JV p. 149.

salepati. ragiono saletha. thurigium. hepatir. vsion. hatamas. hotonas. harayn.

XVIII

Lux mundi, Deus inmense, pater eternitatis, largitor sapiencie et totius gracie spiritualis pie et inestimabilis dispensator noscens omnia, priusquam fiant, faciens tenebras et lucem,

(2) mitte manum tuam et tange animam meam et corpus meum et pone illam ut gladium furbitum ad visionem tuam habendam et fac eam ut sagittam electam et granum tritici reconditum ad contemplandum tuam mirabilem faciem (3) et emitte Spiritum sanctum tuum, Domine, in cor meum ad istud donum percipiendum et in animam meam ad emundandum et in conscienciam meam ad speculandum. (4) Per iuramentum cordis[4] [*coheredis] tui, id est per dexteram pie sciencie tue, misericorditer, clementer et leniter in me graciam tuam inspira et doce et instrue (5) et instaura introitum et exitum sensuum meorum, et doceas me et clarifices me et mundifices me et corrigas me cum disciplina tua usque in finem, (6) ut visionem tuam facialiter optineam, et adiuvet me consilium altissimum per infinitam sapienciam tuam et misericordiam tuam. Amen.

XIX

Si autem velles impetrare aliquam scienciam vel sacrare librum vel invocare spiritus, mutares peticionem oracionis precedentis sic:

(2) "mitte manum tuam et tange os meum et pone illud ut gladium acutum ad ennarandum et eloquendum hec sancta verba et fac linguam meam ut sagittam electam ad ennarrandum mirabilia tua et ad pronunciandum ea et memoriter retinendum."

(3) Sic petes pro sciencia impetranda. Set pro consecrando librum sic: "ut gladium acutum ad consecrandum et sanctificandum hec tam sancta quam alia verba ... ut sagittam electam ad confirmandum in veritate mirabilia tua et ad pronunciandum ea et pro libito impetrandum."

---

4 *Cordis:* reading *coheredis.*

rasahanay. gelgemana. semana. harasymihon. salepatir. salepati. ragiono saletha. thurigium. hepatir. vsion. hatamas. hotonas. harayn.

XVIII.[30]

O light of the World, O God immeasurable, the father of eternity, the granter of wisdom and of all spiritual grace; O pious and inestimable dispenser of all, knowing all things before they happen, making the darkness and the light.

(2) Reach out your hand, and touch my body and soul, and make them like a burnished sword,[31] that I may attain the vision of you, and make me like a chosen arrow and hidden grain of wheat, for observing your wonderful face, (3) and send your Holy Spirit, O Lord, into my heart to receive this gift, and into my soul to cleanse it, and into my conscience to watch over it. (4) Through the oath of your heart,[32] that is, through the right hand of your holy knowledge, mercifully, lovingly, and gently inspire your grace into me, and teach, instruct, (5) and renew the coming in and going out of my senses, and teach me, and clarify and cleanse me, and correct me with your teaching, until the end, (6) in order to attain the vision of your self face to face, and may your most high assembly help me, through your infinite wisdom and mercy. Amen.

XIX.

If however you wish to obtain some knowledge, or to consecrate the book, or to call upon a spirit, you should alter the petition in the preceding prayer thus:

(2) "Stretch out your hand and touch my mouth, and make it like a sharp sword for describing and speaking out these holy words, and make my tongue like a chosen arrow, for describing your miracles, and for pronouncing them, and retaining them in my memory."

(3) But if you wish to obtain knowledge for consecrating the book, say: "... like a sharp sword, for consecrating and sanctifying these most holy words, and all the other words ... like a chosen arrow to confirm the truth of your miracles both for pronouncing them, and for obtaining my desire."

---

30 Ars. Not. II, JV p. 151.
31 Compare Isaiah 49:2.
32 GH, following Sl. 1712, reads "coheredis tui" (of your co-heir), but "cordis tui" (of your heart) is also attested in *Ars Notoria* manuscripts.

(4) Si pro vocando spiritus agis, pete sic: "... acutum ad eloquendum hec verba tam sancta quam alia ad coartandum et cogendum venire, respondere, stare, recedere, obedire spiritus tales N michi tali N, filio talis N (5) ... electam ad ostendendum mirabilia sancte potencie tue et ad pronunciandum verba et gladialiter et flammee tuos tales spiritus N coartandum."

(6) Si aliud pecieris quam illa, que dicta sunt, simili modo secundum naturam illius peticionem mutares et non solum in hac oracione, immo in omnibus Latinis, in quibus aliqua peticio reperitur.

XX Oracio

Assaylemaht. rasay. semaht. azahat. haraaht. lameth. hazabat. hamat. hamae. gesemon. grephemyon. zelamye. relamye. hazatha. hamatha. hazaremehal. hazanebal. helial. zebial. (2) seziol. Semyhor. hamissiton. fintiugon. tintiugethe. hamissirion. sebarnay. halmoht. alymyon. gemail. halmiot. sadail. hehomail. neomail. Cristos. thiothot. sepha. taphamal. (3) paphalios. sicrogramon. laupdau. laupta. iothim. iothileta. lazahemor. iemeamor. lotahemor. fitcomegal. haemor. giselector. gilzelerethon. glereleon. gamasgay. semagar. semalgay. (4) semasgyy. balua. arethon. iesamahel. gegemahelay. hala. hela. iemay. semethay. may. semnay. geles. syney. iolehemey. iesmar. samennay. bariactoca. cariactera. tharihetha. socalmata. (5) getimay. socalma. socagamal. helgezamay. balma. hailoso halos. zaynos. ienenegal. sarimalip. sarmalaip. sacramalaip. tamygel. thamahel. sathabynhel. sathabinal. samal. maga. samalanga. (6) saminaga. satalmagu. silimal. salmana. saguaht. silimythu. semalsay. gahit. galiht. gezamannay. sabal. zegahathon. zahanphaton. iezanycrathon. ietuaphaton. iezemo. iezelem. (7) ioselimen. hatanathos. hathanathay. semaht. zemehet. iezorahel. checorab. Hel. gerozabal. craton. hariabal. hariagal. hanagai. hariagil. parithomegos. samazihel. simazihel. leosemmaht. (8) leosamaty. themiathol. genynatol. gemizacol. hebalthe. halabee. hamisschon. sebanay. halmye. gemail. sadail. neomahil. cristolepha. caphanial. hazaron. gezamel. haymal. hayhala. (9) sememay. gehesmoy. thariattha. gemiazai. zohanphaton. ielesamen. hatanathay. gemaht. iesomabel. haynosiel. halabethen. iabaioge. halabeht. ebalohe. nyphos. phabos. phelior. phobos. Ydolmassay. (10) predolmassay. pholihor. negioggen. neginather. pharampnee. pharanehe. scomico-

(4) And if you strive to call forth spirits, modify the petition thus: "... for sharply speaking out these holy words and others, for constraining and compelling the spirit (such and such) to come, answer, remain, depart, and obey me N. son of N. (5) ... chosen arrow for showing the holy miracles of your power, both for pronouncing the words as with your flaming sword, for constraining the spirit N."

(6) If your aim is other than these examples, alter the petition in a similar way according to the nature of your request. This should be done not only for this prayer, but for all the Latin ones, in which any petition is found.

XX. Prayer.[33]

Assaylemaht. rasay. semaht. azahat. haraaht. lameth. hazabat. hamat. hamae. gesemon. grephemyon. zelamye. relamye. hazatha. hamatha. hazaremehal. hazanebal. helial. zebial. (2) seziol. Semyhor. hamissiton. fintiugon. tintiugethe. hamissirion. sebarnay. halmoht. alymyon. gemail. halmiot. sadail. hehomail. neomail. Cristos. thiothot. sepha. taphamal. (3) paphalios. sicrogramon. laupdau. laupta. iothim. iothileta. lazahemor. iemeamor. lotahemor. fitcomegal. haemor. giselector. gilzelerethon. glereleon. gamasgay. semagar. semalgay. (4) semasgyy. balua. arethon. iesamahel. gegemahelay. hala. hela. iemay. semethay. may. semnay. geles. syney. iolehemey. iesmar. samennay. bariactoca. cariactera. tharihetha. socalmata. (5) getimay. socalma. socagamal. helgezamay. balma. hailoso halos. zaynos. ienenegal. sarimalip. sarmalaip. sacramalaip. tamygel. thamahel. sathabynhel. sathabinal. samal. maga. samalanga. (6) saminaga. satalmagu. silimal. salmana. saguaht. silimythu. semalsay. gahit. galiht. gezamannay. sabal. zegahathon. zahanphaton. iezanycrathon. ietuaphaton. iezemo. iezelem. (7) ioselimen. hatanathos. hathanathay. semaht. zemehet. iezorahel. checorab. Hel. gerozabal. craton. hariabal. hariagal. hanagai. hariagil. parithomegos. samazihel. simazihel. leosemmaht. (8) leosamaty. themiathol. genynatol. gemizacol. hebalthe. halabee. hamisschon. sebanay. halmye. gemail. sadail. neomahil. cristolepha. caphanial. hazaron. gezamel. haymal. hayhala. (9) sememay. gehesmoy. thariattha. gemiazai. zohanphaton. ielesamen. hatanathay. gemaht. iesomabel. haynosiel. halabethen. iabaioge. halabeht. ebalohe. nyphos. phabos. phelior. phobos. Ydolmassay. (10) predolmassay. pholihor. negioggen. neginather. pharampnee.

---

[33] Ars. Not. 16, JV p. 154.

poten. sohomychepoten. hymaliassenon. ymiamos. manyahas. geromay. iemay. ietathamazai. passamaht. Theon. beht. bon. (11) sathamat hagynol. naragal. semozihot. nerothinay. raguathi. raguali. ranal. ragahal. hagmal. hagamal. fagomossyn. fagemesym. domogentha. theomogen. theromogen. Salmatha. (12) salamaht. zalamatha. Hon. bolon. halon. sephezimu. sapynon. saphiamon. hamon. harion. usion. gemession. sepha. phalymyt. sebanay. hamyssithon. thyutyugren. hactou. rogoubon. lon. usion. Amen.

XXI Oracio

Hazailemaht. lemaht. azat. gessemon. thelamoht. hazab. halatal. haebal. sezior. sicromagal. gigoro. mogal. gielocheon. samagoy. (2) haphiles. pamphilos. sicragalmon. laupda. iothim. haiual. hailos. halua. geneuogal. samanlay. tacayhelthamyel. secalmana. (3) hesemolas. hesomelaht. gethasam. cethalsam. scilmon. saibaiol. semalsay. crathon. hanaguil. pancomnegos. tyngeny. hamissitoy. (4) sebarnay. hassimilop. thenaly. soday. henaly. halaco. meahil. crihicos. sepha. caphaual. hazaron. cezamahal. haila. saramnay. gelior. synoy. bariachacha. (5) gehemyzai. iecrafagon. legelyme. hathamathay. senac. gromyhazay. sothal. magaal. iemazay. zehemphagon. hasihezamay. legelime. hacama. ieizobol. (6) ierozabal. symaliel. seymaly. seihel. leosamaht. gemyhacal. halabre. cyhophagros. Theos. phabos. ycolmazai. negen. (7) pharameht. nehihahon. sehon. gethorem. nehehom. helisemaht. saratihai. ierafiai. hynaliha. sememanos. gezamai. iecremai. (8) passamaht. thagail. hagamal. fagamesy. fagamesym. themegoman. zemegamary. salamatha. salomothono. bon. lon. sepizihon. harion. usyon. semession. tegon. Amen.

XXII Oracio

Lemaht. sebanthe. helitihay. gozogam. romasim. hegetti. gozimal. exiophiam. sorathim. salathaam. besapha. saphiez. haculam. samiht. senaiho. phethaloym. harissim. genges. lethos. Amen.

pharanehe. scomicopoten. sohomychepoten. hymaliassenon. ymiamos. manyahas. geromay. iemay. ietathamazai. passamaht. Theon. beht. bon. (11) sathamat hagynol. naragal. semozihot. nerothinay. raguathi. raguali. ranal. ragahal. hagmal. hagamal. fagomossyn. fagemesym. domogentha. theomogen. theromogen. Salmatha. (12) salamaht. zalamatha. Hon. bolon. halon. sephezimu. sapynon. saphiamon. hamon. harion. usion. gemession. sepha. phalymyt. sebanay. hamyssithon. thyutyugren. hactou. rogoubon. lon. usion. Amen.

XXI. Prayer.[34]

Hazailemaht. lemaht. azat. gessemon. thelamoht. hazab. halatal. haebal. sezior. sicromagal. gigoro. mogal. gielocheon. samagoy. (2) haphiles. pamphilos. sicragalmon. laupda. iothim. haiual. hailos. halua. geneuogal. samanlay. tacayhelthamyel. secalmana. (3) hesemolas. hesomelaht. gethasam. cethalsam. scilmon. saibaiol. semalsay. crathon. hanaguil. pancomnegos. tyngeny. hamissitoy. (4) sebarnay. hassimilop. thenaly. soday. henaly. halaco. meahil. crihicos. sepha. caphaual. hazaron. cezamahal. haila. saramnay. gelior. synoy. bariachacha. (5) gehemyzai. iecrafagon. legelyme. hathamathay. senac. gromyhazay. sothal. magaal. iemazay. zehemphagon. hasihezamay. legelime. hacama. ieizobol. (6) ierozabal. symaliel. seymaly. seihel. leosamaht. gemyhacal. halabre. cyhophagros. Theos. phabos. ycolmazai. negen. (7) pharameht. nehihahon. sehon. gethorem. nehehom. helisemaht. saratihai. ierafiai. hynaliha. sememanos. gezamai. iecremai. (8) passamaht. thagail. hagamal. fagamesy. fagamesym. themegoman. zemegamary. salamatha. salomothono. bon. lon. sepizihon. harion. usyon. semession. tegon. Amen.

XXII. Prayer.[35]

Lemaht. sebanthe. helitihay. gozogam. romasim. hegetti. gozimal. exiophiam. sorathim. salathaam. besapha. saphiez. haculam. samiht. senaiho. phethaloym. harissim. genges. lethos. Amen.

---

34 This seems to be another variant of Ars. Not. 16, namely var. 3. See JV p. 157.
35 Ars. Not. 16 var. 4, JV p. 159.

XXIII

Lameht. lenat. lemahat. semaht. selmahat. helmay. helymam. helmamy. zezetta. zezegta. gezegatha. zozogam. remasym. themaremasym. ieranyhel. phuerezo. gamyhal. zecegomyhal. hezetogamyhal. (2) heziephiat. hozoperbiar. iosaithyn. iosathyn. iosany. gosamyn. salaht. salatoham. salatehen. salatambel. hen. henbem. habena. henlezepha. bosephar. thamar. sahaletromar. (3) hafartitmar. thimas. tirimar. namor. semyhot. semohit. zemyhot. semoiz. lemdihon. lemahat. phethalon. hamiht. phethalonamie. zomye. zamiht. prihiti. philei. haphyn. gergeon. gergohen. (4) ierthon. lothios. lothos. semyhot. lemahat. zemohit. lemaiho. phetalon. hamye. hamyphyn. pethio. gergion. lecton. iergohen. thothios. lectos. Amen.

XXIV Oracio

Deus summe, Deus invisibilis, Theos. Patir. behemnos. lehernnyos. behenny. te rogamus, ymos. per sanctissimos angelos tuos, qui sunt Michael, id est medicina Dei, Raphael, fortitudo Dei, Gabriel, ardens, (2) et seraphyn. helipha. massay. cherubyn. ielomynctos. gadabany. zedabanay. gederanay. saramany. lomtety. loctosy. gerohanathon. zahamany. lomyht. gedanabasy. setemanay. seremanay. henlothant. helomyht. henboramyht. samanazay. gedebaudi. (3) [de] plenitudine sciencie, cherubyn et seraphyn, vos suppliciter rogamus et te, Iesu Christe, per omnes sanctos [arch]angelos tuos gloriosos, quorum nomina a Deo consecrata sunt, que a nobis proferri non debent, que sunt hec: (4) Deihel. Dehel. Depymo. Dein. Hel. Exluso. Depymon. Helynon. Exmogon. Parineos. Exmegan. Pheleneos. Nauagen. Hosyel. Dragon. Garbona. Rathion. Monyham. Megonhamos.

XXV

Te queso, Domine mi: Illustra et clarifica animam et conscienciam meam splendore luminis tui et illustra et confirma intellectum meum odore suavitatis Spiritus tui sancti, ut optinere valeam gloriosam visionem tuam, quam nunc humiliter deposco. (2) Adorna, Domine, animam meam, ut

XXIII.[36]

Lameht. lenat. lemahat. semaht. selmahat. helmay. helymam. helmamy. zezetta. zezegta. gezegatha. zozogam. remasym. themaremasym. ieranyhel. phuerezo. gamyhal. zecegomyhal. hezetogamyhal. (2) heziephiat. hozoperbiar. iosaithyn. iosathyn. iosany. gosamyn. salaht. salatoham. salatehen. salatambel. hen. henbem. habena. henlezepha. bosephar. thamar. sahaletromar. (3) hafartitmar. thimas. tirimar. namor. semyhot. semohit. zemyhot. semoiz. lemdihon. lemahat. phethalon. hamiht. phethalonamie. zomye. zamiht. prihiti. philei. haphyn. gergeon. gergohen. (4) ierthon. lothios. lothos. semyhot. lemahat. zemohit. lemaiho. phetalon. hamye. hamyphyn. pethio. gergion. lecton. iergohen. thothios. lectos. Amen.

XXIV. Prayer.

O God, the most high, invisible God. Theos. Patir. behemnos. lehernnyos. behenny. We ask you, Ymos, through your most holy angels, who are Michael, i.e. the medicine of God, Raphael, the Strength of God, Gabriel, burning, (2) and Seraphim: helipha. massay. Cherubim: ielomynctos. gadabany. zedabanay. gederanay. saramany. lomtety. loctosy. gerohanathon. zahamany. lomyht. gedanabasy. setemanay. seremanay. henlothant. helomyht. henboramyht. samanazay. gedebaudi.

(3) [From] the fullness of the knowledge, we humbly ask you cherubim and seraphim, and you, O Jesus Christ, through all your saints and glorious [arch]angels, the names of which are consecrated by God, which must not be spoken by us, which are these: (4) Deihel. Dehel. Depymo. Dein. Hel. Exluso. Depymon. Helynon. Exmogon. Parineos. Exmegan. Pheleneos. Nauagen. Hosyel. Dragon. Garbona. Rathion. Monyham. Megonhamos.

XXV.[37]

I beseech you, O my Lord: illuminate and clarify my soul and conscience with the brilliance of your light and you illuminate and strengthen my understanding with the sweet scent of your Holy Spirit, that I may successfully attain to your glorious vision, which I now humbly ask for. (2) O Lord, adorn my soul

---

36 Ars. Not. 22, JV p. 162.
37 Ars. Not. 25, JV p. 42.

videam faciem tuam, videam et audiam gloriam tuam et laudem tuam. (3) Reforma, Domine, cor meum. Instaura, Domine, sensum meum. Placa, piissime, memoriam meam ad aspiciendam visionem facialem tuam et beatam. (4) Tempera, benignissime, animam et linguam meam ad habendam hanc visionem per gloriosa et ineffabilia nomina tua, tu, qui es fons bonitatis et tocius pietatis origo. (5) Habeas, queso, Domine, pacienciam in me et memoriam et graciam tuam da michi, ut accipere valeam hanc visionem beatam, (6) et quod a te pecii in hac sancta oracione da michi et largire. Tu, qui peccantem statim non iudicas set ad penitenciam misertus expectas, (7) te queso indignus peccator, ut facinora et peccata mea et delictorum meorum scelera abstergas et penitus extinguas, ut aptus efficiar, Domine, sancta visione tua, (8) et me peticione tanta per sanctorum angelorum et archangelorum tuorum virtutem, de quibus prefatus sum, dignum et efficacem facias per gloriosam maiestatem tuam, tu, qui es trinus et unus [et] verus Deus omnipotens. Amen.

XXVI Oracio

Iesu, Dei filius incomprehensibilis, hancor. hanacor. hanylos. iehorna. theodonos. helyothos. heliotheos. phagor. corphandonos. norizaue. corithico. hanosae. helsezope. phagora.

XXVII Oracio

Eleminator. candones. helos. helee. resphaga. thephagayn. thetendyn. thahonos. Ulcemya. heortahonos. uelos. behebos. belhores. hacaphagan. belehothol. ortophagon. corphandonos. (2) humane natus pro nobis peccatoribus, et vos, Heliothos. Phagnora. angeli sancti, adestote, advertite et docete me et regi te me ad visionem Dei sanctam perveniendam, habendam, optinendam (3) per gloriosum, clementissimum et omnipotentissimum creatorem, Dominum nostrum vivum, sanctum et inmensum, pium et eternum, cui est laus et honor et gloria per infinita secula. Amen.

that I may see your form, see and hear your glory and praise. (3) Transform my heart, O Lord. Renew, O Lord, my perception. Reconcile, O most holy one, my memory, to look upon the vision of your blessed shape. (4) Temper, O most kind one, my soul and my tongue, for having this vision through your glorious and ineffable names, you who are the fountain of goodness and source of all piety. (5) Have patience with me, I beg you O Lord, and give me a good memory and your grace, that I may have the strength to receive this blessed vision. (6) and which I have asked you to give and bestow on me in this holy prayer. You, who does not immediately judge a sinner, but pities him, awaiting his repentance. (7) Though I am unworthy, I beseech you to wipe away my crimes and sins and extinguish them inwardly, that I may be worthy to achieve, O Lord, your holy vision, (8) and grant me these my petitions, by the virtue of your holy angels and archangels, being fit and effective through the aforesaid through your glorious majesty, you are three and one, and true God almighty. Amen.

XXVI. Prayer.[38]

Jesus, son of the incomprehensible God, hancor. hanacor. hanylos. iehorna. theodonos. helyothos. heliotheos. phagor. corphandonos. norizaue. corithico. hanosae. helsezope. phagora.

XXVII. Prayer.[39]

Eleminator. candones. helos. helee. resphaga. thephagayn. thetendyn. thahonos. Ulcemya. heortahonos. uelos. behebos. belhores. hacaphagan. belehothol. ortophagon. corphandonos. (2) born human for us sinners, and you holy angels Heliothos. Phagnora. aid, guide, and teach me, and direct me towards reaching, having, and maintaining the vision of God, (3) through the glorious, most merciful and all-powerful creator, our living Lord, sacred and immeasurable, holy and eternal, to whom be the praise, honor, and glory, through the infinite worlds. Amen.

---

38 Ars. Not. 29a, JV p. 166.
39 Ars. Not. 29b, JV p. 167.

XXVIII Oracio

Lameht. ragua. ragahel. ragia. ragiomab. hagnaht. hoguolam. exactodan. heractodam. hanthonomos. hethaeneho. (2) hemones. iothe. lothensezaiha. sazaratha. hensazatha. serail. marab. mynathil. marathal. mairathal. brihamocon. thahamathon. (3) leprodoz. lephoris. leprohoc. lephorijs. hesacro: hesacohen. corquenal. choremal. guoyemal. ualiaiol. salail. salaiz. (4) salaior. halaiz. salquihel. gessidomy. gesseuazi. iessonay. hazoroz. hazarob. tharahal. bostihal. hamol. hamalamyn. Amen.

XXIX

Semeht. seghehalt. raguaht. reloymal. haguliaz. exhator. hanthomos. lezen. saccail. marab. brihamathon. lephez. hiefacto. themay. salaihel. agessomay. arathotamal.

XXX Oracio

Memoria irreprehensibilis, sapiencia incontradicibilis et incommutabilis Deus, eterni consilii angelus, amplectetur hodie cor meum dextera tua, et adimpleat conscienciam meam memoria tua (2) et odor unguentorum tuorum, et dulcedo gracie tue muniat mentem meam splendore Spiritus sancti et claritate, qua angeli faciem tuam, Domine, cum omnibus celi virtutibus intueri sine fine desiderant, (3) ut valeam cum ipsis te, clementissime, facialiter intueri, sapiencia, qua omnia [fecisti, intelligencia, qua omnia] reparasti, beatitudinis perseverancia, qua angelos restituisti, dileccione, qua hominem lapsum ad celestia traxisti, doctrina, qua Adam omnem scienciam docere dignatus es. (4) Informa, reple, instrue, instaura, corrige, clarifica et refice me, ut fiam novus in mandatis tuis intelligendis et suscipienda hac visione tua beata in salutem corporis et anime mee et omnium fidelium credencium in nomine tuo, quod est benedictum in secula seculorum. Amen.

XXVIII. Prayer.[40]

Lameht. ragua. ragahel. ragia. ragiomab. hagnaht. hoguolam. exactodan. heractodam. hanthonomos. hethaeneho. (2) hemones. iothe. lothensezaiha. sazaratha. hensazatha. serail. marab. mynathil. marathal. mairathal. brihamocon. thahamathon. (3) leprodoz. lephoris. leprohoc. lephorijs. hesacro: hesacohen. corquenal. choremal. guoyemal. ualiaiol. salail. salaiz. (4) salaior. halaiz. salquihel. gessidomy. gesseuazi. iessonay. hazoroz. hazarob. tharahal. bostihal. hamol. hamalamyn. Amen.

XXIX.[41]

Semeht. seghehalt. raguaht. reloymal. haguliaz. exhator. hanthomos. lezen. saccail. marab. brihamathon. lephez. hiefacto. themay. salaihel. agessomay. arathotamal.

XXX. Prayer.[42]

O irreprehensible memory, O uncontradictable wisdom, and unchangeable God, the angel of eternal council, hold my heart today with your right hand, and fill up my conscience with memory of you, (2) and with the scent of your oils, and may the sweetness of your grace strengthen my mind with the brilliance and clarity of the Holy Spirit, with which, O Lord, the angels, with all the powers of heaven, desire to look on your form always, (3) that I, like them, may be able to behold your face, most mercifully, with the wisdom [with which you have created all things, with the intelligence] with which you have renewed all things, with the steadfast blessedness, with which you have restored the angels, with the love, with which you have drawn man back to the heavens, who had fallen, with the teachings, and with which you deemed Adam worthy to be taught all knowledge. (4) Shape, complete, prepare, renew, correct, clarify, and rebuild me, that I may be made new to understand your commandments, and undertake this blessed vision of you, for the salvation of my body and soul, and of all faithful believers in your name, which is blessed, world without end. Amen.

---

40 Ars. Not. 34, JV p. 170
41 Ars. Not. 35, var. 5, JV p. 172.
42 Ars Not. 36, JV p. 46.

XXXI Oracio

Hazaram. hihel. hehelilem. hethelilem. theiihem. hazagatha. agruazcor. hizguor. liaiah. isenesan. zezor. iesar. ysail. (2) et vos, angeli, quorum nomina scribuntur in libro vite et ibi recitantur, iasym. horos. helsa. heremogos. myrecagil. resaym. lemay. lemar. rasamen. lemar. themamoht. irasim. (3) iemamoht. themamoht. secray. sotthaht. sehan. hanamar. thau. sechay. helymaht. iosoihel. helymoht. sattamaht. helymyhot. iosey. theodony. iasamaht. pharene. panetheneos. phateneynehos. (4) haramen. Theos. hathanaym. hanataiphar. hatanazar. basiactor. ieseuemay. iesamana. iesamanay. haziactor. hamynosia. zezamanay. hamos. hamynos. hiatregilos. cahegilihos. zaguhel. zatahel.

XXXII

Hielma. helma. helymat. heuina. hytanathas. hemyna. hitanathois. helsa. hebos. hiebros. helda. hagasa. hoccomegos. raitotagum. coictagon. myheragyn.

XXXIII

Confirma, consolida, elucida, abba. Theos. behetimyhat. hehem. ruhos. bethar. husuruhunt. hetarius. Theos. Deus Pater, Deus Fili, Deus Spiritus sancte, <o>racionem nostram. (2) Confirma et intellectum et animam meam et memoriam meam ad suscipiendam, cognoscendam, videndam, intuendam visionem et faciem tuam beatam et gloriosam. Amen.

XXXIV

Agloros. theomythos. themyros. sehocodothos. zehocodos. hattihamel. sozena. haptamygel. sozihenzia. hemya. gettahol. (2) helyna. sothoneya. geherahel. halimyz. zezoray. gezetiz. gerehona. hazihal. hazai. meguos. megalos. usyon. saduhc.

XXXI. Prayer.[43]

Hazaram. hihel. hehelilem. hethelilem. theiihem. hazagatha. agruazcor. hizguor. liaiah. isenesan. zezor. iesar. ysail. (2) and you angels, whose names are written in the *Book of Life* and there they are read aloud, iasym. horos. helsa. heremogos. myrecagil. resaym. lemay. lemar. rasamen. lemar. themamoht. irasim. (3) iemamoht. themamoht. secray. sotthaht. sehan. hanamar. thau. sechay. helymaht. iosoihel. helymoht. sattamaht. helymyhot. iosey. theodony. iasamaht. pharene. panetheneos. phateneynehos. (4) haramen. Theos. hathanaym. hanataiphar. hatanazar. basiactor. ieseuemay. iesamana. iesamanay. haziactor. hamynosia. zezamanay. hamos. hamynos. hiatregilos. cahegilihos. zaguhel. zatahel.

XXXII.[44]

Hielma. helma. helymat. heuina. hytanathas. hemyna. hitanathois. helsa. hebos. hiebros. helda. hagasa. hoccomegos. raitotagum. coictagon. myheragyn.

XXXIII.[45]

Strengthen, solidify, enlighten, Abba. Theos. behetimyhat. hehem. ruhos. bethar. husuruhunt. hetarius. Theos. God the Father, God the Son, God the Holy Spirit, strengthen our reasoning (2) and comprehension, and my soul and memory, to receive, retain, see and contemplate the vision and of your blessed and glorious face. Amen.

XXXIV.[46]

Agloros. theomythos. themyros. sehocodothos. zehocodos. hattihamel. sozena. haptamygel. sozihenzia. hemya. gettahol. (2) helyna. sothoneya. geherahel. halimyz. zezoray. gezetiz. gerehona. hazihal. hazai. meguos. megalos. usyon. saduhc.

---

43 Ars. Not. 43, JV p. 174.
44 Ars. Not. 46, JV p. 176.
45 Ars. Not. 47, JV p. 49.
46 Ars. Not. 50, JV p. 50.

XXXIVb

[Deus omnium, qui es Deus meus, qui in principio omnia ex nichilo creasti, qui in Spiritu tuo omnia reformasti, comple, restaura, sana intellectum meum, ut glorificem te per omnia opera cogitacionum et verborum meorum.]

XXXV Oracio

Megal. agal. iegal. hariothos. handos. hanathos. hanathoios. hauothos. lemazai. semezai. lamezai. lethonas. (2) iethonay. zemazphar. zeomaspar. zeomaphar. tetragramos. thethagranys. hatammar. hazaamahar. zahamyr. (3) iechosaphor. zethesaphir. gethor. saphor. hasagitha. hasacapha. hasamypa. haragaia. hazaguy. phasamar. samar. saleht. salym. salmeht. (4) sameht. saloht. sillezaleht. sadayne. neothatir. neodamy. hadozamyr. zozena. belymoht. hazat. helyhot.

XXXVI Oracio

Veritas, lux, via et vita omnium creaturarum, iuste Deus, vivifica me, visita me et intellectum meum et animam meam confirma et instaura conscienciam meam et clarifica et purga, (2) sicut Iohanni et Paulo [promisisti], quando rapuisti eos ad visionem tuam eis ostendendam, ut sic, Domine, meo vivente corpore possit te anima mea inspicere facialiter et videre.

XXXVII

Hamycchiahel. hamsahel. dalihir. hair. halel. zedach. hazarach. zedaizh. hazaias. lezorihal. zezorias. iechori. alsemaia. ysamyha. zama. ysa. (2) samma. ysarai. ysameht. ysathay. lemyhel. nehel. semehel. iemymehel. mythynab. nybahal. mychyn. mybancaiab. hamyly. mynab. heliasal. hometibymal. helymal. hymbos. zebracal. zelimal. (3) iechro. samaril. zezocha. iecrosahal. melos. zalimebor. zalymylos. zaguhel. mychathomos. myheromos. mycracosmos. nycromyhos. Amen.

XXXIVb.[47]

[O God of all, you who are my God, who in the beginning created all out of nothing, who in your Spirit has transformed all, fill, restore, and cure my comprehension, that I may glorify you through all my thoughts, words, and deeds.]

XXXV. Prayer.[48]

Megal. agal. iegal. hariothos. handos. hanathos. hanathoios. hauothos. lemazai. semezai. lamezai. lethonas. (2) iethonay. zemazphar. zeomaspar. zeomaphar. tetragramos. thethagranys. hatammar. hazaamahar. zahamyr. (3) iechosaphor. zethesaphir. gethor. saphor. hasagitha. hasacapha. hasamypa. haragaia. hazaguy. phasamar. samar. saleht. salym. salmeht. (4) sameht. saloht. sillezaleht. sadayne. neothatir. neodamy. hadozamyr. zozena. belymoht. hazat. helyhot.

XXXVI. Prayer.[49]

The truth, the light, the way, and the life of all creatures, O just God, vivify me, visit me and strengthen my comprehension, and my soul, and renew my conscience, and glorify and purge it, (2) as [you promised] John and Paul, when you snatched them away to show them the vision of you, so too, O Lord, while my body is yet living, may I be able to behold your face, and live.

XXXVII.[50]

Hamycchiahel. hamsahel. dalihir. hair. halel. zedach. hazarach. zedaizh. hazaias. lezorihal. zezorias. iechori. alsemaia. ysamyha. zama. ysa. (2) samma. ysarai. ysameht. ysathay. lemyhel. nehel. semehel. iemymehel. mythynab. nybahal. mychyn. mybancaiab. hamyly. mynab. heliasal. hometibymal. helymal. hymbos. zebracal. zelimal. (3) iechro. samaril. zezocha. iecrosahal. melos. zalimebor. zalymylos. zaguhel. mychathomos. myheromos. mycracosmos. nycromyhos. Amen.

---

47 Ars. Not. 51, JV p. 51. Apparently omitted by accident, but see LI 9; see also XV.6.
48 Ars. Not. 52, JV p. 177.
49 Ars Not. 53, JV p. 51.
50 Ars Not. 54, JV p. 178.

XXXVIII

Ego in conspectu tuo, Domine, Deus meus, in cuius nutu omnia nuda sunt et aperta, et in cuius manu omnia sunt munda et pura—mundifica et depura me, Deus omnipotens -, hec enim loquor, (2) ut ablato infidelitatis et infeccionis errore et labe adiuvet me Spiritus tuus bonus, sanctus, vivificans omnia, et +vivificet+ omnem incredulitatem et labem meam, (3) ut visionem tuam sanctissimam, licet indignus, propter tuam misericordiam valeam efficaciter et absque defectu iam optinere. Amen.

XXXIX

Semoth. gehel. helymoht. hemeb. sabahel. zerothay. zabahel. gerozay. hebel. crosaihamagra. hatchagra. rageu. seromay. zehez. hezehengon. iezomay. hemehegon. hamagrata. cezozoy. gesommay. (2) hesehenguon. lethomay. Halla. hathanaton. hagigel. hatamyhel. hathomas. hecohay. zemohay. theageta. theal. regon. hagem. iezeregal. zehalragem. geht. zeregal. hamabihat. hezegon. (3) gethage. madiaaios. zadanchios. exhedon. pallathoros. zallachatos. thelthis. trehodios. zezochthiam. pallititacos. nethi. delthis. heremodios. helmelazar. helyne. zazar. haron. (4) gezero. mymyhel. henthon. hermelazar. sython. genithon. hezemyhel. heymemy. helmelazar. cremymyhel. exheruz. zorol. mothora. rabihel. samyb. lamely. melion. sarabihel. samyl. tamyl. Samyhel. Amen.

XL

Omnipotens, sempiterne Deus et misericors Pater ante omnia secula benedicte, qui nobis, eterne Deus incomprehensibilis et incommutabilis, remedium salutare contulisti, (2) qui propter omnipotenciam maiestatis tue nobis facultatem laudandi, glorificandi, videndi facialiter maiestatem tuam concessisti ceteris<que> animalibus negatam, cuius disposicio in sui providencia non fallitur, (3) cuius eciam natura eterna est et consubstancialis deitati sue et trinitati sue, que est Pater et Filius et Spiritus sanctus, que

XXXVIII.[51]

I speak these things in your presence, O Lord my God, at whose command all things are naked and open, and in whose hand all things are clean and pure; cleanse and purify me, almighty God, (2) so that the error and stain of unbelief and deception being taken away, your good holy Spirit may help me, making me live, and *living, help my unbelief[52] and all my faults, (3) that I may be permitted your most holy vision, although unworthy, through your mercy may I prevail effectually and prevail now without failure. Amen.

XXXIX.[53]

Semoth. gehel. helymoht. hemeb. sabahel. zerothay. zabahel. gerozay. hebel. crosaihamagra. hatchagra. rageu. seromay. zehez. hezehengon. iezomay. hemehegon. hamagrata. cezozoy. gesommay. (2) hesehenguon. lethomay. Halla. hathanaton. hagigel. hatamyhel. hathomas. hecohay. zemohay. theageta. theal. regon. hagem. iezeregal. zehalragem. geht. zeregal. hamabihat. hezegon. (3) gethage. madiaaios. zadanchios. exhedon. pallathoros. zallachatos. thelthis. trehodios. zezochthiam. pallititacos. nethi. delthis. heremodios. helmelazar. helyne. zazar. haron. (4) gezero. mymyhel. henthon. hermelazar. sython. genithon. hezemyhel. heymemy. helmelazar. cremymyhel. exheruz. zorol. mothora. rabihel. samyb. lamely. melion. sarabihel. samyl. tamyl. Samyhel. Amen.

XL.[54]

Almighty, eternal God, and merciful Father, you who are blessed before all worlds, who has granted us, O God eternal, incomprehensible, and unchangeable, the medicine of salvation, (2) which because of the omnipotence of your majesty you have permitted us the ability to praise, glorify, and behold your majesty face to face, which is denied to other creatures, the disposition of whose destiny is unfailing, (3) whose nature is both eternal and of one substance, deity and trinity, which is the Father, Son, and Holy Spirit, who is

---

51 Ars. Not. 55, JV p. 52.
52 Cp. Mark 9.24.
53 Ars. Not. 62, JV p. 181.
54 Ars Not. 64, JV p. 56..

est exaltata super omne celum, ubi divinitas et deitas corporaliter habitat, (4) deprecor maiestatem tuam, Domine, et omnipotenciam tuam glorifico et eternitatis tue virtutem, ac magnificenciam tuam summam et eternam cum nimia imploracione intencionis flagitans deposco. (5) Te, Deus meus, sapiencia inestimabilis et ineffabilis, vita angelorum, Deus incomprehensibilis, in cuius conspectu chorus angelorum consistit, te deprecor et flagito, (6) ut per sanctum et gloriosum nomen tuum et per conspectum angelorum tuorum et principatus celestes michi graciam tuam dones huius sancte visionis (7) et statim subvenias michi et sanctitatem michi tribuas et subtilitatem visionis tante et intellectus tui puritatem et perseveranciam concedas, (8) ut te facialiter videre valeam, qui vivis et regnas eternaliter per omnia secula seculorum in conspectu omnium virtutum celestium nunc et semper et ubique. Amen.

XLI

Semoht lamen. lezahel. salmatihal. zamatihel. mahazihel. zamazihal. ezeleaz. mahatihoten. hezoleam. megos. hemol. (2) hemnoleha. methos. hazamegos. halzamyhol. alzamoy. menrnanittos. memomittos. zely. marayhathol. zolmazathol. zemeney. iemenay. lameley. zethemalo. zethenaran. labdaio. lodeho. zabday. hoton. (3) ladaiedon. lapdaihadon. lothanan. hizemazihe. izthamhihe. iotha. uahuzuzif. zihanatihephomos. zeherem. zehe. ziehelmos. hiehanathihe. homos. zeherem. hessimathal. hessicomal. Ono (4) chehe. sihotil. magal. hesiothil. mytho., halpha. husale. ouus. flum. falso hallemassay. alesemonoy. salemanasai. helemasay. zazaico. semanay. nachairo. natham. gemehol. yetulmassay. gemahol. (5) iezemalo. magul. gehamas. senadar. iezama. salpha. secramagay. iehennagay. zehetyn. zemadazan. iehir. ramagay. geiama. salpha. gemama. suphu. ioher. iohabos. haymal. hamanal. thanocbomas. (6) iobohe. hamynal. zanogromos. nyzozoroba. nygerozoma. negero. robali. negora. hohalym. uytheromachum. tho. lymchay. tolomay. loynar. tholinngay. zenolozihon. hisonomelihon. Samyhel. giethi. (7) sicrozegamal. thonehos. carmolehos. samhel. geiszefihor. iezolnohit. phicrose. gramaht. theonthos. carmelos. lainyhel. harmanail. gesezihor. semarnail. zaarmatihail. heliozo. thahel. samail. Amen.

exalted above all heaven, where the divinity and deity physically dwells, (4) I beg your majesty, O Lord, and I glorify your omnipotence and the eternity of your power, and I beseech with great imploring of your greatness, most high and eternal. (5) O my God, inestimable and ineffable wisdom, O life of the angels, incomprehensible God, in whose sight the choir of angels stand, I beg and beseech you, (6) through your holy and glorious name, and through the sight of your angels and heavenly principalities, that you grant to me the grace of this holy vision of you (7) and forthwith come to my aid and bestow to me the sanctity and correctness of the great vision, and grant me the purity of your comprehension, and may it persist, (8) so I may succeed in seeing you face to face, you who lives and reigns forever through all the ages of the ages in the sight of all heavenly virtues, now and always and everywhere. Amen.

XLI.[55]

Semoht lamen. lezahel. salmatihal. zamatihel. mahazihel. zamazihal. ezeleaz. mahatihoten. hezoleam. megos. hemol. (2) hemnoleha. methos. hazamegos. halzamyhol. alzamoy. menrnanittos. memomittos. zely. marayhathol. zolmazathol. zemeney. iemenay. lameley. zethemalo. zethenaran. labdaio. lodeho. zabday. hoton. (3) ladaiedon. lapdaihadon. lothanan. hizemazihe. izthamhihe. iotha. uahuzuzif. zihanatihephomos. zeherem. zehe. ziehelmos. hiehanathihe. homos. zeherem. hessimathal. hessicomal. Ono (4) chehe. sihotil. magal. hesiothil. mytho., halpha. husale. ouus. flum. falso hallemassay. alesemonoy. salemanasai. helemasay. zazaico. semanay. nachairo. natham. gemehol. yetulmassay. gemahol. (5) iezemalo. magul. gehamas. senadar. iezama. salpha. secramagay. iehennagay. zehetyn. zemadazan. iehir. ramagay. geiama. salpha. gemama. suphu. ioher. iohabos. haymal. hamanal. thanocbomas. (6) iobohe. hamynal. zanogromos. nyzozoroba. nygerozoma. negero. robali. negora. hohalym. uytheromachum. tho. lymchay. tolomay. loynar. tholinngay. zenolozihon. hisonomelihon. Samyhel. giethi. (7) sicrozegamal. thonehos. carmolehos. samhel. geiszefihor. iezolnohit. phicrose. gramaht. theonthos. carmelos. lainyhel. harmanail. gesezihor. semarnail. zaarmatihail. heliozo. thahel. samail. Amen.

---

[55] Ars Not. 69, JV p. 183-4.

XLII Primus terminus

Genealogon. reealologon. tenealogo. saphay. zazaiham. saphia. zede. zemoziham. zomonrihel. sanaman. sanma. gegnognal. Samyhel. ieremyhel. horaciotos. hetha. siothos. sepharaym. (2) henemos. genozabal. ieremabal. hethemel. genotheram. genorabal. semyha. senma. mynarom. yninathon. geristel. hymacton. chalos. phabal. resaram. marachihel. naratheos. ietrinantho. iezibathel. (3) sephoros. thesirara. zepharonay. hazana. messihel. Sother. hazihel. semicros. chiel. hamacal. hator. zemothor. sauaday. morothochiel. semenos. satabis. themay. horel. remay. renay. zenel. hasa. gemol. (4) zemelaza. iemozihel. zemei. zemeihaton. zechor. helycos. semysemie. hiacon. iethor.-d| mehohin. hazenethon. semase. mepathon. zemolym. sistos. Eloy. semegey. manos. helypos. hemyclopos. geys. seray. sephet. sephamanay. (5) helihothos. cherobalym. hassenethon. hisistos. domengos. iemyrohal. samanathos. semeham. behenos. megon. hanythel. iechomeros. ielamagar. remelthet. genay. domathamos. hathamyr. seryhon. senon. zaralamay. sabayhon.

XLIII Secundus terminus

Geolym. hazenethon. ysistos. Eloy. sephei. manay. helyhotas. ierobalym. semalet. gonay. heliothos. domathamos. hathamyr. seryhon. hamynyr. senoz. magamagol. (2) sethar. senam. magel. Hel. helymothos. helseron. zeron. phamal. iegromos. herymyhothon. lauthamos. heramathon. laudamos. lanaymos. seplatihel. sephatihel. hagenalis. legenale. hegernar. (3) stanazihel. stanithel. hathanathos. hegrogebal. rogor. heremynar. {hen}ecyman. marothon. iethar{naym}. {heno.z}ios. {i}ezeduhos. gezconas. satam. g{ort}aray. helycychcym. helestymeym. sephalzna. mathar. (4) saphar. manatham. bezazay. samay. sephay. syhemathon. balair. {s}amamar. hamyhel. marmamor. h {en}emos. gegohomos. samar. sabar. {hami}hel. gezamahel. sacramay. iezama{mel}. {ha}mansamel. (5) hamazamoly. geromol. lezemon. sycromal. iezabal. sanma. zama. hatanathos. Theos. helyhene. zelym. helyhem. hezelym. cromemon. henethemos. gegeguol. hemthemos. iamam. harathinam. megon. (6) meguoncemon. scrymay. hethemel. hemel. sethor. helsethor. sophornay. behelthron. sesalihel. tanahel. homyhal. iezahel. zemahel. komal. guomaguos. sennyr. iechor. nomemal. gehamguo. (7) genayr. iecomame. malihaguathos. hachamol. iecromaguos. maguarht.

XLII. First Terminus.[56]

Genealogon. reealologon. tenealogo. saphay. zazaiham. saphia. zede. zemoziham. zomonrihel. sanaman. sanma. gegnognal. Samyhel. ieremyhel. horaciotos. hetha. siothos. sepharaym. (2) henemos. genozabal. ieremabal. hethemel. genotheram. genorabal. semyha. senma. mynarom. yninathon. geristel. hymacton. chalos. phabal. resaram. marachihel. naratheos. ietrinantho. iezibathel. (3) sephoros. thesirara. zepharonay. hazana. messihel. Sother. hazihel. semicros. chiel. hamacal. hator. zemothor. sauaday. morothochiel. semenos. satabis. themay. horel. remay. renay. zenel. hasa. gemol. (4) zemelaza. iemozihel. zemei. zemeihaton. zechor. helycos. semysemie. hiacon. iethor.-d| mehohin. hazenethon. semase. mepathon. zemolym. sistos. Eloy. semegey. manos. helypos. hemyclopos. geys. seray. sephet. sephamanay. (5) helihothos. cherobalym. hassenethon. hisistos. domengos. iemyrohal. samanathos. semeham. behenos. megon. hanythel. iechomeros. ielamagar. remelthet. genay. domathamos. hathamyr. seryhon. senon. zaralamay. sabayhon.

XLIII. Second Terminus.[57]

Geolym. hazenethon. ysistos. Eloy. sephei. manay. helyhotas. ierobalym. semalet. gonay. heliothos. domathamos. hathamyr. seryhon. hamynyr. senoz. magamagol. (2) sethar. senam. magel. Hel. helymothos. helseron. zeron. phamal. iegromos. herymyhothon. lauthamos. heramathon. laudamos. lanaymos. seplatihel. sephatihel. hagenalis. legenale. hegernar. (3) stanazihel. stanithel. hathanathos. hegrogebal. rogor. heremynar. {hen}ecyman. marothon. iethar{naym}. {heno.z}ios. {i}ezeduhos. gezconas. satam. g{ort} aray. helycychcym. helestymeym. sephalzna. mathar. (4) saphar. manatham. bezazay. samay. sephay. syhemathon. balair. {s}amamar. hamyhel. marmamor. h {en}emos. gegohomos. samar. sabar. {hami}hel. gezamahel. sacramay. iezama{mel}. {ha}mansamel. (5) hamazamoly. geromol. lezemon. sycromal. iezabal. sanma. zama. hatanathos. Theos. helyhene. zelym. helyhem. hezelym. cromemon. henethemos. gegeguol. hemthemos. iamam. harathinam. megon. (6) meguoncemon. scrymay. hethemel. hemel. sethor. helsethor. sophornay. behelthor. sesalihel. tanahel. homyhal. iezahel. zemahel. komal. guomaguos. sennyr. iechor. nomemal. gehamguo. (7) genayr. iecomame. malihaguathos.

---

56 Ars Not. 127a, JV p. 84–5.
57 Cf. Ars Not. 127b, V p. 232–3.

noynemal. haguathos. hamathalis. iecoraguos. sammazihel. ieconail. hesuogem. chocorim. mynarntanamaytha. (8) thanaym. raymara. senayhel. honrnon. genthon. lauarnyhel. gehemguor. gemyhothar. iamnamyhel. sezihel. magol. samanay. haganal. menya. ferimay. sarranay. lanamyhel. guohemguor. gemothar. larnmyhel. (9) sezihel. maguol. samanay. hagamal. mena. ferimay. sarranay. lacham. lyhares. lethanagihel. nathes. samairliazer. egihel. thamazihel. hacacaros. cazaihel. hacaraz. hacatoharena. Semyday. (10) hacca. choharon. semelay. iamye. iazabal. lauerecabal. iammeze. thabal. cumachoros. hacoronathos. sathanael. hariharn. zathhar. harathar. haziler. zechar. hazihem. hazachar. Loenigemar. (11) hazanathar. hameguar. semal. geheu. negemar. hemeguol. semam. hathamanos. latimairos. rechiharnos. larnogual. semar. temnalamos. sebranay. selarnnay. baructhata. ialon. hespuhos. ramel. Semal. (12) renylsemar. ielamacrom. ielama. crymyzaiber. segher. sayher. ierologuos. iegemaguolon. geiemamaguosam. hamynos. iamozia. iozihon. iacuhosia. haguyhosio. yecologos. hazeoyon. hamynos. (13) hamyr. matharihon. mathanon. senos. heliothon. zenos. semear. lauar. lamar. setronalon. gemal. secromaguol. sacromehal. lamagil. sethoham. sechoiro. maihol. socromoguol. Genos. thomegen. nycheos.

XLIV 3[us] TERMINUS

Agenos. theomogenos. Theos. hatanathos. kirihel. ypolis. ypile. karihel. cristopholis. Hon. ymalihor. ymas. harethena. chenathon. leonbon. boho. usyon. ieromeguos. hagenoy. (2) hysichou. geromagol. hagyhamal. latham. zarchamal. senar. peconahal. lacramagral. sehar. sehan. iezetom. genomoloy. genomos. iezoro. nomeros. henahihel. gemehagate. gemyha. iethenmahos. myhayhos. (3) semana. hahel. semahel. hoteihos. hatazaihos. saphar. nemenomos. hoheihos. hataz. ayhos. caphar. nemenomos. horihos. hataz. haihoz. seiha. chomo. chomothanay. lamam. lamnamyr. lamyhar. (4) lamanazamyr. lemyar. hagramos. generamosehc. senyha. exagal. hamagron. semaharon. semyr. harauma. mamail. hararncha. mothana. Ramay. iose. ramaht. hauaramay. Iole. Christus. hamyriscos. (5) hamirrios. tharathos. caratheos. saleht. semamarim. iasol. salem. semyhamaym. hallehuma. haristeiz. bohem. ruhos. Halla. samyey. syloht. Samyhel. hallenomay. samythi. methonomos. iethonomos. gedonomay.

hachamol. iecromaguos. maguarht. noynemal. haguathos. hamathalis. iecoraguos. sammazihel. iceonail. hesuogem. chocorim. mynarntanamaytha. (8) thanaym. raymara. senayhel. honrnon. genthon. lauarnyhel. gehemguor. gemyhothar. iamnamyhel. sezihel. magol. samanay. haganal. menya. ferimay. sarranay. lanamyhel. guohemguor. gemothar. larnmyhel. (9) sezihel. maguol. samanay. hagamal. mena. ferimay. sarranay. lacham. lyhares. lethanagihel. nathes. samairliazer. egihel. thamazihel. hacacaros. cazaihel. hacaraz. hacatoharena. Semyday. (10) hacca. choharon. semelay. iamye. iazabal. lauerecabal. iammeze. thabal. cumachoros. hacoronathos. sathanael. hariharn. zathhar. harathar. haziler. zechar. hazihem. hazachar. Loenigemar. (11) hazanathar. hameguar. semal. geheu. negemar. hemeguol. semam. hathamanos. latimairos. rechiharnos. larnogual. semar. temnalamos. sebranay. selarnnay. baructhata. ialon. hespuhos. ramel. Semal. (12) renylsemar. ielamacrom. ielama. crymyzaiber. segher. sayher. ierologuos. iegemaguolon. geiemamaguosam. hamynos. iamozia. iozihon. iacuhosia. haguyhosio. yecologos. hazeoyon. hamynos. (13) hamyr. matharihon. mathanon. senos. heliothon. zenos. semear. lauar. lamar. setronalon. gemal. secromaguol. sacromehal. lamagil. sethoham. sechoiro. maihol. socromoguol. Genos. thomegen. nycheos.

XLIV. Third Terminus.[58]

Agenos. theomogenos. Theos. hatanathos. kirihel. ypolis. ypile. karihel. cristopholis. Hon. ymalihor. ymas. harethena. chenathon. leonbon. boho. usyon. ieromeguos. hagenoy. (2) hysichou. geromagol. hagyhamal. latham. zarchamal. senar. peconahal. lacramagral. sehar. sehan. iezetom. genomoloy. genomos. iezoro. nomeros. henahihel. gemehagate. gemyha. iethenmahos. myhayhos. (3) semana. hahel. semahel. hoteihos. hatazaihos. saphar. nemenomos. hoheihos. hataz. ayhos. caphar. nemenomos. horihos. hataz. haihoz. seiha. chomo. chomothanay. lamam. lamnamyr. lamyhar. (4) lamanazamyr. lemyar. hagramos. generamosehc. senyha. exagal. hamagron. semaharon. semyr. harauma. mamail. hararncha. mothana. Ramay. iose. ramaht. hauaramay. Iole. Christus. hamyriscos. (5) hamirrios. tharathos. caratheos. saleht. semamarim. iasol. salem. semyhamaym. hallehuma. haristeiz. bohem. ruhos. Halla. samyey. syloht. Samyhel. hallenomay. samythi. methonomos. iethonomos. gedonomay.

---

58 Ars Not. 127c. JV p. 233.

XLV 4ᵘˢ TERMINUS

Geuathores. sanamathotos. guanatores. zanothoros. genomos. ienazar. seuma. marathos. seuather. sematheher. senachar. gerub. iamam. exihel. chublalaman. (2) hesihel. sethei. semylihel. zomyhel. genocomel. thanyham. machar. hachay. hazanathay. Theos. hamanatar. hazanethar. theconay. chiathar. theohon. namacar. (3) senuales. samyha. hesaca. semaly. hesamen. semyhahes. sarcihate. nazihatel. hanaziathachel. hasilihacel. pamylihel. haziliatel. hageuoron. hageuorem. (4) hageuorozom. samaht. samoht. habisumaht. hendon. habysanahat. tyngehen. cragohem. hazamgeri. hazamaguhem. lemehot. hasomgeri. iomoyhot. semiha. riahacton. semymarithaton. (5) semynar. zihoton. zaguam. horay. honethe. hoparathos. nahamala. rochos. hazata. helralacos. horetha. horalacos. horetha. horalothos. haralo. lethos. geno. zabahal. (6) lemaht. hazocha. lematalmay. halmay. iemalis. secomathal. harmarlemaht. sethemaesal. rabasadail. semnazliel. lethom. hagihal. legos. patis. iethomagihal. genomychos. (7) samayhas. ieuemeros. samma. zasamar. hazamyha. hasaymam. thaguoro. bandethepharon. thagromathon. laudoches. pharen. decarpe. medyhos. decapocheu. duhomelathus. decaponde. dihamelathos. semyhariht. (8) samyhan. genathely. zazamar. myremoht. satharios. gemiliam. sacrehos. saphorenam. saphoro. megon. hassahamynel. hazaa. myrahel. gerizo. ieristosymythos. hothos. hymicros. Otheos.

XLVI 5[ᵘˢ] TERMINUS

Demathy. motheham. semathyotheos. hesapopa. hesaphopanos. gramyhel. garamanas. saphomoron. gelbaray. ieblaray. hetidiham. henzan. hezidiham. canazpharis. (2) hanthesion. cauastphasis. holithos. hosschihon. samatihel. ramaihel. semiramoht. Sathanos. gecabal. Hostosion. lemeliham. saphara. negon. zaramyhel. zamyrel. geriston. (3) zymphoros. hocho. hadalomob. uagem. nagenay. megos. naymogos. semazihar. helaph. herlo. holophemo. lopheo. hornobahoceo. Nydeht. herihegil. roguhon. nydocricib. (4) uegal. neguabel. memoht. hemel. gemoht. saguanar. clarapalos. zenozmyhel. iosagat. genoz. hamel. guaramaziel. gerathar. sathamyanos. sahamuham. gnamazihel. machelaglilos. (5) geraguaht. sathamyham. hurihel. phalomagos. phalomgros. iotho. megom. saraht. saaysac. horamylichos. carmeli-

XLV. Fourth Terminus.[59]

Geuathores. sanamathotos. guanatores. zanothoros. genomos. ienazar. seuma. marathos. seuather. sematheher. senachar. gerub. iamam. exihel. chublalaman. (2) hesihel. sethei. semylihel. zomyhel. genocomel. thanyham. machar. hachay. hazanathay. Theos. hamanatar. hazanethar. theconay. chiathar. theohon. namacar. (3) senuales. samyha. hesaca. semaly. hesamen. semyhahes. sarcihate. nazihatel. hanaziathachel. hasilihacel. pamylihel. haziliatel. hageuoron. hageuorem. (4) hageuorozom. samaht. samoht. habisumaht. hendon. habysanahat. tyngehen. cragohem. hazamgeri. hazamaguhem. lemehot. hasomgeri. iomoyhot. semiha. riahacton. semymarithaton. (5) semynar. zihoton. zaguam. horay. honethe. hoparathos. nahamala. rochos. hazata. helralacos. horetha. horalacos. horetha. horalothos. haralo. lethos. geno. zabahal. (6) lemaht. hazocha. lematalmay. halmay. iemalis. secomathal. harmarlemaht. sethemaesal. rabasadail. semnazliel. lethom. hagihal. legos. patis. iethomagihal. genomychos. (7) samayhas. ieuemeros. samma. zasamar. hazamyha. hasaymam. thaguoro. bandethepharon. thagromathon. laudoches. pharen. decarpe. medyhos. decapocheu. duhomelathus. decaponde. dihamelathos. semyhariht. (8) samyhan. genathely. zazamar. myremoht. satharios. gemiliam. sacrehos. saphorenam. saphoro. megon. hassahamynel. hazaa. myrahel. gerizo. ieristosymythos. hothos. hymicros. Otheos.

XLVI. Fifth Terminus.[60]

Demathy. motheham. semathyotheos. hesapopa. hesaphopanos. gramyhel. garamanas. saphomoron. gelbaray. ieblaray. hetidiham. henzan. hezidiham. canazpharis. (2) hanthesion. cauastphasis. holithos. hosschihon. samatihel. ramaihel. semiramoht. Sathanos. gecabal. Hostosion. lemeliham. saphara. negon. zaramyhel. zamyrel. geriston. (3) zymphoros. hocho. hadalomob. uagem. nagenay. megos. naymogos. semazihar. helaph. herlo. holophemo. lopheo. hornobahoceo. Nydeht. herihegil. roguhon. nydocricib. (4) uegal. neguabel. memoht. hemel. gemoht. saguanar. clarapalos. zenozmyhel. iosagat. genoz. hamel. guaramaziel. gerathar. sathamyanos. sahamuham. gnamazihel. machelaglilos. (5) geraguaht. sathamyham. hurihel. phalomagos. phalomgros.

---

59 Ars Not. 127d, JV p. 233–4.
60 Ars. Not. 127e, JV p. 234.

chos. hezaladuha. hezeladam. hisihel. hemal. Usyon. lamal. raguam. sablathom. Sabsacom.

XLVII 6ᵘˢ TERMINUS

Derogueguos. geronehos. samanachor. sazanachoray. zamachoray. sauatihel. lamathios. sauazihel. thamyquiol. zazarahel. kyrion. zamynel. kyris. crememon. caristonmon. sacronomay. (2) soromono. hestimpandos. iechampanydos. ietham. panydos. methelamathon. merasamaty. sabarna. heluhama. guathamal. hemdamyhos. thega. myhabal. teguamathal. chathanathel. (3) thehogethos. cehoguos. sanazihel. cathanathel. tehogethos. tehoguos. canazay. teneloihos. zenelyhos. cathaliel. theomeguos. lapdamylon. laudamelyhon. ierothihon. lapda. mozihon. (4) homen. samal. samochia. homy. samal. samaziho. sathamenay. samohaia. sathomonay. geromazihel. hoctho. macalon. hothomegalon. genetazamanay. hazatamel. hazabanas. iechro. tynoguale. sehor. gehoraia. (5) haramanay. harathacihel. hazabamoht. hamython. lapdas. hazathan. thihel. hazabanos. hamacon. hamamalyhon. samalyhon. samalerihon. usiologihon. legyn. heleis. hymon. machitilon. (6) Theos. heloty. sarrainazili. samachili. helamon. chihamon. Hel. lamochiamou. lagay. lemechiel. semezihel. laymos. lanoso hazamathon. themohan. thanathon. Theon. natharathon.

XLVIII 7ᵘˢ TERMINUS

Maguus. maguol. nazihacol. uazihathos. heliam. mathon. saphar. nazachon. gemehihel. iomorihel. sanayhel. sazanyhel. saramel. semyhel. sezimel. (2) lebachon. iarachon. iaratham. basihas. lamnay. rouala. matliathon. rasihos. layna. choro. laymatham. labynegual. scomycros. bazihos. lainna. labunegas. herezemyhel. (3) pheamicros. negemezihol. relmalaguoram. hanamyhos. hanomos. gracosihos. gracomessihos. sothiron. genozepha. chelahel. zopascanelios. zepasconomos. hamarazihos. hamarizihos. (4) zenazihel. geramathihel. gecramathihol. hasaguar. hasagiri. paramyhot. hapasiry. haranamar. Senales. hasaguanamar. sennagel. secastologihon. geuaguolos. hageuolo. thegos. sozor. (5) hamay. seroguomay. sorosamay. iamaramos. remolithos. lammaramos. zenon. serolen. zabay. peripaton. harihat. hanan-

iotho. megom. saraht. saaysac. horamylichos. carmelichos. hezaladuha. hezeladam. hisihel. hemal. Usyon. lamal. raguam. sablathom. sabsacom.

XLVII. Sixth Terminus.[61]

Derogueguos. geronehos. samanachor. sazanachoray. zamachoray. sauatihel. lamathios. sauazihel. thamyquiol. zazarahel. kyrion. zamynel. kyris. crememon. caristonmon. sacronomay. (2) soromono. hestimpandos. iechampanydos. ietham. panydos. methelamathon. merasamaty. sabarna. heluhama. guathamal. hemdamyhos. thega. myhabal. teguamathal. chathanathel. (3) thehogethos. cehoguos. sanazihel. cathanathel. tehogethos. tehoguos. canazay. teneloihos. zenelyhos. cathaliel. theomeguos. lapdamylon. laudamelyhon. ierothihon. lapda. mozihon. (4) homen. samal. samochia. homy. samal. samazihо. sathamenay. samohaia. sathomonay. geromazihel. hoctho. macalon. hothomegalon. genetazamanay. hazatamel. hazabanas. iechro. tynoguale. sehor. gehoraia. (5) haramanay. harathacihel. hazabamoht. hamython. lapdas. hazathan. thihel. hazabanos. hamacon. hamamalyhon. samalyhon. samalerihon. usiologihon. legyn. heleis. hymon. machitilon. (6) Theos. heloty. sarrainazili. samachili. helamon. chihamon. Hel. lamochiamou. lagay. lemechiel. semezihel. laymos. lanoso hazamathon. themohan. thanathon. Theon. natharathon.

XLVIII. Seventh Terminus.[62]

Maguus. maguol. nazihacol. uazihathos. heliam. mathon. saphar. nazachon. gemehihel. iomorihel. sanayhel. sazanyhel. saramel. semyhel. sezimel. (2) lebachon. iarachon. iaratham. basihas. lamnay. rouala. matliathon. rasihos. layna. choro. laymatham. labynegual. scomycros. bazihos. lainna. labunegas. herezemyhel. (3) pheamicros. negemezihol. relmalaguoram. hanamyhos. hanomos. gracosihos. gracomessihos. sothiron. genozepha. chelahel. zopascanelios. zepasconomos. hamarazihos. hamarizihos. (4) zenazihel. geramathihel. gecramathihol. hasaguar. hasagiri. paramyhot. hapasiry. haranamar. Senales. hasaguanamar. sennagel. secastologihon. geuaguolos. hageuolo. thegos. sozor. (5) hamay. seroguomay. sorosamay. iamaramos. remolithos. lammaramos. zenon. serolen. zabay. peripaton. harihat. hananyhos. crascrosihos. graguomoysihos.

---

61 Ars Not. 127f, JV p. 234.
62 Ars Not. 127g, JV p. 235.

yhos. crascrosihos. graguomoysihos. sichiron. genozem. pha. zehahel. (6) sephastaneos. hamaristigos. senazihel. geramacihel. pazamyhol. haphasy. zihazanagar. senasel. secasehogyhon. genaguolos. hegonele. thegos. sorozamay. sozor. hamay. iamaramos. zelihon. iezolen.

XLIX 8ᵘˢ TERMINUS

Remolithos. ypomehiles. hazimelos. samal. hazaramagos. gelomyhel. gezeno. megual. hauacristos. hanaipos. gemotheon. samahot. helihemon. hialamum. salamyhym. haminos. gezelihos. sartharay. sarthamy. (2) gechora. maray. gethoramy. ieguoram. myhamy. Theos. agios. crehanrnos. Yskiros. athanathos. probihos. meguon. hacazamazay. hecohy. uryhel. iebozihel. sarib. rogay. halomora. sarahihel. hechamazihel. sezamagua. iechar.

L

Novem oraciones sunt in principio posite usque ad illam oracionem: "Heliscemaht, hazaram ...," quarum octo sunt preparacio vie ad operandum et preparacio operis ad optinendum, set nona est prima oracio de intrincesitate [*intrinsecitate] operis huius. (2) De octo dico tibi, quod summo mane paululum ante crepusculum matutinum ante incepcionem operis cuiuslibet diei ipse sunt proferende, et non oportet de tota die amplius.

(3) De nona dico, quod semper in principio orandi per oraciones alias ab illis octo predictis et in fine est proferenda.

(4) Octo oraciones sunt in fine posite, que octo termini nuncupantur, et de illis dico, quod valent ad habendum divinum concessum.

(5) Sic primo una die Veneris, postquam eris vere penitens et confessus, ieiunabis pane et aqua. (6) Et summo mane circa principium crepusculi matutini dices decem oraciones, quas invenies infra, scilicet 23, 24, 25, 26, 27, 28, 29, 30, 31, 32, suaviter et intente atque sedule prorumpendo. (7) Deinde facto parvo intervallo postulative cogitando dices illos 8 terminos, intervallum similiter parvum et postulativum in fine cuiuslibet termini faciendo.

sichiron. genozem. pha. zehahel. (6) sephastaneos. hamaristigos. senazihel. geramacihel. pazamyhol. haphasy. zihazanagar. senasel. secasehogyhon. genaguolos. hegonele. thegos. sorozamay. sozor. hamay. iamaramos. zelihon. iezolen.

XLIX. Eighth Terminus.[63]

Remolithos. ypomehiles. hazimelos. samal. hazaramagos. gelomyhel. gezeno. megual. hauacristos. hanaipos. gemotheon. samahot. helihemon. hialamum. salamyhym. haminos. gezelihos. sartharay. sarthamy. (2) gechora. maray. gethoramy. ieguoram. myhamy. Theos. agios. crehanrnos. Yskiros. athanathos. probihos. meguon. hacazamazay. hecohy. uryhel. iebozihel. sarib. rogay. halomora. sarahihel. hechamazihel. sezamagua. iechar.

L.

Nine prayers are placed in the beginning, up to the prayer "**Heliscemaht, hazaram...**," of which eight are preparation of the way to work, and preparation of the work for obtaining, but the ninth is the first prayer that is intrinsic to this work. (2) Concerning the eight I say to you, they should be said early in the morning, a little before morning twilight, before beginning the day's work, and should be said no more the rest of the day.

(3) Concerning the ninth, I tell you, it should always be said before beginning the prayers which follow those eight, and at the end.

(4) The eight prayers are placed at the end, which are called the eight *Termini* (or "Ends"), and regarding them I say, that they are effective for obtaining divine consent.

(5) Thus to begin, one Friday, after sincerely repenting and confessing, you must fast on bread and water. (6) And in the early morning around morning twilight, say the ten prayers which you will discover below, namely, numbers 23, 24, 25, 26, 27, 28, 29, 30, 31, and 32, pleasantly and attentively, while projecting the words purposefully. (7) Then you must pause for a short time, thinking about your request, then say those eight *Termini*, taking a similar pause after each *Terminus* to repeat your request.

---

63 Ars Not. 127h, JV p. 235.

(8) Deinde, eum mane semel dixeris, eodem modo penitus circa terciam semel dices et similiter circa meridiem semel et tune poteris prandere.

(9) In crastino, scilicet in die sabbati, eodem modo penitus facies. In die Dominica similiter, nisi quod non ieiunabis, immo quod vis, vel pisces vel carnes, comedere quibis post meridiem, scilicet finita tercia vice orandi.

(10) Tunc in nocte sequenti in sompnis revelabitur tibi per angelum concessus vel repulsa. Si concessus, facies ut docebitur in hoc libro. (11) Si repulsa, spectabis aliud tempus, in quo iterum queres concessum, et tunc te melius preparato apud Deum, unde veniet concessus.

(12) Set nota, quod illa oracio: "Iesu, Dei filius ..." cum illa: "Eleminator...," que est pars eiusdem oracionis, nisi quod ibi debet fieri minimum intervallum postulativum, debet dici ter submisse post quamlibet vicem orandi horis predictis. (13) Si autem repulsam habueris, fac ut dictum est die Veneris, sabbati et Dominico, nisi quod in die Dominico loco ieiunii debes dare tres elemosinas tribus pauperibus misericorditer et devote.

(14) Deinde prima luna, scilicet in die Lune sequenti, fac ut prius penitus et eodem modo similiter luna 2^a et luna 3^a et luna 4^a et sic usque ad finem. (15) Et sic forte Deus miserebitur tui. Tamen in oracionibus Latinis tunc oporteret peticionem mutare, scilicet peticionem concessus in peticionem miseracionis.

(16) Et nota, quod qui tales oraciones vult dicere debet esse castus et mundus et devote proferre, et qui aliter fecerit procul dubio punicionem manifestam videbit. (17) In illis enim oracionibus Grecis, Hebraicis et Caldaicis sunt sacratissima nomina Dei et angelorum, que non nisi ex misericordia ab homine proferri permitterentur.

(18) Et quando tibi accidit repulsa, non debes desperare set confiteri et renes magis perscrutari et elemosinas multas lete largiri et missas diversas facere celebrari et oraciones diversas genibus flexis ad Dominum alloqui sive fari et tempestivis et protervis fletibus et oracionibus Dominum hortari et amplecti. Hec solent facere sapientes, ut veniant ad effectum.

(8) Then, having said this once in the morning, you must repeat the same around Terce, and again around noon, whereupon you can eat your first meal.

(9) On the following day, namely, the Sabbath,[64] you must do in the exact same manner. Do the same again on Sunday, except it is not necessary to fast, and in fact you can eat fish or meat as you prefer, but after noon, namely after you have finished praying for the third time.

(10) Then on the following night as you sleep, it will be revealed to you by an angel, whether your request will be permitted or rejected. If permitted, you will do as will be taught in this book, (11) but if rejected, consider another time in which to seek permission, and then prepare yourself better before God, from whom permission will come.

(12) But note, that the prayer, "Jesus, son of God…" (XXVI) with this one: **"Eleminator,"** (XXVII) which is part of the same prayer, should be said three times softly, except there should be a short petition interval, after each time of praying.—(13) If however your petition is rejected, do as described for Friday, Saturday, and Sunday, with the exception that on Sunday, instead of fasting you must give three alms to three poor persons, with compassion and devotion.

(14) Then, in the first moon, namely the following Monday, do as you did earlier, and so too for the second, third, and fourth Monday, and thus all the way to the end. (15) And thus perhaps God will be merciful to you. But in the Latin[65] prayers you should alter the petition, namely you should ask for mercy, not for granting your desire.

(16) And note that whoever wishes to say those prayers must be chaste and clean, and offer them with devotion, and anyone who does otherwise will undoubtedly see punishment. (17) In fact, those Greek, Hebrew, and Chaldean prayers include the most holy names of God and the angels, which must not be spoken by anyone except through his mercy.

(18) And when your request has been rejected, you must not despair, but confess and search your inner feelings more, and cheerfully give many alms, and have diverse Masses celebrated, and different prayers on bent knees addressed to the Lord, or speak suitable and passionate prayers with tears, exhorting and embracing the Lord. These are the things the wise men are accustomed to doing, in order to achieve success.

---

64 Here obviously meaning Saturday.
65 As opposed to those consisting of mystical words and names.

LI Prima mundacio

Si Adonay largiente concessum habueris et opereris secundum modum subscriptum, luna 4ª, 8ª, 12ª, 16ª, 20ª, 24ª, 28ª, 32ª in die circa matutinum semel, circa terciam semel, circa nonam semel, circa vesperas semel dices has oraciones prescriptas, (2) scilicet "Assaylemah t ..." et "Hazailemaht ...," que est secunda pars eius, et ["Lemaht ..." et] "Lameht lemaht ..." et "Deus summe, Deus ..." et "Te queso, Domine ...," <et> que est prologus eius, scilicet "Deus summe, Deus ...," nisi quod ille tres oraciones prime de intraneitate artis: (3) "Alpha et Ω ..." et "Heliscemaht ..." et "Theos megale Patir ..." cum suo prologo "Lux mundi ...," que post eam debet dici, prius dicantur, et post ille: "Hassailemaht ..." [et "Hazailemaht ..."] dicantur facto tamen intervallo postulativo.

(4) Illa autem sanctissima oracio: "Lameht ragua ..." cum sua particula "Semeht segaht [*segheahlt] ..." et cum suo prologo debet dici luna prima quater, scilicet summo mane semel, circa terciam semel, circa meridiem ter, circa nonam ter.

(5) Luna 3ª proferatur ter: Circa mane semel, circa meridiem semel, circa nonam semel.

Luna 6ª proferatur bis in mane, bis in meridie, bis in nona.

Luna 9ª proferatur ter in mane, ter in meridie, ter in nona.

(6) In 12ª luna proferatur ter in mane, ter in meridie, ter in nona, ter in vesperis.

Luna 15ª proferatur [in] mane ter, in tercia ter, in meridie ter, in nona ter, in vesperis ter.

In 18ª luna 21 et 23, 26 et 29 et 30 legantur similiter sicut in 15ª.

LI. The first purification.

If Adonay generously grants that you might have permission, then proceed according to the method described below. On the 4th, 8th, 12th, 16th, 20th, 24th, 28th, and 32nd of the moon, the following prayers should be said once around Matins, once around Terce, once around None, and once around Vesper, (2) namely "Assaylemaht..." (XX) and "Hazailemaht ...," (XXI) which is the second part of it, and "[Lemaht ..." (XXII), and] "Lameht lemaht ..." (XXIII), and "God the highest, God ..." (XXIV), and "I beseech you, O my Lord ..." (XXV), <and> which is its prologue, namely, "God the highest, God ...," except that those three first prayers from the essence of the art: (3) "Alpha and Omega ..." (XV) and "Heliscemaht ..." (XVI) and "Theos megale Patir ..." (XVII) with its prologue "the light of the world ...", (XVIII) which must be said *after* that which should be said first, and after that, say "Hassailemaht ..." (XX) [and "Hazailemaht...."] (XXI) yet they should be said with a petition interval.

(4) But that most holy prayer: "Lameht ragua..." with its part "Semeht segaht [*segheahlt] ..." and with its prologue should be said on the *Luna Prima*[66] four times, namely once very early in the morning, once around Terce, three times around noon, three times around None.

(5) On the third day of the moon it should be recited three times: Once in the morning, once around noon, and once around None.

On the sixth day of the moon it should be recited twice in the morning, twice at noon, and twice at None.

On the ninth day of the moon it should be recited three times in the morning, three times at noon, and three times at None.

(6) On the twelfth day of the moon it should be recited three times in the morning, three times at noon, and three times at Vespers.

On the fifteenth day of the moon it should be recited three times in the morning, three times at Terce, three times at noon, three times at None, and three times at Vespers.

On the eighteenth day of the moon, 21, 23, 26, 29, and 30 are to be read similarly as on the fifteenth.[67]

---

66 *Luna Prima*: The first day of the lunar calendar, i.e. the new moon.
67 Hedegård (p. 33) interprets this to mean that prayers 21, 23, etc. as found later in the book, are to be recited on the 18th day of the moon. The other interpretation is that the same prayers are to be recited on the 18th, 21st, etc. day of the moon. This is how MS R

(7) Set nota, quod ista oracio in castitate et in mundicia et fide prolata valet similiter ad pericula ignis, bestiarum vel demonum, et tunc nichil de horis vel lunacionibus respicere oportet.

(8) Illa autem oracio sanctissima: "Hazaram hihel ..." cum suis particulis 4, que sunt "Hihelma helma" et cetera, "Agloros theomythos" et cetera, "Megal agal" et cetera, "Hamicchiahel" et cetera, cum suis similiter prologis, (9) scilicet "Confirma, consolida" et cetera, "Deus omnium, qui es" et cetera, "Veritas, lux" et cetera, "Ego in conspectu tuo" et cetera, seriatim, ut prius iacent, debent prorumpi suaviter et intente post illam predictam: (10) "Lameht ragua ..." eisdem diebus et horis nisi in uno casu, scilicet quando pro magno negocio petitur, puta loqui cum spiritibus vel videre Deum. Tunc ipsa non debet dici nisi semel, scilicet circa mane. (11) Set quando petitur sciencia vel tutela a malis vel cognicio celorum et angelorum et sigillorum et cetera, tunc sicut dictum est de "Lameht ragua ..." est faciendum. (12) Et hec oracio eandem efficaciam cum "Lameht ragua ..." habet et aliquid plus in speciali vel, quod melius est, in casu, (13) quo petitur fieri a spiritibus celestibus aliquid arduum et magnum eis approbatum, scilicet descendere et homini loqui vel cogere spiritus aereos et terreos ad veniendum et obediendum.

(14) Illa autem oracio: "Semoht gechel..." et illa: "Omnipotens, sempiteme Deus ..." et illa: "Semoht lamen ..." proferantur cum illa: "Iesu, Dei filius ..." in illis diebus, (15) in quibus alie predicte proferri non debent, sicut dictum est supra, quod non debent proferri luna 2a nec 5a nec 7a nec 14a, et sic de aliis, ut prius patet.

(16) Et nota, quod si coram iudice habet magnam causam, que non possit ad finem produci, et ieiunet precedenti die qua ibit ad curiam propositum causam suam pane et aqua, postea proferat basse bis illas tres oraciones: "Semoht..." et "Omnipotens ..." et "Semoht ...;" (17) tanta enim

(7) But note, that this same prayer offered in chastity and cleanness and faith has power over dangers from fire, wild beasts, or daemons, and then no specific time of day or month need be observed.

(8) But that most holy prayer: "Hazaram hihel …" (XXXI) with its four parts, which are "Hihelma helma" etc. (XXXII), "Agloros theomythos" etc. (XXXIV), "Megal agal" etc. (XXXV) "Hamicchiahel" etc. (XXXVII), similarly with its prologues, (9) namely, "Strengthen, solidify" etc. (XXXIII), 'O God of all, you who are' etc. (XXXIVb), "the Truth, the Light" etc. (XXXVI), "I speak these things in your presence" etc. (XXXVIII), as set down in order earlier. They must be projected pleasantly and attentively after that one preceding: (10) "Lameht ragua …" (XXVIII) the same days and with the hours, except in the one case, namely when your petition is for some great undertaking, for example to speak with the spirits or to see God. Then it must be said only once, namely around morning. (11) But when your petition is for knowledge, or protection from evil, or learning about the heavens and the angels, and the seals, etc., then you must do as said concerning "Lameht ragua …" (XXVIII). (12) And this prayer has the same effectiveness as "Lameht ragua," and is even somewhat more specific, which is better in the case (13) that you desire the celestial spirits to approve some great or difficult task, such as them descending and speaking to people, or to compel the spirits of the air and the earth into coming and obeying.

(14) Therefore this prayer must be offered: "Semoht gechel …" (XXXIX), and this: "Omnipotent, eternal God …" (XL), and this: "Semoht lamen …" (XLI), with this one: "Jesus, the Son of God …" (XXVI) on those days, (15) in which the others preceding must not be offered, as explained above, because they must not be offered on the second day of the moon, nor the fifth, seventh, nor the fourteenth, and so for the others as appears earlier.

(16) And note, that if someone has a major case before a judge, the end of which cannot be determined, he should fast on bread and water the day before he is to plead his case, and afterwards he should recite quietly those three prayers, two times: "Semoht …" (XXXIX) and "Almighty …" (XL) and

---

interpreted it. I am inclined to go with the latter interpretation, for three reasons. First, the first interpretation would mean that a good portion of the month would have no recitations. Second, the fact that it only goes up to 30 is another clue that days of the moon are intended. Finally, the fact that those prayers hadn't yet been given is another clue.

sapiencia et eloquencia dabitur sibi in proponendo causam suam, quod breviter optinebit, nisi quod oportet <te> esse bene mundum et castum. (18) Similiter hanc oracionem valet dicere, quando aliquis spiritus vocatus venit, cum illa: "Lameht ragua ..." pro evitando periculum et acquirendo sapienciam et eloquenciam affandi audacter spiritu advocato.

LII

Cum igitur nichil aliud fecerit vel aliquod peccatum cogitaverit, roget continue Deum aliis horis a primis 6ª, 10ª, 12ª oracione et in mane vadat ad missam et eundo dicat 16, (2) in templo dicat 22, item 14, 24,[5] 21, 32, 33, 34, 29, 30 et ita faciat continue per 20 dies cavens sibi diligenter, ne incidat in peccatum. (3) Si tamen casualiter in peccatum inciderit, immediate peniteat et confiteatur; ieiunet, si possit, continue. (4) Si non, de duobus unum relaxet. Set per 7 dies ordine retrogrado procedendo ab omni morticinio ieiunet.

(5) Tunc habeat sacerdotem cautum et fidelem, qui sibi matutinam, primam et terciam et missam de Spiritu sancto cantet dicens in introitu 13, post offertorium 9. (6) Tunc accipiat thus et suffumiget, ut pertinet ad altare, dicens primam. Et quia beati patres in illis gloriosis sanctis ibidem nominatis sperabant, ideo sic fecerunt. (7) Operans autem, si in aliquibus aliis sanctis maiorem devocionem habeat, mutet nomen pro nomine, quia fides operatur ut predixi. (8) 2ª oracio immediate dicatur et post "Te igitur ..." 3, 4, 5, 7, 8, et sic in sacrando corpus Christi petat pro

---

5 SSM reads "23."

"Semoht ..." (XLI). (17) For such great wisdom and eloquence will be given to him for pleading his cause, that it will be obtained quickly, except you must be very clean and abstinent. (18) Similarly it is powerful to say this prayer when an invoked spirit has come, with this one: "Lameht ragua ..." (XXVIII) in order to avoid danger and acquire wisdom and eloquence in speaking boldly with the spirit that is called.

LII.

Now, provided that he has not done anything else, nor intended to sin, he should continuously ask God, in all other hours except Prime, with the sixth, tenth, and twelfth prayers,[68] and in the morning he should go to mass and while going he should say sixteen; (2) in the church he should say 22, likewise, 14, 24,[69] 21, 32, 33, 34, 29, 30, and he should do thus continuously for twenty days, taking careful precautions against falling into sin. (3) If however he accidentally sins, he must immediately repent and confess; if he can let him fast continuously, (4) but if he is unable to, he may relax that to fasting every other day. But for seven days consecutive going back prior, he must fast and abstain from (eating) all dead matter.[70]

(5) Then he should have a cautious and faithful priest, who should sing for him Matins, Prime, Terce, and a Mass of the Holy Spirit. During the *introit* he should say 13,[71] and after the offertory he should say 9.[72] (6) Then he should take incense and fumigate as he approaches the altar, saying the first.[73] And note that those famous saints were named therein because the blessed fathers had faith in them, (7) But if the operator has greater devotion to any other saints, he may replace the names therein with those of the other saints, because faith works, as I have said before.[74] (8) The second prayer should be said immediately and after "*te igitur*" 3, 4, 5, 7, 8, and thus in consecrating the

---

68 LVIII, LXV, and LXVII.
69 SSM reads "23."
70 Compare SSM L.4.f.15: *nil mortuum comedas, nec tangas* ("you should consume nothing dead, nor touch any"). The Royal ms misinterprets this as abstaining from all deadly sin.
71 LXVIII.
72 LXIV.
73 LIII.
74 This passage, starting with "and note" seems to be an example of an interpolation by the "London" redactor, since it isn't found in SSM. See Veenstra 2012 p. 156–7.

operante sacerdos, ut effectum peticionum suarum per divinam graciam assequatur. (9) Et ita intellige de omnibus oracionibus, que pertinent ad sacerdotem et ad operacionem, quia sunt generales ad omnes peticiones habendas. (10) Set nichil aliis addas. Item post communionem dicat sacerdos 26, post missam vero recipiat operans eucaristiam dicendo 19, 20. (11) Et caveat, ne corpus Christi accipiat pro effectu malo, quia non esset salus immo mors, unde quidam intitulaverunt librum istum sic: "Incipit mors anime." (12) Et hoc est verum male operantibus et propter effectum malum, et non propter scienciam. Nam ait Dominus: "Petite, et dabitur vobis. Querite et invenietis." (13) Et alibi dicit Dominus: "Ubi duo vel tres congregati fuerint in nomine meo, ibi sum in medio" et "De omni re, quam pecierint in nomine meo, fiet illis a patre meo."

LIII

Oraciones prenominate et post nominande numero sunt hec, scilicet:

Prima oracio

Agla, lux, veritas, vita, via, iudex misericors, misericordia, fortitudo, paciencia, conserva et iuva me in hac sancta visione et miserere mei (2) propter misericordiam tuam et servicium huius sancti suffumigii et sancti sacrificii Domini nostri Iesu Christi et propter meritum gloriose semper virginis Marie, matris Domini nostri Iesu Christi, (3) et meritum apostolo-

body of Christ, the priest should petition on behalf of the operator, that he may obtain success in his petition through divine grace. (9) And so too you should understand regarding all the prayers, which pertains to the priest and for the operation, because in general they are required for all petitions. (10) But nothing else should be added. Likewise after the mass the priest should say 26, and after Mass in truth he should receive the Eucharist, saying 19 and 20. (11) And he must beware, not to receive the body of Christ for any evil purpose, because then it would be ineffective, and might even be deadly, from which some have entitled that book "The death of the soul."[75] (12) And this is truly bad for those who would operate for an evil purpose, and not on behalf of knowledge. For the Lord has said: "Ask and you will receive. Seek and you will find."[76] (13) And elsewhere the Lord says: "Where two or three are gathered together in my name, there I am in the midst of them"[77] and "anything which they ask for in my name, it will be done for them by my father."[78]

LIII.

The prayers previously named, and named afterwards, with their number, are these:[79]

First Prayer.[80]

Agla, the light, the truth, the life, the way, merciful, mercy, the strength, patience, preserve and help me in this sacred vision, and pity me (2) because of your compassion, and the service of this holy suffumigation, and the holy sacrifice of our Lord Jesus Christ, and because of the merit of the glorious and eternal virgin Mary, mother of our Lord Jesus Christ, (3) and the merits

---

75 Compare Bern, Statbibliothek, Handshriften 260, f 227 vb, listed by Klaassen and by Thorndike under necromancy in list of incip. Cp Boudet *Entre* p. 94.
76 Matt. 7:7.
77 Matt. 18:20.
78 Matt. 18:19. This concludes the "First Purification;" the instructions for the second are found in chapter XCVIII. The intervening chapters, the prayers mentioned in the text, seem to be inserted here for convenience. They don't break the narrative in SSM, which is evidence the London Honorius prototype was adapted from an earlier text.
79 These following prayers each begin with one of the 100 names of God, in the same order as enumerated in chapters C and CI. See chapter XCVII. Compare Gollancz 1914 pp. V ff.
80 Ars. Not. 53, JV p. 51.

rum Petri et Pauli, Andree, Iacobi, Iohanis, Thome, Iacobi, Philippi, Bartholomei, Mathei, Symonis et Thadei, Lini, Cleti, Clementis, Sixti, Cornelii, Cipriani, (4) Laurencii, Grisogoni, Iohanis et Pauli, Cosme et Damiani et omnium sanctorum tuorum, quorum meritis et precibus concedas hanc sanctam tuam visionem per eundem Dominum nostrum.

LIV 2ᴬ ORACIO

Monhon, Domine, sancte Pater, omnipotens, sempiterne Deus, in cuius conspectu omnia sunt visibilium et invisibilium fundamenta creaturarum omnium, cuius oculi imperfectum meum viderunt, cuius caritatis dulcedine pleni sunt celi et terra, (2) cuius aures omnia audiunt, qui omnia vidisti, antequam fierent, in cuius libro omnes formati sunt dies et homines inscripti, respice hodie super famulum tuum tibi tota mente et toto corde subiectum. (3) Per Spiritum sanctum tuum confirma me, ut te videam. Benedic hodie et protege omnes actus meos hodiernos et hanc inspeccionem et constancia tue visitacionis me illustra. Amen.

LV 3ᴬ ORACIO

Tetragramathon, respice, Domine, Deus, clemens Pater, omnium eterne dispositor <omnium> virtutum. Operaciones meas hodie considera, tu, qui es actuum hominum et angelorum inspector atque discretor. (2) Ideo te rogo, ut admirabilis gracia promissionis tue in me dignetur subitam adimplere virtutem huius sancte visionis, et in me tantam efficaciam nomini sancto tuo et magno infundas, tu, qui laudem tuam in ore te diligencium imponis et infundis. Amen.

LVI 4ᴬ ORACIO

Hely Deus, creator, Adonay, omnium [visibilium et] invisibilium creaturarum Pater piissime, qui incircumscripto lumine habitas eternaliter <et> ante principium mundi omnia ineffabiliter disponens atque gubernans, (2) eternitatem tuam atque incomprehensibilem pietatem verbis supplican-

of the apostles Peter and Paul, Andrew, Jacob, John, Thomas, Jacob, Philip, Bartholomew, Matthew, Simon, Thaddeus, Linus, Cletus, Clement, Sixtus, of Cornelius, Cyprian, (4) Laurence, Grisogone, John and Paul, Cosme and Damian, and all your saints, through whose merits and prayers may you grant this holy vision of yourself, through the same our Lord.

LIV. Prayer 2.[81]

Monhon, O Lord, O holy Father, all-powerful, eternal God, in whose sight are the foundations of all creatures visible and invisible, whose eyes have seen my imperfections, whose sweet charity fills the heavens and the earth, (2) whose ears hear all things, who sees all things before they are made, in whose book all days are formed, and all men inscribed, look upon your servant this day, whose whole mind and heart are exposed to you. (3) Through your Holy Spirit strengthen me, in order that I may see you. Bless me today and in this inspection protect all my actions, and illuminate me with the constancy of your visitation. Amen.

LV. Prayer 3.[82]

Tetragrammaton, Look upon me, O Lord, God, merciful Father, eternal disposer of all virtues. Examine my works today, you who are the inspector and judge of all acts of men and of angels. (2) Therefore I ask you that the wonderful grace of your promise may be deemed worthy to fulfill the sudden power of this holy vision, and pour into me such great effectiveness to your holy and great name you, who infuse and pour your praise into the mouth of those who love you. Amen.

LVI. Prayer 4.[83]

Hely Deus, the creator, Adonay, of all [visible and] invisible creations, O most holy Father, who dwells forever in infinite light <and> before the beginning of the world, ineffably disposing and governing all things, (2) I approach your infiniteness and incomprehensible piety with words of supplication, so

---

81 Ars. Not. 128, JV p. 87.
82 Ars. Not. 129, JV p. 87.
83 Ars. Not. 130, JV p. 87.

tibus aggredior, ut huius sacramentalis atque mistici operis in me et per tui et sanctorum angelorum potenciam efficacia, tui visio et consideracio, clarescat (3) atque per eorundem sanctorum angelorum nomina in memoria et mente habundet, atque sancta opera tua facialis tue sancte visionis in me cum stabilitate clarescant. Amen.

LVII 5ᴬ ORACIO

Hocleiste, sancte Deus, Pater pie et indissolubilis argumentacio cordis, qui celum et terram, mare et abissos et omnia, que in eis sunt, stabiliri voluisti, (2) in cuius conspectu omnis racio, sermo, opus et sanctitas subsistit, per hec preciosa sacramenta angelorum tuorum da michi ea, que desidero et credo, visionis huius absque malignitatis intencione gloriam et graciam. Amen.

LVIII 6ᴬ ORACIO

Hamphynethon, Heloy, clementissime creator et inspirator et reformator omnium animarum viciatarum et omnium bonarum voluntatum approbator et ordinator, (2) deprecacionem gloriosus intende et mentem meam respice benignus, ut quod ex humilitate deprecor, sicut a te promissum est, michi de tue magnificencie largitate concedas. Amen.

LIX 7ᴬ ORACIO

Lamyhara, omnipotens, misericors Pater, omnium creaturarum ordinator, [iuste] iudex, eterne rex regum et Domine dominancium, qui tuis sanctis sapienciam, sanctitatem et gloriam conferre dignatus es, (2) concede michi, ut possim te videre mirabiliter, qui omnia diiudicas et discernis. (3) Illumina hodie cor meum fulgore claritatis et mundicie atque sanctificencie, ut cognoscam et intelligam et facialiter videam te et tuam gloriam. Et quod huius gloriam videre merear, exopto. Amen.

that the power and effectiveness of this sacramental and mystical work may manifest in me through you and your holy angels, the vision and contemplation of you may be illuminated with effectiveness (3) and, by the names of the same holy angels, may it abound in my memory and mind, and your holy works of the vision of your presence may be illuminated in me in an enduring way. Amen.

LVII. Prayer 5.[84]

Hocleiste, O holy God, blessed Father and imperishable evidence of the heart, who has determined to establish Heaven and Earth, the sea, and the abysses and everything that is in them, (2) in whose sight subsists the plans, words, deeds, and piety of all, by these precious sacraments of your angels grant unto me those things which I desire and I believe, the glory and grace of this vision, without any ill intent. Amen.

LVIII. Prayer 6.[85]

Hamphynethon, Heloy, most merciful creator, inspirer and reformer of all corrupted souls and approver and arranger of all good wills, (2) look mercifully in your glory on my earnest prayer and kindly consider my intent, that what I ask for with humility, you might grant to me from the abundance of your greatness, as you have promised. Amen.

LIX. Prayer 7.[86]

Lamyhara, almighty, merciful Father, the ordainer of the all creatures, [just] judge, eternal king of kings and Lord of Lords, who has deigned to grant to your saints wisdom, sanctity, and glory, (2) grant to me that I may miraculously be able to behold you, who sees and decides all things. (3) Illuminate my heart this day with the brightness of your splendor and purity and sanctity, that I may be able to comprehend and understand and see your face and your glory. And that I may be worthy to see this glory, I long for.[87] Amen.

---

84 Ars. Not. 135, JV p. 90.
85 Ars. Not. 137, JV p. 91.
86 Ars. Not. 138, JV p. 92.
87 Note the adaptation of the *Ars Notoria* material is a bit awkward at times.

LX 8ᴬ Oracio

Hanazay. zarahoron. hubisenaar. ghu. hirbaionay. gynbar. zanailc. selchora. zelmora. hiramay. iethohal. ylaramel. hamatha. mathois. iaboha. (2) gethos. cozomerag. zosomeraht. hamy. phodel. denos. gerot. hagalos. meliha. tagahel. sechamy. salihelethon. monocogristes. lememon. hachagnon. hamyhon.

LXI Oracio de precedenti Latina

Ianemyer, unus, magnus, mirabilis, eterne Deus, eterni consilii angelus, dispositor omnium virtutum et compositor atque ordinator, (2) adorna hodie intelligenciam meam et multiplica in me racionem penitendi et clarificandi et cognicionem ac claritatem, quam in proferendis nominibus celestium angelorum tuis creaturis contulisti, (3) et eandem scienciam et puritatem secundum promissionem tuam michi concede et da michi huius visionis tue efficaciam et discrecionem. Amen.

LXII Oracio

Hadyon, usyon, omnium potestatum atque regnorum et iudiciorum eterna conspiracione conspicuus, omnium administrans +thema+[6] glorie et tue visionis, (2) in cuius regimine nullum impedimentum dabis, instaura, queso, habitam innocenciam et repetitam et adhuc maiorem, cor meum, voluntatem meam, linguam meam, opus meum (3) ad mei animam mundificandam, absolvendam et tui faciem facialiter videndam et ad habendum que in hac arte necessaria auctoritas divina commendat, ut in me perfecte compleantur. Amen.

LXIII Oracio Hebraica

{H}ely. azelethias. uelozeosmohan. zama. saruelo. hatehus. saguaht. Adonay. zoma. lenozothos. lithon. iezemothon. sadahot. et tu, Deus,

---

6 The ++ is used by GH to indicate *turbata*, i.e. disturbed/corrupted. *Ars Notoria* reads *zeuma*. i.e. *zeugma* ("bond, yoking"). C: zema; ed in Agrippa reads *schemata* i.e. "outline, shapes".

LX. Prayer 8.[88]

Hanazay. zarahoron. hubisenaar. ghu. hirbaionay. gynbar. zanailc. selchora. zelmora. hiramay. iethohal. ylaramel. hamatha. mathois. iaboha. (2) gethos. cozomerag. zosomeraht. hamy. phodel. denos. gerot. hagalos. meliha. tagahel. sechamy. salihelethon. monocogristes. lememon. hachagnon. hamyhon.

LXI. The meaning of the preceding Prayer.[89]

Ianemyer, One, great, wonderful, and eternal God, angel of eternal council, disposer of all virtues and composer and ordainer, (2) adorn my intelligence this day, and multiply in me a penitent and clarifying reasoning, and understanding and clarity which you have conferred on creatures for pronouncing the names of your heavenly angels, (3) and grant to me the same knowledge and purity according to your promise, and give me the effectiveness and discernment of this vision of you. Amen.

LXII. Prayer.[90]

Hadyon,[91] **usyon**, illustrious with eternal harmony of all powers, rulers, and courts, administering +the theme+ of all glory, and of the vision of yourself, (2) in the control of which you make no obstacles; renew, I beg you the well-kept and repeated innocence, and even more so, my heart, my will, my tongue, my work (3) for the purification and absolution of my soul, and for seeing you in person, and for having those things which divine authority commends are necessary for this art, in order that they are fulfilled in me fully. Amen.

LXIII. Hebrew Prayer.[92]

{H}ely. azelethias. uelozeosmohan. zama. saruelo. hatehus. saguaht. Adonay. zoma. lenozothos. lithon. iezemothon. Sadahot, and you, O God, be favor-

---

88 Ars. Not. Glose de la version B, § 140, V p. 197.
89 Ars. Not. 139, JV p. 92.
90 Ars. Not. 141, JV pp. 92–3.
91 This name is not found in Chapters C and CI, which give the next name as "Sadyon." but that is used in LXIV below.
92 Ars. Not. 141 glose de la version B, var. 7, JV pp. 197–198.

propicius in me promissiones confirma, sicut confirmasti per eosdem sermones regi Salomoni et preter eosdem Iohanni et Paulo. (2) Emitte michi, Domine, virtutem de celis, que cor meum et mentem meam illuminet et confirmet, et conforta, Deus, intellectum meum et animam meam. (3) Innova me et lava me aquis, que super celos sunt, et effunde de Spiritu tuo super carnem meam et in visceribus meis ad facienda et componenda iudicia tua humilitate et caritate, qua celum et terram fecisti et hominem ad ymaginem et similitudinem tua m creasti et formasti. (4) Infunde claritatis tue lumen intellectui meo, ut fundatus et radicatus in misericordia tua diligam nomen tuum, cognoscam et videam et adorem te et optineam et intelligam omnes vias huius artis habendi visionem tuam, (5) ob quam hec data a Deo et insignita et emissa per manus sanctorum angelorum sunt figurarum et sanctitatum misteria, que omnia in corde meo et intellectu mentis mee habeam et cognoscam, et huius artis vere et efficaciter effectum habeam nominis sancti tui et gloriosi prevalente consilio. Amen.

LXIV 9ᴬ ORACIO

Sadyon, scio enim, quia delector in factura tua magna, mirabili et ineffabili, [et] dabis michi visionem, quam per hoc opus habentibus pollicitus es secundum magnam et incomprehensibilem veritatem tuam, (2) Theon. hatagamagon. haramalon. zamoyma. thamasal. ieconomaril. harionathor. iecomagol. gelamagos. remelihot. remanathar. hariomagalathar. hananehos. uelouianathar. haiozoroy. iebasaly. (3) Per hec sacratissima Dei et gloriosissima et profunda misteria et preciosissimam mundiciam virtutem et visionis tue graciam auge in me et comple quod incepisti et reforma quod ostendisti in me. (4) zemabar. henoranaht. grenetail. samzatham. iecornazay. fundamentum altissime omnium bonitatum et scienciarum atque virtutum, (5) tribue famulo tuo tibi displicencia vitare contagia et lavare, et tua veritate pura et intencione sancta possim saciari, (6) ut tuam

ably inclined to confirm in me the promises, as you confirmed them by the same words to King Solomon, and moreover by the same to John and Paul. (2) Send out to me, O Lord, the power from Heaven, which will illuminate and strengthen my heart and my mind, and strengthen, O God, my understanding and my soul. (3) Renew me and wash me with the waters which are above the heavens, and pour out from your spirit over my flesh and into my vital organs, for accomplishing and arranging your judgments with humility and affection, with which you have made Heaven and Earth, and created people after your own image and likeness. (4) Pour the light of your brightness into my understanding, that being grounded and rooted in your mercy I may love your name, recognize and see and honor you, and that I may obtain and understand all the ways of this art of having the vision of you, (5) for the sake of which these are given by God and made known, and are sent out from the hands of the holy angels the mysteries of the figures[93] and holiness, all which may I receive and in my heart the understanding of my mind, and comprehend, and may I attain the true and efficacious accomplishment of this art, with the prevailing counsel of your sacred and glorious name. Amen.

LXIV. Prayer 9.

Sadyon,[94] I know indeed, that I delight in your great handiwork, wonderful and indescribable, [and] the vision that you will give to me, which you have promised those doing this work, according to your great and incomprehensible truth, (2) Theon. hatagamagon. haramalon. zamoyma. thamasal. ieconomaril. harionathor. iecomagol. gelamagos. remelihot. remanathar. hariomagalathar. hananehos. uelouianathar. haiozoroy. iebasaly. (3) Through these most sacred and most glorious and profound mysteries of God and by the most precious purity, power, and grace of your vision, increase in me and fulfill that which you have begun, and restore that which you have revealed in me. (4) zemabar. henoranaht. grenetail. samzatham. iecornazay The highest foundation of all goodnesses, knowledge, and virtues, (5) enable your servant to avoid contagions displeasing to yourself, and to be washed clean, and filled with your pure truth and holy striving, (6) just as your promise, longing with all my heart and possessing virtue and purity in all things, as well as the

---

93 In *Ars Notoria* this refers no doubt to the *notae* or mystical drawings which are the centerpiece of that art.
94 Seems to repeat names 9 and 10. See Ars. Not. Glose de la version B, Var. 8, JV p. 198.

promissionem toto corde desiderans et possidens in omnibus tam virtutibus quam puritatibus et viciorum absolucionibus precipue per hec sancta misteria videar et cognoscar adipisci et bene in ista arte perficiar penitus,[7] laudabilis ac pro sancta visione mundus.

LXV 10ᴬ ORACIO

Hely, reverende, potens et dominans superioribus angelis et archangelis omnibusque celestibus creaturis [et] tam infernalibus quam terrestribus, de cuius magnificencia plenitudinis venit, (2) ut tibi a nobis digne famuletur, cuius a mundi 4 partibus regnat potestas, qui [ex carne], ossibus, anima et spiritu hominem ad ymaginem et similitudinem tuam formasti, (3) da michi huius artis sciencium et visionis effectum coroborans me in ipsius facultate visionis sancte et sciencie. Amen.

LXVI XIᴬ ORACIO

Horlon, Deus, qui omnia numero, pondere et mensura fecisti, de cuius munere omne capud hominis desiderans elevabitur, in cuius ordine omnium momentorum sive dierum patens est et aperta dimencio, (2) qui eciam solus stellarum nomina numeras et nominas, menti mee constantem tribue visionis tue efficaciam, ut in huius artis cognicione et operacione te diligam et videam et tue pietatis munus agnoscam facialis visionis. Amen.

LXVII 12ᴬ ORACIO

Porrenthimon, mediator omnium operacionum et creaturarum, a quo omnia exeunt naturaliter bona et omnium [virtutum] dona, a quo omne, quod est solidum et perfectum, (2) cuius omnis sermo recens est et de regalibus sedibus venit gracia in corda nostra, dum medium tenerent omnia silencium media, (3) racione et mente me tua caritate

---

7 GH reads *peritus* (expert), but I think this is a simple typo. Sl. 3854 123r, R 50r, and Ars. Not: all read *penitus*.

forgiveness of faults, especially for seeing these sacred mysteries, and gaining comprehension, and that I may be made thoroughly complete in this art of yours, praiseworthy, and pure for the sacred vision.

LXV. Prayer 10.[95]

Hely, O One most worthy to be revered, mighty, master of angels and archangels, and all celestial creatures, both infernal and earthly, whose vast abundance enables us (2) to serve you worthily, whose power rules from the four parts of the world, who made mankind after your own image and likeness, out of [flesh,] bones, soul, and spirit, (3) grant to me the knowledge of this art, and the effect of the vision, strengthening me its ability of the sacred vision and knowledge. Amen.

LXVI. Prayer 11.[96]

Horlon, God, who ordered all things in number, weight, and measure,[97] from whose gift the longing head of every person will be lifted up, who has arranged all moments or days are well known, and dimensions measured, (2) you who alone number the stars and name them,[98] grant to my mind the constant effectiveness of the vision of yourself, in order that in learning and practice of this art I may see and love you, and acknowledge the gift of your piety of the vision of your face. Amen.

LXVII. Prayer 12.[99]

Porrenthimon, O mediator of all operations and creatures, from whom naturally emerges all good things and the gifts of all [virtues], which is unbroken and perfect, (2) whose every word is fresh, and comes from the royal throne, and by grace comes into our hearts, while all things were in quiet silence,[100] (3) by reason of your love and my mind, that my understanding may be sufficient

---

95 Compare *Ars Notoria*, 142 [version A]— glose, JV p. 199.
96 This prayer is the only one that is never mentioned in the descriptions of the rituals. See GH, p. 49. Compare Ars. Not. 144 [version A]—glose, JV p. 199.
97 Wis. 11:21.
98 Ps. 146:4. KJV 147:4.
99 Ars. Not. 145, JV p. 94.
100 Compare Wis. 18:14-15.

[in] intellectum bonum construe ad perficiendum hec tanta tam[que] excellentissima misteria,[8] huius artis, sancte tue visionis et istorum sacramentorum perfectum consequar effectum. Amen.

LXVIII 13ᴬ ORACIO

[Ihelur], iudex omnipotens, Pater, qui notum nobis fecisti salutare tuum et in conspectu gencium revelasti iusticiam tuam, revela oculos meos et cor meum illustra salutari iusticia tua, ut mirabilia de tuis tam gloriosissimis videam [sacramentis], (2) quatinus per ea tantam in hac arte consequar innocenciam et intelligencie clarificenciam, ut te prestante, qui solus mirabilia facis magna, in ipsa opera subitus celebs efficiar, (3) ut mea celebitate et innocencia cum puritate et caritate recepta te speculando speculer et te videndo videam et tuam sanctam visionem videam et intercessione virtutum celestium honorem te in secula seculorum. Amen.

LXIX 14ᴬ ORACIO

Gofgameli, omnis sapiencie Deus et sciencie donator illis, in quibus peccatum non est, omnis discipline spiritualis magister et doni spiritualis cuiusque largitor, macule omnis elimator, (2) te, Domine, per angelos et archangelos tuos, per tronos et [dominaciones], potestates, principatus et virtutes, per cherubin et seraphin, per 24 seniores, per omnem miliciam celestis excercitus (3) adoro, invoco, flagito, vereor, glorifico et exalto nomen tuum sanctissimum, terribile et mitissimum et te queso, Domine, ut hodie cor meum Spiritus sancti lumine et gracia tue visitacionis fecundatum, clarificatum et caritate coroboratum illustres, tu, qui es trinus et unus. Amen.

LXX 15ᴬ ORACIO

Emanuel, adoro te, rex regum et Deus meus et substancia mea, salus et revelacio mea, memoria et virtus mea, qui hora una diversarum genera lin-

---

8 GH adds "<ut>."

for attaining such great and excellent mysteries of this art, of the sacred vision of you, and of those sacraments of yours I might achieve the perfect completion. Amen.

LXVIII. Prayer 13.[101]

[**Ihelur**],[102] almighty judge, O Father, who has shown to us your salvation, and revealed your justice in the sight of the nations, open my eyes and illuminate my heart with your saving justice, in order that I may see the miracles from your glorious [sacraments], (2) as far as through those I may obtain such great innocence and clarity of understanding in this art, so that with your graciousness, who alone performs great miracles, I may suddenly be made celibate in this work, (3) that through my celibacy and innocence, with purity and charity received, that by looking for you, I may look at you, and by striving to see you, I may see you, and I may see your holy vision, and with the intervention of heavenly powers I may honor you forever and ever. Amen.

LXIX. Prayer 14.[103]

Gofgameli, God of all wisdom and giver of this science to those without sin, master of all spiritual teachings, and bountiful giver of all spiritual gifts, cleanser of all stains, (2) to you, O Lord, through your Angels and Archangels, Thrones and [Dominations], Potestates, Principalities and Virtues, through the Cherubim and Seraphim, through the twenty-four Elders, by all the host of the celestial army, (3) I honor, invoke, entreat, revere, glorify, and exalt your most holy name, terrifying yet most gentle, I beg you, O Lord, that today my heart may be made fruitful with the light of the Holy Spirit, and the grace of your visitation, and made clear and bright with your love, you who are threefold and one. Amen.

LXX. Prayer 15.[104]

Emanuel, I honor you, the king of kings, and my God, and my substance, my salvation and my revelation, my memory and my strength, who in a sin-

---

101 Ars. Not. 143, JV p. 93.
102 Name 13 seems to have been omitted by mistake.
103 Ars. Not. 146, JV p. 94.
104 Compare Ars. Not. 146 [version A] Var. 9, JV p. 200.

guarum edificantibus turrim dedisti (2) et qui sanctis apostolis tuis uncciōnem septiformis Spiritus sancti infudisti et illis ediomata, qui nos docerent de omnibus linguis eisdem repente loqui, tribuisti per virtutem verbi tui, in quo omnia creasti, (3) per potenciam huius sacramenti inspira cor meum et infunde in illud rorem gracie tue, ut subito tui Spiritus sancti afflatus lumine efficaciam huius operacionis, (4) innocenciam et purificacionem anime et harum sanctarum visionum capax voluntatem subtilem et ingeniosam et mentem clarificatam valeam consequi. Amen.

LXXI 16ᴬ ORACIO

{H}on. ezethomos. iezemonos. hazalathon. azaithon. hentynethel. hezemtynethel. zamayzathon. hamanzathon. zamarzathon. (2) hezemeguor. zecromanda. iecomancha. ieraphay. zaraphamy. phalezethon. phaboghecon. seremyhal. sacramyzan. (3) iethemathon. sacramazaym. se{cr}anal. sacramathan. iezemy. halathon. hathezihacos. ieceley. mathan. ateriathos. zai. mazay. (4) zamma. zazay. guygucheibib. gigithios. guahiros. megalon. senegalon. heracruhit. ciarihuht. haracrihuz. [Amen].

LXXII Oracio Latina

Domine, Deus incomprehensibilis, invisibilis, immortalis et intelligibilis, cuius vultum angeli et archangeli et celestes virtutes ardenter videre desiderant, (2) cuius maiestatem eternaliter desidero adorare atque continue pro posse meo exerceo adorans te Deum vivum in secula seculorum. Amen.

LXXIII 17ᴬ ORACIO

Admyhel, Domine, Deus, sancte Pater omnipotens, exaudi preces meas hodie et inclina aurem tuam ad oraciones meas, (2) chemon. gezomelyhon.

gle hour gave diverse languages to the builders of the tower,[105] (2) and who infused into your holy apostles with the seven-fold anointing of the Holy Spirit and with speaking in tongues, you granted that they might teach us to suddenly speak in all the same languages, by the power of your Word, through which you created all things. (3) By the power of this sacrament, inspire my heart and pour into it the dew of your grace, that suddenly inspired with the light of your Holy Spirit, I may have the strength, the effectiveness of this operation, (4) the innocence, and the purification of the soul, and fit for these holy visions, and able to achieve a subtle and clever will, and a clarified mind. Amen.

LXXI. Prayer 16.[106]

{H}on. ezethomos. iezemonos. hazalathon. azaithon. hentynethel. hezemtynethel. zamayzathon. hamanzathon. zamarzathon. (2) hezemeguor. zecromanda. iecomancha. ieraphay. zaraphamy. phalezethon. phaboghecon. seremyhal. sacramyzan. (3) iethemathon. sacramazaym. se{cr}anal. sacramathan. iezemy. halathon. hathezihacos. ieceley. mathan. ateriathos. zai. mazay. (4) zamma. zazay. guygucheibib. gigithios. guahiros. megalon. senegalon. heracruhit. ciarihuht. haracrihuz. [Amen].

LXXII. Latin Prayer.[107]

O Lord God, incomprehensible, invisible, immortal, and intelligible, whose face the angels and archangels, and heavenly powers passionately desire to see, (2) whose majesty I desire to honor forever and continuously, enforcing it to the extent of my powers, honoring you, the living God, forever and ever. Amen.

LXXIII. Prayer 17.[108]

Admyhel, O Lord, God, holy and almighty Father, hear my prayers today, and bend your ear towards my prayers, (2) chemon. gezomelyhon. samaht.

---

105 I.e. the Tower of Babel. Gen. 11:4–9.
106 Ars. Not. 90, JV p. 205.
107 Ars. Not. 91, JV p. 67.
108 Ars. Not. 92, JV p. 205

samaht. gezagam. iezehator. lesehator. sezehacon. saymanda. samay. gezihel. gulahentihel. iezel. iezetihel. galetihel. gazay. hetihel.

LXXIV Oracio Latina

Deus, semper via, vita, veritas, da lucem tuam florere per virtutem sancti Spiritus in conscienciam meam et mentem meam et concede, (2) ut fulgeat et clarescat donum operacionis tue et donum gracie tue in cor meum et animam meam nunc et per omnia secula seculorum. Amen.

LXXV 18ᴬ oracio

Honzmorb. lemogethon. hegemothon. hazathay. hazathar. hazamathar. hazatha. hazamathar. iazamathan. zegomothay. gohathay. zachana. legomothay. iachama. legomezon. legornezon. lemdomethon. hathanathios. (2) lamdomathon. iegomaday. hathamam. zachamos. hathanayos. hellesscymon. zelezion. uaderabar. uagedaroin. lauinauaht. lamandi. gemechor. guomon. gehor. genamchor. hellemay. iezecromay. iecromal. iecrahaly. tholomanos. colomaithos.

LXXVI Oracio Latina

Vita hominum et omnium creaturarum visibilium et invisibilium, claritas eterna celestium spirituum, omnium hominum salus indeficiensque pietatis origo, (2) qui omnia novisti, antequam fiant, qui iudicas omnia, que videntur [et non sunt et que non videntur] et sunt, [et] ineffabili disposicione discernis, glorifica sanctum nomen tuum et ineffabile hodie. (3) Corrobora cor meum et intellectum meum et animam meam et auge innocenciam meam et confirma precem meam et a viciis expeditam redde animam meam, clarificatam in virtutibus et penitenciis et fletibus et innocenciis, (4) ut facultate puritatis et innocencie a te michi collata et lima penitencie et tue gracie laudem te et cognoscam te sine enigmate et videam facialiter te et glorificem nomen tuum ad laudem tuam in secula seculorum. Amen.

gezagam. iezehator. lesehator. sezehacon. saymanda. samay. gezihel. gulahentihel. iezel. iezetihel. galetihel. gazay. hetihel.

LXXIV Latin Prayer.[109]

O God, always the way, the truth, and the life, give your light to flourish in my conscience and my mind through the virtue of the Holy Spirit, and grant (2) that the gift of your operation, and the gift of your grace, shines brightly in my heart and soul, now and forever. Amen.

LXXV. Prayer 18.[110]

Honzmorb. lemogethon. hegemothon. hazathay. hazathar. hazamathar. hazatha. hazamathar. iazamathan. zegomothay. gohathay. zachana. legomothay. iachama. legomezon. legornezon. lemdomethon. hathanathios. (2) lamdomathon. iegomaday. hathamam. zachamos. hathanayos. hellesscymon. zelezion. uaderabar. uagedaroin. lauinauaht. lamandi. gemechor. guomon. gehor. genamchor. hellemay. iezecromay. iecromal. iecrahaly. tholomanos. colomaithos.

LXXVI. Latin Prayer.[111]

O life of men and all creatures visible and invisible, the eternal clarity of the heavenly spirits, the salvation of all men, and the unfailing origin of piety, (2) who knows all things before they happen, who judges all things visible [and invisible], and you see with indescribable disposition, glorify your holy and ineffable name today. (3) Strengthen my heart, and my understanding, and my soul, and increase my innocence, and strengthen my prayer, and release my soul from sin, clarified in the virtues and with penance, weeping, and innocence, (4) so that with the quality of purity and innocence from you to me, brought together and the polish of penitence, and your grace, I may praise you and recognize you without obscurity, and see you face to face, and glorify your name, to your praise, through the ages of the ages. Amen.

---

109 Ars. Not. 93, JV p. 68.
110 Ars. Not. 94, JV pp. 205–6.
111 Ars. Not. 95, JV p. 68.

LXXVII 19ᴬ ORACIO

Joht. omaza. behea. Theon. megal. menehon. exhehal. tirigel. harapheiocon. semenoyn. sehmneny. (2) hachemathan. hiemarayn. gemehehon. lucharanochyn. exnotheyn. themelihen. segyhon. hihoueuyr. hacrisientheon.

LXXVIII Oracio Latina

Rex regum, Deus infinite misericordie et maiestatis inmense, largitor ac dispositor atque dispensator, stabilitor omnium fundamentorum, (2) pone fundamentum omnium tuarum virtutum in me et aufer a me insipienciam cordis mei, ut stabiliantur sensus mei in dileccione caritatis tue, (3) et informetur Spiritus sanctus in me secundum [re]creacionem et innovacionem voluntatis tue, ut habeam efficaciter tuam facialem visionem, qui vivis et regnas Deus per omnia secula seculorum. Amen.

LXXIX 20ᴬ ORACIO

Hofob, Deus, Pater inmense, a quo procedit omne, quod bonum est, cuius magnitudo [misericordie] incomprehensibilis est, exaudi hodie preces meas, quas in conspectu tuo refero, et concede michi donum, quod a te peto. (2) Redde michi leticiam salutaris tui, ut deleam iniquitates meas hodie et accipiam vias tuas et semitas scienciarum tuarum, et convertantur ad te rebelles et increduli, ut quod corde repeto et ore commemoro in me radicitus habeat fundamentum, et in operibus tuis efficax videar et adiutus. Amen.

LXXVII. Prayer 19.[112]

Ioht. omaza. behea. Theon. megal. menehon. exhehal. tirigel. harapheiocon. semenoyn. sehmneny. (2) hachemathan. hiemarayn. gemehehon. lucharanochyn. exnotheyn. themelihen. segyhon. hihoueuyr. hacrisientheon.

LXXVIII. Latin Prayer.[113]

O king of kings, God of infinite mercy and immeasurable greatness, granter, arranger, and disposer, you who make firm all foundations, (2) you lay the foundation of all your virtues in me, and remove from me the foolishness of my heart, that my feelings may be made firm in the love of your charity, (3) and the Holy Spirit may be shaped in me, according to the restoration and renewal of your will, in order that I may have effectually the vision of your face, you who lives and reigns, God through the ages of the ages. Amen.

LXXIX. Prayer 20.[114]

Hofob, O God, infinitely great Father, from whom proceeds all good, the greatness of [your mercy] is incomprehensible. Hear my prayers today, which I offer in your sight, and grant me the gift which I beg from you. (2) Grant to me the joy of your salvation, that I may erase my iniquities today and follow your ways, and the paths of your knowledge, and convert the rebels and unbelievers towards you, that what I repeat in my heart and commemorate with my mouth will take root in me and become my foundation, and in your works I may be seen as effective and of help. Amen.

---

[112] Ars. Not. 95 var. 10, JV p. 206.
[113] Ars Not. 96, JV p. 68.
[114] Ars. Not. 98, JV p. 69.

LXXX 21ᴬ ORACIO

Messamarathon. gezomothon. ezomathon. haihatha. hagihar. hagiathar. haihatha. lethasiel. lechisihel. gethiduhal. geguhay. iethonay. samazataht. samazarel. zamazthel. sergomazar. hazomathan. hazothynathon. iesomathon. (2) iezochor. heihazay. heihazar. samy. zamyn. helihel. samehelihel. siloth. silereht. gezemathal. iecoronay. iecomenay. samyhahel. hesemyhel. secozomay. sedomasay. sethothamay. sanna. rabihathos. hamnos. hamnas. Amen.

LXXXI Oracio Latina

Rex, eterne Deus, iudex et discretor omnium conscienciarum bonarum, tu hodie clarifica me propter nomen sanctum tuum et per hec sancta sacramenta tua purifica mentem meam, (2) ut intret innocencia tua [in] interiora mea sicut aqua fluens de celo et sicut oleum in ossibus meis per te, Deus, salvator omnium, qui es fons bonitatis et tocius pietatis origo. (3) Dirige me et promove me in ista sancta faciali visione, quam deposco, tu, qui es trinus et unus. Amen.

LXXXII 22ᴬ·oracio

Hanethi, Deus, tocius pietatis auctor et fundamentum, omnium salus eterna et redempcio populorum, inspirator omnium graciarum et sanctitatum, omnium purarum operacionum largitor inmense, (2) de cuius munere et misericordia venit, ut tantum nobis famulis tuis indulgenciarum inspirare digneris augmentum, qui eciam michi misero peccatori tua concessisti scire sacramenta, (3) tuere, Domine, defende et clarifica animam meam et libera cor meum de pravis huius mundi cogitacionibus et incentiva libidinis voluptate et omnis fornicacionis desideri a in me potenter extingue et reprime, (4) ut puritatibus tuis et actibus misticis ac virtutibus[9] delecter in eis, et des michi peticionem cordis mei, ut in glorificacione tua confirmatus et delectatus diligam te, (5) quod valeam efficaciter tuam facialem visionem et sanctam meo vivente corpusculo optinere, et augeatur in me virtus sancti Spiritus per salutem tuam et remuneracionem fidelium in salutem anime mee et corporis mei. Amen.

---

9 GH adds "<*intentus*>" ("eager, intent") per Ars. Not.

LXXX. Prayer 21.[115]

Messamarathon. gezomothon. ezomathon. haihatha. hagihar. hagiathar. haihatha. lethasiel. lechisihel. gethiduhal. geguhay. iethonay. samazataht. samazarel. zamazthel. sergomazar. hazomathan. hazothynathon. iesomathon. (2) iezochor. heihazay. heihazar. samy. zamyn. helihel. samehelihel. siloth. silereht. gezemathal. iecoronay. iecomenay. samyhahel. hesemyhel. secozomay. sedomasay. sethothamay. sanna. rabihathos. hamnos. hamnas. Amen.

LXXXI. Latin Prayer.[116]

O King, eternal God, judge and discerner of all good consciences, clarify me this day, because of your holy name, and through these holy sacraments purify my mind, (2) that your innocence may enter into my interior, like water flowing from the sky, and like oil into my bones, through you, O God, the savior of all things, who are the fountain of goodness, and the source of all piety. (3) Guide me and move me forward in this holy vision of your form, which I beseech of you, who are threefold and one. Amen.

LXXXII. Prayer 22.[117]

Hanethi, O God, the author and foundation of all piety, the eternal health and redemption of all people, inspirer of all graces and sanctity, the generous immeasurable giver of all pure operations, (2) from whose gift and mercy your servants are granted such great indulgences, your servants, which you have even permitted me, a miserable sinner to know your sacraments, (3) O Lord, watch, defend, and clarify my soul, and free my heart from faulty thinking of this world, and the allure of the desire for physical pleasure, and extinguish and potently restrain in me all lust for fornication, (4) that with your purifications and mystical acts and powers, I may delight in them, and grant to me the petition of my heart, that I may be strengthened in your glorification, and love you, (5) and that I may have the ability to attain the vision of your holy face while my body lives, and may the virtue of the Holy Spirit increase in me, through your deliverance and the reward of the faithful, for the health of my soul and of my body. Amen.

---

115 Ars. Not. 99, JV p. 207.
116 Ars. Not. 100, JV p. 70.
117 Ars. Not. 101, JV p. 70.

LXXXIII

Deus, Pater inmense, a quo procedit omne, quod bonum est, misericordissime, omnipotentissime Deus, ure renes meos[10] ex gracia Spiritus sancti et igne visitacionis tue visita me hodie (2) et propicius esto michi misericordiamque tuam concede, ut potem et sacier de fonte, qui Deus est, et sciam voluntatem tuam, benignissime, et psallam et videam mirabilia tua, tu, qui es Deus trinus et unus. Amen.

LXXXIV 23·ORACIO

Heriona, omnipotens, incomprehensibilis, invisibilis et indivisibilis Deus, adoro hodie nomen sanctum tuum ego, indignus et miserimus peccator, (2) extollens oracionem meam et intellectum meum et racionem meam ad templum sanctum tuum celestis Ierusalem et assisto tibi hodie, Deus meus, ostendens te Deum meum, creatorem meum et salvatorem meum. (3) Et ego, creatura racionabilis, invoco hodie gloriosam clemenciam tuam, ut visitet[11] hodie Spiritus sanctus infirmitatem meam.

(4) Et tu, Domine, Deus meus, qui Moysi et Abrahe, servis tuis, per fidem et puritatem visionis tue graciam contulisti, (5) confer michi hodie graciam superioris dulcedinis tue, qua rorasti servos tuos, et investigacionis,[12] qua investigasti eosdem per prophetas, et sicut voluisti eis momentaneam conferre graciam, (6) adhibe michi innocencie graciam, quam desidero, et emunda conscienciam meam ab operibus mortuis[13] et mitte cor meum in viam rectam et aperi illud ad te videndum.

---

10 Ps. 26.2. (Vulgate 25.2): Proba me Domine et tempta me ure renes meos et cor meum ("Prove me, O Lord, and try me; burn my reins [i.e. mind] and my heart.")
11 Vivificet T.
12 Ars. Not.: instigasti.
13 Heb. 9:14.

LXXXIII.[118]

O God, infinitely great Father, from whom all things proceed,[119] who is good, most merciful, and all-powerful God, test my heart and my mind[120] with the grace of the Holy Spirit, and visit me today with the fire of your inspection (2) and look favorably on me, and grant your mercy, in order that I may drink and be satisfied from the spring, which is God, and know your most generous will, and that I may sing the Psalms and see your miracles, you, who are the three-fold and one God. Amen.

LXXXIV. Prayer 23.[121]

Heriona, Almighty, incomprehensible, the invisible and indivisible God, I honor today your holy name. I, am unworthy and wretched sinner (2) lift up my prayers and my understanding, and my reasoning towards your holy temple of heavenly Jerusalem, and I stand before you this day, my God, making it clear that you are my God, my creator, and my savior. (3) And I, a rational creature, call upon your glorious mercy today, that the Holy Spirit may witness my weakness today.

(4) And you, O Lord, my God, who bestowed grace upon Moses and Abraham,[122] your servants, through faith and the purity of your vision, (5) bestow today your grace of superior sweetness upon me, wherewith you have moistened your servants, and invest what you have invested through the same prophets, and as you intended to instantly confer grace on them, (6) so too extend the grace of innocence to me, which I desire, and cleanse my conscience from dead works,[123] and send my heart onto the right path, and uncover it for seeing yourself.

---

118 Compare LXXIX above, and Ars. Not. 98, JV p. 69.
119 Cp. Opening of prayer LXXIX.
120 Lit. "burn my reins and my heart." The wording coincides with Ps. 26.2.
121 Ars. Not. 115, JV pp. 77–8.
122 Ars. Not.: Aaron.
123 Heb. 9:14.

(7) Destina intellectum meum ad viam sanctam, tu, Domine, Deus, qui me ad ymaginem et similitudinem tuam creare dignatus es. (8) Exaudi me in tua iusticia et doce me in tua veritate et reple animam meam gracia tua secundum magnam misericordiam tuam, (9) ut in multitudine miseracionum tuarum amplius <me> delecter et in operibus tuis magnis et complaceam in administracione mandatorum tuorum (10) et secundum opera gracie tue adiutus et restauratus exaltato corde et consciencia mea emundata confidam in te et epuler in conspectu tuo et exaltem nomen tuum, quod bonum est, (11) o Domine, in conspectu sanctorum tuorum. Sanctifica me hodie, ut in fide viva et spe perfecta et caritate constanti visionis, (12) quam desidero, adepta gracia exaltatus, coroboratus et illuminatus diligam te et cognoscam te facialiter (13) et innocenciam, sapienciam et purificenciam de sedibus tuis moncium eternitatis, que hominibus [dona] donanda promisisti, et sanctimoniam firmiter habeam et memoriter retineam.

(14) Iesu Christe, fili Dei unigenite, cui ante secula dedit Pater omnia in manus, da michi hodie propter nomen sanctum tuum gloriosum et ineffabile nutrimentum corporis et anime. (15) Ydoneam presta michi et perspicuam voluntatem et animam liberam et expeditam, ut quicquid postulavero in tua misericordia et veritate pro voluntate disponatur, et omnis oracio mea et accio mea in beneplacito tuo radicata et confirmata existat.[14] (16) Aperi, Domine, Deus meus et Pater vite mee, fundamentum visionis, quam desidero. (17) Aperi michi, Domine, fontem, quem aperuisti prothoplausto Ade et quem aperuisti servis tuis Abraham, Ysac et Iacob ad credendum, diligendum, obediendum, clarificandum et sanctificandum. (18) Suscipe pro me hodie preces et oraciones, Domine, omnium sanctorum et omnium sanctarum celestium virtutum, [ut] omnium sanctimoniarum tuarum docibilis constanter efficiar. Amen.

LXXXV 24ᴬ ORACIO

Yvestre, adoro te, rex regum et Domine dominancium, rex eterne impermutabilis; intellige hodie clamorem meum et spiritus mei et cordis mei

---

14 Ars. Not.: da michi hodie propter nomen tuum gloriosum et ineffabile instrumentum anime et corporis ydoneam et perspicax linguam expeditam et liberam et absolutam, ut quicquid postulavero in tua misericordia et voluntate disponatur, et omnis actio mea in beneplacito tuo radicata et confirmata consistat.

(7) Send my understanding towards the holy path, you, O Lord, God, who deigned to create me in your image and likeness. (8) Hear me clearly in your justice, and teach me in your truth, and replenish my soul with your grace according to your great mercy, (9) that I might delight more in your many mercies <towards me>, and in your great works, and I may take pleasure in fulfilling your commands (10) and being helped by your works of grace, and restored, with heart raised up, and my conscience purified, I will trust in you and dine sumptuously in your sight, and I may exalt your name, which is good (11) O Lord, in the sight of your saints. Sanctify me today, that I may live in faith and perfect hope and with the constant love of the vision, (12) which I desire, and being raised up by the grace received, strengthened, and illuminated, I will love you and recognize you face to face (13) and that I may really have the innocence, wisdom, and purification which you promised to give to mankind, from your seats of the everlasting mountains, and that I may have the sanctity and retain it in memory unshakeably.

(14) O Jesus Christ, only-begotten son of God, into whose hands the Father placed all things before the ages began; grant to me today for the sake of your holy name,[124] glorious and ineffable nourishment of the body and the soul, (15) grant me a suitable and clear will, and a free and unburdened soul, that whatever I have asked for in your mercy and truth, may be disposed according to your will, and all my prayers and deeds, coming to pass rooted and strengthened in your good pleasure. (16) Reveal, O Lord, my God and Father of my life, the foundation of the vision, which I desire. (17) Reveal to me, O Lord, the spring, which you revealed to the first man Adam, and which you revealed to your servants, Abraham, Isaac, and Jacob that they might believe, love, obey, glorify, and sanctify you. (18) O Lord, accept on my behalf the prayers and prayers of all the saints, and of all holy heavenly virtues, [that] I may be as fit to be taught as any of your holy ones. Amen.

LXXXV. Prayer 24.[125]

Yvestre, I worship you, king of kings and Lord of Lords, eternally unchangeable king; hear this day my cries, and the moaning of my spirit and my heart, that I may enjoy a respite in you, with my understanding changed, and a heart

---

124 Compare (KJV) Ps. 79:8–9.
125 Ars. Not. 116, JV p. 78.

gemitum, ut commutato intellectu meo et dato michi corde carneo pro lapideo respirem in te, Dominum et Salvatorem meum. (2) Lava, Domine, interiora mea Spiritu tuo novo. Pro intellectu carnis mee malo pone, Domine, intellectum tuum sanctum bonum et aufer a me quod malum est commutans me in hominem novum, ut dileccione, qua reformasti mundum, reformes me, et salus tua sancta michi tue sanctimonie tribuat incrementum. (3) Exaudi hodie, Domine, preces meas, quibus clamo ad te, et revela oculos carnis mee, [ut] considerans, intelligens et custodiens mirabilia de glorificaturis et purificaturis gracie tue spiritualis (4) et vivificatus in iustificacionibus tuis prevaleam in conspectu adversarii fidelium Diaboli. Exaudi me, Domine, Deus meus, et propicius esto michi, qui plasmasti me. (5) Ostende michi hodie misericordiam tuam et porrige michi vas salutare, ut potem et sacier de fonte gracie tue, tu, qui Deus es, ut de sanctificaturis et de visionis tue facialis monstraturis, (6) quas desidero et adopto, hodie psallam cum intellectu et anima et intuer et stem et fruar in via immaculata visionis tue, et veniat hodie de celo gracia Spiritus sancti et requiescat in me. Amen.

LXXXVI 25ᴬ ORACIO

Saday, Domine, confiteor tibi ego reus hodie, Pater celi et terre, Deus, conditor omnium visibilium et invisibilium creaturarum atque virtutum omnium et graciarum bonarum dispensator atque largitor, (2) qui custodis sapienciam tuam, scienciam, humilitatem tuam et caritatem tuam a superbis et reprobis et revelas parvulis. (3) Humilia hodie, Domine, cor meum et intellectum meum stabilem facias et mentem meam firmam et intelligenciam meam et conscienciam meam augmenta, ut te diligam, intelligam et videam. (4) Signa hodie, Domine, lumen vultus tui super me, ut prorsus innovatus et mundatus ab omnibus operibus mortuis et a peccatis meis prevaleam in visionibus et speculaturis tuis. (5) Proba me, misericordissime et omnipotentissime Deus, et ure renes meos. Corrobora hodie cor meum et illustra gracia Spiritus sancti et igne gracie visitacionis tue visita

of flesh given to me in place of a heart of stone, O my Lord and Savior. (2) O Lord, wash my inner self with your new Spirit. In place of the bad understanding of my flesh, O Lord, give me your good, sacred understanding, and remove from me whatever is bad, and changing me into a new person, and transform me with the love wherewith you have transformed the world, and may your holy salvation grant to me the growth of sanctity. (3) Hear my prayers today, O Lord, wherewith I cry to you, and reveal to my eyes of flesh [that] I may examine, understand, and guard the miracles involving the glorification and purification of your spiritual grace (4) and being brought back to life by your justifications, I may prevail in the face of the devil, the enemy of the faithful. Hear me, O Lord, my God, and be favorable to me, you who has formed me. (5) Show me your mercy today, and extend to me the vessel of salvation, that I may drink and be satisfied from the fountain of your grace, you, who are God, that I will be sanctified and shown the vision of you face to face, (6) which I desire and choose today, and that I may sing Psalms with understanding and soul and that I may enjoy and stand in the immaculate path of the vision of you, and may the grace of the Holy Spirit come today from heaven, and may it rest in me. Amen.

LXXXI. Prayer 25.[126]

Saday, O Lord, I a sinner confess to you today, O Father of Heaven and Earth, O God, maker of all visible and invisible creatures, and of all virtue and good grace, you dispense and give bountifully, (2) who guards your wisdom, knowledge, humility, and your love from the arrogant and the false ones, and show them to the little ones. (3) O Lord, humble my heart today, and make my understanding stable, and my mind strong, and increase my intelligence and conscience, that I may love, perceive, and see you. (4) O Lord, mark the light of your face upon me today, that being renewed and cleansed completely from all dead works and from all my sins,[127] I may prevail in the vision and observation of you. (5) Test me, O all merciful and almighty God, and burn my reins.[128] Strengthen my heart today, and illuminate it with the grace of the Holy Spirit, and visit me with the fire of the grace of your visitation, and

---

126 Ars. Not. 117, JV p. 79.
127 Cf. Heb. 6:1.
128 See Ps. 25:2 (KJV 26).

me et illumina mentem meam (6) et fortitudine stabilitatis tue precinge lumbos meos et baculum confortacionis tue da in dexteram meam et in lavaturis stillarum tuarum me lotum facias (7) et in sanctimoniis tuis dirige mentem meam et in opera manuum tuarum. Confirma spiritum meum, ut eradicatis viciis omnibus et sordibus peccatorum meorum prevaleam fortiter in dileccione misericordiarum tuarum. (8) Inspira michi, Domine, hodie spiraculum vite et auge mentem meam et intellectum meum et racionem meam per Spiritus sancti firmitatem et constanciam, ut in operibus laudum et visurarum tuarum exercitatus spiritus meus confortetur et augeatur. (9) Vide, Domine, et considera hodie laborem mentis mee, et fiat voluntas tua benigna in me, et de celo mitte in terra in michi consolatorem Spiritum sanctum, (10) ut me stabilitate perfecta muniat et auxilium michi conferat in videndis visionibus tuis et laudandis laudibus tuis et fruendis fruicionibus tuis, quas desidero, que sunt gracia et gloria et defensio mea. Amen.

LXXXVII 26ᴬ ORACIO

Maloht. Otheos. hatamagiel. hataha. marihel. gezozay. iezoray. gezozay. saziel. sazamay. iezoramp. zazamanp. sacamap. zachamay. iecornamas. (2) iecohoruampda. salatihel. gezomel. zarachiel. megalis. nachama. nechamyha. sazamaym. sophonaym. lazamair. mehisrampna. hamamyl. (3) zamanyl. sihel. |c- deloth. hamamyn. hazemeloch. moys. ramna. secoram. hanasichonea. seronea. zaramahem. sacromohem. iegonomay. (4) zaramohem. chades. bachuc. iezemeloht. harugo. semorgizechon. malaparos. malapatas. helatay. helahenay. methay. meray.

LXXXVIII Oracio Latina

Pie Deus, misericors Deus, clemens Deus omnipotens omnia dans, fac michi credenti hodie omnia possibilia et adiuva hodie incredulitatem meam et miserere mei hodie, (2) sicut misertus es Ade penitenti, qui ei subitaneam per omnipotencie tue misericordiam multarum virtutum contulisti graciam. (3) Confer michi hodie per omnipotencie tue misericordiam graciam, quam desidero, ut in magnificencia operum tuorum

illuminate my mind (6) and gird my loins with the strength of your stability, and give the staff of your comfort into my right hand, and may you wash me along with those who will be washed in your drops, (7) and direct my mind in your sanctities and in the work of your hands. Strengthen my spirit, that having rooted out all vices and the filth of my sins, I may prevail strongly in the joy of your mercy. (8) Breathe into me, O Lord, today with the breath of life, and increase my mind, my understanding, and my reasoning, through the firmness and perseverance of the Holy Spirit, that my spirit may be consoled and increase in works of praise, and the sight of you. (9) Consider, O Lord, and examine today the effort of my mind, and let your will rejoice in me, and send the Comforter, the Holy Spirit, from Heaven to me on the Earth, (10) that he will fortify me with perfect stability, and bring his assistance to me for seeing the vision of you, and praising you with praises, and delighting in your delights, which I desire, which are my grace, my glory, and my defense. Amen.

LXXXVII. Prayer 26.[129]

Maloht. Otheos. hatamagiel. hataha. marihel. gezozay. iezoray. gezozay. saziel. sazamay. iezoramp. zazamanp. sacamap. zachamay. iecornamas. (2) iecohoruampda. salatihel. gezomel. zarachiel. megalis. nachama. nechamyha. sazamaym. sophonaym. lazamair. mehisrampna. hamamyl. (3) zamanyl. sihel. |c- deloth. hamamyn. hazemeloch. moys. ramna. secoram. hanasichonea. seronea. zaramahem. sacromohem. iegonomay. (4) zaramohem. chades. bachuc. iezemeloht. harugo. semorgizechon. malaparos. malapatas. helatay. helahenay. methay. meray.

LXXXVIII. Latin Prayer.[130]

O holy God, O merciful God, O gentle God, O almighty God, giver of all, make all things possible today, to me, a believer, and help my disbelief today, and have mercy on me today, (2) just as you had mercy on Adam when he repented, whereby you gave to him the grace of many virtues, through the mercy of your omnipotence, in an instant. (3) Grant to me this day the grace which I desire, through your omnipotence, that I, delighted in the greatness of your works, may succeed in achieving the vision of you, which I desire.

---

129 Ars. Not. 118, JV p. 79.
130 Ars. Not. 119, JV p. 80.

delectatus potestate tue virtutis efficaciam facialis visionis, quam desidero, valeam adipisci. (4) Adesto, clementissime Pater, hodie operi meo et clarifica me, benigne, alme, clementissime unigenite fili Dei. Confirma me. (5) Aspira me flamine Spiritus sancti, omnipotens, sancte Deus. Consolida hodie opus meum et doce me, ut ambulem in innocencia tui ipsius Dei gloriosi et glorier in multitudine effluentis gracie tue, (6) et impetus fluminis sanctissimi Spiritus civitatem cordis mei letificet et depuret in fide visionis sancte et in spe efficacie et innocencie, pro qua laboro, (7) et cor meum caritatis largitate repleat et instauret et radiis Spiritus sancti vivificet et muniat c[l]aritate eterna[15] affluentis misericordie. (8) Et non sit in me vacua, te queso, Deus meus, gracia tua, que maneat semper et multipliciter in me. (9) Sana, Domine, animam meam pietate clemencie tue ineffabilis et inestimabilis, quia peccavi tibi, et conforta cor meum hodie, (10) ut quod michi trades intranee recipiam et teneam et aptitudinem facialis et sancte tue visionis habeam per hec sacramenta tua sanctissima prefata cooperante gracia Patris et Filii et Spiritus sancti. Amen.

LXXXIX 27ᴬ ORACIO

Sechce, pie Pater, misericors Fili, clemens Spiritus sancte, Deus, rex ineffabilis et inestimabilis, trinus et unus Deus, adoro te, invoco te et deprecor te et sanctum nomen tuum et supereffluentem equitatem tuam operantem omnia, (2) quatinus ignoscas, indulgeas et miserearis michi, peccatori misero presumenti, et officium, quod aggressus sum, de visione videnda in me senciam et cognoscam, (3) et +tu, Domine mi, ut+ gracia, quam desidero, efficaciter in me vigeat et convalescat. Aperi in me, Domine, aures meas potenter, ut audiam. (4) Conforta manus meas, ut operer. Exterge luctum oculorum meorum, ut videam. Dilata circumspeccionem meam, ut proficiam et lucescam. Confirma pedes meos, ut ambulem. (5) Expedi nares meas et os meum, ut olfaciam et senciam et loquar tibi placita nunc et semper ad honorem nominis tui, quod est benedictum in secula. Amen.

---

15 Ars. Not. JV p. 80: caritate largotatis repleat, claritate eterna.

(4) O most gentle Father, assist my work today, and clarify me with kindness; O you who are most giving and most gentle, the only-begotten son of God, strengthen me. (5) Breathe into me the breath of the Holy Spirit, almighty and holy God. Solidify today my work, and teach me, that I may walk in innocence before glorious God himself and rejoice in the abundant outpouring of your grace, (6) and may the onslaught of the outpouring of the most Holy Spirit delight and purify the citadel of my heart in the faith of the holy vision and in the hope of the effectiveness and innocence, for which I work, (7) and may it renew and refill my heart with an abundance of love, and may I be invigorated and fortified with the rays of the Holy Spirit and the eternal clarity[131] of abundant mercy. (8) And may your grace not be empty in me, I beg you, O my God, but always remain and grow in me. (9) O Lord, heal my soul with your ineffable and inestimable tenderness of mercy, because I have sinned against you, and comfort my heart this day, (10) that I may receive inwardly that which you will give, and retain and be suited for having the vision of your person, through these your most holy sacraments aforesaid, along with the grace of the Father, and of the Son, and of the Holy Spirit. Amen.

LXXXIX. Prayer 27.[132]

Sechce, O tender Father, O merciful Son, O gentle Holy Spirit, O God, ineffable and inestimable king, threefold and one God, I honor you, I call upon you and beg you and your holy name and your overflowing justice performing all things, (2) O how great is your forgiveness, leniency, and pity for me, a poor sinner presuming to undertake this ceremony, for seeing and recognizing this vision. (3) And may the grace which I desire take root in me, O my Lord, thriving and growing strong in me. O Lord, potently open within me my ears, so I may hear. (4) Strengthen my hands, that I may labor. Wipe the grief from my eyes, that I may see. Broaden my foresight, that I may make advance and grow bright. Strengthen my feet, that I may walk. (5) Set my nostrils and mouth free, that I may smell and perceive and speak what will please you, now and always to the honor of your name, which is blessed forever. Amen.

---

131 So GH, following Ars. Not. *Claritate*. The LIH manuscripts read *caritate* ("with love").
132 Ars. Not. 120, JV pp. 80–1.

XC 28ᴬ ORACIO

Elscha, extollo sensus carnis [et anime] mee ad te hodie, Domine, Deus meus, et elevo [*eleva]¹⁶ hodie cor meum ad te, ut placeant tibi, Domine, hodie gemitus mei et represententur in conspectu tuo, (2) et complaceant verba et opera mea in conspectu tuo, et refulgeat hodie omnipotencia tua et misericordia tua in visceribus meis, et clarificetur mens mea efficaciter in operibus tuis, (3) et concrescat glorificacio in anima mea, et germinet gracia tua in corde meo et ore meo, ut quod commisero vel peccavero ita diluam, sicut beata Maria Magdalena diluit, (4) et ita in tuo dono gracie quod a te recepero perficiam, sicut sanctus apostolus tuus Paulus perfecit, et sicut custodivit Abraham, ita custodiam, (5) sicut memoriter tenuit Jacob, teneam, ut in purificaturarum tuarum virtute fundatus et radicatus in me tue misericordie fundamentum confirmatum glorier acquisisse (6) et delectatus in operibus manuum tuarum iusticiam et pacem mentis mee et corporis et paulo post sanctam visionem perseveranter adoptem et adipiscar et custodiam, (7) et Spiritus sancti tui, Domine, plenarie in me operante gracia hostium, sive visibilium, sive invisibilium, michi adversancium insidias atque versutias gaudeam superasse. Amen.

XCI 29ᴬ ORACIO

Abbadya, omnium regnorum sive potestatum visibilium sive invisibilium dispensator atque dispositor, Deus, et omnium bonarum voluntatum ordinator, (2) tu, Domine, consilio tui boni Spiritus dispone voluntatem meam et vivifica hodie potestatem meam debilem et imbecillitatem meam et inordinacionem mentis mee. (3) Ordina, Domine, voluntatem meam in bonum et in beneplacito tuo et michi graciam tua in multiformem in benignitate dispensacionis largire propicius non ad multitudinem peccatorum meorum respiciens (4) set michi que desidero, voluntatem tibi conformem, sensum in te iubilantem, anime graciam clarificantem in me, confirma et effectum meum cum gracia tua anime mee accomoda (5) et visita me visitacione Spiritus sancti, ut <et> quod ex carnis macula sive

---

16 As in Ars. Not. Sl. 3854 125v.

XC. Prayer 28.[133]

Elscha, lift up this day the senses of my body [and soul], O Lord my God, and lift up my heart to you, so that they are pleasing to you, O Lord, let my lamenting be manifest and known to your sight today, (2) and may my words and deeds be pleasing in your sight, and may your omnipotence and mercy shine brightly within me this day, and may my mind be effectually made clear in your works, (3) and may the glorification become more rooted in my soul, and your grace sprout forth in my heart and mouth, in order that whatever wrong I may have done or committed will thus be washed away, even as the blessed Mary Magdalen washed it away,[134] (4) and thus I will have received and completed it through the gift of grace that I have received from you, even as your apostle Paul did, and even as Abraham kept it, so will I also keep it, (5) even as Jacob kept it in his memory, so will I also keep it, so that being founded and rooted in the power of your purification, strengthened in the foundation of your mercy, I rejoice to acquire (6) and delight in the works of your hands, justice and peace of my mind and body, and soon after I may attain the holy vision, and steadfastly choose and keep, (7) and with the grace of your Holy Spirit working fully in me, O Lord, I may overcome all my enemies, whether visible or invisible, and rejoice over any treacherous and cunning adversaries. Amen.

XCI. Prayer 29.[135]

Abbadya, O God, dispenser and disposer of all kingdoms, whether visible or invisible, and ordainer and arranger of all good wills, (2) dispose my will, through the counsel of your good spirit, and bring to life my weak power today and the weakness and disorder of my mind. (3) Arrange O Lord, my will into good and what is pleasing to you, and grant me your manifold grace, dispensed with kindness, not considering the multitude of my sins (4) but a will conformable to yours, rejoicing in the perception of you, making manifest in me the grace of my soul, and confirming it, and inclining my work with your grace (5) and visit me with the visitation of the Holy Spirit, that the stain

---

133 Ars. Not. 121, JV p. 81.
134 See Luke 7:47. After washing Jesus' feet, he declared "Her sins, which are many, are forgiven; for she loved much." (KJV)
135 Ars. Not. 122, JV pp. 81–2.

quod ex nativitate aut ex peccati labe contraxi divina tua [illa] ineffabilis pietas aboleat, (6) qua in principio celum et terram creare voluisti, illa spiritualis magna misericordia tua restauret, (7) qua hominem perditum ad gracie pristinum statum amissum revocare dignatus es, cui iudicium Sathane facultatem visionis abstulit et intellectus.

(8) Tu, Domine, cuius sensus atque sapiencia et claritas est attingens a fine usque ad finem fortiter et disponens omnia suaviter et misericorditer, omnem sinceritatem atque puritatem in me restituas, (9) ut ego, indignus peccator et miser, in omnibus operibus tuis confirmatus in hiis, que desidero, habilis efficiar et perspicuus et claribundus triplici et septemplici Patris et Filii et Spiritus sancti largitate efficiar (10) ad optinendum sanctam facialem sancte et gloriose trinitatis visionem meo vivente corpusculo Deo prestante et administrante, cooperante sua sanctissima gracia, qui vivit et regnat trinus et unus. Amen.

XCII 30ᴬ ORACIO

Alpha et Ω, Deus, vivorum dominator et omnium visibilium et invisibilium administrator, fecundator omnibus omnia singulis singula tribuens secundum nature sue facultatem, (2) pro [e]qualitate meritorum angelorum et hominum gracie celestis largitatem in me infunde, ut gracia Spiritus sancti hodie cor meum et animam meam illustret, (3) et tu, Domine, multiplica in me dona Spiritus sancti et corrobora et innova [in] me interiorem hominem et fecunda me rore tue gracie, qua angelos rorasti, (4) et adorna me largitate innocencie tue, qua a principio fideles tuos adornasti, ut operentur in me septiformis gracie munera Spiritus sancti tui, (5) et aque superioris fluminis Ierusalem cum impetu fluentes puteum consciencie mee et animum meum irrigent, repleant et exuberent caritate, (6) qua de celo venisti super aquas, maiestatis tue. Huius puri sacramenti in me confirma magnalia [ac] huius sancte visionis. Amen.

which I have because of my flesh, or because of my birth, or incurred through sin, may be wiped out through your divine ineffable kindness, (6) whereby in the beginning you willed to create Heaven and Earth, that your spiritual and great mercy may deign to restore (7) to its former state of grace, that which mankind has lost, which ability of seeing and comprehending the judgment of Satan has stolen away.

(8) You, O Lord, whose understanding, wisdom, and clarity powerfully reach from one end to the other, and administering all things graciously and mercifully, may you restore all integrity and purity in me, (9) that I, an unworthy and wretched sinner, being strengthened in all your works, which I desire, that I may be able to attain the threefold and sevenfold abundance of the Father, Son, and Holy Spirit, which makes things clear and apparent (10) for attaining the holy vision of your sacred and glorious Trinity in person, while my body lives, God willing and administering by his most holy grace, who lives and reigns threefold and one. Amen.

XCII. Prayer 30.[136]

Alpha and Omega, God, ruler of the living, and director of all visible and invisible things, you make all things fertile, giving to each one according to its natural ability, (2) for the sake of the [e]quality of the merits of angels and people, pour into me the abundance of the heavenly grace, that the grace of the Holy Spirit will illuminate my heart and my soul today, (3) and O Lord, multiply the gifts of the Holy Spirit in me and strengthen and alter [in] me the inner man, and make me fertile with the dew of your grace, with which you have bedewed the angels, (4) and adorn me with the abundance of your righteousness, with which you have adorned your faithful from the beginning, so that the sevenfold gifts of grace of your Holy Spirit may work in me, (5) and the waters of the higher river of Jerusalem, flowing with force, and fill up the well of my conscience and my soul, that they may refill and surge up with the greatness of your love, (6) wherewith you came from heaven over the waters.[137] Confirm in me the mighty works of this pure sacrament [and] of this sacred vision. Amen.

---

136 Ars. Not. 123, JV p. 82.
137 Gen. 1:2.

XCIII 31ᴬ ORACIO

Leyste, profiteor tibi hodie, Deus, Pater omnium, qui secreta celestia ostendisti. Te deprecor suppliciter et maiestatem tuam precor et exoro, (2) ut, sicut tu es rex et princeps cogitacionum, voluntatum et animarum et omnium virtutum aliarum, hodie exaudi preces meas, (3) et dirigantur operaciones mee in conspectu tuo, et acciones mee in conspectu celestium virtutum prevaleant. (4) Clamo hodie ad te, Deus meus; nunc exaudi clamorem meum. Ingemisco ad te; hodie exaudi gemitus cordis mei. (5) Et ego commendo hodie spiritum meum, corpus meum et animam meam et cogitaciones meas in manus tuas, Pater mi et Deus meus, (6) et ne me a te senciam derelictum set misericordia in tuam in me [senciam], et exaltetur nomen tuum in me, clementissime Spiritus sancte, Deus, (7) cuius bonitas est eterna, cuius misericordia est incomprehensibilis, cuius perpetua claritas, cuius possessione pleni sunt celi et terra, (8) aspira et respice in me, Domine, et [intende] ad hanc operacionem meam, et quod in tue laudis honore devote postulo michi concede, ut in me omnis profectus[17] facialis et sancte visione dispensacione divina compleatur. (9) Doce me, Domine, quia in te pono me docendum. Purifica me, Domine, quia in te pono me purificandum. Clarifica me, Domine, quia in te pono me clarificandum. (10) Mundifica me, Domine, quia in te pono me mundificandum. Innocentifica me, Domine, quia in te pono me innocentificandum. Glorifica me, Domine, quia in te pono me glorificandum. (11) Rege me, Domine, quia in te pono me regendum, et in me gracie tue fidem infunde et fige, ut Spiritus tuus sanctus in me veniat, regnet et imperet pro hac sancta visione divina. Amen.

XCIV 32ᴬ ORACIO

Horistion, Domine, quia ego servus tuus sum, servio tibi hodie et confiteor coram maiestate glorie tue, in cuius conspectu omnis magnificencia et sanctimonia est, (2) et deprecor sanctum et ineffabile nomen tuum, quatinus ad tante operacionis mee effectum hodie aures tue pietatis inclines et oculos tue maiestatis accomodes, (3) ut aperiente te manum tuam gracia\<m\>, quam desidero, sacier et fecunder caritate et claritate, qua

---

17 So Sl. 3854 126r col. 2. Sl. 3885 (C): perfectis; Sl. 313 (B): perfeccio. Sl. 3885 135v: et in me omnis profectus huius operacionis dispensacione diuina compleatur.

XCIII. Prayer 31.[138]

Leyste, I declare to you today, O God, Father of all things, who revealed the heavenly secrets. I humbly beg you and pray and entreat your greatness, (2) that since you are the king and ruler of thoughts, intentions, and souls, and of all other virtues, hear my prayers this day, (3) and may my operations be directed in your sight, and may my actions prevail in the sight of your heavenly powers. (4) I cry out to you today, my God; hear now my cry. I grieve to you; hear now the grieving of my heart. (5) And I entrust today my spirit, my body, and my soul, and my thoughts into your hands, O my Father and my God, (6) and let me never feel abandoned by you, but rather sense your compassion in me, and may your name be exalted in me, O most merciful Holy Spirit O God, (7) whose goodness is eternal, whose mercy is incomprehensible, whose brightness is everlasting, whose substance fills Heaven and Earth, (8) breathe into me and look upon me, O Lord, and this operation of mine, and for your praise and honor grant my devout request, I beg you, that all progress in this sacred vision may be fulfilled in me with divine guidance. (9) Teach me, O Lord, in whom I entrust myself for teaching. Purify me, O Lord, in whom I entrust myself to be purified. Clarify me, O Lord, for I entrust myself in you to be clarified. (10) Cleanse me, O Lord, in whom I entrust myself to be cleansed. Make me innocent, O Lord, for I entrust myself to be made innocent by you. Glorify me, O Lord, in whom I entrust myself to be made glorious. (11) Guide me, O Lord, in whom I entrust myself to be guided, and pour into me the faith of your grace, and secure it so that your Holy Spirit may come into me, and may rule and command me for the sake of this holy divine vision. Amen.

XCIV. Prayer 32.[139]

Horistion, O Lord, because I am your servant, I serve you today, and I confess before the majesty of your glory, in whose sight is all generosity and purity, (2) and I beg your holy and ineffable name, that this day you might turn the ears of your piety to the successful completion of my operation, and apply the eyes of your majesty, (3) that as you open your hand by the grace which I desire, I may be satisfied and made fertile with charity and with clarity, with which

---

138 Ars. Not. 124, JV p. 83.
139 Ars. Not. 125, JV p. 83.

celum fundasti et terram, te, Pater piissime, largiente, qui vivis et regnas solus per omnia secula seculorum. Amen.

XCV 33ᴀ ORACIO

Jeremon, clementissime Domine, Deus meus, et miserere mei et parce malis meis. Sana animam meam, quia peccavi tibi. Non abneges uni quod pluribus contulisti. (2) Exaudi, Deus, oracionem famuli tui N, et in quacumque die invocavero te. Velociter exaudi me, sicut exaudisti sanctam Mariam Magdalenam. (3) Suscipe, Domine, clamorem confitentis ad te, audi vocem precantis et per oraciones beatissime Marie virginis, matris tue, atque omnium sanctorum tuorum, (4) ut oraciones et preces perveniant ad aures pietatis tue, quas ego, N, pro hac sancta visione effundo coram te in hac hora, ut per tua sanctissima nomina et sacramenta, (5) que sunt Hosel. Iesel. Hazaiacol. Iosel. Authiachar. Hazacol. Gezor. Gezamyhor. Namathar. Senales. Iole. Tarotheos. Lochos. Genos. Halla. Samyhel. Ramay. Sacharios. Logos. Patir. Sarahc. Iothosym. (6) mundatus, purificatus, clarificatus, innocentificatus et consecratus ad hanc gloriam et sacram tui facialem visionem pervenire merear prestante Domino nostro Iesu Christo, qui vivit et regnat per omnia secula seculorum. Amen.

XCVI 34ᴀ ORACIO

Hofbor, excelse Domine, Deus invisibilis, Deus inestimabilis, Deus ineffabilis, Deus incommutabilis, Deus incorruptibilis, Deus piisime, Deus dulcissime, Deus excelse, Deus gloriose, Deus inmense, Deus omnipotens, Deus, Pater tocius misericordie, (2) ego, licet indignus et plenus iniquitate, dolo et malicia, suplex ad tuam venio misericordiam orans et deprecans, ut non respicias ad universa et innumerabilia peccata mea set, sicut consuevisti peccatorum misereri et preces humilium exaudire, (3) ita me, famulum tuum N, licet indignum, exaudire digneris clamantem ad te pro hac sanctissima visione divina humiliter et desiderantissime a te postulata prece tuis sanctis sacramentis insignita, que sunt Hosel, Iesel et cetera,

you have generously established heaven and earth, you, O most holy Father, who lives and reigns alone, forever and ever. Amen.

XCV. Prayer 33.[140]

Jeremon, most generous, my Lord and my God, have mercy on me, and consider my faults. "Heal my soul, because I have sinned against you."[141] Do not deny to the one that which you have given to the many. (2) Hear, O God, the prayer of your servant N., and in whichever day I will call upon you, quickly hear me, as you heard the holy Mary Magdalen. (3) Accept, O Lord, the cries of him who confesses to you; hear the voice of the praying and by the prayers of the blessed virgin Mary, your mother, and all of your saints, (4) that these prayers and pleas for this holy vision, which I, N., pour out personally to you right now, may reach the ears of your piety, that through your most holy names and sacraments, (5) which are: Hosel. Iesel. Hazaiacol. Iosel. Authiachar. Hazacol. Gezor. Gezamyhor. Namathar. Senales. Iole. Tarotheos. Lochos. Genos. Halla. Samyhel. Ramay. Sacharios. Logos. Patir. Sarahc. Iothosym. (6) being cleaned, purified, glorified, made innocent and consecrated, and I may be worthy to attain the vision of your glorious and sacred shape, with our Lord Jesus Christ as our guide, who lives and reigns forever and ever. Amen.

XCVI. Prayer 34.

Hofbor, O Lord, who dwells on high, invisible God, inestimable God, ineffable God, unchangeable God, incorruptible God, O God most-pious, O God most sweet, O God most high, O glorious God, O immeasurable God, O almighty God, O God, the Father of all mercy, (2) I, although unworthy and full of iniquity, deceit, and vice, I come humbly begging and pleading for your mercy, that you don't consider all my countless sins, but just as you are accustomed to show mercy on sinners, and to hear the prayers of the humble, (3) so too deign to hear me, your servant N., although unworthy, crying to you for this most holy and divine vision, humbly and most earnestly, asking it of you

---

140 A variation of this prayer can be found in BoO p. 100, also in *Forbidden Rites*, p. 259. The holy names, Hosel, Iesel, etc. are found in Ars. Not, JV p. 211. Apart from this, neither prayer 33 nor 34 seem to occur in Ars. Not.
141 Ps. 40:5 (Vulgate).

(4) ut virtutem et graciam, quam pro tanta visione habere debeo, habeam, scilicet puritatem et innocenciam et claritatem, sapienciam et sanctitatem, (5) caritatem et sinceritatem et humilitatem et firmitatem et bonam voluntatem, te ipso prestante, qui sedes in altissimis, cui laus est atque gloria et honor per infinita secula seculorum. Amen.

XCVII

Si seriem harum oracionum scire vis, respice seriem 100 nominum Dei huius libri, quia per illa semper incipiunt oraciones. (2) Et nota, quod illa sacra Dei nomina predicta: Hosel, Iesel et cetera, debent dici paulo post principium orandi eciam in principio cuiuslibet oracionis.

XCVIII Incipit 2^A mundacio in visione divina.

Mundato igitur et macerato corpore volentis videre celeste palacium ipsum mundissimum esse iubemus et in omnibus virtutibus esse vestitum, (2) et semper cogitet et deprecetur Dominum de suorum absolucione peccatorum, quia iustus eciam debet timere, quia qui non timet, non diligit, testante Salomone et dicente: "Inicium sapiencie timor Domini,"[18] (3) unde quilibet debet timere, quia nemo ex sua condicione vel dignitate meretur vel consequitur gloriam vel salutem nec potest videre Deum absque gracia salvatoris.

(4) Et iterum alios 12 dies in pane et aqua integre sine aliqua relaxacione ieiunet faciens ut fecerat in predictis, donec veniat ad 13^{am} diem, que sit dies Iovis, et tunc iterum, si quid in se mali senserit, emundet et tunc iterum corpus Christi recipiat dicendo:

---

18 Sir. 1:16, based on Proverbs 9:10.

with prayers and embellished with holy sacraments, which are Hosel, Iesel, etc. (4) that I may have the virtue and the grace which are needed to attain such a great vision, namely purity, innocence, clarity, wisdom, and piety, (5) love, sincerity, humility, determination, and good will, through you, who sits on high, to whom be praise, glory, and honor, forever and ever. Amen.

XCVII.

If you wish to know the sequence of these prayers, consider the sequence of the one hundred names of God in this book, because the prayers always begin with those. (2) And note, that those preceding sacred names of God: **Hosel, Iesel,** and the rest, must be said soon after beginning worship, and also in the beginning of any specific prayer.

XCVIII. Here begins the second purification for the Divine Vision.[142]

Thereupon, with the body purified and softened,[143] he that wishes to see the heavenly palace, we command him to keep himself most clean to be clothed with all virtues, (2) and he should always contemplate the Lord, and pray for the forgiveness of sins, for the Lord is just and must be feared, for if you don't fear him, you don't love him, as Solomon testified when he said: "The beginning of wisdom is the fear of the Lord,"[144] (3) Therefore, everyone should fear him, because nobody attains glory, or salvation, or the sight of God, of his own merit, without the grace of the savior.

(4) And again he should fast another twelve days on bread and water and nothing else, without any relaxation as he did before, until he comes to the thirteenth day, which should be a Thursday, and then again, if he perceives any evil in himself he should cleanse it, and then again he should receive the body of Christ, saying:

---

142 The instructions for the first purification are given in chapters li-lii.
143 Namely, the physical passions conquered.
144 Sir. 1:16, based on Proverbs 9:10. Compare *Key of Solomon*, chapter 1. http://esotericarchives.com/solomon/ksol.htm#chap1 (retrieved October 15, 2015)

(5) Oracio ante recepcionem Christi

"Tu, Domine Iesu Christe, salvator omnium, qui pro me, miserimo peccatore, et aliis in seculo viventibus voluisti corpus tuum salubriter immolare, (6) qui 5ª die, scilicet Iovis [vel] Cenacionis, beatos apostolos tuos de tuo precioso corpore et sanguine saciasti precipiens, ut in nomine tuo sancta mater ecclesia sacratissimum corpus tuum et sanguinem consecraret, ut fieret salus et vita animarum in te credencium. (7) Ego, licet indignus, te, Domine Iesu Christe, recipiens, sciens et confitens te Dominum meum et creatorem meum, quem in carne mea visurus sum ego ipse et non alius, quem expecto iudicem meum venturum, (8) concede michi propicius et in virtute huius sacri misterii, quod sicut corporeis oculis tuam spiritualem et corporalem potenciam ac eciam divinitatem visibiliter confiteor et agnosco per redempcionem huius sacratissimi corporis et sanguinis tui, (9) sic corpus meum clarificare et mundare digneris, ut abluto corpore te visibiliter cum tuis novem angelorum ordinibus me vivente mea possit anima collaudare, qui vivis et regnas Deus per omnia secula seculorum. Amen."

XCIX

Quo recepto recedas ad domum et taliter opus incipies.

Placacio divine maiestatis

Dices illa die Iovis semel psalterium et letaniam cum propriis eam sequentibus oracionibus. Post dices 25, 26, 31 et ibi addes:

(2) "Ut tu, Domine, per annunciacionem, concepcionem, nativitatem, circumcisionem, predicacionem, baptismum, resurreccionem, ascensionem beatissimi filii tui, Domini nostri Iesu Christi, (3) corpus meum clarificare et mundare digneris, ut abluto corpore te visibiliter cum tuis novem dictis angelorum ordinibus me vivente mea possit anima collaudare," (4)— conclusio:—"quoniam tu es Deus potens et super omnia misericors, qui

(5) Prayer before receiving Christ.

"You, O Lord Jesus Christ, the savior of all, who were willing to sacrifice your body, on behalf of me, a wretched sinner, and others living in the world, (6) you who on the fifth day, namely Thursday, the Last Supper, fed your blessed apostles with your precious body and blood, teaching them that they should consecrate your most holy body and blood in the name of the holy mother church, in order that it might be the salvation and life of the souls believing in you. (7) I, although unworthy to receive you, O Lord Jesus Christ, knowing and confessing you to be my Lord and my creator, whom I shall see, and no other, while my body lives, whom I await to judge me soon, (8) grant me your favor, and by the virtue of this sacred mystery, that as I am able to recognize visibly and acknowledge with my physical eyes your spiritual and physical power, and even your divinity, through the redemption[145] of this your most sacred body and blood, (9) so design to clarify and cleanse my body, that with my body being washed, my soul will able to praise you visibly, while I live, along with your nine orders of angels, you who lives and reigns, God, world without end. Amen."

XCIX.

Once this[146] has been received, you may retire to your house and begin the work in such a manner.

The placating of the Divine Majesty.

The same Thursday, you will say the psalter and litany with its special prayers following it. After that you will say 25, 26,[147] 31 then add: (2) "... that you, O Lord, by the annunciation, conception, birth, circumcision, proclamation, baptism,[148] resurrection, and ascension of your most blessed son, our Lord Jesus Christ, (3) deign to make my body lustrous and pure, that with my body washed pure, my soul may be able to praise you visibly, while I live, alongside your aforesaid nine orders of angels," (4) The conclusion: "Because

---

145 SSM: *receptionem* ("reception"), referring to the eucharist, which seems to fit better.
146 I.e. the Eucharist. SSM: The Body of Christ.
147 SSM: 28.
148 SSM adds: "fasting, dining, suffering."

vivis et regnas Deus in unitate et trinitate, Pater et Filius et Spiritus sanctus, et regnaturus es per infinita secula seculorum. Amen."

C *Separacio*

Ex nunc eris in loco concluso, ubi non sit frequentacio personarum, et qualibet die dices istas oraciones, que secuntur, cum precedentibus, que pertinent operanti, et cum hoc dices hec nomina, que secuntur. (2) "Agla, Monhon, Tetragramaton, Ely Deus, Ocleiste, Amphynethon, Lamyara, Ianemyer, Sadyon, Hely, Horlon, Porrenthimon, (3) Yelur, Gofgameli, Emanuel, On, Admyel, Honzmorb, Ioht, Hophob, Mesamarathon, Anethy, Eryona, Yuestre, Saday, Maloht, Sechce."

(4) Post hoc dices:

Oracio

"Deus meus, Pater omnipotens eterne potestatis, potens facere mundum de immundo conceptum semine, Primellus, Principium, Primogenitus, Sapiencia, Virtus, Sol, Splendor, Gloria, Pax, Lux, Panis, Os, (5) Verbum, Salus, Angelus, Sponsus, Propheta, Agnus, Ovis, Vitulus, Serpens, Aries, Leo, Vermis, exaudi propicius oraciones et invocaciones servi tui, ut in virtute horum sanctorum nominum tuorum corpus meum" et cetera.

(6) Postea dices ista alia nomina, que secuntur. "Elscha fortis, Abbadia iuste, Alpha et Ω piissime, Leiste dulcissime, Oristyon potentissime, Yeremon excellentissime, Hofbor excelse, Merkerpon adiutor, Elzephares

you, O God, are mighty and merciful over all, who lives and reigns, God in unity and trinity, Father, Son, and Holy Spirit, and will reign forever, world without end. Amen."[149]

C. Separation.

From this time on you should be in a place where access can be restricted, where people do not frequent, and each day say those prayers which follow, along with those preceding, which are pertinent to the work,[150] and with this you should say these names, which follow: (2) "Agla, Monhon, Tetragramaton, Ely Deus, Ocleiste, Amphynethon, Lamyara, Ianemyer, Sadyon, Hely, Horlon, Porrenthimon, (3) Yelur, Gofgameli, Emanuel, On, Admyel, Honzmorb, Ioht, Hophob, Mesamarathon, Anethy, Eryona, Yuestre, Saday, Maloht, Sechce."[151]

(4) After this, say:

Prayer.

"O my God, almighty Father, eternal power, who can make pure that which was conceived of unclean seed, Primellus, the Beginning, the First-Born, the Wisdom, the Virtue, the Sun, the Brilliance, the Glory, the Peace, the Light, the Bread,[152] the Mouth, (5) the Word, the Salvation, the Angel, the Bridegroom, the Prophet, the Lamb, the Sheep, the Calf, the Serpent, Aries, Leo, the Worm, hear clearly the propitious prayers and invocations of your servant, that through the power of your holy names, that with my body" etc.[153]

(6) Then say these additional names which follow: "Strong Elscha, just Abbadia, most pious Alpha and Omega, sweetest Leiste, most potent Oristyon, most excellent Yeremon, lofty Hofbor,[154] Merkerpon the helper, Elzephares the defender, Egyryon the protector, Pheta the generous, (7) hear

---

149 The wording of this prayer should be adapted to the situation; in this case, for the divine vision. See CII, and Veenstra 2012 pp. 166–167.
150 SSM adds: "and not to the priesthood."
151 Compare with similar lists of names of God in chapters C.2, CI.2–8.
152 GH following S. 3854 127r reads "Patris," but SSM L.4.f.17, Sl. 313, Sl. 3853 144r, and R all read "Panis," which is also consistent with BoO p. 35.
153 As in XCVIII.9.
154 So GH. Sl. 3854 127r reads "Hosbor," but see XCVI 1 and CI.4. SSM: Hospr; Sl. 3885: hostor.

defensor, Egyryon protector, Pheta largitor, (7) exaudi benigne deprecaciones servi tui, ut ex dono gracie tue per intercessiones beate genitricis tue virginis Marie et angelorum et archangelorum tuorum Michaelis, Gabrielis, Urielis et Raphaelis et omnium aliorum celestium angelorum (8) et apostolorum tuorum Petri et Pauli, Iohannis et Iacobi, Andree, Mathie, Symonis, Iude, Philippi, Thome, Bartholomei et Barnabe corpus meum" et cetera.

(9) Postea dices ista sequencia nomina Dei. "Ombonar ineffabilis, Stimulamathon in substancia invisibilis, Oryon inestimabilis, Erion inpermutabilis, Noymos clementissime, Pep incommensurabilis, Nathanatay incorruptibilis, Theon inmense, Ysiston gloriose, Porho tocius misericordie."[19]

(10) Postea dices hanc oracionem:

Oracio

"Respice humiliter preces humilis servi tui non aspiciens neque vindicans inennarrabiles iniquitates, quas contra te feci; quoniam, 'si iniquitates observaveris, quis sustinebit?' (11) Set tu, Domine, 'suscitans a terra inopem et de stercore erigens pauperem' in virtute sancte humilitatis et obediencie tue, sicut dicitur: (12) 'factus est obediens usque ad mortem'—et alibi: 'Ego autem humiliatus sum nimis'—quam pro peccatoribus humiliter pati atque recipere voluisti, sic preces meas placatus recipias—(13) quia confiteor et scio, quia tu es misericors tocius creature te firmiter invocantis, testante David et dicente: 'Cor contritum et humiliatum Deus non despicies,' (14) et alibi: 'Prope est Dominus omnibus invocantibus eum in veritate'—ut animam meam a tenebris corpusculi mei suscitare et a stercore peccatorum meorum erigere digneris, ut abluto corpore" et cetera.

(15) Et postea dices hec nomina hanc sequentem oracionem constituencia.

---

19 SSM: ... Eryon incomutabilis, Nomyx, clementissime, Pele, incommensurabilis, Nathanatoy incorruptibilis, Theon inmense, ysyston, gloriose, Porhe tocius misericordie

kindly the supplications of your servant, so that from your gift of grace through the intercession of your blessed mother, the virgin Mary, and of your angels and archangels Michael, Gabriel, Uriel, and Raphael, and all other celestial angels (8) and of your apostles Peter and Paul, John and Jacob, Andrew, Matthew, Simon, Jude, Philip, Thomas, Bartholomew, and Barnabus, that with my body ..." etc.[155]

(9) Then say these following names of God: "Ombonar ineffable, Stimulamathon in substance invisible, Oryon inestimable, Erion unchangeable, Noymos most merciful, Pep immeasurable, Nathanatay incorruptible, Theon immeasurable, Hysiston glorious, Porho altogether merciful."

(10) Then say this prayer:

Prayer.

"Look favorably on the prayers of your humble servant, not considering or punishing the many sins which I have committed against you; for, 'if you consider our sins, who could measure up?'[156] (11) But you, O Lord, 'raise up the needy from the dust, and the poor from the filth'[157] by virtue of holy humility and obedience to you, as it is said: (12) 'He became obedient even unto death'[158] and elsewhere: 'moreover I have been greatly humbled'[159]—which you humbly allowed and wished to receive for sinners, so may you favorably receive my prayers—(13) because I confess and know that you are merciful to all creatures who call upon you sincerely, which David testified when he said: 'A contrite and humbled heart, O God, you will not look down on,'[160] (14) and elsewhere: 'The Lord is nearby to all who faithfully call upon him'[161]— that you may deign to awaken my soul from the darkness of my body, and raise it up from the foulness of my sins, that with my body being washed" and so on.[162]

(15) And then say these names composed in the following prayer:

---

155 Adding your petition, as in XCVIII.9.
156 Ps. 129:3 (KJV 130:3).
157 Ps. 112:7 (KJV 113:7).
158 Phi. 2:8.
159 Ps. 115:1 (KJV 116:10).
160 Ps. 50:19 (KJV 51:17).
161 Ps. 144:18 (KJV 145:18).
162 As in XCVIII.9.

Nomina Dei vivi

"**Fothon**, celi et terre conditor; **Lethellete**, qui celum super altitudinem nubium extendisti; **Ysmas**, qui terram super aquas in sua stabilitate fundasti; (16) **Adonay**, qui mari terminum suum, quem preterire non poterit, tribuisti; **Hachionadabir**, qui Solem et Lunam et omnes stellas celi in summa arce collocasti; **Omytheon**, qui omnia in sapiencia fecisti; (17) **Hofga**, qui sexta die hominem ad ymaginem et similitudinem tuam creasti; **Leyndra**, qui Adam una cum Eva, quam sibi comitem dederas, in paradiso voluptatis collocasti, quos propter mandati tui prevaricacionem mox de paradiso eiecisti; **Nosulaceps**, qui victimam Abel conspexisti;

(18) **Tutheon**, qui mundum propter sui scelera in aqua diluvii perdidisti; **Gelemoht**, qui Noe et eos, qui cum eo erant in aqua diluvii, salvasti, unde genus humanum restituisti; (19) **Paraclitus**, qui Abrahe, servo tuo, sub triplici persona ad radicem Mambre aparuisti; **Occynonerion**, qui Enoch et Helyam ad pugnandum contra tirannum in celis rapuisti; **Ectothas**, qui Loth, servum tuum, de submersione Sodome et Gomorre misericorditer liberasti; (20) **Abracio**, qui Moysi, servo tuo, in medio rubi locutus fuisti in flamma ignis; **Anephenethon**, qui virgam Aaron frondere, florere et fructum producere fecisti; (21) **Abdon**, qui populum tuum de terra Egypti de captivitate potenter abduxisti; **Melthe**, qui, ut siccis pedibus transirent, per medium mare viam aperuisti; **Sother**, qui in monte Synay populo tuo per manum Moysi legem dedisti;

(22) **Usyrion**, qui populo scicienti de petra sicca nimias aquas exire fecisti; **Baruch**, qui Danielem prophetam de lacu leonum sanum et incolumem eripuisti; **Sporgongo**, qui tres pueros Sydrac, Misaac et Abdenago, qui sunt Ananyas, Azarias et Mysael, de camino ignis ardentis illesos abire

Names of the Living God.

"**Fothon**, creator of Heaven and Earth; **Lethelletus**, whereby you stretched out Heaven above the height of the clouds; **Ysmas**, whereby you set the lands firmly upon the waters; (16) **Adonay**, whereby you separated the sea from her bounds, which she is not able to go beyond; **Hachionadabir**, whereby you arranged the Sun and Moon and all the stars in the highest height of Heaven; **Omytheon**, whereby you made all things in wisdom;[163] (17) **Hofga**, Whereby on the sixth day you created mankind in your own image and likeness; **Leyndra**, whereby you put Adam into the Paradise of pleasure, together with Eve, whom you gave as his companion, whereby you also soon expelled them from Paradise for transgressing your commandment; **Nosulaceps**, whereby you accepted Abel's offering;

(18) **Tutheon**, whereby you caused a flood of water to destroy the world, on account of its corruption; **Gelemoht**, whereby you saved Noah, and those who were with him, from the destruction of the flood, and whereby you restored mankind; (19) **Paraclitus**, whereby you appeared to Abraham, your servant, in the guise of three persons, in the plains of Mamre;[164] **Occynonerion**, whereby you took Enoch and Elijah to Heaven for fighting against the tyrant;[165] **Ectothas**, whereby Lot, your servant, was mercifully spared from the destruction of Sodom and Gomorrah;[166] (20) **Abracio**, whereby you spoke to Moses, your servant, in the midst of the burning bush; **Anephenethon**, whereby you made the staff of Aaron sprout leaves and produce fruit;[167] (21) **Abdon**, whereby you forcefully led your people out of the land of Egypt, and out of captivity; **Melthe**, whereby you opened a path through the middle of the sea, allowing them to cross with dry feet; **Sother**, whereby you gave your people the Law at Mount Sinai, through the hand of Moses;

(22) **Usyrion**, whereby you produced much water for your thirsty people, from a dry rock; **Baruch**, whereby you released the prophet Daniel from lions' den safe and unharmed;[168] **Sporgongo**, whereby the three children Shadrach, Meshach, and Abedenego, who were Hananiah, Azariah and

---

163 Ps. 103:24 (KJV 104:24).
164 Gen. 18:1–2.
165 Gen. 5:24; II Kings 2:11.
166 Gen 19.
167 Num. 17:8.
168 Dan. 6.

fecisti; (23) **Genouem,** qui Susannam bonam fiduciam atque spem in te habentem de falso crimine falsorum iudicum liberasti; **Messias,** qui Ionam prophetam in ventre ceti tribus diebus et tribus noctibus commorantem incolumem conservasti; (24) **Pantheon,** qui David prophetam de manibus Golie invictum evadere fecisti; Deus iustus, fortis et paciens, **agyos, Otheos, Hiskyros, athanathos, eleyson ymas, Christus,** Deus fortis, omnipotens et immortalis, (25) Iesus Nazarenus, et multum misericors, qui solum ex vera cordis contricione peccatorem mundificas, exaudi clemens et propicius oraciones servi tui, (26) quas in virtute sublimitatis tue profero, ut per misericordiam tuam <et> graciam, quam sanctis tuis tribuisti, michi largiri digneris.

(27) Descendat ergo, Domine, super me, famulum tuum, quamvis multis criminibus irretitum tamen a te creatum, virtus Spiritus sancti, que meorum indulgenciam faciat peccatorum, ut ex rore celesti mei corpusculi macule deleantur, ut abluto corpore" et cetera.

(28) Hec oracio supradicta debet pro ferri in omni periculo, quoniam sanos custodit, infirmos sanat, peccata relaxat, iratos pacificat, amicicias nutrit, (29) desperantes confortat, pauperes fovet, iram Domini mitigat, omnes tribulaciones et perversitates vincit, tempestates fugat, incantaciones solvit, spiritus constringit et ligat. (30) Debet proferri ieiuno stomacho, flexis genibus cum devocione maxima, et eius abstinencia est, quod operans debet esse humilis, paciens et pudicus. (31) Taliter igitur diebus Veneris, sabbati, Dominico, Lune, Martis, Mercurii sequentibus hec omnia, et ter in qualibet die, scilicet mane, meridie et sero, integre recitabis.

CI Perfeccio operis

Die vero Iovis sumo mane dicat ut dixerat in predictis et tunc super cineres de fece mundatos de feno cubile faciat, et in circuitu lecti sint in cineribus scripta centum nomina Dei.

Mishael, were able to come forth uninjured from the fiery furnace;[169] (23) **Genovem**, whereby the good and faithful Susanna, having hope in you, was freed from false accusations of false judges; **Messias**, whereby you preserved the prophet Jonah unharmed for three days and three nights in the stomach of a whale; (24) **Pantheon**, whereby you made the prophet David escape the hands of Goliath unconquered;[170] O Just God, strong and patient, **Agios, Iskiros, Athanatos, Eleyson ymas, Christus**, strong God, all-powerful and immortal, (25) Jesus of Nazareth, most merciful, who cleanses us of sins only through a truly contrite heart, O merciful and generous one, hear the prayers of your servant, (26) which I offer through the virtue of your sublimity, so that through your mercy, you would deign to grant to me the grace which you have granted to your saints.

(27) Therefore, O Lord, may the power of the Holy Spirit descend upon me, your servant, in spite of my many faults, yet created by you, who may show leniency for my sins, that the stains of my body are erased by the heavenly dew, that my body being washed" etc.

(28) This above-mentioned prayer should used in all dangers, because it protects the health, cures the sick, forgives sins, calms anger, nurtures friendship, (29) comforts those despairing, warms the poor, mitigates the wrath of the Lord, conquers all troubles and perversities, drives away storms, breaks enchantments, and constrains and binds spirits. (30) It should be said after fasting and abstinence, kneeling with the greatest devotion, and the one who performs it must be humble, patient, and chaste. (31) Therefore you should recite all of these in their entirety in the same way on the following Friday, Saturday, Sunday, Monday, Tuesday, and Wednesday, and three times every day, namely in the morning, at noon, and at night.

CI. The Completion of the Work.

On Thursday begin in the morning; saying as you said on the preceding, and then you should make a bed of hay, on top of ashes which you should make clean from the dregs, and around the bed, in the ashes, should be written the one hundred names of God.[171]

---

169 Dan. 3.25.
170 1 Sam. 17.
171 In SSM, the seventy-two letters from the Seal of God are used instead.

(2) 100 Dei vivi nomina

1. Agla, 2. Monon, 3. Tetragramaton, 4. Ely Deus, 5. Ocleiste, 6. Amphynethon, 7. Lamyara, 8. Ianemyer, 9. Sadyon, 10. Hely, 11. Horlon, 12. Porrenthimon, 13. Ihelur, (3) 14. Gofgameli, 15. Emanuel, 16. On, 17. Admyhel, 18. Honzmorb, 19. Ioht, 20. Hofob, 21. Mesamarathon, 22. Anethy, 23. Eryhona, 24. Iuestre, 25. Saday, 26. Maloht, 27. Sechce, 28. Elscha, (4) 29. Abbadia, 30. Alpha et Ω, 31. Leiste, 32. Oristion, 33. Jeremon, 34. Hofbor, 35. Merkerpon, 36. Elzephares, 37. Egyrion, 38. Pheta, 39. Hombonar, 40. Stimulamathon, 41. Orion, 42. Eryon, (5) 43. Noymos, 44. Pep, 45. Nathanathay, 46. Theon, 47. Ysiston, 48. Porho, 49. Fothon, 50. Letellethe, 51. Ysmas, 52. Adonay, 53. Achionadabir, 54. Omytheon, 55. Hofga, 56. Leyndra, (6) 57. Nosulaceps, 58. Tutheon, 59. Gelemoht, 60. Paraclitus, 61. Occynoneryon, 62. Ecthothas, 63. Abracio, 64. Anephenethon, 65. Abdon, 66. Melthe, 67. Sother, 68. Usirion, 69. Baruch, (7) 70. Sporgongo, 71. Genouem, 72. Messias, 73. Pantheon, 74. Zabuather, 75. Rabarmas, 76. Yschiros, 77. Kyrios, 78. Gelon, 79. Hel, 80. Techel, 81. Nothi, 82. Ymeynlethon, 83. Karex, 84. Sabaoth, (8) 85. Sellah, 86. Cirrhos, 87. Opiron, 88. Nomygon, 89. Orihel, 90. Theos, 91. Va, 92. Horha, 93. Christus, 94. Hospesk, 95. Gofgar, 96. Occynnomos, 97. Elyorem, 98. Heloy, 99. Archima, 100. Rabur.

(9) Quo facto comedat, et quando comederit, opus istud ita incipiat. Accipiat aquam claram fontis frigidam, de qua se abluat dicens:

(10) "Domine, sancte Pater, omnipotens, eterne Deus, cuius ante creacionem seculi Spiritus ferebatur super aquas, qui in mundi creacione una cum aliis elementis eas benedictas fecisti, (11) qui populo sicienti has in alimento dedisti, et ut sordide mundi exteriores macule per eas lavarentur, qui in flumine Iordanis per Iohannem baptistam baptizari voluisti, (12) ut per misterium sacratissimi corporis tui flumina omnium aquarum tua benediccione crescerent, ut sicut per eas exteriora lavantur, (13) ita interiora per ipsas et Spiritum sanctum lavarentur peccata testante propheta David et dicente: 'Asparges me, Domine, ysopo, et mundabor. Lavabis me, et super nivem dealbabor,' (14) qui beatis apostolis tuis in huius sacri commemoracione misterii pedes eorum lavasti, qui nobis ad saturacionem

(2) The 100 Names of the Living God.

1. Agla, 2. Monon, 3. Tetragramaton, 4. Ely Deus, 5. Ocleiste, 6. Amphynethon, 7. Lamyara, 8. Ianemyer, 9. Sadyon, 10. Hely, 11. Horlon, 12. Porrenthimon, 13. Ihelur, (3) 14. Gofgameli, 15. Emanuel, 16. On, 17. Admyhel, 18. Honzmorb, 19. Ioht, 20. Hofob, 21. Mesamarathon, 22. Anethy, 23. Eryhona, 24. Iuestre, 25. Saday, 26. Maloht, 27. Sechce, 28. Elscha, (4) 29. Abbadia, 30. Alpha et Ω, 31. Leiste, 32. Oristion, 33. Jeremon, 34. Hofbor, 35. Merkerpon, 36. Elzephares, 37. Egyrion, 38. Pheta, 39. Hombonar, 40. Stimulamathon, 41. Orion, 42. Eryon, (5) 43. Noymos, 44. Pep [*Pele?], 45. Nathanathay, 46. Theon, 47. Ysiston, 48. Porho, 49. Fothon, 50. Letellethe, 51. Ysmas, 52. Adonay, 53. Achionadabir, 54. Omytheon, 55. Hofga, 56. Leyndra, (6) 57. Nosulaceps, 58. Tutheon, 59. Gelemoht, 60. Paraclitus, 61. Occynoneryon, 62. Ecthothas, 63. Abracio, 64. Anephenethon, 65. Abdon, 66. Melthe, 67. Sother, 68. Usirion, 69. Baruch, (7) 70. Sporgongo, 71. Genouem, 72. Messias, 73. Pantheon, 74. Zabuather, 75. Rabarmas, 76. Yschiros, 77. Kyrios, 78. Gelon, 79. Hel, 80. Techel, 81. Nothi, 82. Ymeynlethon, 83. Karex, 84. Sabaoth, (8) 85. Sellah, 86. Cirrhos, 87. Opiron, 88. Nomygon, 89. Orihel, 90. Theos, 91. Va, 92. Horha, 93. Christus, 94. Hospesk, 95. Gofgar, 96. Occynnomos, 97. Elyorem, 98. Heloy, 99. Archima, 100. Rabur.

(9) When this has been done, he should eat, and after eating, he should begin the work as follows: He should take clear cold spring water, and wash himself, saying:

(10) "O Lord, holy Father, almighty and eternal God, whose spirit moved over the waters before the creation of the world, who in the creation of the world, made water blessed with the other elements, (11) who gave water to the thirsty people for their nourishment, and in order that they could wash their outward stains clean with it, who wished to be baptized in the river Jordan by John the Baptist, (12) in order that through the mystery of your most sacred body the rivers of all waters will increase with your blessing, so that, even as we are washed on the outside by it, and by the Holy Spirit, (13) so too will we be washed inside and cleansed of our sins, as the prophet David testified when he said: 'Sprinkle me, O Lord, with hyssop, and I will be clean; wash me, and I will be whiter than snow,' (14) which in remembrance of this sacred mystery, you washed the feet of your blessed apostles,[172] who offered us water

---

172 See John 13:12.

anime aquam de tuo precioso latere in potum tribuisti et propter nos lancea latus acriter perforari voluisti, concede propicius, (15) quod sicut huius mei miseri corpusculi per hanc aquam exteriora lavantur, sic per virtutem tui sacri baptismatis, quod in me nomine tuo recepi, super me tue future gracie rorem descendere concedas, per quam mea interiora laventur peccata, ut abluto corpore" et cetera.

(16) Et scias, quod nullus vacans circa terrena potest hoc facere, quia anima racione obscenitatis terrene a divinis secretis est penitus sequestrata et ideo cum difficultate intelligit. (17) Tamen secundum quod caro magis vult operacionibus anime consentire, cicius intelligit et clarius. (18) Et ideo illi, qui sciencias inveniebant, magis in locis secretis habitabant, quia nolebant per temptaciones carnales a suis operacionibus sequestrari. (19) Nec non si aliquis operari voluerit eciam pro acquisicione parcium, eum convenit a terrenis sequestrari. Pro acquisitione tocius multo magis forciusque debet operans terre dimittere vanitatem.

(20) Tunc indutus cilicio et nigris vestibus chorum[20] intret, in quo sedeat. Tunc incipiat psalterium cum letania et oracionibus propriis et aliis, ut predixi, et cum totum compleverit, dicat hec nomina, que secuntur. (21) "Zabuather, Rabarmas, Yskiros, Kyrios, Gelon, Hel, Techel, Nothi, Ymeinlethon, Karex, Sabaoth, Sella, Chiros, Opiron, Nomygon, Oriel, Theos, Ya."

(22) Oracio

"Deus fortis et potens in prelio, rex eterne glorie, cuius claritatis dulcedine pleni sunt celi et terra, quem angeli et archangeli tremunt et colunt laudando et dicunt: (23) 'Sanctus, sanctus, sanctus Dominus Deus Sabaoth; pleni sunt celi et terra gloria tua. Ossanna in excelsis,'

---

20 SSM: thorum.

to drink from your precious side for quenching the thirst in our souls, and for our sakes allowed the lance to savagely pierce your side, graciously grant (15) that as this water washes my wretched body outwardly, so too by virtue of your sacred baptism, which I have received in your name, grant that the dew of your grace may descend upon me, by which my inner faults may be washed away, that my body being washed," etc.

(16) And you should know, that nobody who is idle with worldly things can attain to this work, for the soul, because of the obscenity of worldly things, is isolated inwardly from divine secrets, and therefore it understands them with difficulty. (17) Yet when the flesh is willing to consent with the operations of the soul, it understands more quickly and more clearly. (18) And therefore those who first discovered this knowledge lived more in hidden places, because they were unwilling to let carnal temptations isolate them from their operations. (19) And certainly if anybody has determined to work to acquire only parts of this science, should isolate himself from worldly things. And how much more strongly should he dismiss the emptiness of the world for the sake of performing the whole of it.

(20) Then he should put on a sackcloth[173] and black garments, then enter the choir,[174] in which he should sit. Then he should begin the Psalter with the litany, and with the proper prayers and the rest as mentioned before, and when all is complete, he should say these names which follow: (21) "Zabuather, Rabarmas, Yskiros, Kyrios, Gelon, Hel, Techel, Nothi, Ymeinlethon, Karex, Sabaoth, Sella, Chiros, Opiron, Nomygon, Oriel, Theos, Ya."[175]

(22) Prayer.

"O mighty God, and powerful in battle, and eternally glorious king, the sweetness of whose clarity fills Heaven and Earth, before whom the angels and archangels tremble and praise, saying: (23) 'Holy, Holy, Holy, Lord God of hosts, Heaven and Earth are full of your glory. Hosannah in the highest,'

---

173 I.e. Cilice.
174 SSM: *thorum* ("bed").
175 Cp. CI.7 (names 74 ff.). SSM L.4.f.18-19: Zabuather, <u>rabarbas</u>, yskyros, kyryos, gelon, el, techel, <u>nochy</u>, <u>ymeymlethon</u>, karex, sabaoth, <u>sellah</u>, <u>cyrros</u>, <u>opron</u>, nomygon, oryel, theos, ya.

qui pro dominacione[21] humani generis revocanda de celis ad terram descendisti.

(24) **Orha**, qui per Gabrielem beate Marie virgini, genetrici tue, nuncium tue incarnacionis in templo Ierusalem premisisti.

Christus, qui sicut sol per vitrum in eius utero et sine corupcionis contagio obumbrasti.

(25) **Hospesk**, qui in manibus Ioseph virgam siccam florere fecisti.

Gofgar, qui adventus tui per Iohannem baptistam populo tuo Israel testimonium et precognicionem misisti, (26) predicandaque dicta erant de te per prophetas, qui nativitatis tue tuis sanctis hominibus in tenebris stantibus lumen misisti, per quod tuum sanctum adventum cognoverunt.

(27) **Occynnomos**, qui tribus regibus te adorare volentibus, Caspar, Melchior, Balthasar, stellam previam transmisisti et eorum munera recepisti te verum Deum et hominem mortalem eis esse demonstrans (28) et eis per angelum tuum falsitatem Herodis in sompnis manifestans, qui beatos innocentes pro tuo nomine cruciatos in celi palacio sublimiter coronasti.

(29) **Eliorem**, qui in templo Salomonis in manibus Symeonis Domino presentatus ipsi Symeoni dedisti cognicionis effectum, ut asserit dicens: 'Nunc dimittis servum tuum, Domine, in pace, (30) quia viderunt oculi mei salutare tuum, quod parasti ante faciem omnium populorum lumen ad revelacionem gencium et gloriam plebis tue Israel.'

Heloy, qui ad architriclini nupcias aquam in vinum convertisti.

(31) **Archima**, qui 32 annis populo tuo fidem catholicam predicasti, qui Petrum, Iacobum et Iohannem, Bartholomeum, Thomam et ceteros discipulos in sciencia et gracia perfectos condidisti.

(32) **Rabur**, qui 40 dierum spacio in deserto ieiunasti et a demone temptatus es, qui eciam beate Marie Magdalene super pedes tuos flenti

---

21 Sl. 3885, SSM: dampnatione.

which for the sake of mastery to redeem mankind[176] you descended from the heavens to Earth.

(24) **Orha**, whereby you sent ahead Gabriel to the temple at Jerusalem, to announce to the blessed virgin Mary, your mother, your incarnation.

Christ, whereby you overshadowed yourself in her womb, like the sun shining through glass, and without the touch of corruption.

(25) **Hospesk**, whereby you made the dry staff sprout flowers in the hands of Joseph.[177]

Gofgar, whereby you sent foreknowledge and testimony of your arrival through John the Baptist to your people Israel, (26) and the things preached about you by the prophets, and of your birth, whereby you sent a light to your holy ones standing in darkness, by which they recognized your holy arrival.

(27) **Occynnomos**, whereby you sent a star to lead the three kings, Caspar, Melchior, Balthazar, wishing to honor you, and you received their gifts, showing yourself to them to be true God and mortal man (28) and you revealed to them through your angel, in a dream, the deception of Herod, and whereby in the heavenly palace you sublimely crowned the blessed innocent persons tormented on behalf of your name.

(29) **Eliorem**, whereby when Jesus was being presented to the Lord in the temple of Solomon, brought realization to Simeon, when he took him up in his arms,[178] as he asserts saying: 'Now dismiss your servant in peace, O Lord, (30) because my eyes have seen your salvation, which you have prepared before the face of all peoples: A light to the revelation of the Gentiles, and the glory to your people Israel.'[179]

Heloy, whereby you turned water into wine at the wedding of a certain person hosting a feast.

(31) **Archima**, whereby for thirty-two years you preached to your people the catholic faith, whereby you preserved the knowledge in Peter, Jacob and John, Bartholomew, Thomas and the other disciples, and with perfect grace.

(32) **Rabur**, Whereby you fasted for the space of forty days in the desert, and were tempted by the demon; whereby also you forgave the sins of the blessed Mary Magdalen weeping most bitterly over your feet, and dry-

---

176 Sl. 3885, SSM: for the sake of redeeming mankind from damnation.
177 See the expanded infancy narrative in the apocryphal Gospel of James.
178 See Luke 2:25 ff.
179 Luke 2:29-32.

amarissime et capillis tergenti et unguenti sua dulcissime peccata remisisti (33) et Lazarum, fratrem suum, quatriduanum mortuum a mortuis suscitasti et ceco nato visum tribuisti et propter nos corpus tuum immolari, detrahi, ferociter accipi, turpiter iudicari ac eciam blasphemari, duris corrigiis amariter flagellari, (34) alapis et sputis vexari, spinis coronari, in cruce affigi, clavis acutis pedes et manus perforari, felle et aceto potari, lancea latus aperiri, et in sepulcro poni et a militibus custodiri voluisti, (35) qui per summam tuam potenciam ac signo tue sancte crucis, de quo meis me signo manibus †, in nomine Patris et Filii et Spiritus sancti scilicet, portas ereas confregisti et amicos tuos de tenebrosis locis inferni eripuisti. (36) Item, Domine, per fidem et credenciam, quam in hiis sanctis misteriis confiteor et scio et habeo, ita et animam meam a corporis mei tenebris eripias, (37) ut indestructo corpore te visibiliter cum tuis novem angelorum ordinibus me vivente mea possit anima collaudare, aspicere et glorificare. (38) Tu igitur, Domine, qui tercia die resurrexisti a mortuis et resurreccionem per angelum Marie Magdalene, [Marie] Iacobi et Salomee et tuis discipulis revelasti (39) et beato Thome tua vulnera demonstrasti et post trium dierum spacium ad celos ascendisti, unde discipulis tuis Spiritum sanctum misisti et eis pacem tuam dedisti.

(40) Tu eciam, Domine, Paulo, apostolo tuo, atque Iohanni evangeliste secreta demonstrasti et beato Stephano, dum lapidabatur, celos aperuisti, (41) ut asserit se vidisse tuam corporalibus oculis maiestatem dicens: 'Ecce video celos apertos et Filium hominis stantem a dextris virtutis Dei,' (42) qui martiribus tuis tormenta pacienter recipere concessisti, qui venturus es iudicare vivos et mortuos et seculum per ignem, respice super me et exaudi preces meas, (43) ut per graciam tuam et virtutem sanctorum nominum

ing them with her hair, and anointing them most sweetly; (33) and you woke Lazarus, her brother, after he had been dead for four days, and you gave sight to one who was born blind, and for our sake you gave your body to be sacrificed, and allowed yourself to be dragged away, viciously taken, shamefully judged and even blasphemed, and savagely whipped with hard lashes, (34) abused with slaps and spitting, crowned with thorns, fastened to the cross with sharp nails piercing your hands and feet, given gall and vinegar to drink, pierced in the side with a lance, and placed in a grave and guarded by soldiers, (35) which through your most high power, and with the sign of your holy cross, the sign of which I make now with my own hands ✝, In the name of the Father, and of the Son, and of the Holy Spirit, that is to say, you have shattered the gates of bronze,[180] and rescued your friends from the darkness of hell. (36) Likewise, O Lord, through the faith and belief in these holy mysteries which I confess and know and have, and so snatch away my soul from the darkness of my body, (37) in order that, with an indestructible[181] body, my soul is able to praise you visibly, along with your nine orders of angels, that my soul is able to praise you, look upon you, and glorify you while I am yet alive. (38) Therefore, O Lord, who on the third day appeared again from the dead, and you revealed your resurrection through an angel to Mary Magdalen, [Mary the mother of] James and Salome,[182] and your disciples (39) and showed your wounds to saint Thomas, and after the space of three days[183] you ascended to Heaven, from which you sent the Holy Spirit to your disciples, and gave your peace to them.

(40) You also, O Lord, showed the secrets to Paul, your apostle, and John the Evangelist, and Saint Stephen, to whom you opened up the Heavens as he was being stoned, (41) as he asserts having seen your greatness with his physical eyes, saying: 'Behold I see the heavens opening up, and the Son of Man standing at the right hand of the power of God,'[184] (42) and you enabled him to patiently endure the torture, as the other martyrs, you who will soon come to judge the living and the dead and the world through fire. Look upon me and hear my prayers, (43) so that, through your grace and the virtue of your

---

180 Ps. 106:16 (Ps. 107:16 in the KJV).
181 Sl. 3885: *destructo* ("destructible"), which is also consistent with J.
182 See Mark 16:1.
183 Sl. 313 and SSM read "40 days," which is consistent with the biblical account in Acts 1:3.
184 Acts 7:55.

tuorum animam meam a tenebris mei corpusculi suscitare et a stercore peccatorum meorum erigere digneris, (44) quia in te facio consummacionem vite mee, Deus meus, **Hto exor abalay. qci. ystalgaouofularite kspfyomomanaremiarelatedacononaoyleyot**, qui dixisti in cruce: 'Consummatum est.'"

(45) Tunc dormiat et de cetero non loquatur, et sic fiet, quod videbit celeste palacium et maiestatem in gloria sua, ordines angelorum et agmina spirituum beatorum. (46) Set dicet aliquis: 'Cum Dominus dicat: "Non videbit me homo et vivet," sequitur ergo, quod si quis Deum videat, oportet, quod in corpore moriatur. (47) Ergo de cetero usque ad diem iudicii non resurget, quia nemo bis corpore moritur.' Set falsum est, quod quis in corpore in visione divina moriatur, set spiritus in celo rapitur, et corpus in terra cibo angelico reficitur. (48) Nam de multis raptis in spiritu legitur, quibus multa secreta celesti a fuerunt revelata, et eciam in passione Domini nostri Iesu Christi multa corpora resurrexerunt, ut legitur.

(49) Operans debet esse in voluntate operis desiderans et mundatus ab omni sorde penitus, et quanto plus pacietur, tanto plus optinebit, (50) quia si superior, id est Christus, pro suis subditis et inferioribus voluit pati, ut eos in conspectu suo et gloria feliciter collocaret, multo forcius inferior debet pro se ipso pati, (51) ut possit placere suo Domino, quoniam nisi cum difficultate habebitur divina visio et cum puritate perfecta, quia non est super ipsum coaccio immo preces, et eciam cum difficultate habetur, (52) quia Dominus dedit terram homini et cognicionem sue legis testante David et dicente: "Celum celi Domino terram autem dedit filiis hominum." (53) Alibi: "Attendite, popule meus, legem meam.' Et quia 'fides non habet

holy names, you may awaken my soul from the darkness of my meager body, and deign to raise it up from the filth of my sins, (44) because in you I make my life complete, O my God, **Hto exor abalay. qci. ystalgaouofularite ksp fyomomanaremiarelatedacononaoyleyot**,[185] you who said on the cross: 'It is finished.'"

(45) Then he should sleep, speaking to no one, and thus it will happen, that he will see the heavenly palace, and the greatness of his glory, the orders of angels and the multitudes of blessed spirits. (46) But some may say: "When Lord says, 'no one can see me and live,'[186] it follows therefore, that if one sees God, the body must die. (47) Therefore he will not rise up again until the day of the judgment, because nobody's body dies twice." But it is not true, that one's body must die in the divine vision, because the spirit is carried up to Heaven, and the body is sustained on Earth with angelic food. (48) For we read of many who are carried up in spirit, to whom many celestial secrets are revealed, and even during the passion of our Lord Jesus Christ, many bodies were raised again, as it is written.[187]

(49) The operator must have a great will to perform the work, and must be cleansed inwardly from all filth, and the more he endures,[188] the more he will achieve, (50) because if our superior, namely Christ, allowed himself to suffer on behalf of his inferiors and subjects, in order to glorify them in his sight, even more strongly should the inferiors suffer on their own behalf, (51) in order to please their Lord, because the divine vision cannot be attained without difficulty and perfect purity, because a superior cannot be coerced, but rather entreated, and even then is only achieved with difficulty, (52) because the Lord has given the Earth to mankind, and recognition of his law, as David testified when he said, "Heaven and all of the celestial realm are the Lord's, but the Earth he has given to the children of men."[189] (53) And elsewhere, "Pay heed, O my people, to my law."[190] And "because faith has no

---

185 SSM: T. o. e. x. o. r. a. b. a. ¶layqtiyst. ¶Algaonosu. ¶laryceksp. ¶fyomemana. ¶Renugarel. ¶Atedatono. ¶Naoyleyot

186 Exodus 33:20.

187 Matt. 27:52. This section defending the possibility of a divine vision is not found in SSM, and another indication that it was a later addition in reaction to the actions of Pope John XXII.

188 Or "suffers."

189 Ps. 115:16 (KJV).

190 Ps. 78:1 (KJV)

meritum, ubi racio prebet exemplum," ideo homini difficillimum est cognoscere divinam maiestatem.

(54) In hoc opere non debet homo cogitare de morte, quia virtute oracionum et virtute Dei, in quo totaliter habet fiduciam, corpus efficitur quasi spirituale et saturatur cibo celesti, (55) sicut fiunt pulli corvorum, quibus misericordia succurrit Dei testante David et dicente: "Qui dat iumentis escam ipsorum et pullis corvorum invocantibus eum."

(56) Set cavendum est operanti, ne sit in peccato mortali, quia de cetero esset insanus, et causa est, quia intellectus procedit a parte anime, que intendit videre in quo delectatur, (57) et cum non videt id delectabiliter propter impedimentum peccati, de cetero ad nil aliud cogitabit, et sic in corpore non erit humana racionabilitas. (58) Et similiter videmus in pluribus, quod inanimati efficiuntur eo, quod intellectus procedens a parte anime non pervenit ad optata. (59) Concedat ergo nobis divina virtus graciam visionis, qui in trinitate vivit et regnat per omnia secula seculorum. Amen.

CII De capitulis primi libri

Divina visione cathezizata de cognicione potestatis divine, de absolucione peccatorum, de confirmacione non irruendi in peccatum mortale, de redempcione trium animarum de purgatorio est cathezizandum, (2) quoniam si aliquid istorum 4 volueris, fac sicut dictum est de divina visione mutando verumptamen peticionem visionis in peticionem cognicionis potestatis divine (3) vel absolucionis peccatorum vel confirmacionis in gracia immobiliter vel redempcionis trium animarum de purgatorio, set sic procul dubio similiter et adhuc facilius optinebis.

value, if human reasoning can provide experimental proof,"[191] for that reason it is most difficult for one to perceive the Divine Majesty.

(54) In this work one must not think about death, because with the virtue of prayer and the virtue of God, in whom he has placed all his trust, the body becomes like a spiritual body, and is nourished by heavenly food, (55) as young ravens are, when nourished by the mercy of God, as David testified when he said, "he gives his food to beasts, and to young ravens who cry out."[192]

(56) But the operator must beware, lest he is in mortal sin, because if so, he will go insane, and the cause is that, comprehension comes from part of the soul, which strives to see what it delights in, (57) and when he doesn't see it because of the hindrance of sin, henceforth will think of nothing else, and so the body will have no human reasoning. (58) And similarly we see many who become inanimate thereby, because the comprehension coming from part of the soul has not reached its wishes. (59) May the Divine Power therefore grant us the grace to achieve the divine vision, who lives and reigns in trinity through all the ages of the ages. Amen.

CII. *The topics of the first book.*

Having examined the divine vision, we have also examined understanding of divine power, the absolution of sins, confirmation against mortal sin, and the redemption of three souls from purgatory, (2) because if you wish to accomplish any of those four, do as said regarding the divine vision, but simply change the petition to "understanding of divine power (3) or "absolution of sins" or "confirmation in perpetual grace" or "the redemption of three souls from purgatory," and so without doubt you will more easily achieve them similarly.

---

191 St. Gregory, Homilies on the Gospels, number 26. Also quoted by Thomas Aquinas in *Summa Theologica* question 1, art. 8.
192 Ps. 147:6 (KJV).

(4) Et nota, quod, si vis, in omnibus predictis potes qualibet die dicere predictos 8 terminos cum illis 10 oracionibus, que sunt 23, 24, 25, 26, 27, 28, 29, 30, 31, 32, (5) quia in eis non oportet respicere diem neque lunacionem neque de necessitate horam, licet presertim circa mane, circa terciam circaque meridiem proferantur, (6) unde iste oraciones reducunt in bonum quicquid homo erravit per fragilitatem in operacione, et quanto plus et frequencius dicuntur, tanto magis erratum corrigitur et errandum prohibetur.

CIII Incipit secundus tractatus libri sacri.

Expleto primo tractatu huius libri sacri et Domini secreti subditur secundus, qui, sicut primus 6 capitula habebat, de quibus Hely gracia est desertum, ita iste 27 habet, scilicet hec:

(2) De cognicione celorum;

De cognicione angelorum cuiuslibet celi;

De cognicione cuiuslibet angeli et nominis et potestatis eius;

De cognicione sigillorum cuiuslibet angeli et virtutis eorum;

(3) De cognicione superiorum cuiuslibet angeli;

De cognicione officii cuiuslibet angeli;

De invocacione et associacione cuiuslibet angeli;

De impetracione voluntatis per quemlibet angelum;

(4) De impetracione omnium sciencarum;

De hora mortis scienda;

De omnibus presentibus, preteritis et futuris sciendis;

De cognicione planetarum et stellarum;

(5) De cognicione virtutum planetarum et stellarum et quid habent influere;

De influenciis planetarum [et stellarum] mutandis;

De mutacione noctis in diem et diei in noctem;

(6) De cognicione spirituum ignis et nominum et superiorum et sigillorum et potestatum et virtutum eorum;

(4) And note that, if you wish, for all those preceding things, on any day you can say the preceding eight *Termini* (or "ends") with these ten prayers, which are 23, 24, 25, 26, 27, 28, 29, 30, 31, 32 (5) because with them it is not necessary to consider the day of the week, nor the lunation, nor the hour; it is permitted to offer them especially in the morning, around terce, and around noon, (6) whereby any faults in the operation can be corrected by these prayers, and the more times and more often they are said, the better the error will be corrected and further errors prevented.

CIII. Here begins the Second Treatise of the Sacred Book.

Having completed the first treatise of this Sacred Book and secrets of the Lord, here follows the second, which, just as the first had six topics completed with the grace of HELY, so this one has twenty-seven topics as follows:

1. (2) Concerning the knowledge of the Heavens;
2. Concerning the knowledge of the angels of each of the Heavens;
3. Concerning the knowledge of each angel's name and powers;
4. Concerning the knowledge of the seals of each angel, and their virtues;
5. (3) Concerning the knowledge of the superiors of each angel;
6. To know the office of any angel;
7. Regarding the invocation of any angel, and associating with them;
8. To obtain your wishes through any angel;
(4) 9. To obtain all knowledge;
10. To know the hour of death;
11. To know all things past, present, and future;
12. To know the planets and stars;
(5) 13. To know the virtues of the planets and stars and their influences;
14. To change the influences of the planets [and stars];
15. To change night into day and day into night;
(6) 16. To know the spirits of the fire, their names, superiors, seals, powers, and virtues;

De cognicione spirituum et animalium aeris; De cognicione nominum et virtutum et superiorum eorum;

(7) De cognicione sigillorum et virtutum eorum;

De cognicione mixtionis et transmutacionis elementorum et corporum ex hiis mixtorum;

(8) De cognicione omnium herbarum et plantarum et omnium animalium existencium super terram et virtutum eorum;

De cognicione humane nature et omnium factorum hominum, que sunt abscondita et ignota;

(9) De cognicione aquaticorum spirituum et animalium et virtutum eorum et superiorum eorum;

De cognicione terrenorum et infernorum spirituum;

(10) De visione purgatorii et inferni et cognicione animarum ibidem existencium;

De ablacione[22] corporis vel anime revocanda;

De consecracione huius libri.

CIV Hic tractat de natura et officio horum angelorum.

Completo de visione divina et novem ordinum angelorum de secundis angelis incipiamus tractatum, quorum natura talis est, quod serviunt Deo per prius et naturatis per posterius. (2) Homines et eorum naturam diligunt regnantque in speris stellarum. Corpus igneum accipiunt, quando ad mandatum Domini hominibus mundatis et purificatis tamquam sociando, ut eos consolentur, mittuntur. (3) Et istorum sunt 7 modi, de quibus debet natura precognosci, quoniam quilibet suum proprium habet officium predestinatum, quamvis omnibus aliis serviciis possent deservire.

---

22 SSM: *obligatione*, which is also reflected in R.

[17. To know their seals] and virtues.

18. To know the spirits and creatures of the air;[193] knowing their names, *powers*, and their superiors;

(7) 19. To know the seals and their virtues;

20. To know the mixture and transmutation of the elements and of the bodies mixed from these;

(8) 21. To know all herbs and plants, and of all animals existing on the earth, and their virtues;

22. To know human nature and all the deeds of mankind, which are hidden and unknown;

(9) 23. To know the aquatic spirits and animals, and of their virtues, and their superiors;

24. To know the earthly and infernal spirits;

(10) 25. Concerning the vision of Purgatory and Hell, and acquiring knowledge of the souls therein.

26. Concerning the removal of the body or the restoration of the soul.[194]

27. Concerning the consecration of this book.

CIV. *Here we treat of the natures and offices of these angels.*

Having completed the discussion on the divine vision, and the nine orders of angels, we now commence a treatise on the second type of angels, whose nature is that they serve God first, and created things second. (2) They love men and their nature, and reign in the spheres of the stars. They take a fiery body, when they are sent according to the Lord's mandate to people, in order to comfort them, being cleansed and purified for associating with them. (3) And there are seven categories of them, from which their nature can be known beforehand, because each has its own predestined office, even though they may serve all other services as well.

---

193 Compare II.8.
194 Compare the list at the beginning of the book: *de obligacione corporis et anime ad revertendum*.

CV (De spiritibus Saturninis).

Istorum autem quidam sunt et vocantur Saturnini et isti sunt **Bohel, Cafziel, Mich[r]athon, Satquiel**, et eorum natura est tristicias et iras et odia promovere, nives et glacies concreare, (2) et sua corpora sunt longa et gracilia, pallida vel flava, et sua regio est septemtrio, et habent sub se 5 demones, scilicet unum regem et 4 eius ministros, quibus omnes alii demones Saturnini subsunt. (3) Isti sunt Maymon rex, Assaibi, Albunalich, Haibalidech, Yasfla, qui demones in ventis Affrico subditis, qui sunt 3, Mextyura, Alchibany, Alflas, penantur[23] vel requiescunt.

CVI De spiritibus Iovialibus.

Alii sunt Ioviales et sunt isti **Satquiel, Raphael, Pahamcocihel, Asassaiel**, et eorum natura est gaudium, amorem, leticiam, benivolenciam et graciam attribuere operanti omnium personarum, rores, flores, herbas et folia procreare et amovere, (2) et sua regio est inter austrum et orientem, et habent 4 demones sub se, scilicet unum regem et tres eius ministros, quibus omnes alii demones Iovis subiugantur, et isti sunt **Formione** rex, **Guth, Maguth et Guthryn**, (3) qui demones in ventis boree subditis et subsolano, qui sunt 5, **Harith, Iesse, Ryon, Nesaph, Naadob**, penantur vel requiescunt. Sua corpora sunt medie stature, et colar eorum quasi color celi vel cristalli.

---

23 See GH's note on "penantur," p. 50.

(CV.) (Concerning the Spirits of Saturn.)[195]

But of those certain ones are called Saturnians, and these are: **Bohel, Cafziel, Michrathon, Satquiel [*Saterquiel]**,[196] and their nature is to cause sadness, anger, and hatred, to create snow and ice together, (2) and their bodies are long and slender, pale or yellow, and their region is the North.[197]

And five daemons are under these, namely one king and his four attendants, with which all other daemons of Saturn are subjugated. (3) They are these: **Maymon** the king, **Assaibi, Albunalich, Haibalidech, Yasfla**, which daemons are subordinate to the Southwest Winds, which are three: **Mextyura, Alchibany, Alflas;** they may be compelled to serve,[198] or they rest.

CVI. Concerning the Spirits of Jupiter.

Others are Jovial and are these: **Satquiel, Raphael, Pahamcocihel, Asassaiel**, and their nature is joy, love, gladness, and grant favor and influence of all persons to the operator, and to produce or take away dews, flowers, herbs and leaves, (2) and their region is between the south and east, and four daemons are under these, namely one king and his three attendants, with which all other daemons of Jupiter are subjugated, and they are **Formione** the king, **Guth, Maguth, and Guthryn**, (3) which three daemons are subject to the North and East winds, which are five: **Harith, Iesse, Ryon, Nesaph, Naadob**, they may be compelled to serve, or they rest. Their bodies are of medium stature, and their color is like the color of the sky, or of crystal.

---

195 Compare chapters CV–CXI with a slightly more elaborate catalog of spirits in chapters CXIX-CXXVI.
196 Should probably read Saterquiel. Satquiel is one of the seven angels in the Sigillum Dei.
197 Note the natures of these planetary "angels" or "spirits" is similar but not identical to the natures of the aerial spirits or "daemons" which are given in CXIX–CXXVI. SSM does not have exact parallels to these chapters, but rather "oblique correspondence." The physical descriptions of the angels found here have parallels in SSM L.2.f.11 ff prayers to the planetary angels or spirits.
198 Regarding the problematic word "penantur" (here translated "compelled to serve"), see introduction, p. 41 and GH, p. 50.

CVII De spiritibus Martis.

Alii sunt Martis et sunt isti **Samahel, Satihel, Yturahihel, Amabiel**, et natura eorum est guerras, occisiones, destrucciones et mortalitates gencium et omnium terrenorum provocare, et sua corpora sunt medie stature, sicca et macra. (2) Color eorum materialis est rubeus sicut carbones accensi bene rubei, et sua regio est austrum, et habent 4 demones sub se, scilicet unum regem et tres eius ministros, quibus omnes alii demones Martis totaliter subiugantur, (3) et isti sunt **Iammax** rex, **Carmox, Ycanohl, Pasfran,** qui demones in ventis subsolano subditis, qui sunt isti 5: **Atraurbiabilis, Yachonaababur, Carmehal, Innyhal, Proathophas**, penantur vel requiescunt.

CVIII De spiritibus Solaribus.

Alii sunt Solis et sunt isti **Raphael, Cafhael, Dardihel, Hurathaphel**, et eorum natura est amorem, graciam, divicias homini communicare et virtutem, similiter sanum custodire, rores, herbas, flores et fructus in instanti dare. (2) Corpora eorum magna et ampla, omnis benivolencie plena, color eorum lucidus vel citrinus sicut Sol vel aurum, et sua regio est oriens, et habent 4 demones sub se, scilicet unum regem et tres eius ministros, quibus omnes alii demones Solis subiugantur, (3) et isti sunt **Barthan** rex, **Thaadas, Chaudas, Ialchal**, qui demones in ventis boree subditis, qui sunt 4, **Baxhathau, Gahathus, Caudes, Iarabal**, penantur vel requiescunt.

CIX De spiritibus Veneris

Alii sunt Veneris et sunt isti **Hanahel, Raquiel, Salguyel**, et natura eorum est risus, lacivias, desideria in amorem conversa cum mulieribus, floribus et fructibus tribuere, (2) et corpora eorum sunt medie stature in omnibus, quia neque parva neque magna neque pinguia neque macra, et eorum

CVII. Concerning the Spirits of Mars.

Others are of Mars and are these: **Samahel, Satihel, Yturahihel, Amabiel**, and their nature is to provoke wars, murder, destruction, and mortality of people, and all earthly things, and their bodies are of medium stature, dry and thin. (2) The color of their material is red, such as red-hot coals kindled well, and their region is the South.

And four daemons are under these, namely one king and his three ministers, to whom all other daemons of Mars are subjugated, (3) and they are these: **Iammax** the king, **Carmox, Ycanohl, Pasfran,** which daemons are subject to the East winds, which are these five: **Atraurbiabilis, Hyachonaababur, Carmehal, Innyhal, Proathophas**, they may be compelled to serve, or they rest.

CVIII. Concerning the Spirits of the Sun.

Others are of the Sun, and they are **Raphael, Cafhael, Dardihel, Hurathaphel,**[199] and their nature is provide love, gratitude, and wealth to man, and virtue, similarly to guard his health, and to instantly give dew, herbs, flowers, and fruits. (2) Their bodies are great and large, and full of all benevolence. Their colors are bright or citrus, or like the Sun or gold, and their region is the East.

And four daemons are under them, namely one king and three of his ministers, to whom all other daemons of the Sun are subjugated, (3) and they are these: **Barthan** the king, **Thaadas, Chaudas, Ialchal,** and those daemons are subject to the North winds, which are four: **Baxhathau, Gahathus, Caudes, Iarabal,** they may be compelled to serve, or they rest.

CIX. Concerning the Spirits of Venus.

Others are of Venus, and they are these: **Hanahel, Raquiel, Salguyel,** and their nature is to cause laughter, lust, desire, and to turn women to love, and to give flowers and fruit. (2) Their bodies are of medium stature in all ways, because they are neither small nor large, nor fat nor thin, and their form is

---

199 In CXXXIII.27 these are spelled Raphael, Caphael, Dardiel, and Hurathaphel; SSM: Raphael, Caphael, Dardyel, Huracaphel.

forma est graciosa, alba sicut nix. (3) Sua regio est inter austrum et occidentem, et habent 3 demones sub se, unum regem et duos eius ministros, quibus omnes alii demones Veneris subiugantur, (4) et isti sunt **Sarabocres** rex, **Nassar, Cynassa**, qui demones in ventis subsolano et zephiro subditis, qui sunt 4, scilicet **Cambores, Trachathath, Nassar, Naasa**, penantur vel requiescunt.

CX De spiritibus Mercurii

Alii sunt Mercurii et sunt isti **Mychael, Myhel, Sarapiel**, et eorum natura est bonos, eciam se ipsos, <in> aliis subiugare. (2) Respondent de preteritis, presentibus et futuris. Docent secreta facta vel facienda, que debent accidere in hoc mundo. Revelant secreta omnium aliorum. (3) Possunt eciam facere, quando eis coniunguntur, penitus quod hii possunt, et ipsi una cum Luna referunt consilia secretorum omnium aliorum, et sua forma est mobilis, clara ad modum vitri vel flamme ignis albe. (4) Sua regio est inter occidentem et septemtrionem, et habent 5 demones sub se, unum regem et 4 eius ministros, quibus omnes alii demones Mercurii subiugantur, (5) et isti sunt **Habaa** rex, **Hyyci, Quyron, Zach, Eladeb**, <eladab>, qui demones in ventis zephiro et Affrico subditis, qui sunt 4, scilicet **Zobha, Drohas, Palas, Sambas**, penantur vel requiescunt.

CXI De spiritibus Lune

Alii sunt Lune et sunt isti **Gabriel, Michael, Samyel, Atithael**, et eorum natura est voluntates et cogitaciones mutare, itinera properare, verba referre, pluvias provocare. (2) Sua corpora sunt longa et ampla. Sua forma est obscura et alba sicut cristallus vel ensis furbitus vel sicut glacies vel nubes obscura. (3) Sua regio est occidens, et habent 4 demones sub se, unum regem et tres eius ministros, quibus omnes alii demones Lune obediunt et eciam supponuntur, (4) et isti sunt **Harthan** rex, **Bileth, Milalu, Abucaba**, qui demones in ventis zephiro subditis, [qui] sunt 5, **Hebethel, Amochap, Oylol, Milau, Abuchaba,** penantur vel requiescunt.

agreeable, and is as white as snow. (3) Their region is between the south and the west.

And there are three daemons under them, one king, and his two ministers, and all the other daemons of Venus are subject to these, (4) and they are: **Sarabocres** the king, **Nassar, Cynassa**, which rule the daemons of the East and West winds [sic], which are four, namely **Cambores, Trachathath, Nassar,** and **Naasa**; they may be compelled to serve, or they rest.

CX. Concerning the Spirits of Mercury.

Others are of Mercury, and they are these: **Mychael, Myhel, Sarapiel,** and their nature is to subjugate themselves and other good spirits to others. (2) They give answer regarding the past, present, and future. They teach the secret deeds or doings, which must come to pass in this world. They reveal the secrets of all of the others. (3) They can also, when constrained, do what the others can do, and together with the moon they can reveal the secret councils of all the others, and their forms are changeable, clear like glass, or like a flame of white fire. (4) Their region is between the west and the north.

And there are five daemons under them: one king, and his four ministers, to which all other daemons of Mercury are subjugated, (5) and they are these: **Habaa** the king, **Hyyci, Quyron, Zach, Eladeb,** which rule the daemons of the West and Southwest winds, which are four, namely: **Zobha, Drohas, Palas, Sambas**, they may be compelled to serve, or they rest.

CXI. Concerning the Spirits of the Moon.

Others are of the Moon, and they are these: **Gabriel, Michael, Samyel, Atithael,** and their nature is to move the will and thinking, to speed journeys, to recall words, and to cause it to rain. (2) Their bodies are long and large. Their forms are dark and white like crystal or of a burnished sword, or like ice or dark clouds. (3) Their region is the West.

And there are four daemons under them: a king and his three ministers, and all the other daemons of the moon are obedient to those, and placed under them, (4) and they are these: **Harthan**, the king, **Bileth, Milalu, Abucaba,** which rule the daemons of the West winds, which are five: **Hebethel, Amochap, Oylol, Milau, Abuchaba;** they may be compelled to serve, or they rest.

CXII *Formacio circuli*

Habita igitur eorum secundum naturam, dominium, regionem et formam cognicione debita dum eos invocare volueris, sic facies. (2) Accipe lapides duros et equales, in quibus non sint foramina vel ruptura, vel tegulas specialiter ad hoc factas. (3) Operans vero sit a pollucione purgatus et habeat calcem et arenam litoris mixtam, cum quibus lapides vel tegule coniungantur.

(4) Tunc fiet ex eis locus, in quo protrahetur circulus, et iste locus taliter formabitur. Primo fiet circulus equalis terre habens in longitudine et latitudine 9 pedes, (5) infra quem fiat circulus gibbosus ad modum semicirculi, alcior quam sit alter, in longitudine et latitudine continens 7 pedes et in altitudine tres pedes cum dimidio. (6) Tamen paupertatis oppressio permittit locum hunc de terra munda fieri, si optime decoquatur, dum tamen ibi non fuerit disiunctura.

(7) Peracto vero loco circuli operans, ut diximus, sit mundatus, ut in prima mundicia continetur. Set mutetur peticio questionum sic. Sacerdos, dum conficit corpus Christi, dicat:

(8) Oracio

"Tu, Domine Iesu Christe, Deus et homo, qui voluisti per te ipsum fidelem populum tuum medicabiliter visitare, te suppliciter exoro, precor et postulo temet ipsum, (9) quem nunc hic in manibus meis teneo pro famulo tuo N, ut ex dono ac permissione gracie tue omnes illos angelos, quos invocaverit, (10) ut per eos benigniter consulatur, sibi mittere ac constringere digneris, ut te mediante possit cum ipsis misericorditer consociari."

CXII. Construction of the Circle.

Having therefore due knowledge of their nature, dominion, region, and form, when you wish to call upon them, you should do thus: (2) Take hard and uniform stones, which have no holes or cracks, or otherwise you can use tiles made specifically for this purpose. (3) And the one who makes them must be purified from all defilement. And he should have a mixture of lime and beach sand, with which to mortar the stones or tiles together.

(4) Then make a place from them in which to draw the circle, and that place should be formed in the following manner: First, let the circle be level with the ground, and nine[200] feet in width, (5) below which make a humped circle (i.e. a mound) like a semi-circle, higher than the other, seven feet in length and width and in height three and a half feet.[201] (6) Yet in the case of extreme poverty, this place can be made (paved) with clean earth (or clay), if it is thoroughly boiled, as long as it is not about to fall apart.

(7) The place for the circle having been duly finished, as we have said, it should be cleaned, as described for the first cleaning. But the petition should be changed thus. The priest, while consecrating the body of Christ, should say:

(8) Prayer.

"You, O Lord Jesus Christ, God and man, who wished to visit your faithful people in person, for their healing, I humbly beseech you, I pray and ask you, even your own self (9) which I now hold in my hands, for the sake of your servant N., that from the gift and permission of your grace, all those angels which he shall call upon (10) graciously for council, may you deign to send and constrain them, so that with your mediation he may be able to associate with them mercifully."

---

200 SSM L.3.f.2: ten feet. R reads "in length and breadth 14 feet." S3: "4^{or} pedes."
201 R seems to interpret this second circle or mound as being within the first, but rather it seems to be outside the first, and a place for the spirits to appear. Compare below where the terrestrial spirits are evoked, where a pit is dug apart from the operator's circle of protection.

CXIII Prima dies

Qui dum, ut diximus, receperit corpus Christi, exiens de ecclesia continue dicat 17 et eam, donec ad locum circuli venerit, recitabit.

(2) BENEDICCIO LOCI CIRCULI

Tunc locum circuli benedicat dicens 15 nec illa die plus faciat.

CXIV Secunda dies

In crastino ecclesiam similiter visitabit et post completorium ibit ad circulum 17 iterum dicendo. (2) Et tunc habeat margaritas super prunas in thuribulo positas, de quibus pars invocatoria et 4 mundi partes, celum et terra [suffumigentur], ter dicendo primam et secundam oracionem.

(3) Hoc facto ter circueundo et suffumigando circulum incipiendo a parte invocatoria et terminans in eadem nominabis angelos, (4) de quibus volueris operari, cum angelis diei et hore, mensis, temporis et faciei, in qua operari volueris, sic dicendo:

(5) "**Michael, Miel, Saripiel, Gabriel, Michael, Samyel, Athitael, Boel, Cafziel, Mich\<r\>athon, Sathquyel, Raphael, Pahamcociel, Assassayel, Samael, Satiel, Yturaihel, Amabihel, Raphael, Caphael,** (6) **Dardiel, Hurathapel, Hanael, Raquiel, Salguiel,**

CXIII. *The First Day.*

Then, as we have said, having received the body of Christ, you should leave the church, continuously saying prayer 17, reading it out loud, until you come to the place of the circle.

(2) THE BLESSING OF THE PLACE FOR THE CIRCLE.

Then he should bless the place for the circle, saying Prayer 15, and that day he should do nothing more.

CXIV. *The Second Day.*

The following day you should similarly visit the church, and after the evening prayer service, you should go to the circle saying again the seventeenth prayer. (2) And then you should place pearls on glowing charcoal in the censer, which [will be suffumigated][202] from the place (or direction) of invocation,[203] and the four parts of the world, heaven, and earth, saying three times the first and second prayer.

(3) With this done three-times, circling and suffumigating the circle, beginning from the place (or direction) of invocation and ending at the same, you should name the angels (4) with which you desire to work, with the angels of the day and hour, month, time, and aspect,[204] in which you desire to work, saying thus:

(5) "**Michael, Miel, Saripiel, Gabriel, Michael, Samyel, Athitael, Boel, Cafziel, Michathon, Sathquyel, Raphael, Pahamcociel, Assassayel, Samael, Satiel, Yturaihel, Amabihel, Raphael, Caphael,** (6) **Dardiel, Hurathapel, Hanael, Raquiel, Salguiel.**[205]

---

202 So SSM L.3.f.3. See also CXXVIII.2 and CXXXI.1.
203 The invocatory place, namely, the direction you will be facing while invoking, as appropriate for the type of angel being invoked.
204 Aspect (or face): i.e. decan. Compare below CXXVII.8: "scribes nomina angelorum diei, et hore mensis, temporis faciei" and CXL.10: Angeli hore sunt qui regnant in hora operis, angeli diei qui in die operis, angeli mensis angeli Lune vel principii mensis, angeli faciei qui regnant facie, ubi est eorum dominium, ascendente, temporis omnes insimul, ...
205 Michael, Miel (variants Mihel, Myhel), Saripiel: Aerial spirits of Mercury. Gabriel, Michael, Samyel, Athitael (variant Atithael): Aerial spirits of the Moon. Boel (var. Bohel), Cafziel, Michrathon, Sathquyel (var. Satquiel): Aerial spirits of Saturn. [Satquiel,]

pax vincit, munus subiugat, paciencia superat, humilitas concordiam nutrit. Ego igitur N, filius N et N, vobiscum humilis pacem meam do vobis. (7) Faciens [*paciens]²⁴ istud meum munusculum confero vobis, ut vos pacificati, pacientes et placati questiones, quas a vobis petiero, michi benigniter intercedente Domino faciatis."

(8) Quo facto protrahe duos circulos, quorum unus distet ab altero per unum pedem, et fiat cum cultello²⁵ novo, et scribe in circuitu nomina angelorum hore, diei, mensis, temporis et faciei dicendo:

(9) "Venite, vos omnes, N, ad pacem super sedem **Samaym**, quam precepit Dominus tribubus Israel ad exaltacionem laudis sue. Unde invoco vos, N, ut precepit Zebedeie suis subditis obedire, veniatis."

CXV 3ª dies

Tercia vero die balneatus ac mundis canabinisque et albis indutus vestibus, a pilis corporis denudatus, habens faciem versus partem, que pertinet questioni, extra circulum erectus sic incipies.

---

24 So SSM.
25 SSM: *cultro*.

Peace conquers, service subjugates, tolerance overcomes, humility nurtures harmony. Therefore I, N., son of N. and N., give my peace to you with humility. (7) With tolerance, I bring this small gift to you, that you will be pacified, tolerant, and your complaints appeased, that you will kindly grant me that which I have asked for, with the Lord's intercession."

(8) With this completed, draw two circles, with one separated from the other by one foot, doing this with a new knife,[206] and write around the circumference the names of the angels of the hour, day, month, time, and aspect, saying:

(9) "Come all of you, N., in peace, upon the seat of **Samaym**,[207] as the Lord commanded[208] to the tribes of Israel, to the exaltation of his praise. From whence I invoke upon you, N, as Zebedee ordered his subordinates to obey, come."[209]

CXV. *The Third Day.*

The third day, being bathed and putting on garments of clean white hemp, and the hairs from your body clean shaved, facing whichever direction which relates to your question, standing upright outside the circle, you should begin thus:

Raphael, Pahamcociel (var. Pahamcocihel), Assassayel (var. Assassaiel): Aerial spirits of Jupiter. Samael (var. Samahel), Satiel (var. Satihel), Yturaihel (Yturahihel), Amabihel (Amabiel): Aerial spirits of Mars. Raphael, Caphael (var. Cafhael), Dardiel (var. Dardihel), Hurathapel (var. Huarthaphel): Aerial spirits of the Sun. Hanael (var. Hanahel), Raquiel, Salguiel (var. Salguyel): Aerial spirits of Venus. Note that Satquiel is assigned to two planets in the preceding chapters. SSM reads: mychael, myel, sarypyel, gabriel, mychial, samyel, acythael, boel, cafzyel, mycrathon, satriquyel, Satquyel, raphyel, paamtotyel, asassayel, samael, sathyel, yturayel, annabyl, raphael, caphael, dardyel, hurachaphel, anael, raquiel, salguyel.
206 Or dagger. SSM reads *cultro* (knife), while LIH reads *cultello* ("small knife").
207 According to SSM L.3.f.3, this is the second circle, placed next to the circle of the operator. See Veenstra 2012 p. 173-175. Shamayim is the Hebrew word for heaven. In medieval Jewish Merkabah literature it is the name of the First Heaven. See Raziel, 6/7Moses in Peterson 2008 p. 265.
208 The Lord: Perhaps a corruption for *Solomon. Compare CV below, with note.
209 See Matt. 4:21-22.

(2) Preparacio ad invocandum

Habeas signum Domini in manu tua dextera munde compositum et sacratum et suffumigabis circulum faciendo et dicendo ut iam dixi. (3) Post hoc suffumiga signum et eciam temet ipsum et tunc flexis genibus dicas 31 cum oracione Salomonis "49, celi et terre conditor" et cetera.

(4) Addicio

Et addas in fine cuiuscumque: "ut tuis sanctissimis angelis valeam amicabiliter sociari, qui ex permissione tue dulcissime voluntatis mea velint iusta desideria penitus adimplere."

(5) Finitis igitur oracionibus taliter invocabis:

Invocacio angelorum

"O vos angeli potentes Saturni, Iovis, Martis, Solis, Veneris, Mercurii, Lune: (6) Boel, Cafziel, Micrathon, [Saterquiel,] Satquiel, Raphael, Paamchociel, Asassaiel, Samael, Satiel, Yturaiel, Amabiel, Raphael, Caphael, Dardiel, Hurathaphel, Anael, Raquiel, Salguyel, Michael, (7) Miel, Sarapiel, Gabriel, Michael, Samyel, Athithael, potentes in celis, nubibus et abissis."

Hic erigat signum Dei manu aperta versus celum dicens:

"Ecce formacionem seculi. Spiritus autem spiritum vocat. (8) Amor Dei nos coniungat, sua potencia nos dirigat, sua misericordia nos coniunctos misericorditer custodiat. Vos igitur nomine illius Dei vivi et veri, qui vos et me verbo creavit, (9) cuius nomina sunt tremenda, que sunt 1, 2, 3, 4, 5, 6, 7, 8, 9, 10, 11, 12, 13, 14, 15, 16, 17, 18, 19, 20, 21, 22, 23, 24, 25, 26,

(2) Preparation for the invocation.

You must have the Sign of the Lord in your right hand, neatly composed and consecrated, and then fumigate the circle, doing and saying as I have said. (3) After this suffumigate the seal and also yourself, and then kneel and say 31 with the oration of Solomon "49, Heaven and Earth preserve" etc.[210]

(4) An addition.

Then you must add at the end of each: "that I may be able to associate with your most holy angels in a friendly manner, who may, by your permission, wish to fulfill most pleasantly my lawful desires."[211]

(5) With the orations thus finished, invoke them in the following manner:

Invocation of the Angels.

"O you mighty angels of Saturn, Jupiter, Mars, the Sun, Venus, Mercury, and the Moon: (6) **Boel, Cafziel, Micrathon, [Saterquiel,]**[212] **Satquiel, Raphael, Paamchociel, Asassaiel, Samael, Satiel, Yturaiel, Amabiel, Raphael, Caphael, Dardiel, Hurathaphel, Anael, Raquiel, Salguyel, Michael, (7) Miel, Sarapiel, Gabriel, Michael, Samyel, Athithael,**[213] mighty in heaven, in the clouds, and in the abyss."

Here, with an open hand, raise the Sign of God towards heaven, saying:

"Behold the design of the world. Whereupon the Spirit calls the spirit. (8) May the love of God join us, may his power direct us, may his mercy mercifully guard our union. You therefore, through the name of that living and true God, who created you and me with the word, (9) whose names are terrible, which are 1, 2, 3, 4, 5, 6, 7, 8, 9, 10, 11, 12, 13, 14, 15, 16, 17, 18, 19, 20, 21,

---

210 C.15.
211 R omits all the rest of the *Sworn Book* proper, but substitutes excerpts from Agrippa, Petrus de Abano, and other material.
212 So SSM L.3.f.4. This is the correct name for the last angel of Saturn, but it has been accidentally omitted here because of the similarity with the Satquiel, the first angel of Jupiter. See CXV.44. Sl. 313 22r has this correction in the margin. Heptameron: Seraquiel.
213 SSM L.3.f.4: boel, cafzyel, mycrathon, satriquyel, Satquyel, raphyel, paamtotyel, asassayel, samael, sathyel, yturayel, annabyl, raphael, caphael, dardyel, hurachaphel, anael, raquiel, salguyel, mychael, (7) myel, sarypyel, gabriel, mychial, samyel, acythael.

27, 28, 29, 30, 31, 32, 33, 34, 35, 36, 37, 38, (10) quoniam magnus, altissimus, sanctissimus, excellentissimus, potentissimus, fortis, iustus, pius, clemens, dulcis, adiutor, protector, defensor, largitor, misericors, (11) cuius potencia ineffabilis, cuius substancia indivisibilis, sciencia inestimabilis, veritas incommutabilis, misericordia incommensurabilis, essencia incorruptibilis, (12) cuius gloriose gracie pleni sunt celi et terra, cuius forti potencie genuflectuntur omnia celestia, terrestria et infernalia, vos invoco humiliter et deposco, (13) ut vos infra circulos hic circumscriptos descendere dignemini apparentes in forma benivola, de omnibus quesitis michi veritatem respondentes. Per virtutem illius vobis precipio, cuius nomine signatur. Amen."

(14) Sigillum et ligacio

"Vos igitur, sanctissimos angelos, peticionibus meis obedire sigillo, deposco, invoco et eciam coniuro sigillo sanctorum nominum Dei, (15) quo Dominus humane creature servire sigillavit, dicere et facere que licita sunt et honesta. **Ya, Ya, Ya, Laaaa, Adonay, Sabaoth, Heloy, Genouem, Merquerpon, Usye, Achedion, Zebedio, Greba.** (16) Cum istis et per ista sacratissima [nomina] iterum ad concordiam vos appello. Vos meis peticionibus obedire et coniuro atque virtute Dei precipio, (17) ut vos meo placati munusculo prompti michi in omnibus locis honestis obedire[26] super

---

26 SSM: in omnibus licitis & honestis obedire.

22, 23, 24, 25, 26, 27, 28, 29, 30, 31, 32, 33, 34, 35, 36, 37, 38,[214] (10) Because the great, most high, most holy, most distinguished, most powerful, strong, just, blessed, merciful, sweet, helper, protector, defender, generous giver, merciful, (11) whose power is indescribable, whose nature is indivisible, whose knowledge is priceless, whose truth is unchangeable, whose mercy is immeasurable, whose essence is incorruptible, (12) of whose glorious grace the heavens and earth are full,[215] before whose mighty power all the heavens, lands, and infernal realms genuflect,[216] I humbly invoke and beseech you, (13) that you may condescend to come down and appear here before this circle in a perceptible and agreeable form, to answer truly all my questions. I command you through the virtue of that one, whose name is marked. Amen."

(14) Seal and binding.

"Therefore, O most sacred angels, I seal, beseech, invoke, and also conjure you to obey my petitions, through the seal of the sacred names of God, (15) which the Lord sealed to serve human creatures, which are lawful and honorable to say and to make. **Ya, Ya, Ya, Laaaa, Adonay, Sabaoth, Heloy, Genouem, Merquerpon, Usye, Achedion, Zebedio, Greba.**[217] (16) With those same and through those same most sacred [names] I again call you to union, to obey my petitions, and I conjure and with the virtue of God I order, (17) that you will be appeased with the small present which I have presented, to obey me in all honest places[218] upon the seat of **Samaym**[219] to the circles here

---

214 SSM lists out the names, here spelled thus: Agla, monon, tetragramathon, gly'deus, ocleyste, amphymeton, lamyara, Ianenuer, sadyon, hely, orlon, porrentymon, yelur, gofgamel, hemanuel, on, admyel, honzmorb, yoth, offeb, resamarathon, amethy, eryona, yuestre, saday, meloth, setthe, elscha, abbadya, alpha & Ω, leyste, orystyon, yeremon, hospr, mesquerpon, elzephares, egyryon, pectha.
215 From the *Sanctus* prayer, adapted from Isaiah 6:3.
216 Genufection as a formal gesture of respect for a superior, is a tradition dating from early times.
217 SSM L.3.f.4: ya ya ya, laaaaadonarum, sabaoth, heloy, Genonem, mesquerpon, usye, athedyon, zebedye, greba.
218 Honest place: i.e. one suited to the dignity of the occasion. See "sacred space" in introduction to David Postles, *Social Geographies in England (1200–1640)*. Washington, DC: New Academia Pub, 2007. SSM: in all lawful and honest things. This reading is also consistent with the wording later in the paragraph.
219 i.e. Shamayim, the common Hebrew word for heaven or sky. It is specifically

sedem **Samaym** hic infra circulos hic circumscriptos (18) a Saturninis, Iovinis, Martialibus, Solaribus, Venereis, Mercurialibus, Lunaribus speris descendere dignemini, que sunt iste: **Bacalgar, Totalg, Yfarselogon, Alchedion, Meremieca, Ureleguyger, Ioath, Somongargmas, Iohena**. (19) Obedite ergo Zebedeie, qui vos Salomoni et tribubus Israel sibi fidelibus ad laudem et honorem sui sancti nominis Sabaoth, quod est "exercitus angelorum," in honestis et licitis obedire precepit, (20) et vobis super hoc et ad hoc nomine suo me munitum optime represento, quoniam misericors est, non ex nostris meritis, set ex sue gracia largitatis.

(21) Nomine igitur ipsius vos, N, placatos sub hiis sanctis nominibus iterum appello: **Legemoth, Gonathaym, Maloth, Yhoston, Hemonege, Anephene<s>ton, Stobr, Otheos, Tutheon, Thereis, Chatheon, Agla**. (22) In hiis igitur perfeccione sigilli quamvis vos sciencia vestra cum humilitate preceptis [precepit] obedire creatoris,[27] (23) tamen ego, N, filius N, pollutus viciorum meorum contagio vestrum amittere timeo iuvamentum; humilitatis tamen indutus cilicio obedire peticionibus meis vos deprecor et invoco. (24) Set virtute creatoris eterni ferens insignium[28] vos nomine illius summi creatoris obedire michi, famulo suo, precipio et coniuro, ut sitis meis in omnibus licitis et honestis peticionibus obedire parati."

Finit ligacio.

(25) INCIPIT CONIURACIO.

"Vos igitur, sanctos angelos, me vestris imponens officiis, quamvis humilitatis ac paciencie vestre indutus cilicio, (26) qui sicut Filius altissimi creatoris in nomine illius, qui **Loke Heuaf Hese** [*Ioth, He, Vaf, He, se][29]

---

27 GH hypothesizes that the word *"precepit"* is missing, but SSM reads "In huius igitur perfectione sigilli quamuis vos sciam vestri cum humilitate preceptis obedire creatoris."
28 So Sl. 313 21v; Sl. 3854 131r col. 1: *in signium* or *insignium*. Sl. 3885 92v: *in signum*.
29 My reading follows SSM L.3.f.5: "ioth, he, vau, he, se Moysi nominavit...." GH: "loke, henaf, hese." Sl. 3854 131r seems to be a simple corruption.

circumscribed, (18) to deign to descend from the Saturnian, Jovian, Martial, Solar, Venusian, Mercurial, and Lunar spheres, which are these: **Bacalgar, Totalg, Yfarselogon, Alchedion, Meremieca, Ureleguyger, Ioath, Somongargmas, Iohena**.[220] (19) Obey therefore Zebedee,[221] whereby you commanded Solomon, and the tribes of Israel who were loyal to him, to honestly and lawfully obey, for the praise and honor of his holy name **Sabaoth**, which is "the army of angels," (20) and with his name, which I accurately set forth, protecting me, because he is merciful, not because of our merits, but because of the abundance of his grace.

(21) With his name therefore I again appeal to you N, placated by these sacred names: **Legemoth, Gonathaym, Maloth, Yhoston, Hemonege, Anepheneton, Stobr, Otheos, Tutheon, Thereis, Chatheon, Agla**.[222] (22) Therefore by the perfection of this Seal, I know that you will obey the commandments of the Creator with humility, (23) nevertheless I N. son of N., fear losing your help, polluted by the influence of my sins; and so, putting on the hair-shirt of humility, I entreat and call on you to obey my petitions. (24) But with the virtue of the emblems of the eternal Creator bringing you, with the name of that most high Creator I entreat you to obey me, his servant, I direct and conjure, that you be prepared to obey me in all my lawful and honest petitions."

The end of the binding.

(25) THE BEGINNING OF THE CONJURATION.

"Therefore, O you sacred angels, with me imposing upon your duties, although putting on the garment of humility and suffering, (26) who like the Son of the most high Creator in his names, **Loke Heuaf Hese [*Ioth He Vau**

---

associated with the Moon and Monday in *Heptameron*.
220 SSM L.3.f.4-5: bacalgar, totalg, yfarselogon, <u>athedyon</u>, <u>meremieta</u>, <u>vrelegnyger</u>, ioach, <u>Sommangarginas</u>, iohena.
221 Zebedei: This name also appears in the list of names of God at the beginning of this paragraph, and in the magic circle. The sense seems to be that this is the name of God which Solomon invoked to command the loyalty of the people of Israel. *Hebrew* "Gift of God". Also the name of various biblical personalities. In CXIV.9 the spirits are exhorted to "obey as Zebedee ordered his subjects to obey," apparently based on Matt. 4:21-22. It is possible the current passage is a mutilated version of that.
222 SSM: Legemoth, gonathaym, maloth, <u>ysyston</u>, <u>homonege</u>, anepheneston, <u>febr</u>, <u>octreys</u>, <u>derheys</u>, tutheon, agla.

Moysi nominavit, quamvis sub meo nomine sublimitatis imperium non valeam deprecare, (27) humiliter deprecor, obedienter precipio per iustum **Ombonar**, per verum **Stimulamathon**, per sanctum **Orion**, per sanctissimum **Eryon**, per magnum **Noymos**, per festinantem **Pep** et per alia Dei nomina pura, (28) que propter sue celsitudinis magnitudinem nulla deberet, nisi concederetur a Domino, humanitas nominare, (29) que sunt 45, 46, 47, 48, 49, 50, 51, 52, 53, 54, 55, 56, 57, 58, 59, 60, 61, 62, 63, 64, 65, 66, 67, 68, 69, 70, 71, 72, 73, 74, 75, 76, 77, 78, 79, (30) quatinus a Saturninis, Iovinis, Marcialibus, Solaribus, Venereis, Mercurialibus, Lunaribus speris[30] descendere dignemini."

(31) Placacio

"O[31] vos, angeli benignissimi, potentissimi ac fideles, **Bohel, Cafziel** et ceteri, qui obediencie ac humilitatis vinculo gubernamen[32] celorum cum omnibus subditis eorundem recipere a Domino meruistis, (32) quibus omnis sciencia revelatur, quibus data est potestas plenaria[33] terreas cum infernalibus subiugare creaturas,[34] nocere vel iuvare, (33) quoniam Dominus in omnibus fideles, humiles ac cum paciencia iustos a vestra creacione primaria vos cognovit; (34) ego enim, licet immeritus, tamen vestram implorando graciam humiliter vos deprecor et invoco, (35) ut meis prompti peticionibus, in forma benivola atque meo placati munusculo, prompti michi in omnibus licitis et honestis obedire super sedem Samaym hic infra circulos hic circumscriptos a Saturninis, Iovinis et ceteris speris descendere dignemini, (36) et ad hoc igitur nomine vivi et veri Dei, qui vobis graciam tribuit non peccandi, vos invoco atque potenter impero per eius sacra nomina, que sunt ista: [80], 81, 82, 83, 84, 85, 86, 87, 88, 89, 90, 91, 92, 93, 94, 95, 96, 97, 98, 99. (37) Obedite ergo Zebedeie et michi nomine ipsius. Invoco vos, potestates celorum, et invocando coniuro per **Ab**, per **Gap**, per

---

30 Sl. 3854 omits, but see below, along with CIV.2 and CXV.18.
31 GH omits.
32 i.e. regimen.
33 SSM adds: aereas.
34 Compare IV.58-63.

He], which Moses himself named, although under my own name I may not have power to entreat the Lofty Empire, (27) I humbly beg, I obediently order through the just **Ombonar**, through the true **Stimulamathon**, through the holy **Orion**, through the most sacred **Eryon**, Through the great **Noymos**,[223] through the hastening **Pep**,[224] and through the other pure names of God, (28) which on account of the greatness of his height, no one should name, unless compassion has been granted by the Lord, (29) which are 45, 46, 47, 48, 49, 50, 51, 52, 53, 54, 55, 56, 57, 58, 59, 60, 61, 62, 63, 64, 65, 66, 67, 68, 69, 70, 71, 72, 73, 74, 75, 76, 77, 78, 79, (30) so that you may deign to descend from the spheres of Saturn, Jupiter, Mars, the Sun, Venus, Mercury, and the Moon."

(31) THE PLACATING.

"O you, most kind angels, most powerful and faithful, **Bohel, Cafziel,** and the rest, who with the chain of obedience and humility have merited the control of the heavens, with your subordinates receiving the same from the Lord, (32) to whom all knowledge is revealed, to whom is given complete power to subjugate earthly creatures, along with the infernal ones, to harm or to help, (33) because the Lord has recognized you faithful in all things, humbly and with patience just from your first creation; (34) for I, though unworthy, nevertheless humbly ask for your grace, and entreat and call upon you, (35) in an agreeable form, and appeased by my small present, to obey me in all things presented in my petitions that are lawful and worthy, upon the seat of Samaym[225] to the circles drawn here, may you deign to descend from Saturn, Jupiter, and the other spheres, (36) and for this reason therefore, in the name of the living and true God, who has granted you the grace of being without sin, I call upon and potently command you, through his sacred names, which are these: [80,] 81, 82, 83, 84, 85, 86, 87, 88, 89, 90, 91, 92, 93, 94, 95, 96, 97, 98, 99. (37) Obey therefore Zebedei[226] and me in his name. I invoke you, heavenly powers, and conjure you with the invocation, through **Ab**, through **Gap**, through **Abx**, through **Abra**, through **Abraca**, through **Gebra**, through **Abr-**

---

223 SSM: nomyx.
224 SSM: pele. On PELE, see Agrippa, OP3.11. Also used by John Dee. See Peterson, *John Dee's Five Books of Mystery* (York Beach ME: Weiser, 2003, pp. 79-80, 152.)
225 Compare CXIV.
226 Is this an indication that the biblical quote has been misunderstood?

Abx, per **Abra,** per **Abraca,** per **Gebra,** per **Abracala,** per **Abracasap,** per **Abracaleus,** per **Zargon,** per **Abrion,** per **Eleyon,** per **Sargion.**

(38) Vos igitur, potentes angeli, invoco et invocando coniuro. Superne maiestatis imperii potentes potenter imparo per eum, qui dixit, et factum est, cui omnes excercitus angelorum celestium, terrestrium et infernorum subduntur et obediunt, (39) et per nomen eius ineffabile **Tetragramaton,** quod in fronte tulit Aaron, quod angelice dicitur **Agla,** Hebraice **Heloy,** Arabice **Iaym,** Grece **Theos,** quod **Deus** Latine vocatur, (40) quo audito omnes exercitus celestes, terrestres et infernales tremunt et colunt, et per ista, que sunt **Rethala, Rabam, Cauthalee, Durhulo, Archyma, Rabur,** (41) quatinus a Saturninis, Iovinis, Marcialibus, Solaribus, Venereis, Mercurialibus, Lunaribus speris omni occasione et malivolencia cessante in forma benivola atque meo placati munusculo (42) michi in omnibus licitis et honestis obedire parati super sedem Samaym hic infra circulos hic circumscriptos descendere dignemini per virtutem humilitatis, quam nunc vobis offero,"—hic debet crucifigi in terra clausis oculis dicens:—(43) "et in virtute vivi et veri Dei, qui vos in iusticia et in equitate in sempiterno permanere concessit, cui sit gloria, laus et honor atque victoria per infinita secula seculorum. Amen."

(44) "**Boel, Cafziel, Micrathon, Saterquiel, Satquiel, Raphael, Paamcociel, Asassaiel, Samael, Sathiel, Yturaiel, Amabiel, Raphael, Caphael, Dardiel, Hurathaphel, Anael, Raquiel, Salguyel, Michael, Myel, Sarapiel, Gabriel, Mychael, Samyel, Athithael,** (45) venite, venite, venite letantes vestro obedire creatori et michi nomine ipsius, coniurati per nomen suum excellentissimum, quod super capud meum vobis omnibus ostendo"—hic ponat manum inversam super capud suum et eis signum ostendat.

acala, through **Abracasap**, through **Abracaleus**, through **Zargon**, through **Abrion**, through **Eleyon**, through **Sargion**.[227]

(38) Therefore, O powerful angels, I invoke you, and with the invocation I conjure you by the authority of the Supreme Majesty, I strongly command you, by him who spoke and it was done, and to whom all hosts of celestial, terrestrial, and infernal angels are subjugated and obey, (39) and by his ineffable name **Tetragrammaton**, which Aaron wore on his forehead,[228] which in English is called **Agla**, in Hebrew **Heloy**, in Arabic **Iaym**, in Greek **Theos**, which in Latin is called *Deus* ("God"), (40) which when heard, all heavenly, earthly, and infernal hosts tremble and worship,[229] and by these, which are **Rethala, Rabam, Cauthalee, Durhulo, Archyma, Rabur**,[230] (41) that by the spheres of Saturn, Jupiter, Mars, the Sun, Venus, Mercury, the Moon, at every opportunity and without ill-will, in an agreeable form, and appeased with my small gift, (42) prepared to obey me in all things lawful and honest, you shall deign to descend from upon the seat of Samaym to these circles drawn here below, through the power of humility, which I offer to you now,"—here make the sign of the cross on the ground, with eyes closed, saying: (43) "And in the power of the living and true God, who has granted you to endure in perpetual justice and equality, to whom be glory, praise, honor, and victory, forever and ever. Amen."

(44) "Boel, Cafziel, Micrathon, Saterquiel,[231] Satquiel, Raphael, Paamcociel, Asassaiel, Samael, Sathiel, Yturaiel, Amabiel, Raphael, Caphael, Dardiel, Hurathaphel, Anael, Raquiel, Salguyel, Michael, Myel, Sarapiel, Gabriel, Mychael, Samyel, Athithael, (45) Come! Come!, Come! be glad to obey your creator and me in his name, conjuring through his most excellent name, which I show you all now over my head"—here he should hold his hand inverted over his head, and show the sign[232] to them.

---

227 SSM L.3.f.15-16: per **ab**, per **gab**, per **abr**, per **abra**, per **abraca**, per **greba**, per **abracala**, per **abracasap**, per **abracaleus**, per **sargon**, per **abryon**, per **helyon**, per **sargyon**.
228 This perhaps echoes the poem *de divinis nominibus* of Abbott Sigo of St Florent de Saumur (d. 1070). See Wilkinson, Robert J. *Tetragrammaton: Western Christians and the Hebrew Name of God : from the Beginnings to the Seventeenth Century*. 2015, p. 219.
229 See Philem. 2:10.
230 SSM L.3.f.16: <u>Bethala</u>, rabam, <u>canthalee</u>, <u>durule</u>, archyma, rabur.
231 So too SSM. GH marked this name as extraneous by comparison with CXIV.5 and CXV.6, but rather its omission from those passages seems to be the mistake.
232 SSM: the Divine Sign.

(46) Et immediate cum taliter ter invocaveris, si non prima vice venerint vel 2ª, audies quasi fulgur descendens de celo, et erit color eorum nitidissimus. (47) Set non debent alloqui nec aspici, donec ipsi primo loquantur, qui dicent: "Amice, quid petis?" Tunc dicat: "Pacem et amiciciam vestram." (48) Et si recte mundatus fueris, immediate concedent et dicent: "Surge et respice graciam virtutis Dei. Pete, et complebitur tibi, quia te misericordia Domini visitavit." Tunc pete quod volueris, et habebis.

(49) Quocienscumque aliquid de 27 predictis capitulis volueris, ut iam predictum est, voca hos angelos celestes sanctos mundum et totam naturam regentes in racione amantis et desiderantis Deum gloriosum. (50) Et quando venerint et te interogaverint: "Quid vis?," postquam responderis: "Pacem et amiciciam vestram," petas illud de 27, quod in oracionibus mundacionis petivisti, (51) cognicionem celorum, si hanc quesivisti, vel mutacionem diei in noctem et e contrario, si hoc petisti, vel consecracionem libri, si hanc voluisti, vel utramque simul, (52) si de tanto fueris una operacione dignus, et sic quodlibet de 27 dante Domino facere quibis. Quod ipse nobis concedat, qui vivit et regnat per infinita secula seculorum. Amen.

(Tercium opus vel tractatus)

CXVI. Incipiunt capitula tercii tractatus huius operis, qui est de spiritibus aeris.

De constriccione spirituum per verba; De constriccione spirituum per sigilla; (2) De constriccione spirituum per tabulas; De forma imponenda cuilibet spiritui; De inclusione spirituum; De incluso spiritu ut non respondeat; De fulgure et tonitruo provocando; (3) De combustione facienda; De

(46) And immediately when you have invoked them three times in this manner, if not after the first or second time, you will hear a sound like lightning descending from heaven, and their color will be most shining. (47) But you must not address them or look at them, until they themselves have first spoken. They will say: "O friend, what do you desire?" Then he should say: "Peace and your friendship." (48) And if you have been properly cleaned, they will immediately concede and say: "Arise and contemplate the grace and virtue of God. Ask, and it will be granted to you, because the mercy of the Lord has visited you." Then ask what you wish, and you shall have it.

(49) However often you might desire something from the preceding twenty-seven topics, as covered earlier, call these holy celestial angels ruling the world and all of nature because of the loving and greatly desired glorious God.[233] (50) And when they have come and asked you: "what do you want?" whereupon you should respond "Peace, and your friendship." ask one of the twenty-seven, which you have sought in the prayers of purification, (51) knowledge of the heavens, if you have asked for this, even changing day into night and the opposite, if you have desired this, or consecrating a book, if you wish it, or likewise the others, (52) if you have been worthy to such an extent in one operation, you will be able to accomplish any of the twenty-seven, Lord granting. Because he grants it to us himself, who lives and reigns world without end. Amen.

[The Third Work or Treatise]

CXVI. Here begins the topics of the Third Treatise of this Work, which is about the Spirits of the Air.

Concerning the constraint of spirits through words. Concerning the constraint of spirits through seals. (2) Concerning the constraint of spirits through tables. Concerning imposing a form to any spirit. Concerning the confinement of spirits. Concerning a confined spirit, whether or not it will answer. Calling forth lightning and thunder. (3) Concerning the required

---

233 Is this a quote from Simon of Faversham (c. 1260–1306) , *Quaestiones super De motu animalium*. http://cimagl.saxo.ku.dk/download/84/84Christensen93-128.pdf p. 109 or Peter of Auvergne (died 1304)? Compare "in ratione amantis et desiderantis" and "in ratione amati et desiderati" in Petrus, and Griet Galle. *Questions on Aristotle's De caelo*. Leuven (Belgium): Leuven University Press, 2003, p. *204.

purificacione aeris; De corrupcione aeris; De nive et gelu facienda; De rore et pluvia facienda; De floribus et fructibus provocandis; De invisibilitate; (4) De equo, qui una nocte te portabit et reportabit ubi volueris; De absente quod veniat una hora sanus; De re, que deferatur in momento ubicumque volueris; De subtraccione rei; De revocacione rei; (5) De transfiguracione cuiuscumque; De flumine provocando in terra sicca; De commocione regni contra dominum; De regno vel imperio destruendo; De habenda potestate super quemlibet; (6) De habendis mille militibus armatis; De formacione castri indestructibilis; De speculo perverso; De destruccione loci vel inimici per speculum perversum; De speculo aparicionis mundi; (7) De fure et furto revocando; De ceraturis aperiendis; De discordia facienda; De concordia provocanda; De habenda gracia omnium personarum et benivolencia; De mulieribus habendis ad libitum; (8) De diviciis habendis; De curacione cuiuslibet infirmitatis; De dando infirmitatem cuilibet et qualemcumque placuerit operanti; De interficiendo quemlibet; De tempestate et periculo terre et maris fuganda; (9) De nave retenta in mari per adamantem vel aliter rehabenda; De omni periculo evitando; De congregacione et accepcione avium; De piscibus congregandis et accipiendis; (10) De animalibus silvestribus et domesticis congregandis et accipiendis; De bello faciendo inter aves vel homines vel pisces vel animalia; (11) De apparencia combustionis; De apparencia ioculatorum et puellarum balancium;[35] De apparencia gardinorum vel castrorum; De apparencia militum pugnancium; De apparencia griffonum et draconum; (12) De apparencia omnium ferarum; De apparencia venatorum cum canibus; De apparencia hominis quod sit alibi quam est; De apparencia tocius voluptatis.

---

35 Cap II: psallencium; SSM: ballancium.

burnings; Concerning the purification of the air. Concerning the corruption of the air. To make snow and frost. To make dew and rain. To call forth flowers and fruit. Concerning invisibility. (4) Concerning a horse, which will carry you anywhere you wish in a single night. To bring an absent person back safely in an hour. To transport something wherever you wish, in a moment. To have something removed. To recall something. (5) To transfigure anything. To cause a river on dry land. To incite a kingdom against its ruler. To destroy a kingdom or state. To have power over anyone. (6) To have a thousand armed soldiers. To form an indestructible fortress. How to make a mirror of destruction. How to destroy a place or an enemy using the mirror of destruction. The apparition of the world in a mirror (or glass). (7) To return anything which a thief has stolen. To open locks. To cause discord. To cause agreement. To have the good will and favor of all persons. To have the desire of women. (8) To have wealth. To cure any sickness. To make anyone sick, whenever you wish. To kill anyone. To hold back storms and dangers of the earth and sea. (9) To hold back a ship at sea using the adamant stone, or otherwise to bring it back again. To avoid all danger. To flock birds together, and collect them. To cause fish to gather and be caught. (10) To cause woodland and domestic animals to gather and be caught. To cause war between the birds, or people, or fish, or animals. (11) To make burning appear. To make appear jesters and girls babbling.[234] To make gardens or fortresses appear. To make appear soldiers fighting. To make griffins and dragons appear. (12) To make all wild beasts appear. To make hunters appear with dogs. To make someone appear as if they were somewhere other than where they actually are. To make all pleasures appear.

---

[234] Chap 2: psallencium ("singing psalms"); SSM: ballancium ("dancing").

CXVII Finitis capitulis incipit prohemium in spiritibus aereis.

Cum igitur ignoratis superioribus angelorum illos constringere sit impossibile, (2) nomina spirituum aeris et ventorum in precedenti posuimus capitulo; ut sui superiores clarius viderentur, et a quibus poterat quilibet subiugari. (3) Nunc autem de natura aeris et omnium spirituum in ipso residencium hic faciemus tractatum.

(4) Aer est elementum corruptibile, liquidum et subtile inter cetera nobilius passibiles recipiens qualitates et est simpliciter invisibilis set ipso composito videtur. (5) In quo sunt spiritus, quos sancta mater ecclesia dampnatos appellat, set ipsi oppositum asserunt esse verum, et ideo eos neque bonos neque malos volumus appellare. (6) Et illi spiritus in aere reguntur secundum ipsius aeris qualitates, et ideo eius qualitates videamus.

(7) Aer igitur in quantum elementum a planetarum influenciis gubernatur. Bene igitur accipit diversas complexiones, quas nunc dicemus, (8) quia quidam sunt demones ad tribulacionem aeris constituti, quos ventos Salomon appellavit, quoniam ventos excitant, et secundum quemlibet mutatur aer. (9) Et penatur spiritus illius partis, unde quilibet debet aspicere ventum sue operacioni competentem, quia tunc illius partis demones excitantur. (10) Set non semper invenitur ventus invocacioni habilis. Ideo eos precipimus excitari, qui <tunc> aere sereno vocantur indifferenter. (11) Et ideo cum angelis ventos ponemus, ut in eis veniant et vincantur; quorum opera in subsequentibus sunt dicenda.

CXVIII Divisio spirituum aeris

Aereorum vero spirituum duo sunt modi, quoniam quidam sunt boni, quidam mali, quidam mites, quidam feroces. (2) Boni, mites et fideles sunt

CXVII. End of the topics, and beginning of the preface on the aerial spirits.

Know therefore, since it is impossible to bind those higher angels without knowledge about them, (2) we have listed the names of the spirits of the air and winds in the preceding chapter; in order that the superiors might be clearly seen, and through which anyone can be subjugated. (3) Therefore we now will prepare a treatise concerning the nature of the air and all the spirits residing in it.

(4) The air is a corruptible element, fluid, and subtle, capable of receiving qualities from the others, and is plainly invisible, but it is seen to be composed of parts of itself. (5) In which are spirits, which the holy mother church calls damned, but they themselves assert the opposite to be true, and therefore we prefer to call them neither good nor evil. (6) And those spirits that are governed by air act according to the nature of air itself, and therefore we can understand their nature.

(7) The air therefore, insofar as an element, is governed by the influences of the planets. It therefore readily takes on diverse combinations, which we will now describe, (8) for there are certain daemons established for the disturbance of the air, which Solomon has called winds, because they raise up the winds, and behind which the air is moved. (9) And a spirit of that part may be compelled to serve, hence each one should consider which wind is suitable for the operation, because the daemons of that part are awakened then. (10) But the wind for the invocation is not always easily discovered. Therefore we order them to be raised up, which <then> are indiscriminately called calm air. (11) And therefore we will place the winds with the angels, in order that they may come to them and be conquered; their works are spoken of in the following sections.

CXVIII. Divisions of the spirits of the air.

There are two kinds of aerial spirits, for some are good while others are evil; some are mild, others wild.[235] (2) The good, mild, and faithful ones are the eastern and western ones, and are called good, because operations with them

---

235 Or cruel.

illi orientales et occidentales et dicuntur boni, quia operaciones eorum iuvant in bono, et vix nocent alicui, nisi ad hoc cogantur divina virtute.

(3) Mali sunt et cum superbia feroces australes et septemtrionales et dicuntur mali, quia opera eorum sunt mala in omnibus, et nocent libenter omnibus et vix aliquid, quod sequatur, ad bonum faciunt, nisi ad hoc superiori virtute cogantur.

(4) Set inter istos sunt alii collaterales istis, qui neque boni neque mali dicuntur, quoniam in omnibus obediunt invocanti, sive in bono fuerit sive in malo. De quibus hic est cognicio cuiuscumque.

CXIX De spiritibus orientalibus

Istorum autem 4 sunt in oriente regnantes et sunt subditi Soli et vento eius, qui boreas dicitur. Et excitantes eum sunt isti 4: **Baxhatau** <rex>, **Gahatus, Caudes, Iarabal,** (2) et habent hos 4 demones et eorum subditos excitare, congregare, dispergere, constringere et in loco proprio ligare, quorum **Barthan** est rex, **Taadas, Caudas, Yalcal** sunt ministri, (3) et eorum natura est aurum dare cum carbunculis ad libitum, divicias, graciam et benivolenciam gencium impetrare, inimicicias hominum mortales vel alias dissolvere, homines in summis honoribus sublimare, infirmitates tribuere vel auferre.

(4) Sua corpora sunt magna et ampla, sanguinea et grosa, color eorum sicut aurum brunitum[36] sanguine depictum. Motus eorum est celi coruschacio. Signum eorum est invocanti commovere sudores.

---

36 Du Cange: Politus, levigatus ("polished, smoothed"). http://ducange.enc.sorbonne.fr/BRUNITUS accessed June 28, 2015.

help in good, and they rarely harm anyone, unless they are forced with divine strength.

(3) The evil, arrogant, and wild ones are the southern and northern ones, and are called evil, because their works are evil in everything, and they willingly harm anyone, and will scarcely do good for anyone unless they are forced with superior strength.

(4) But between those, there are others on both sides of them, which are said to be neither of good nor of evil, because they obey in everything when invoked, whether it be for good or evil. Concerning these, here is the information on each:

CXIX. Concerning the Spirits of the East.

But of those there are four governing in the East, and they are subordinate to the Sun and its wind, which is called the North wind. And there are four (spirits) raising it up: **Baxhatau, Gahatus, Caudes, Iarabal**, (2) and they have these four daemons and their subordinates to raise up, congregate, scatter, constrain, and bind to their proper place, of which **Barthan** is the king, **Taadas, Caudas, Yalcal** are the ministers, (3) and their nature is to give gold with carbuncles as desired; also to obtain wealth, gratitude, and good will of the population; likewise to dissolve the hostility of people and other beings; and to raise people to high honors, and to grant or take away weaknesses.

(4) Their bodies are great and large, bloody and thick;[236] their color is like polished gold, painted with blood. Their movement is like the glittering of the sky. The sign that they have appeared is that the one who calls them will break into a sweat.

---

236 S3853: *gratiosa* ("agreeable").

CXX De spiritibus occidentalibus

Occidentales sunt illi 4, quibus omnes alii regionis demones subduntur, quorum **Harthan** est rex, **Bileth, Milalu, Habuchaba** eius ministri, et sunt subditi Lune et vento eius, qui zephirus dicitur. (2) Et excitantes [eum] sunt isti: **Hebethel, Amocap, Oilol, Myla<l>u, Abuchaba,** et habent hos 4 demones et eorum subditos excitare, congregare, dispergere, constringere ac in loco proprio ligare, (3) quorum natura est argentum ad libitum dare, res de loco ad locum deferre, equum velocitatis tribuere, facta et secreta presencia atque preterita dicere personarum.

(4) Sua corpora sunt magna et ampla, mollia et fleumatica, color eorum sicut nubes obscura et tenebrosa, et habent multum inflatum, oculos rubeos aqua plenos, non habent pilos in capite, et dentes ut aper. (5) Motus eorum est sicut magna maris ruina, et signum est, quod magna pluvia iuxta circulum cadere videbitur invocanti.

CXXI De spiritibus meridionalibus

Meridionales sunt isti: **Iammax** rex, **Carmox, Ichanol, Pasfran,** quibus omnes alii regionis demones subduntur, et sunt subditi Marti et vento eius, qui subsolanus dicitur. (2) Et excitantes eum sunt isti 5: **Atraurbiabilis, Yaconaababur, Carmeal, Innial, Proathophas,** et habent hos demones et eorum subditos excitare, constringere, dispergere, congregare ac in loco proprio ligare. (3) Sua natura est guerras et mortalitates, occisiones, prodiciones et combustiones facere, mille milites cum suis famulis, que sunt duo milia, ad tempus dare et mortem tribuere, cuicumque infirmitatem et sanitatem tribuere.

(4) Sua corpora sunt parva, macra, colerica, in aspectu turpissima, color eorum sicut cuprum ignitum modicum denigratum. Habent cornua ad modum cervi, ungues ad modum grifonum. (5) Ululant sicut tauri insani. Motus eorum quasi combustionis partis sue realis aspeccio. Signum est, quod fulgur et tonitruum iuxta circulum cadere videbitur invocanti.

CXX. Concerning the Spirits of the West.

The western ones are four, and all other daemons of the region are under them, of which **Harthan** is the king, **Bileth, Milalu,** and **Habuchaba** are his ministers, and they are subordinate to the Moon and its wind, which is called Zephyr. (2) And raising it up are these: **Hebethel, Amocap, Oilol, Mylau,** and **Abuchaba**, and they have these four daemons and their subordinates to raise up, congregate, scatter, constrain, and bind to their proper place. (3) Their nature is to give silver as desired; they also carry things from place to place; they grant speed to horses; they tell the secrets of persons present and past.

(4) Their bodies are large and ample, soft and phlegmatic, their color resembles dark and obscure clouds, and they have red eyes full of water, greatly inflated; they have no hair on their heads, and their teeth are like those of a boar. (5) Their movement is like a great rushing down of the sea, and the sign is that great rainfall will be seen near the circle when they are invoked.

CXXI. Concerning the Spirits of South.[237]

Those of the South are these: **Iammax** the king, **Carmox, Ichanol, Pasfran**, to whom all other daemons of the region are subordinate, and they are subordinate to Mars and its wind, which is called the Eastern wind. (2) And raising it up are these five: **Atraurbiabilis, Yaconaababur, Carmeal, Innial, Proathophas**, and they have these daemons and their subordinates to raise up, constrain, disperse, congregate, and bind in proper place. (3) Their nature is to cause war, and plague, murders, treasons, and burnings; they also temporarily give one thousand soldiers with their servants, which are two thousand, and they grant death; they also grant sickness or health to anyone.

(4) Their bodies are small, thin, choleric, and very ugly in appearance, their color is like copper that has been blackened a little by fire. They have horns like those of a stag, and nails like a griffin. (5) They howl like mad bulls. Their movement is somewhat like the burning of part of their true appearance.[238] The sign is that lightning and thunder will be seen to fall near the circle when they are invoked.

---

237 Cp. CVII.
238 Compare OP4: Apparebunt longo corpore, cholerico, et aspectum turpissimo:

CXXII De spiritibus septemtrionalibus

Septemtrionales sunt isti: **Maymon** rex, **Albunalich**, **Assaibi**, **Haibalidech**, **Yasfla**, quibus omnes alii demones regionis subduntur, et sunt subditi Saturno et vento eius, qui Affricus dicitur. (2) Et excitantes eum sunt isti 3: **Mextyura, Alcybany, Alflas**, et habent hos 5 demones et eorum subditos congregare, dispergere, constringere ac in loco proprio ligare. (3) Sua natura est seminare discordias, odia generare, malas cogitaciones, furta et avaricias, dare cum libito plumbum, quemlibet interficere et membrorum quodlibet destruere.

(4) Sua corpora sunt longa et gracilia, cum ira et rancore plena. Habent vultus 4, unum a parte anteriori et alterum a parte posteriori, in quibus sunt duo rostra ampla et longa ad mensuram trium pedum, (5) et videntur duos serpentes devorare, et in duobus genibus alios duos, qui cum merore maximo flere videntur, et sunt in colore nigra et lucencia sicut speculum furbitum. (6) Motus eorum est ventorum agitacio cum apparencia terremotus. Signum eorum est, quod terra alba nive tecta videbitur invocanti.

CXXIII

Cum igitur de perfecte bonis et malis diximus, de mediocribus hinc dicamus. (2) Set est advertendum, quod operans non debet operari in istis nec pro perfecte bono nec pro perfecte malo. (3) Set in rebus mobilibus sicut in itinere, in revocacione et subtraccione et similibus operantur.

CXXII. Concerning the Spirits of the North.[239]

The Northern ones are these: **Maymon** the king, **Albunalich, Assaibi, Haibalidech,** and **Yasfla**, and all other daemons of the region are placed under these, and they are subordinate to Saturn and its wind, which is called Africus (or the "southwest wind"). (2) And raising it up are these three: **Mextyura, Alcybany, Alflas,** and they have these five daemons and their subordinates to congregate, disperse, constrain, and bind to their proper place. (3) Their nature is[240] to sow discord, create hatred, evil thoughts, theft, and greed; they give lead if desired, kill anyone, and destroy limbs.

(4) Their bodies[241] are long and slender, full of wrath and anger. They have four faces: one is forward, another behind, which have two large and long beaks measuring three feet, (5) which can be seen devouring two serpents. The other two faces are on the two knees, which appear to be crying with most great mourning, and they are black in color, and shining like a burnished mirror. (6) Their movement is the moving of the wind with the appearance of an earthquake. Their sign is that the ground will appear to be white, covered with snow when they are invoked.

CXXIII. [Concerning the intermediate spirits.]

Having treated of the spirits which are either fully good or fully evil, we will now talk about the intermediate ones (2) But it should be noted in operating with them, that their actions are neither fully for good nor fully for evil. (3) But they operate in movable things such as in journeys, in the recalling and withdrawing and similar things.

---

colore subfusto, et quasi ruffo, cornibus fere ceruinis, et unguibus griphi: mugiunt instar taurorum insanorum. Motus eorum fit quasi instar ignis comburientis. Signum afferent in specie, fulgur et tonitru iuxta circulum. ("They appear in a tall body, choleric, a filthy countenance, of color brown, swarthy or red, having horns like Harts horns, and gryphon's claws, bellowing like wild Bulls. Their Motion is like fire burning; their sign Thunder and Lightning about the Circle.")

239 Cp. CV, spirits of Saturn.
240 This description is almost identical to that found in de Abano, "considerations of Saturday."
241 Cp. OP 4.5a.

CXXIV De spiritibus inter orientem et meridiem

Dicamus igitur, quod inter orientem et meridiem est una regio, que **consol** appellatur, et sunt in ea angeli, qui dicuntur equinocciales, et sunt isti 4: (2) **Formione** rex, **Guth, Maguth, Gutrhyn** eius ministri, quibus omnes alii regionis illius demones subduntur, et sunt subditi Iovi et ventis eius, qui boreas et subsolanus dicuntur. (3) Et excitantes eos sunt isti 5: **Harit, Iesse, Ryon, Nesaph, Naadob**, et habent hos 4 demones et eorum subditos excitare, congregare, constringere, dispergere ac in loco proprio ligare. (4) Sua natura est amicicias et benivolencias tribuere mulierum non carnali copula. Generant leticias, gaudia, lites pacificant, mitigant inimicos, sanant infirmos, infirmant sanos, auferunt vel inferunt dominium cuicumque.

(5) Sua corpora sunt magna, tam sanguinea quam colerica, medie stature, trementissima in motu, visu mitissima, eloquio blanda, falsa in motu, vultus eorum in forma benivolus, color eorum sicut es non burnitum colore flamme ignis depictum. (6) Motus eorum est choruscacio cum tonitruo. Signum eorum est, quod invocans, ut sibi videbitur, [videbit] iuxta circulum homines a leonibus devorari.

CXXV De spiritibus inter austrum et occidentem

Alii sunt inter austrum et occidentem, et sua regio est nogahem. (2) Qui sunt isti: **Sarabocres** rex, **Nassar, Cynassa** eius ministri, quibus omnes alii demones regionis obediunt et subduntur, et sunt subditi Veneri et ven-

CXXIV. Concerning the Spirits between the East and the South.

We therefore declare, that between the east and south is a single region, which is called "Consol",[242] and in it are angels, which are called "equinoctial", and they are these four: (2) **Formione** the king, and his ministers **Guth, Maguth,** and **Gutrhyn [*Guthryn]**,[243] and all other daemons of this region are placed under these, and they are subordinate to Jupiter and its winds, which are called Borean ("Northerly") and Subsolar ("Easterly"). (3) And raising them up (the winds) are these five: **Harit, Iesse, Ryon, Nesaph,** and **Naadob**, and these have four daemons and their subordinates to raise them up, gather them, disperse them, and bind them to their proper place. (4) Their nature is to grant friendship and favor of women, but not carnal relations. They engender gladness and joy, settle lawsuits (or quarrels) peacefully, make enemies mild, cure the sick, sicken the healthy, and they steal away or obtain ownership of anything.

(5) Their bodies are large, as much sanguine as choleric, of medium stature, very jittery, appearing very mild, their manner of speaking flattering, false in the motion. Their faces have a kindly appearance. Their color is like they are painted with flames of fire, not burnished. (6) Their movement is like flashing with thunder. Their sign is, when invoked, lions will be seen devouring men near the circle.[244]

CXXV. Concerning the Spirits between the South and the West.

Others are between the south and the west, and their area is Nogahem, (2) which are these: **Sarabocres** the king, **Nassar,** and **Cynass**a his ministers, with which all other daemons of the area obey and are subjugated, and they

---

242 SSM: Cosol; Leipzig: Casol.
243 Spelled Guthryn or Guthrin all other passages. SSM: Gutryn.
244 OP4: Apparent corpore sanguineo et cholerico, mediae staturae, horribili motu, visu mitissimo, blando colloquio, <u>colore ferrugineo</u>. Motus eorum, est coruscatio, cum tonitru. Signum eorum, apparebunt iuxta circulum homines, qui in specie a leonibus devorabuntur. Formae autem particulares sunt: ("The spirits of Jupiter do appear with a body sanguine and choleric, of a middle stature, with a horrible fearful motion; but with a middle countenance, a gentle speech, <u>and of the color of iron</u>. The motion of them is flashings of lightning and thunder; their sign is, there will appear men about the circle, who shall seem to be devoured of lions.")

tis eius, qui sunt subsolanus et zephirus. (3) Et excitantes eos sunt isti 4: **Cambores** <rex>, **Trachatat, Nassar, Naassa,** et habent hos tres demones excitare, congregare, dispergere, constringere ac in loco proprio ligare. (4) Et eorum natura est dare argentum, in quo est impressio signata, et stagnum ad libitum hominis calefacere, luxuriam excitare, inimicos per luxuriam concordare, ut matrimonium ostendit, (5) constringere homines in amorem mulierum et ipsas ad hominum voluntates constringi, homines infirmare vel sanare et facere omnia, que moventur.

(6) Sua corpora sunt medie stature, pulcra, dulcia et iocosa, color eorum sicut nix insuper deaurata, motus eorum sicut stella clarissima, signum eorum, quod puelle extra circulum ludere et ipsum vocare videbitur invocanti.

CXXVI De spiritibus inter occidentem et septemtrionem

Alii sunt inter occidentem et septemtrionem, et sua regio est frigicap. (2) Qui sunt isti 5: **Abaa** rex, **Hyici, Quyron, Zach, Eladeb** eius ministri, quibus omnes alii illius regionis demones obediunt et subduntur, et sunt subditi Mercurio et ventis eius, qui zephirus et Affricus dicuntur. (3) Et excitantes eos sunt isti 4: **Zobha** <rex>, **Drohas, Palas, Zambas,** et habent hos 5 demones excitare, congregare, dispergere, constringere ac in loco proprio ligare. (4) Natura eorum est omnia metalla de mundo, quecumque fuerint, literata vel sculpta cum auro et argento ad libitum dare, omnia preterita, presencia et futura terrena revelare, (5) iudices placare in placito, victoriam dare, experimenta et omnes sciencias destructas rectificare et reedificare et eciam docere, (6) corpora eciam ex elementis mixta convertibiliter unum in aliud transmutare et eciam elementa, senem iuvenem facere et e contrario, dare infirmitatem quamlibet vel eciam sanitatem, si placeat invocanti, (7) pauperes sublimare, sublimes opprimere, dignitates dare vel auferre cuicumque, spiritus ligare, ad tempus inclusum impedire, seraturas aperire, transfiguraciones facere. (8) Et isti possunt omnes operaciones aliorum facere, set hoc non ex perfecta potencia vel virtute set sciencia bene.

are subordinate to Venus and its winds, which are easterly and westerly. (3) And there are four spirits which raise them up: **Cambores, Trachatat, Nassar, Naassa,** and they have those three daemons to raise up, bring together, disperse, constrain, and bind them in their own place. (4) And their nature is to give silver, in which the sign is impressed, and tin, for arousing human desire, to cause luxury, to bring harmony to enemies through luxury, as marriage shows, (5) to bind men in love of women, and bind women to the wills of men, to sicken or cure people, and to make all things which are moved.

(6) Their bodies are medium in stature, pretty, pleasant, and merry. Their color is like snow over gilding. Their movements are like the clearest star. Their sign of their presence is that when invoked, a girl will be seen playing outside the circle, and calling to you.

CXXVI. Concerning the Spirits between the West and the North.

Others are between the west and the north, and their area is Frigicap. (2) Which are five: **Abaa** the king, and **Hyici, Quyron, Zach, Eladeb** his ministers, whom all other daemons of the area obey and are subject to, and they are subject to Mercury and his wind, which is the west wind (Zephyr), and they are called African.[245] (3) And raising them up there are these four: **Zobha** <the king>, **Drohas, Palas, Zambas**, and they have five daemons to raise up, congregate, disperse, constrain, and bind them in their own place. (4) Their nature is to give all metals from the earth, whichever exist, lettered or sculpted with gold and silver as desired, to reveal all earthly things pasts, present, and future, (5) to appease judges in a plea, to give victory, to recover and reconstruct experiments and all destroyed knowledge, and also to teach them, (6) also to transmute bodies out of the mixed elements changeably, one into the other, and also the elements, to make an old person young and vice versa, to infect someone with any kind of sickness, and also to make them healthy, if they are placated when invoked, (7) to raise up poor men, bring down the high and mighty, to give dignities to whomever, or take them away, to bind spirits, to hinder imprisonment for a time, to open locks, and to make transfigurations. (8) And these same spirits are able to accomplish all other operations, however not with perfect power or virtue, but with sufficient knowledge.

---

245 *Africus* means either the southwest wind, or from Africa.

(9) Sua corpora sunt medie stature, frigida, humida, veneranda, pulcra, rauca in eloquio, humanam formam habencia ad modum armigeri compti et cucufati, color eorum sicut nubes clara, motus eorum sicut nubes argentea. (10) Signum est, quod horripilacionem tribuunt invocanti. Et isti possunt indifferenter ubicumque vocari.

CXXVII Finita divisione angelorum et spirituum incipit modus operandi in eis.

Si ergo de istis aliquis voluerit operari, sibi primo districte precipimus, (2) ut peroptime mundetur, sicut diximus in predictis, donec venerit ad diem 14^{am}, in qua die convenit ieiunare. (3) Tunc in ea recipiat corpus Christi dicendo 19, 20, et cum missa de sancto Spiritu, ut diximus, igitur celebratur, sacerdos tenendo corpus Christi, antequam gentibus ostendatur, petat pro operante sic dicens:

(4) ORACIO

"Domine Iesu Christe, fili Dei vivi, quem credo firmiter hominem et Deum et iudicem meum venturum, peto te in hoc articulo in virtute istius sacramenti tui, (5) ut talis N ex dono tuo ac tua voluntate sine dampnacione corporis et anime sibi spiritus N in omnibus subiciat, ut apparere, perficere, custodire, respondere eos ad omnia precepta constringat, ut sperat et desiderat. Amen."

(6) Tunc audito completorio, ut dictum est, de ecclesia recedat dicens 17, donec veniat ad locum, in quo debet fieri circulus. Tunc locum benedicat dicens 15. (7) Hoc facto protrahat circulum 9 pedum dicens 18, in quo duos circulos protrahat, quorum unus distet ab alio per unum pedem, inter quos scribes nomina angelorum diei et hore, mensis, temporis, faciei dicendo:

(9) Their bodies are of medium stature, cold, humid, venerable, attractive, and their manner of speaking is hoarse. They have human form, bearing arms and hooded. Their color is like a bright cloud. Their movements are like a silvery cloud. (10) Their sign is that your hair will bristle when they are invoked. And they can be called in any place equally.[246]

CXXVII. End of the divisions of the angels and spirits, and beginning of the manner of working with them.

If therefore anybody wishes to operate with those spirits, we must first warn him strictly (2) that he must be thoroughly purified, as we have said in the preceding, until he comes to the fourteenth day, on which day he must begin his fast. (3) Then when the mass of the Holy Spirit is being said or celebrated, when the operator is receiving the body of Christ (Eucharist), he should say prayers 19 and 20 (LXXVII–LXXIX), as we have said, when the priest is holding up the body of Christ (i.e. the wafer), to reveal it to the congregation, he should pray on behalf of the operator, saying thus:

(4) Prayer.

"O Lord Jesus Christ, son of the living God, whom I truly believe is man and God, and my judge soon to come, I beg you in this critical moment, by the power of your sacraments, (5) in order that such N. by your gift and by your will, without condemnation of body and soul that the spirit N. may make himself subject in all things, that he may constrain them to appear, to complete, to guard, to answer to all orders that he hopes and desires. Amen."

(6) Then having heard the evening prayer service (Compline), as said, retire from the church, saying 17, until you come to the place where the circle has been made. Then bless the place saying 15. (7) With this done, he should draw a circle of nine feet across, saying 18, in which he should draw two circles, where the first is one foot away from the other, between which you should write the names of the angels of the day and hour, of the month, of the time, and of the aspect,[247] saying:

---

246 Cp H p. 146–7.
247 Aspect (face): i.e. decan.

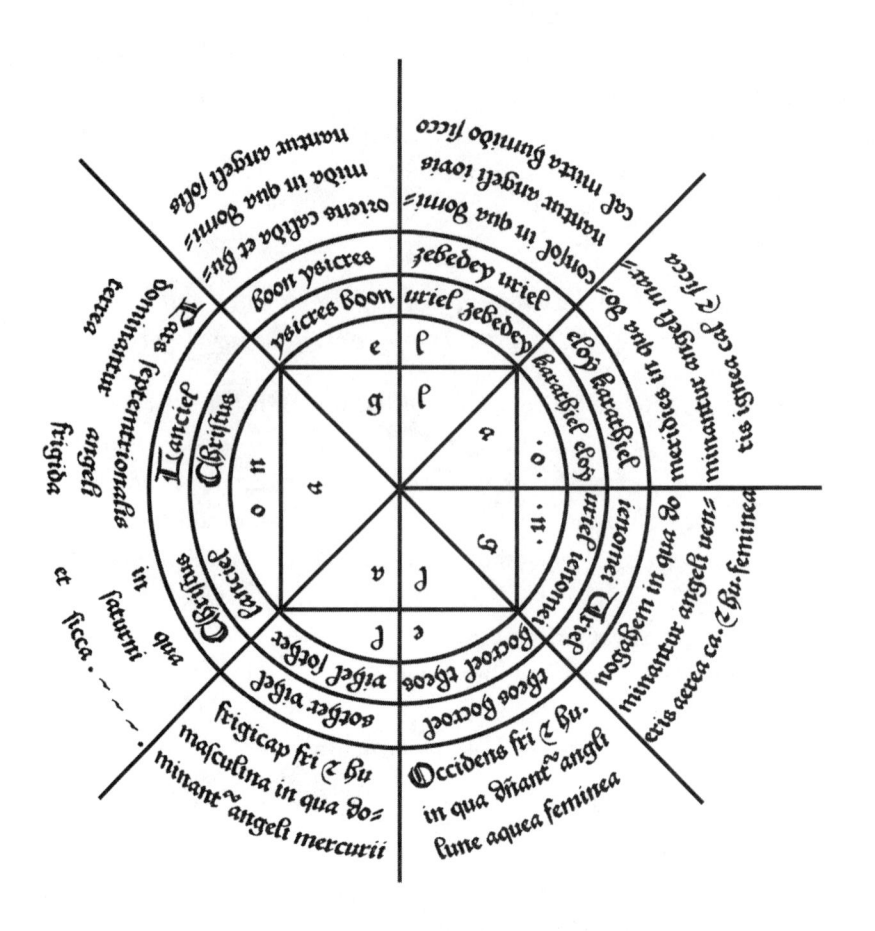

(8) "O vos angeli sancti et potentes, sitis michi in hoc opere adiutores."

(9) Tunc protrahes infra istos duos circulos eptagonum communem omnibus invocacionibus aptum, cuius forma cum parcium suarum dimencionibus et diffinicionibus subsequitur inferius in figura.

Sworn Book of Honorius 241

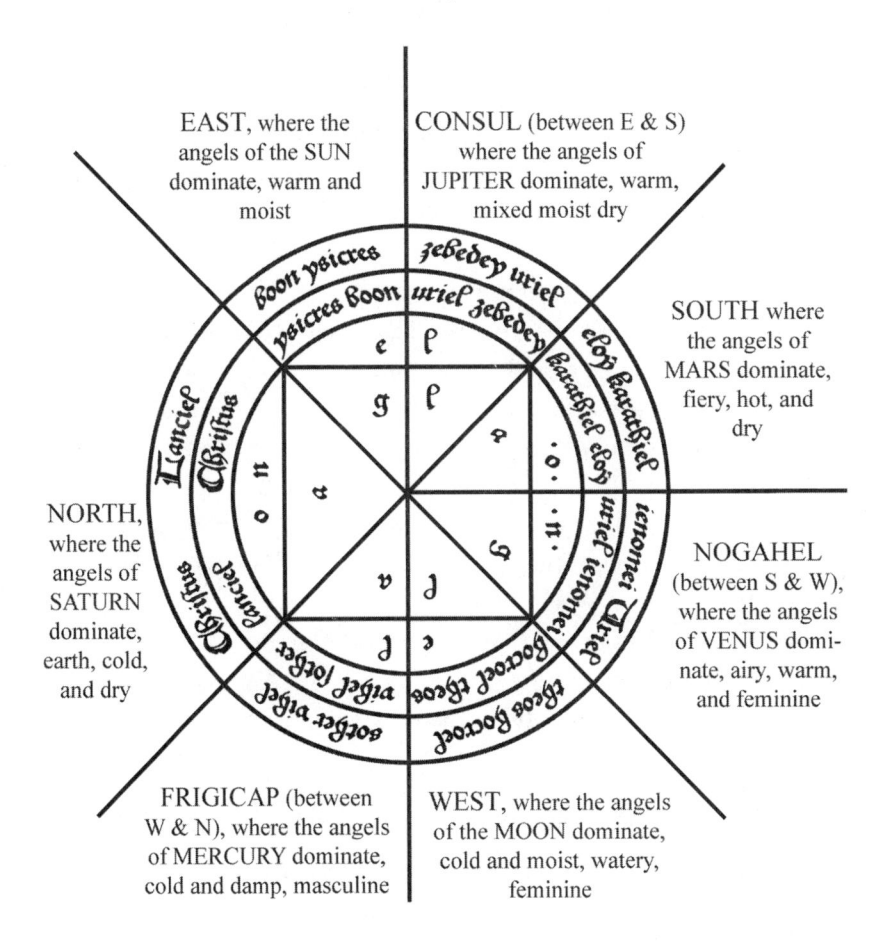

EAST, where the angels of the SUN dominate, warm and moist

CONSUL (between E & S) where the angels of JUPITER dominate, warm, mixed moist dry

SOUTH where the angels of MARS dominate, fiery, hot, and dry

NOGAHEL (between S & W), where the angels of VENUS dominate, airy, warm, and feminine

WEST, where the angels of the MOON dominate, cold and moist, watery, feminine

FRIGICAP (between W & N), where the angels of MERCURY dominate, cold and damp, masculine

NORTH, where the angels of SATURN dominate, earth, cold, and dry

(8) "O you holy and powerful angels, may you be my assistants in this work."

(9) Then draw within those two circles a regular heptagon,[248] suitable for all invocations, the form of which with its parts, dimension, and definitions, is shown in the figure above.[249]

---

248 The drawings in Sl. 3854 amd Sl. 313 do not resemble heptagons, but other exemplars do, e.g. 3853 150v, and SSM L.3.f.29. Leipzig Cod. Mag. 16 p. 112 is similar to Sl. 3854.
249 Figure not found in C or R. B shows North occupying 90 degrees. D and SSM show seven equal segments. L shows the West as occupying 90 degrees. SSM text has slight variations in the order and especially in the names. See Appendix II.

(10) Nota, quod operans debet esse diligens, ut addat ista nomina aliis nominibus, quia durum est homini ignoranti virtutes spirituum et eorum malicias cum eis sine municione maxima aliqualiter habitare, (11) et assimilatur illi, qui vult debellare militem sagacem et ignorat arma eius et quis miles et que virtus militis, quem debellat. (12) Bene igitur sibi caveat, quia ingenium viribus prevalet, et ideo oportet ipsum esse sagacissimum in suo circulo faciendo, quia ibi iacet tuicio operantis.

(13) Primo sic aptetur locus, quod terra sit plana et equa, nec sint ibi lapides aut herbe, et quando eum protraxerit, aerem supra se duobus diametris ubicumque signet dicens: (14) "Signum Salomonis ad salvacionem et defensionem pono supra me, ut sit michi proteccio a facie inimici. In nomine Patris et Filii et Spiritus sancti. Amen." (15) Sic tuo completo circulo exi et extra eum scribe in terra vel in cedulis 7 nomina creatoris, que sunt L[a]ialy, Lialg, Veham, Yalgal, Narath, Libarre, Libares, nec plus facies in hac nocte.

Oriens calida[37] et humida[38] in qua dominantur angeli solis / boon ysicres[39] / ysicres boon

Consol[40] in qua dominantur angeli iovis, ca[lido], mixta humido sicco[41] / Zebedey Uriel[42] / Uriel Zebedei.

Meridies in qua dominantur angeli martis ignea cal[ida] et sicca / Eloy Karathiel / Karathiel Eloy[43]

Nogahem[44] in qua dominantur angeli ueneris **aerea**[45] ca[lida] et hu[midi] feminea / ienomei Uriel / Uriel ienomei[46]

Occidens frigida et hu[mida] in qua dominantur angli lune aquea feminea[47] / theos Hocroel[48] / Hocroel theos

---

37 Calida: SSM: pars calida
38 Humida: SSM adds: masculina
39 boon ysicres: SSM: Beon ysystres
40 Consol: SSM calls this cosol throughout the manuscript.
41 Calido mixta humino sicco: B: mixta cum hu. SSM: mixta calida et sicca
42 Zebedey Uriel: SSM: Zebedye, Vuel
43 Eloy Karathiel / Karathiel Eloy: B: elothi karathi / karathi elothi. SSM: Eloy barachiel / barachyel Eloy
44 Nogahem: B, D: Nogaham. SSM: Nogaem
45 Aerea: D: aerei
46 ienomei Uriel / Uriel ienomei: SSM: Genonem, Uryel / Uriel, genonem
47 Feminea: D: semina
48 Hocroel: B: Ocrohel; D: Hocrohel. SSM: atrohel

(10) NOTE: You must be very careful while working, that you add those names to the other names,[250] because it is hard for a person not knowing the powers of the spirits and their malice, without the greatest fortification to abide with them somehow, (11) and it is like someone who seeks to wage war with a shrewd knight, and disregards his weapons, and who the knight is, and what are the strengths of the knight with whom he wages war. (12) It is well therefore to be cautious, because the nature of the strengths prevail, and therefore it is necessary to be very shrewd when making the circle, because therein lies the defense of the operator.

(13) First you must prepare the place thus, for the earth should be flat and level, and free from stones or vegetation, and when it has been drawn, mark the air above yourself to two diameters every way, saying: (14) "I put the Seal of Solomon over me for salvation and defense, in order that it protect me in the face of the enemy. In the name of the Father and the Son and the Holy Spirit. Amen." (15) Thus with your circle complete, exit and write outside in the earth or on small pieces of paper, the seven names of the creator, which are **L[a]ialy, Lialg, Veham, Yalgal, Narath, Libarre, Libares**,[251] and nothing more is accomplished this night.

[Text of Circle reads as follows:]

East, warm and moist,[252] where the angels of the Sun dominate / Boon Ysicres / Ysicres Boon[253]
Consol,[254] where the angels of **Jupiter** dominate, warm mixed moist dry / Zebedey Uriel / Uriel Zebedei
South in which the angels of **Mars**, fiery, hot and dry, dominate / Eloy Karathiel / Karathiel Eloy
Nogahem, where dominate the angels of **Venus**, airy, warm, and feminine / Ienomei Uriel / Uriel Ienomei
West cold and moist, where the angels of the **Moon** dominate, watery feminine / Theos Hocroel / Hocroel Theos

---

250 That is, to add the names of God, such as "Theos" and "Sother," to that of the appropriate angels of the day etc.
251 SSM: <u>Layaly</u>, lyalg, <u>veham</u>, yalgal, <u>narach</u>, lybarre, lybares. Compare the Seal of God. Compare also Wellcome 110, fol. 45v.
252 SSM adds: masculine.
253 Boon: SSM reads "beon." This name doesn't appear elsewhere in the text.
254 This text is included in the diagram of the circle, and not part of the text.

frigicap frigida et hu[mida] masculina in qua dominantur angeli mercurii / Sother Vihel[49] / Vihel Sother

Pars[50] septemtrionalis in qua dominantur angeli Saturni terrea frigida et sicca / Christus Lanciel / Lanciel Christus[51]

CXXVIII Secunda dies

In crastino, dum matutinam, primam, terciam, missam, meridiem, nonam, vesperas et completorium audieris, venies ad circulum dicendo 17. (2) Tunc habeas thus et thuribulum, in quo sint prune, et ponas thus super prunas et suffumiges circulum dicens 1 et 2 incipiens ab oriente in occidentem, a meridie in septemtrionem, tunc a consol in noghahem et a noghahem in frigicap, et postea celum et terram, et ita ter facies. (3) Set primo debent 7 predicta nomina deleri. Hoc facto suffumigando circulum, ventos novies taliter excitabis.

(4) INCIPIT EXCITACIONIS VENTORUM PRIMUS CIRCULUS INCIPIENS IN ORIENTE ET TERMINANS IN MERIDIE.

(5) "Baxhatau, Gahatus, Caudes, Yarabal, Harit, Iesse, Rion, Nesaph, Naadob, Attraurbiabilis, Yaconaababur, Carmeal, Ynial, Prohathophas, Cambores, Trachatat, Nassar, (6) Naassa, Hebethel, Amocap, Oylol, Mylau, Abucaba, Zobha, Drohas, Palas, Sambas, Mextyura, Alcybany, Alflas, ego vos invoco, ut meis sitis prom[p]ti[52] peticionibus et preceptis. Summa Dei potencia vos obedire constringat".

(7) Secundus circulus incipiens in meridie et terminans in occidente

(8) "Attraurbiabilis, Y[a]conaababur, Carmeal, Innyal, Prohathophas, Cambores, Trachatat, Nassar, Naassa, Hebethel, Amocap, Oylol, Mylau, Abuchaba, Zobha, (9) Drohas, Palas, Sambas, Mextyura, Alcibany, Alflas, Baxatau, Gahatus, [Caudes, Yarabal, Harit], Iesse,

---

49 Vihel: D: Viel. SSM: Vyel
50 Pars: D and SSM omit.
51 Christus Lanciel / Lanciel Christus: D: Christus Lancihel / Lancihel Christus. SSM: Christus, lancyel, Christus / Lancyel, Christus / lancyel (!)
52 Promti: *Prompti. Compare CXXIX 9 and 14 and SSM L.3.f.30.

Frigicap, cold and damp, masculine, where the angels of **Mercury** dominate. / Sother Vihel / Vihel Sother
Northern part, where the angels of **Saturn** dominate, earth cold and dry / Christ Lanciel / Lanciel Christ

CXXVIII. Second day.

On the next day you should hear matins, prime, terce, mass, none, vespers, and compline, then go to the circle saying prayer 17. (2) Then you should have incense and a censer, in which should be glowing charcoals, and you should put the incense over the glowing charcoals, and fumigate the circle saying 1 (LIII) and 2 (LIV), beginning at the East to the West, from the South to the North, then from Consol to Nogahem, and then from Nogahem to Frigicap, and afterwards the sky and the earth, and this you should do three times. (3) But first the seven preceding names must be erased.[255] With this done, suffumigate the circle, and in this way you should raise up the winds nine times.

(4) Here begins the raising up of the winds. The first circle beginning in the east and ending in the south:

(5) "Baxhatau, Gahatus, Caudes, Yarabal, Harit, Iesse, Rion, Nesaph, Naadob, Attraurbiabilis, Yaconaababur, Carmeal, Ynial, Prohathophas, Cambores, Trachatat, Nassar, (6) Naassa, Hebethel, Amocap, Oylol, Mylau, Abucaba, Zobha, Drohas, Palas, Sambas, Mextyura, Alcybany, Alflas,[256] I invoke you, that you allow me those things which are described in my petitions and orders. The power of the most high God constrains you to obey!"

(7) The second circle beginning in the south, and end in the west.

(8) "Attraurbiabilis, Y[a]conaababur, Carmeal, Innyal, Prohathophas, Cambores, Trachatat, Nassar, Naassa, Hebethel, Amocap, Oylol, Mylau, Abuchaba, Zobha, (9) Drohas, Palas, Sambas, Mextyura, Alcibany, Alflas,

---

255 See CXXVII.15.
256 SSM L.3.f.30: <u>Baxahathau, gaatus, candones,</u> yarabal, <u>haryx,</u> yesse, ryon, nesaph, <u>naadobp:</u> <u>atrahurbyabylys,</u> yaconaablaburo, carmeal, <u>iunyal, proathofas:</u> cambores, trachatat, nassar, (6) <u>naassah:</u> hebethel, <u>amocab,</u> oylol, <u>mylalu,</u> abucaba: zobha, drohas, palas, Sambas: Mextyura, <u>Altybany, alphlas.</u>

Ryon, Nesaph, Naadob, angeli Domini vos excitent, qui vos venire constringant."

(10) Tercius circulus incipiens in occidente et terminans in septemtrione

Tunc in occidente dicat: (11) "Hebethel, Amocap, Oylol, Milau, Abucaba, Zobha, Drohas, Palas, Zambas, Mextyura, Alcybany, Alflas, Baxhatau, Gaatus, Caudes, Yarabal, Harit, Iesse, Rion, Nesaph, (12) Naadob, Attraurbiabilis, Yaconaababur, Carmeal, Ynnyal, Proathophas, Cambores, Trachathat, Nassar, Naassa, sciencia Dei et sapiencia Salomonis vos convincat, que vos et ventos vestros excitare faciat."

(13) Quartus circulus incipiens in septemtrione et terminans in consol

Tunc in septemtrione dicat: (14) "Mextyura, Alchibany, Alflas, Baxhatau, Gahatus, Caudes, Iaraba<a>l, Harith, Iesse, Ryon, Nesaph, Naadob, Attraurbiabilis, Iaconaababur, Carmeal, Innyal, Prohathophas, Cambores, (15) Trachathat, Nassar, Naassa, Hebethel, Amocap, Oylol, Myla<l>u, Abucaba, Zobha, Drohas, Palas, Sambas, sancta nomina Dei vos subiugent, que vos et ventos vestros excitare et huc venire constringant."

(16) Quintus circulus incipiens in consol et terminans in nogahem

Tunc in consol dicat: (17) "Harit, Iesse, Ryon, Nesaph, Naadob, Attraurbiabilis, Yaconaababur, Carme[a]l, Innyal, Prohathophas, Cambores, Trachatath, Nassar, Naassa, Hebethel, Amocap, Oylol, (18) Mylau, Abucaba, Zobha, Drohas, Palas, Zambas, [Mextyura, Alcybany, Alflas], Baxhatau, Gaatus, Caudes, Yarabal, capud et corona principis vestri Belzebut vos venire et ventos vestros excitare constringat."

(19) 6us circulus incipiens in nogahem et terminans in frigicap

Tunc in nogahem dicat: (20) "Cambores, Tracatath, Nassar, Naassa, Hebethel, Amocap, Oylol, Mylau, Abucaba, Zobha, Drohas, Palas, Sambas, Mextyura, Alcybany, Alflas, Baxhatau, Gaatus, Caudes, Yarabal, (21) Harith, Iesse, Ryon, Nesaph, Naadob, Attraurbiabilis, Iaconaababur, Carmeal, Ynnyal, Prohathophas, iudicium summi Dei tremendum vos convincat, qui vos et ventos vestros ad mandatum meum venire et obedire constringat."

(22) 7us circulus incipiens in frigicap et terminans in oriente

Baxatau, Gahatus, [Caudes, Yarabal, Harit], Iesse, Ryon, Nesaph, Naadob,[257] may those angels of the Lord raise you up, who compel you to come."

(10) Third, begin the circle in the west, and end in the north.

Then, facing west, say: (11) "Hebethel, Amocap, Oylol, Milau, Abucaba, Zobha, Drohas, Palas, Zambas, Mextyura, Alcybany, Alflas, Baxhatau, Gaatus, Caudes, Yarabal, Harit, Iesse, Rion, Nesaph, (12) Naadob, Attraurbiabilis, Yaconaababur, Carmeal, Ynnyal, Proathophas, Cambores, Trachathat, Nassar, Naassa, the knowledge of God and the wisdom of Solomon conquers you, so that you and your winds are made to rise up."

(13) Fourth, begin the circle in the north, and ending in Consol.

Then, facing north, say: (14) "Mextyura, Alchibany, Alflas, Baxhatau, Gahatus, Caudes, Iarabal, Harith, Iesse, Ryon, Nesaph, Naadob, Attraurbiabilis, Iaconaababur, Carmeal, Innyal, Prohathophas, Cambores, (15) Trachathat, Nassar, Naassa, Hebethel, Amocap, Oylol, Myla<l>u, Abucaba, Zobha, Drohas, Palas, Sambas, the sacred names of God will subjugate you, who compel you and your winds to arise and come here."

(16) Fifth, begin the circle in consol, and end in Nogahem.

Then, in consol, say: (17) "Harit, Iesse, Ryon, Nesaph, Naadob, Attraurbiabilis, Yaconaababur, Carme[a]l, Innyal, Prohathophas, Cambores, Trachatath, Nassar, Naassa, Hebethel, Amocap, Oylol, (18) Mylau, Abucaba, Zobha, Drohas, Palas, Zambas, Mextyura, Alcybany, Alflas, Baxhatau, Gaatus, Caudes, Yarabal, the head and crown of your prince Belzebut compels you to arise and come."

(19) Sixth, begin the circle in Nogahem and end in Frigicap.

Then, towards Nogahem say: (20) "Cambores, Tracatath, Nassar, Naassa, Hebethel, Amocap, Oylol, Mylau, Abucaba, Zobha, Drohas, Palas, Sambas, Mextyura, Alcybany, Alflas, Baxhatau, Gaatus, Caudes, Yarabal, (21) Harith, Iesse, Ryon, Nesaph, Naadob, Attraurbiabilis, Iaconaababur, Carmeal, Ynnyal, Prohathophas, the terrible judgment of the most high God conquers you, which compels you and your winds to come at my command, and obey."

(22) Seventh, begin the circle in frigicap, and end in the East:

---

257 SSM: Hatraurbyabylys, yaconablabur, carmeal, iunyal, prohatofas, cambores, trachatat, nassar, naassah, hebethel, amocab, oylol, mylalu, aabucaba: zobah, (9) drohas, palas, Sambas, mextyura, alcibany, alphlas, baxathau, cahatus, caudones, yarabal, haryth, yesse, ryon, nesaph, naadob.

Tunc in frigicap dicat: (23) "Zobha, Drohas, Palas, Sambas, Mextyura, Alcybany, Alflas, Baxhatau, Gaatus, Caudes, Yarabal, Harith, Iesse, Ryon, (24) Nesaph, Naadob, Attraurbiabilis, Yaconaababur, Carmeal, Innyal, Prohathophas, Cambores, Trachatath, [Nassar, Naassa], Hebethel, Amocap, Oilol, Mylau, Ab<r>ucaba, meo placati suffumigio, (25) timor furoris Domini et ignis ignem devorans vos pacificet et pacificatos mittat cum ventis vobis subditis et demonibus eorundem et missos obedire constringat, quoniam ei debetur ab omni creatura reverencia et obediencia cum timore."

(26) Tunc flexis genibus versus orientem dic: "Unde tu, Domine, 49, celi et terre conditor" et cetera. Et addes in fine: "Te suppliciter exoro et invoco, ut ex dono gracie tue et virtute sanctorum tuorum nominum, (27) ut isti prenominati venti hos demones, quos invocavero, congregent, constringant et ligent eos meis peticionibus penitus obedire, (28) quia tu es Deus potens, pius et misericors, qui vivis et regnas et imperas et regnaturus es per omnia secula seculorum. Amen."

(29) Hoc facto videbis tranquillitatem ab omni parte mundi in nubibus elevari, nec cessabit, donec perfeceris tuum opus, et erunt nubes iuxta circulum circumcirca. (30) Set prius iuxta circulum hec 7 predicta nomina scribantur, quia posset circulus aliter violari.

CXXIX 3ª dies

Tercia vero die<s> visitabis ecclesiam, ut oportet, et tunc habeas ignem, candelam de cera virginea et illa, que tue conveniunt questioni, thuribulum, thus, 7 gladios equales, (2) si possis claros, et si velis habere socios, poteris habere 7. Habeas eciam vinum optimum, de quo bibes, et socii tui, dum cognoveritis motus suos. (3) Et si solus fueris, porta 4 in latere dextro et 3 in sinistro, si tres, porta 3, et quilibet illorum 2, si 5, ferat quilibet unum, et tu 3, si 4, porta unum, et quilibet illorum 2, si 6, porta 2, et quilibet illorum unum.

Then, in Frigicap, say: (23) "Zobha, Drohas, Palas, Sambas, Mextyura, Alcybany, Alflas, Baxhatau, Gaatus, Caudes, Yarabal, Harith, Iesse, Ryon, (24) Nesaph, Naadob, Attraurbiabilis, Yaconaababur, Carmeal, Innyal, Prohathophas, Cambores, Trachatath, [Nassar, Naassa], Hebethel, Amocap, Oilol, Mylau, Ab<r>ucaba, with my pleasing suffumigation, (25) the maddening fear of the Lord, and the fire of fires, pacifies you, and pacified may he send with your winds the subordinates and daemons of the same, and may he bind the messengers to obey, because all creatures owe him reverence and obedience with fear."

(26) Then, bending your knees to the east, say: "From whence you, O Lord, 49, the originator of heaven and earth" etc. And add at the end: "I humbly beg and pray to you, that by the gift of your grace and the power of your holy names, (27) that these daemons of the previously-named wind, which I have called upon, may assemble; may they be constrained and bound to obey my petitions completely, (28) because you are a mighty God, kind and merciful, who lives and reigns and commands through all eternity. Amen."

(29) With this done, you will see a stillness from all parts of the world, rising up to the clouds, nor will it cease until you have completed your work, and the clouds will be all around near the circle. (30) But these seven preceding names should be written next to the circle beforehand, because otherwise they might be able to violate the circle.

CXXIX. The Third Day.

On the third day you should visit the church, as usual, and then you should have a fire, a candle of virgin wax, and those things which are relevant to the inquiry,[258] the censer, the incense, seven equal swords, (2) if possible they should be lustrous, and if you wish to have associates, you can have seven. You may also have a choice wine, which you and your associates can drink while you look for their movements. (3) And if you are alone, carry four swords on your right side, and three on your left. If there are three of you, carry three swords yourself and the others should each carry two; if there are five, carry three yourself, and the others should each carry one; if there are four, carry one yourself, and the others should each carry two.

---

258 GH p. 38: "whatever else suits his purpose."

(4) Tunc XI^a hora die[i], cum fueritis competenter saciati vino et piscibus vel aliquo alio a carne, magister semel excitet ventos incipiendo ab illis, qui habent dominium die illa, et habeat signum Domini in manu sua dextra. Post hoc demones excitabit dicens contra orientem:

(5) EXCITACIO SPIRITUUM SOLIS, QUE FIT IN DIE DOMINICO, QUANDO FIT PARTICULARITER.

"Ubi est Barthan rex, ubi sunt Thaadas, [Caudas], Yalcal eius ministri? (6) Ubi est Formione rex, ubi sunt Guth, Maguth, Guthrin eius ministri? Ubi est Iammax rex, ubi sunt Carmox, Ycanol, Pasfran eius ministri? (7) Ubi est Sarabocres rex, ubi sunt Nassar, Cynassa eius ministri? Ubi est Harthan rex, ubi sunt Bileth, Mylalu, Abucaba eius ministri? (8) Ubi est Abaa rex, ubi sunt Hyici, Quyron, Zach, Eladeb eius ministri? Ubi est Maymon rex, ubi sunt Assaiby, Albunalich, [Haibalidech, Yasfla] eius ministri? (9) Omnes occurrite cicius quam poteritis promti meis peticionibus et preceptis obedire. Summa ac divina maiestas vos convincat, que vos venire constringat."

(10) EXCITACIO DIEI IOVIS ET SPIRITUUM EIUS, QUANDO PARTICULARITER FIT.

[Tunc in consol dicat:] "Ubi est Formione rex, ubi sunt Guth, Maguth, Guthrin eius ministri? (11) Ubi est Iammax rex, ubi sunt Carmox, Ycanol, Pasfran eius ministri? Ubi est Sarabocres rex, ubi sunt Nassar, Cinassa eius ministri? (12) Ubi est Harthan rex, ubi sunt Bileth, Mylalu, Abucaba eius ministri? Ubi est Abaa rex, ubi sunt Hyici, Quiron, Zach, Eladeb eius ministri? (13) Ubi est Maymon rex, ubi sunt Hassaybi, Albunalich, Haibalidech, Yasfla [eius ministri]? Ubi est Barthan rex, ubi sunt Thaadas, Caudas, Yalcal

(4) Then in the eleventh hour of the day, when you have been suitably satisfied with wine and fish, or any other meat, the master should raise up the winds once, beginning with those which have dominion on that day, and he should have the Sign of the Lord in his right hand. After this he should raise up the daemons saying towards the east:

(5) THE RAISING UP OF THE SPIRITS OF THE SUN, WHICH SHOULD PARTICULARLY BE DONE ON A SUNDAY.

"Where is King Barthan?[259] where are Thaadas, [Caudas],[260] and Yalcal his ministers? (6) Where is King Formione? where are Guth, Maguth, and Guthrin his ministers? Where is King Iammax?, where are Carmox, Ycanol, and Pasfran his ministers? (7) Where is King Sarabocres? where are Nassar and Cynassa his ministers? Where is King Harthan? where are Bileth, Mylalu, and Abucaba his ministers? (8) Where is King Abaa? where are his ministers Hyici, Quyron, Zach, and Eladeb? Where is King Maymon? where are his ministers Assaiby, Albunalich, [Haibalidech, and Yasfla]? (9) Come with all haste to meet us, that you are willing and able to obey my petitions and precepts. The Most High and Divine Majesty conquers you, so that you are constrained to come."

(10) THE RAISING UP OF THE DAY OF JUPITER, AND THOSE SPIRITS WHICH ARE PARTICULAR TO IT.

[Then in Consol say:] "Where is King Formione? Where are his ministers Guth, Maguth, and Guthrin? (11) Where is King Iammax? Where are his ministers Carmox, Ycanol, and Pasfran? Where is King Sarabocres? Where are his ministers Nassar and Cinassa? (12) Where is King Harthan? Where are his ministers Bileth, Mylalu, and Abucaba? Where is King Abaa? Where are his ministers Hyici, Quiron, Zach, and Eladeb? (13) Where is King Maymon? Where are [his ministers] Hassaybi, Albunalich, Haibalidech, and Yasfla? Where is King Barthan? Where are his ministers Thaadas, Caudas, and

---

259 Gershom Scholem asserts that this indirect form of addressing the spirits is an indication of Arabic influence ("Some Sources of Jewish-Arabic Demonology," *Journal of Jewish Studies* 15 (1965): 1-13, cited in Mesler 2012 p. 142 n91.)
260 See below, 13, 17, 21, 25, 33, and CXIX.2. SSM L.3.f.31: thaadas, <u>caaudas</u>, <u>yarabal</u>.

eius ministri? (14) Omnes cicius quam poteritis venite cum omnibus subditis vestris promti michi in omnibus obedire. Virtus summi creatoris vos subiuget, que vos venire constringat."

(15) Excitacio diei Martis et spirituum eius, quando perticulariter fit.

Tunc in meridie dicat: "Ubi est Iammax rex, ubi sunt Carmox, Ycanol, Pasfran eius ministri? (16) Ubi est Sarabocres rex, ubi sunt Nassar, Cynassa eius ministri? Ubi est Harthan rex, ubi sunt Bileth, Milalu, Abucaba eius ministri? Ubi est Abaa rex, ubi sunt Hyici, Quyron, Zach, Eladeb eius min[i]stri? (17) Ubi est Maymon rex, ubi sunt Assaibi, Albunalich, Aybalidech, Yasfla eius ministri? Ubi est Barthan rex, ubi sunt Thaadas, Caudas, Yalcal eius ministri? (18) Ubi est Formione rex, ubi sunt Guth, Maguth, Guthryn eius ministri? Vos invoco venire cum excercitu vestro et meis questionibus obedire. Timor furoris Domini vos convincat, qui vos venire et obedire constringat."

(19) Excitacio diei Veneris et spirituum eius, quando particulariter fit.

Tunc in nogahem dicat: "Ubi est Sarabocres rex, ubi sunt Nassar, Cynassa eius ministri? (20) Ubi est Harthan rex, ubi sunt Bileth, Milalu, Abucaba eius ministri? Ubi est Abaa rex, ubi sunt Hyici, Quiron, Zach, Eladeb eius ministri? Ubi est Maymon rex, ubi sunt Assaiby, Albunalich, Haybalidech, Yasfla eius ministri? (21) Ubi est Barthan rex, ubi sunt Taadas, Caudas, Yalcal eius ministri? Ubi est Formione rex, ubi sunt Guth, Maguth, Guthryn eius ministri? Ubi est Iammax rex, ubi sunt Carmox, Ycanol, Pasfran eius ministri? (22) Venite obedientes cum omnibus subditis vestris creatori vestro et michi nomine ipsius. Exercitus angelorum, qui Sabaoth dicitur, vos meis preceptis subiciat."

(23) Excitacio diei Lune et spirituum eius, quando perticulariter fit.

Tunc in occidente dicat: "Ubi est Harthan rex, ubi sunt Bileth, Mylalu, Abucaba eius ministri? (24) Ubi est Abaa rex, ubi sunt Hyici, Quyron, Zach,

Yalcal? (14) Come as quickly as you are able, with all your subordinates, prepared to obey me in all things. The power of the most high Creator subjugates you, that you are constrained to come."

(15) The raising up of the day of Mars, and the spirits which are particular to it.

Then facing south, say: "Where is King Iammax? Where are his ministers Carmox, Ycanol, and Pasfran? (16) Where is King Sarabocres? Where are his ministers Nassar and Cynassa? Where is King Harthan? Where are his ministers Bileth, Milalu, and Abucaba? Where is King Abaa? Where are his ministers Hyici, Quyron, Zach, and Eladeb? (17) Where is King Maymon? Where are his ministers Assaibi, Albunalich, Aybalidech, and Yasfla? Where is King Barthan? Where are his ministers Thaadas, Caudas, and Yalcal? (18) Where is King Formione? Where are his ministers Guth, Maguth, and Guthryn? I call upon you to come with your army and to obey my requests. May the fear of the wrath of the Lord conquer, who binds you to come and obey."

(19) The raising up of the day of Venus, and the spirits particular to it.

Then in Nogahem, say: "Where is King Sarabocres? Where are his ministers Nassar and Cynassa? (20) Where is King Harthan? Where are his ministers Bileth, Milalu, and Abucaba? Where is King Abaa? Where are his ministers Hyici, Quiron, Zach, and Eladeb? Where is King Maymon? Where are his ministers Assaiby, Albunalich, Haybalidech, and Yasfla? (21) Where is King Barthan? Where are his ministers Taadas, Caudas, and Yalcal? Where is King Formione? Where are his ministers Guth, Maguth, and Guthryn? Where is King Iammax? Where are his ministers Carmox, Ycanol, and Pasfran? (22) Come with all your subordinates, obeying your creator and me in his name. The army of angels, which is called *Sabaoth*, makes you subject to my orders."

(23) The raising up of the day of the Moon, and the spirits which are particular to it.

Then, facing west, he should say: "Where is King Harthan? Where are Bileth, Mylalu, Abucaba, his ministers? (24) Where is King Abaa? Where are Hyici,

Eladeb eius ministri? Ubi est Maymon rex, ubi sunt Assaibi, Albunalich, Haibalidech, Yasfla eius ministri? (25) Ubi est Barthan rex, ubi sunt Taadas, Caudas, Yalcal eius ministri? Ubi est Formione rex, ubi sunt Guth, Maguth, Guthrin eius ministri? (26) Ubi est Iammax rex, ubi sunt Carmox, Ycanol, Pasfran eius ministri? Ubi est Sarabocres rex, ubi sunt Nassar, Cynassa eius ministri? (27) <Ubi est harthan rex. Ubi sunt bileth. mylalu. abucaba eius ministri. Ubi est abaa rex. Ubi sunt hyci. quyron. zach. eladeb. eius ministri.> [Venite omnes quam cicius poteritis cum omnibus subditus vestris et ut supra.]⁵³

(28) Excitacio diei Mercurii et spirituum eius, quando particulariter fit.

Tunc in frigicap dicat: "Ubi est Abaa rex, ubi sunt Hyici, Quiron, Zach, Eladeb ministri eius? (29) Ubi est Maymon rex, ubi sunt Assaibi, Albunalich, Haibalidech, Yasfla eius ministri? [Ubi est Barthan rex, ubi sunt Taadas, Caudas, Yalcal eius ministri?] Ubi est Formione rex, ubi sunt Guth, Maguth, Guthryn eius ministri? (30) Ubi est Iammax rex, ubi sunt Carmox, Ycanol, Pasfran eius ministri? Ubi est Sarabocres rex, ubi sunt Nassa[r], Cynassa eius ministri? (31) Ubi est Harthan rex, ubi sunt Bileth, Mylalu, Abucaba eius ministri? Summum Dei tremendum ac reverendum iudicium vos apparere et michi in omnibus obedire constringat."

(32) Excitacio diei sabati et spirituum eius, quando particulariter fit.

Tunc in septemtrione dicat: "Ubi est Maymon rex, ubi sunt Assaibi, Albunalich, Haibalidech, Iasfla eius ministri? (33) Ubi est Barthan rex, ubi sunt Taadas, Caudas, Yalcal eius ministri? Ubi est Formione rex, ubi sunt Guth, Maguth, Guthryn eius ministri? (34) Ubi est Iammax rex, ubi sunt Carmox, Ycanol, Pasfran eius ministri? Ubi est Sarabocres rex, ubi sunt Nassar, Cynassa<r> eius ministri? Ubi [est] Harthan rex, ubi sunt Bileth, Mylalu,

---

53 Namely, "... promti michi in omnibus obedire. Virtus summi creatoris vos subiuget, que vos venire constringat." So Sl. 3853 fol 153r. GH, following Sl, 3854, omits. Compare SSM, which cites Beelzebub. Evidence the London Honorius has had chief daemons redacted out?

Quyron, Zach, Eladeb his ministers? Where is King Maymon? Where are Assaibi, Albunalich, Haibalidech, Yasfla his ministers? (25) Where is King Barthan? Where are Taadas, Caudas, Yalcal his ministers? Where is King Formione? Where are Guth, Maguth, Guthrin his ministers? (26) Where is King Iammax? Where are Carmox, Ycanol, Pasfran his ministers? Where is King Sarabocres? Where are Nassar, Cynassa his ministers? (27) <...> [Come as quickly as you are able, with all your subordinates, prepared to obey me in all things. The power of the most high Creator subjugates you, that you are constrained to come," etc. as above.]

(28) THE RAISING UP OF THE DAY OF MERCURY, AND THE SPIRITS WHICH ARE PARTICULAR TO IT.

Then in frigicap, say: 'Where is King Abaa? Where are his ministers Hyici, Quiron, Zach, and Eladeb? (29) Where is King Maymon? Where are his ministers Assaibi, Albunalich, Haibalidech, and Yasfla? [Where is King Barthan? Where are his ministers Taadas, Caudas, and Yalcal?] Where is King Formione? Where are his ministers Guth, Maguth, and Guthryn? (30) Where is King Iammax? Where are his ministers Carmox, Ycanol, and Pasfran? Where is King Sarabocres? Where are his ministers Nassa[r] and Cynassa? (31) Where is King Harthan? Where are his ministers Bileth, Mylalu, and Abucaba? The most high, terrible, and awe-inspiring judgment of God binds you to appear and to obey me in all things."

(32) THE RAISING UP OF THE SABBATH DAY, AND THE SPIRITS WHICH ARE PARTICULAR TO IT.

Then facing north, say: "Where is King Maymon? Where are his ministers Assaibi, Albunalich, Haibalidech, and Iasfla? (33) Where is King Barthan? Where are his ministers Taadas, Caudas, and Yalcal? Where is King Formione? Where are his ministers Guth, Maguth, and Guthryn? (34) Where is King Iammax? Where are his ministers Carmox, Ycanol, and Pasfran? Where is

Abucaba eius ministri? (35) Ubi est Abaa rex, ubi sunt Hyici, Quyron, Zach, Eladeb ministri eius?"

Hic debet claudere manum et eis pugnum clausum ostendere cum sigillis. Tunc dicat: (36) "Virtus istorum sanctorum nominum Dei et sigillorum vestrorum vos convincat, que vos congregare, venire, apparere, respondere et michi in omnibus obedire constringant."

(37) Hoc dicto videbis eorum motus insurgere, et tunc dicas sociis, quod non dubitent, et fac eos potare, etsi adhuc motus non videris.[54] Set non debent ultra novies excitari.

CXXX Accessus ad circulum— Excitacio ventorum ante eum

Visis eorum motibus ad circulum accedentes ante circulum semel excitabis eos. (2) Tunc intres circulum per partem inter frigicap et occidentem pro meta positam, et tunc socii stantes pedibus in circulo stent, donec recluseris circulos dicens 18. (3) Tunc situa socios et enses in circulo tali modo, set antequam intraverunt, 7 predicta nomina deleantur, quia non possent aliter apparere. (4) Tunc versus quamlibet parcium unus ponatur gladius, et debent in altitudine adequari. Tunc, si solus fueris, versus orientem primo invocabis. (5) Si autem duo,[55] secundus sedeat versus partem contra occidentem, si 3, tercius versus meridiem, si 4, quartus contra septemtrionem, si 5, 5us versus consol, si 6, 6us versus nogahem, si 7, septimus versus faciem contra frigicap situetur. (6) Et habeat quilibet unum scannum ligneum alcius a terra ad digiti spissitudinem, ne scriptura circuli deleatur. Set ultra 3 socios capere non iuvabit.

---

54 Sl. 3853 153v adds: *reitera convocaciones*.
55 Duo: Sl. 3853: "duos socios habueris."

King Sarabocres? Where are his ministers Nassar and Cynassa? Where is King Harthan? Where are his ministers Bileth, Mylalu, and Abucaba? (35) Where is King Abaa? Where are his ministers Hyici, Quyron, Zach, and Eladeb?"

This should be done with your hand closed—show them the closed fist with the seals. Then say: (36) "May the power of these holy names of God and your seals conquer you, which bind you to assemble, to come, to appear, to answer me, and to obey me in all things."

(37) With this said, you will see the movement of them rising up, and then you should say to the associates, that they should not doubt, and make them take a drink, even if thus far you have seen no movements.[261] But they must not be raised up more than nine times.[262]

CXXX. Of the approach towards the circle— the raising up of the winds before it.

When you see their movements approaching the circle, you should summon them once again before the circle. (2) Then you should enter the circle through the part between Frigicap and the West, situated in front of the boundary, and then the associates should stand with their feet inside the circle, reciting 18, until you have re-closed the circles from within. (3) Then situate the associates and the swords in the circle such a manner, but before they have entered, the seven preceding names should be erased, because otherwise they would not be able to appear. (4) Then place one sword towards each direction, and they must be equalized in height. Then, if you are alone, you should invoke first toward the east. (5) If but two, the second one should sit facing toward the western part; if three, the third toward the south; if four, the fourth facing north; if five, the fifth towards Consol; if sixth, the sixth towards Nogahem; if seven, the seventh toward should be situated facing Frigicap. (6) And any of them may have a wooden stool higher than the ground by the thickness of a finger, lest the writing of the circle is erased. But to take more than three associates will not be helpful.

---

261 Sl. 3853 adds: "repeat the convocations."
262 SSM adds: *Quia si infra nouies motus non aperuerit, illa vice frustraris pro tunc. Set corrige te Et in crastino vel post crastino resume opus:* ("Because, if their movements are not revealed after nine times, with that turn you will be disappointed for that time. But you will improve, and on the following day, or the day after that, you may pick up the work again.")

CXXXI *Preparacio ad excitandum spiritus*

Situatis igitur in circulo ensibus et sociis magister habens signum Dei et sigilla in manu sua dextra ponat thus in thuribulo super prunas et suffumiget ter circulum et 7 mundi partes, celum, terram, signum Dei, socios et se ipsum dicens 1 et 2. (2) Tunc flexis genibus versus orientem dicat 25, 27, 28, 31, in quibus applicabit propositum in fine ita dicens:

(3) APPLICACIO

"Ut ille vel illi N spiritus, quos ego invocavero, ad me constricti veniant, sub tali forma N letantes appareant, (4) de omnibus quesitis veritatem respondeant et omnia mea precepta veraciter adimpleant et adimpleta diligenter et sine corupcione custodiant per illum, qui divisit lumen a tenebris, qui diabolis potestatem suam abstulit, (5) sub cuius potestate sunt celestia, terrestria et infernalia, qui vivit et regnat Deus in deitate sua, trinitas, Pater et Filius et Spiritus sancti, Amen."

CXXXII

Hoc facto dicat sociis, quod non timeant et inclinato capite terram et ensem et nichil aliud respiciant et, si siciunt, bibant. (2) Et tunc magister tenens baculum lauri vel coruli illius anni in manu dextra et thuribulum in sinistra incipiens in oriente novies circuiens suffumiget circulum dicens:

(3) EXCITACIO SPIRITUUM

"Barthan, Formione, Iammax, Sarabocres, Harthan, Abaa, Maymon," Quo dicto percuciat orientalem gladium de virgula dicens:

CXXXI. *Preparation for raising up the spirits.*

With the swords and the associates situated in the circle, and the master having the Sign of God and the seals in his right hand, he should place incense on the glowing charcoals in the censer, and he should fumigate the circle three times and the seven parts of the world, the heavens, the earth, the Sign of God, the associates, and he himself, saying prayers one and two. (2) Then kneeling toward the east he should say 25, 27, 28, 31, in which he will apply the intention in the end, saying:

(3) THE APPLICATION.

"That this spirit or these spirits N., whom I have invoked, may come bound to me, appearing cheerfully in the form of N., (4) answering all questions truthfully, and fulfilling all my orders truly and carefully, and may they take care without corruption, through Him who divided light from darknesses, who took away his power from the devils, (5) under whose power are all celestial, earthly, and infernal beings, who lives and reigns God in his deity, the Trinity, the Father, and the Son, and the Holy Spirit, Amen."

CXXXII.

With this done, he should tell the associates not to fear, but to bow their heads, and pay attention to nothing other than the earth and the sword, and if they are thirsty, they may drink. (2) And then the master takes in his right hand a stick of laurel or hazel from that year,[263] and in his left hand the censer. He then begins to suffumigate the circle, starting toward the east, and going around nine times, saying:

(3) THE RAISING UP OF THE SPIRITS.

"Barthan, Formione, Iammax, Sarabocres, Harthan, Abaa, Maymon," Which said he should strike to the east the sword with the wand, saying:

---

263 This is called *baculus* ("a stick or staff") here, but *virgula* ("wand, rod, twig") just below. SSM calls it *virga* below. I have to interpret "from that year" as meaning it should be cut fresh each year, not that it should be of the same year's growth, as the latter would be too small.

(4) "Exeat hic potentissimus rex Barthan cum omnibus suis suffraganeis in virtute celesti meam facere voluntatem,"

Tunc in meridie dicat:

"Iammax, Sarabocres, Harthan, Abaa, Maymon, Barthan, Formione,"

(5) Tunc percuciat meridionalem gladium dicens:

"Exeat hinc[56] fortissimus rex Yammax cum sua inenumerabili[57] caterva virtute divina meam facere voluntatem."

(6) Tunc in occidente dicat:

"Harthan, Abaa, Maymon, Barthan, Formione, Yammax, Sarabocres."

Quo dicto occidentalem gladium percuciat dicens:

"Exeat hic mitissimus Harthan rex cum omnium[58] suorum velocium subditorum caterva angelica virtute meam facere voluntatem."

(7) Tunc in septemtrione dicat:

"Maymon, Barthan, Formione, Iammax, Sarabocres, Harthan, Abaa."

(8) Quo dicto percuciat septemtrionalem gladium de virgula dicens:

"Exeat hic acerbissimus rex Maymon cum omnium suorum aereorum[59] spirituum exercitu virtute obediencie Belzebut ab eis debite meam facere voluntatem."

(9) Tunc in consol dicat:

"Formione, Yammax, Sarabocres, [Harthan], Abaa, Maymon, Barthan,"

Quo dicto consolanem gladium de virgula percuciat dicens:

"Exeat hic pulcherrimus rex Formione cum suis legionibus angelorum virtute timoris summi iudicii meam facere voluntatem,"

(10) Tunc in nogahem dicat:

"Sarabocres, Harthan, Abaa, Maymon, Barthan, Formione, Yammax,"

---

56 *Hinc*: GH corrects to *hic* to be consistent with the other paragraphs, but *hinc* would also fit. SSM L.3.f.34 reads *hinc* for all these paragraphs.

57 SSM L.3.f.34: *inennarrabili* ("indescribable").

58 There is a blank space left in Sl. 3854 of approximately 5-6 characters. There is no indication of a lacuna in Sl. 3853 or SSM.

59 SSM reads *acrium* ("harsh"), which is perhaps more appropriate here, given parallel passages have adjectives that match their office, such as "wise spirits" for Frigicap.

(4) "May this most powerful king Barthan go forth, with all his supporters with the heavenly power, to do my will."

Then, facing North he should say:

"Iammax, Sarabocres, Harthan, Abaa, Maymon, Barthan, Formione."

(5) Then he should strike the sword to the South, saying:

"May this most mighty King Yammax go forth from here, with his innumerable troops with divine power, to do my will."

(6) Then facing West, he should say:

"Harthan, Abaa, Maymon, Barthan, Formione, Yammax, Sarabocres."

Having said this, he should strike the western sword, saying:

"May this most mild King Harthan go forth with the power of all his troops of swift angelic subordinates, to do my will."

(7) Then facing North he should say:

"Maymon, Barthan, Formione, Iammax, Sarabocres, Harthan, Abaa."

(8) Having said this, he should strike the northern sword with the wand, saying:

"May this most harsh king Maymon go forth with all his hosts of aerial [*harsh] spirits, with the power of the obedience they owe Belzebut, to do my will."

(9) Then in Consol he should say:

"O Formione, Yammax, Sarabocres, [Harthan],[264] Abaa, Maymon, Barthan,"

Having said this, he should strike the consol sword with the wand, saying:

"May this most beautiful king Formione go forth with his legions of angels with the power of the fear of the Final Judgment, to do my will."

(10) Then in Nogahem he should say:

"O Sarabocres, Harthan, Abaa, Maymon, Barthan, Formione, and Yammax,"

---

264 Missing in both Sl. 3854 and Sl. 3853, but found in SSM, and needed to be consistent with other parallel passages.

(11) Quo dicto percuciat nogahelem gladium de virgula dicens:

"Exea[t] hic nobilissimus ac fulgentissimus rex Sarabocres cum omnium suorum spirituum fulgencium potencia ac virtute virtute[60] huius celestis suffumigii meam facere voluntatem,"

(12) Tunc in frigicap dicat:

"Abaa, Maymon, Barthan, Formione, Iammax, Sarabocres, Harthan."

Quo dicto percuciat frigicapicem gladium de virgula dicens:

"Exeat hic sapientissimus rex Abaa cum omnium suorum sapientium spirituum exercitu virtute huius sacri [sigilli][61] Dei meam facere voluntatem."

(13) Tunc ponat thuribulum iuxta gladium orientalem. Inclinato capite respiciens crucem ensis dicat hanc oracionem:

(14) Oracio

"Domine Iesu Christe, qui in ligno crucis pro peccatoribus voluisti crucifigi, ut in ipso tua mors mortem nostram destrueret, exaudi clemens et benignus preces servi tui, (15) ut in virtute tua nobis sanctum angelum mittere digneris, qui hoc sacro misterio tuo ac signo nos confirmet, protegat ac defendat, a temptacionibus malis eripiat et in tuo sacro servicio permanere nos doceat, (16) quia tu es pius et misericors Deus, qui vivis et regnas Deus per omnia secula seculorum. Amen."

CXXXIII

Hoc dicto stans pedibus in medio circuli respiciens undique celum taliter invocabit:

---

60 Virtute virtute: So Sl. 3854 135v; Sl. 3853 155r omits second virtute; SSM: cum omnium suorum fulgencium spirituum [in marg: collegio] potenciam et [erased word], virtute huius celestis ....

61 This word is found in SSM.

(11) Having said this, he should strike the nogahel[265] sword with the wand, saying:

"May this most noble and most shining King Sarabocres go forth with the force and power of all his shining spirits, and with the power of this celestial incense, to do my will."

(12) Then in Frigicap he should say:

"O Abaa, Maymon, Barthan, Formione, Iammax, Sarabocres, Harthan."

Having said this, he should strike the frigicap sword with the wand, saying:

"May this most wise King Abaa go forth with the army of all his wise spirits, with the power of this sacred [seal] of God, to do my will."

(13) Then he should put the censer near the eastern sword.

With head bowed, gazing at the cross of the sword, he should say this prayer:

(14) Prayer.

"O Lord Jesus Christ, merciful and kind, who willed yourself to be crucified on a cross of wood for the sake of sinners, in order that through your own death you destroyed our deaths, hear the prayers of your servant, (15) that through your power, you may deign to send to us the sacred angel, who may strengthen us with this your sacred mystery and sign, may it protect and defend, and deliver us from the temptation of evil, and may he teach us to endure in your sacred service, (16) because you are a loving and merciful God, who lives and reigns, God forever and ever. Amen."

CXXXIII.

Having said this, standing with feet in the middle of the circle, gazing in all directions, he should call upon Heaven in this manner:

---

265 SSM: Nogaelem; one would expect "nogahem."

Incipit invocacio.

(2) "{P}er me [*nomen]⁶² et in nomine omnipotentis coroborati Dei vivi et veri Sabaoth, cui omnia patent et cui nulla latent, sub cuius voluntate omnes subiciuntur creature, (3) ego, N et ff filius, quamvis peccator, tamen donum divine suscipio maiestatis et in ipso⁶³ et per ipsum vos Barthan, Thaadas, Caudas, Yalchal, Formione, Guth, Maguth, Guth[r]yn, Iammax, Carmox, (4) Ycanol, Pasfrau, Sarabocres, Nassar, Cynassa, Harthan, Bileth, Milalu, Abucaba, Abaa, Hyici, Quyron, Zach, Eladeb, Maymon, Assaiby, Albunalich, Haybalidech, Yasfla et omnes alios spiritus, animas, demones, ventos, (5) qui vobis serviunt, obediunt et subduntur, excito, coniuro, contestor et constringo per hec sua nomina sancta 1, 2, 3, 4, 5, 6, 7, 8, 9, 10, (6) et ipse Deus super vos excitet, vos tremere, expavescere et timere faciat, ut cum obediencia, leticia, pulcritudine et mansuetudine et veritate vos iuxta circulum venire et apparere const[ri]ngat. (7) Unde adiuro vos per summum nomen 11, per magnum nomen 12, per excelsum 13, per tremendum 14, per colendum 15, per reverendum 16, per piissimum 17, per ineffabile 18, per incommutabile 19, per sempiternum 20, (8) quatinus +ab omnibus mundi partibus unanimes et letantes hic iuxta circulum in forma N non nocentes alicui creature, non ledentes, non frementes, non furientes nec me sociosque meos vel aliquam creaturam terrentes, neminem offendentes set veniatis+ peticionibus meis consulti et providi statim obedire. (9) Et omnia precepta mea absque omni fallacia penitus adimplere per virtutem illius vobis precipio et ad hoc exorciso, quem omnes creature tremunt et colunt, qui vivit et regnat et regnaturus est super omnia et per omnia secula seculorum. Amen."

---

62 GH interprets *mei* as an error for *me*, but Sl. 3853 reads "Per nomen et in nomine." This expression is found frequently in magical texts. See for example, BoO p. 44, Rawl. D252 12v, 87v, Wellcome ms. 110 36r-40v, etc. SSM L.3.f35: "Per N. et in nomine," but in that manuscript N. is often an abbreviation for "nomen;" compare e.g. L.3.f.35 line 10.

63 Sl. 3854 repeats "et in ipso" obviously by mistake. Not found in Sl. 3853 or SSM.

Beginning of the invocation.

(2) "Strengthened by the name and in the name of almighty God, the living and true Sabaoth, to whom all things stand open and to whom nothing is hidden, under whose will all creatures are subject, (3) I, N. the son of ff, although a sinner, yet I receive the gift of divine Majesty, and in Him I call you forth, O Barthan, Thaadas, Caudas, Yalchal, Formione, Guth, Maguth, Guth[r]yn, Iammax, Carmox, (4) Ycanol, Pasfrau, Sarabocres, Nassar, Cynassa, Harthan, Bileth, Milalu, Abucaba, Abaa, Hyici, Quyron, Zach, Eladeb, Maymon, Assaiby, Albunalich, Haybalidech, Yasfla, and all other spirits, souls, daemons, and winds (5) which serve, obey, and are placed under you, I call forth, conjure, call upon you, and bind you through these his holy names: 1, 2, 3, 4, 5, 6, 7, 8, 9, 10, (6) and God himself calls you forth, causing you to tremble, to feel dread and fear, so that you come and are constrained to appear, obedient, cheerful, beautiful, and subdued, and truthful, next to this circle. (7) From which I charge you through the most high name 11, through the great name 12, through the exalted 13, through the terrifying 14, through the name to be worshiped 15, through the awe-inspiring 16, through the most loving 17, through the indescribable 18, through the unchangeable 19, through the perpetual 20, (8) such that you come from all parts of the world, harmonious and cheerful, next to this circle, in the form of N., not harming any creatures, nor striking, roaring, raging, nor frightening me or my associates or any creatures, nor shocking anyone, but prepared to obey my decrees at once. (9) And I order you and exorcise you to thoroughly fulfill all my commands without any deceit, through his power, before whom all creatures tremble and worship, who lives and reigns and will reign over all forever and ever. Amen."

(10) Adiuracio

"Item adiuro vos pernominatos[64] spiritus N et invocando coniuro et coniurando contestor et constringo et viriliter imparo per sanctum nomen 21, per sanctissimum 22, per purum 23 et per iustum 24 et per festinantem 25 et per alia Dei nomina pura, (11) que sunt 26, 27, 28, 29, 30, 31, 32, 33, 34, 35, et per ista novem[65] Dei nomina ineffabilia, que sunt 36, 37, 38, 39, 40, 41, 42, 43, 44, <45,> et per ista nomina Dei pura: [45,] 46, 47, 48, 49, 50, 51, 52, 53, 54, 55, 56, 57, 58, 59, 60, (12) quatinus vos Barthan" et cetera "et omnes spiritus et anime, venti et demones, qui vobis serviunt, obediunt et subduntur, ab omnibus mundi partibus unanimes" et cetera. (13) "Per sanctum igitur, iustum, potentissimum, excellentissimum, piissimum et coroboratum Heloy, fortem et admirabilem, perlaudatum, serviendum, tremendum, colendum, venerandum et terribilem, et per suum sacrum sigillum, quo Maria sigillavit, (14) ego, N, b et f filius, vos prenominatos spiritus N et omnes alios spiritus, animas, ventos et demones unanimiter et letanter cum pulcritudine, mansuetudine et veritate (15) hic iuxta circulum venire, apparere, respondere invoco, contestor, imparo, exorciso, concito,[66] coniuro, constringo et meis preceptis obedire et ea adimplere. (16) Sigillo per hec omnia sancta nomina 61, 62, 63, 64, 65, 66, 67, 68, 69, 70, 71, 72, 73, 74, 75, 76, 77, 78, 79, 80, 81,[67] quatinus vos Barthan" et cetera (17) "et omnes spiritus, anime, venti, demones, qui vobis serviunt, obediu[n]t et subduntur, ab omnibus mundi partibus unanimes et letantes" et cetera.

---

64 GH: *per nominatos*, but see Sl. 3854 135v, Sl. 3853 156r, and SSH L.3.f.35.
65 As GH points out, "novem" ("nine") in Sl. 3854 is inconsistent with the text, which proceeds to list ten names. SSM L.3.f.35 lists names 36-44. S3 (156v) includes name 36 after 35 above, but also reads "decem" ("ten") instead of "novem," and ends with name 46, i.e. "... hofb 34, merkerpon 35, <u>Elzephares 36</u>, et per ista <u>decem</u> dei nomina ineffabilia que sunt Egirion 38 [*37], Betha 38, hombonar 39, Stimulamathon 40, Oryon 41, Eryon 42, Noymos 43, Peb 44, Nathanothay 45, <u>Theon 46</u>." This seems to prove some redacting took place by the scribe of Sl. 3853.
66 GH reads *con[v]icto*. SSM: *excito*; Sl. 3853 157r: *concito*.
67 D does not include 81.

(10) The Adjuration.

"Likewise I adjure you renowned spirits N, and with invoking I conjure, and with conjuring I call upon and constrain and powerfully order you through the holy name 21, through the most holy 22, through the pure 23 and through the just 24 and through the hastening 25 and through the other pure names of God, (11) which are 26, 27, 28, 29, 30, 31, 32, 33, 34, 35, and Through those nine ineffable names of God, which are 36, 37, 38, 39, 40, 41, 42, 43, 44, <45,> and through those pure names of God: [45,] 46, 47, 48, 49, 50, 51, 52, 53, 54, 55, 56, 57, 58, 59, 60," (12) as far as "you, O Barthan" etc.[266] "and the all spirits and the souls, the winds and the daemons, which serve you, they obey and are subdued, from all parts of the world, harmonious" etc. (13) "Therefore, through the holy, just, most powerful, most excellent, most pious and strengthening **Heloy**, strong and wonderful, extolled, served, causing trembling, worship, adoration, and fear, and by your Sacred Seal, with which Mary has sealed, (14) I, N., the child of B. and F., O you previously-named spirits N., and all other spirits, souls, winds, and daemons, I invoke, call upon, order, exorcise, arouse, conjure, and constrain you to come and appear (15) next to this circle, harmoniously and cheerfully, beautiful, subdued, and truthful, to answer, and obey my orders, and fulfill them. (16) I seal you by all these sacred names 61, 62, 63, 64, 65, 66, 67, 68, 69, 70, 71, 72, 73, 74, 75, 76, 77, 78, 79, 80, 81," as far as **Barthan**' etc. (17) "and all spirits, souls, winds, daemons, which serve and obey you, and are subject to you, from all parts of the world, harmonious and cheerful" etc.

---

266 CXXXIII.8 just above.

(18) Sigillum et ligacio

"Bethala suspensus in ethera, payga. permyga. percuretaih. perrenay. atariron. aboaga. convenite et concurrite ab omnibus mundi partibus, (19) ara. aray. pangula. iamtarpa. kauthalae. calcecatas. syray. angyus. sathon. arathon. payn. enrapaelon. edydy. (20) per hoc zeham. Vitale. gysina. genasse. acenich. Vicmat [*Vicinat].[68] ut angi{u}s de sede florigeret super ea, que posita sunt in baldice speris, (21) baldultabrac. flebilis. palmonyam. ynephar. yristix. abyreylazacu. Sella. occurrite ab universi mundi partibus unanimes et letantes cum obediencia, leticia, pulcritudine, mansuetudine et veritate in forma N hic iuxta circulum apparentes, (22) non nocentes alicui creature nec ledentes nec frementes nec furientes nec me sociosque meos vel aliquam creaturam terrentes, (23) neminem offendentes set veniatis peticionibus meis consulti et providi statim obedire et omnia precepta mea absque omni fallacia possitis adimplere. (24) Per virtutem illius vobis precipio et ad hoc exorcizo, quem omnes creature tremunt et colunt, qui vivit et regnat et regnaturus est super omnia benedictus per omnia secula seculorum. Amen."

(25) Tunc novies circumeundo circulum tanges [*tangens][69] singulos gladios dicens: "{I}nvoco vos, aerie potestates in oriente, Barthan, Formione, Iammax," et cetera, sicut fecerat circulos suffumigando, et cum circuierit, (26) reversus in orientem dicat: "... et invocando coniuro vos per Zabuater, Rabarmas, Hiskiros, Kirios, Gelon, [Hel], Techel,

---

68 So Sl. 3853 157r and SSM L.1.f.23.
69 So SSM L.3.f.36 and Sl. 3853 157v.

(18) Seals and bonds.

"Bethala[267] suspended in the ether, **payga. permyga. percuretaih. perrenay. atariron. Aboaga,** convene and assemble from all arts of the Universe, (19) **ara. aray. pangula. iamtarpa. kauthalae. calcecatas. syray. angyus. sathon. arathon. payn. enrapaelon. edydy.** (20) Through this Zeham, Vitale, Gysina, Genasse, Acenich, Vicinath[268] as *angius* from the seat *florigeret*[269] over those, which have been placed in the sphere Baldice, (21) Baldultabrac, Lamentable, Palmonyam, Hynephar, Hyristix, Abyreylazacu, Sella.[270] Come together from all parts of the universe, harmonious and rejoicing with obedience, cheerfully, with beauty, gentleness, and truth, in the form of N., here visible beside this circle, (22) not harmful to any creature, neither hurting nor roaring nor raging against me or my associates, or frightening any creatures, (23) offending nobody, but may you come to respond to the petitions of my decree and provisions, to immediately obey and fulfil all my entreaties without any deceit. (24) I command you, and for this purpose I exorcise you, through his power, whom all creatures fear and worship, who lives and reigns, and will reign over all blessed, forever and ever. Amen."

(25) Then go around the circle nine times, touching each sword once, saying: "I call upon you, O airy powers of the East, Barthan, Formione, Iammax," etc., as you did when suffumigating the circles, and when you have encircled it, (26) you should return to the East and say: "... and invoking I conjure you through **Zabuater, Rabarmas, Hiskiros, Kirios, Gelon, [Hel,] Techel,**

---

267 According to Ganell's text (81r) this prayer is called *Sigillum aereorum* ("the seal of the air"), and reads as follows: "Bethala, suspensus in ethera, per ayga, per myga, per turetac, per renay, ataryron, aboaga. Conuenite et occurrite ab uniuersis mundi partibus, (19) ara, arax, pangula, iamtarpa, kantalee, [L.1.f.23] calcecathos, syray, angyus, sathon, arathon, payn, eurapa, elon, edydy, (20) per hoc zeam, vitale, Gysyna, Genasse, acenyth, Vicinath, ut angius de sede florigereth super ea que posita sunt in baldichye speris [=spheris], (21) baldyutabrac flebilis, palmonyam, Inephar [or Mephar?], yrystyx, abyrey, lazacu, Sella." Compare also BoO p. 167. Compare also *Grimoire of Honorius* Conjuration du roi du Septentrion: "Balandier, *suspensus, iracundus, Origratiumgu, Partus, Olemdemis et Bantatis,* N. je t'exorcise..."
268 GH reads Vicmat, but Vicinat or Vicinath is supported by Sl. 3853 and SSM. Could be read "it is neighboring."
269 Florigeret: "It will bear flowers" (?)
270 Sella could mean "the seat."

Nothi, Ymeynlethon, Karex[70] et per angelos et archangelos, per tronos, dominaciones, per principatus et potestates et virtutes, per cherubyn et seraphyn ...." (27) Tunc semel circuiens circulum tangens gladios dicat: "... et per ista sacra angelorum nomina: Raphael, Caphael, Dardiel, Hurathaphel ...,"[71] in 2° gladio: "... Satquiel, [Raphael], Paamcociel, Asasagel [*Asasayel]...,"[72] (28) in 3[o] gladio: "... Samael, Sat<r>iel, Ituraiel, Am<i>abiel...," in 4[o] gladio: "... Hanahel, Ratquiel [*Raquiel],[73] Salguyel ...," in 5[o] gladio: "... Gabriel, Mychael, Samyel, Atithael ...," (29) in 6[o] gladio: "... Mychael, Myel, Sarapiel ...," in 7° [gladio]: "... [Boel], Cap[h]ciel, Mycraton, Satquiel, quibus non [*vobis] omnibus dominatur, et per omnia, que de Deo sunt dicenda et intelligenda, (30) et per illud signum Salomonis a Domino datum et per capud principis vestri Belzebub, cui debetis obedire, et per ista nomina sacra: (31) [Sabaoth], Sella, 91, Ciros, 92, Ob[i]ron, 93, [Nomygon], Oriel, 94, Theos, 95, Hespelli, 96, quatinus vos Barthan ... et eos spiritus" et cetera.[74]

(32) Tunc flexis genibus contra 4 mundi partes eis coniungitur penitus, quia omnes alii non possunt quod hii possunt, et eciam una cum Luna referunt consilia secretorum omnium in respectu aliorum, et sua forma clara est.

(33) Tunc semel dicat flexis genibus contra 4 mundi partes: "{A}ramorule, Thanthalatisthen, 97, Rabud, Thanthalatisthen, 28, 29, principium et finis, 30, 31, 32, (34) te suppliciter exoro et invoco, ut tuo iudicio convicti et constricti veniant advocati et dent michi responsa vera de quibus interrogavero non nocentes alicui creature,

---

70 Zabuater ... Karex: cfr CI.7.
71 Raphael ... Hurathaphel: cfr CVIII.1.
72 Satquiel ... Asasagel: See CVI.1, where the last name is spelled "Asassaiel." SSM L.3.f.36: Asassayel; Sl, 3853 157v: Assassayel.
73 So CIX, SSM, and corrected *sec. man.* in Sl. 3854. Sl. 3853 157v: Ratha.
74 SSM: "..., 96. Item vos Barchan & c." CXXXIII.8, 12.

Nothi, Ymeynlethon, Karex,²⁷¹ and through the Angels and Archangels, through the Thrones, Dominations, through the Principates and Potestates and Virtutes, through the Cherubyn and Seraphyn ...." (27) Then go around the circle once, touching each sword, saying: "...and by the names of your holy angels: **Raphael, Caphael, Dardiel, Hurathaphel.** At the second sword: "... Satquiel, [Raphael], Paamcociel, Asasagel [*Asasayel]...," (28) at the third sword: "... Samael, Satiel, Ituraiel, Amabiel...," at the fourth sword: "... Hanahel, Raquiel, Salguyel...," at the fifth sword: "... Gabriel, Mychael, Samyel, Atithael...," (29) at the sixth sword: "... Mychael, Myel, Sarapiel...," at the seventh: "... [Boel], Caphciel, Mycraton, Satquiel, who is master of everything with you,²⁷² and by all things which should be said and understood about God, (30) and through that sign of Solomon given by the Lord, and by the head of your prince Belzebub, whom you must obey, and by these holy names of yours: (31) [Sabaoth], Sella, 91, Ciros, 92, Obiron, 93, [Nomygon], Oriel, 94, Theos, 95, Hespelli, 96," as far as "you, O Barthan ... and those spirits" and so forth.²⁷³

(32) Then kneeling towards the four parts of the world, joining with them inwardly,²⁷⁴ because no others can do what these are able to do, and furthermore, together with the moon, they can reveal the secret plans of all the others, and their form is clear.²⁷⁵

(33)²⁷⁶ Then say once towards the four parts of the world with bent knees: "**Aramorul, Thanthalatisthes, 97, Rabud, Thanthalatistha, 28, 29, the beginning and the end, 30, 31, 32, 33,** (34) I humbly beg and call upon you, that by your judgment they may be bound and constrained to come and give true answers to those things which I shall ask them, not hurting any creature,

---

271 i.e. names 74-83 from CI.7, however these were used above. SSM specifies names 82-90, which would be next in the list. It is not clear why Sl. 3854 and Sl. 3853 abandoned the practice of referring to names by their number in this instance.
272 Following D, which reads "qui vobis omnibus dominatur." A has "nō" or "uō" which could easily be a misreading.
273 CXXXIII.8.
274 GH: "After this, he should kneel at the four cardinal points *to meet and join with the spirits*...." It is not clear if *eis* ("with them") refers to the spirits or to the four parts of the world.
275 The last part of this paragraph seem out of place. Compare CX.3: together with the moon they (the spirits of Mercury) can reveal the secret councils of all the others. *Clara* can also mean "bright," but CX.3 adds *ad modum vitri* ("like glass").
276 Compare *Heptameron*: "Amorule...."; BoO pp. 195–196; D252 130r–131r.

(35) non ledentes, non frementes, non furientes[75] nec me sociosque meos vel aliquam creaturam terrentes, neminem offendentes set peticionibus meis [obedientes] pocius et que precepero diligenter adimplentes."

(36) Tunc stans pedibus sibila sepcies percuciat et tunc semel circueat circulum dicens "Bethala" et cetera usque ad "occurrite." (37) Tunc stans in medio circuli aperta manu super aerem eis signum ostendat dicens: "Sigillo Salomonis veniant advocati et dent michi responsum verum."

(38) Incipit placacio spirituum.

"{G}eneolia, Chide, ministri tartaree sedis primathie, principes prepotentes sedis apoloice, potestates maonami{ri}e,[76] (39) ego vos invoco et invocando vos coniuro atque superne maiestatis munitus virtute potenter imparo per eum, qui dixit, et factum est, cui obediunt omnes creature, et per hoc nomen ineffabile 'Tetragramaton:' ioht, he, uau, deleth, (40) in quo plasmatum est omne seculum, quo audito omnes exercitus celestium, terrestrium et infernalium creaturarum tremunt et colunt, (41) quatinus cito et sine mora et omni occasione cessante ab universis mundi partibus adveniatis, racionabiliter de omnibus, quecumque interogavero, respondeatis non nocentes michi nec sociis meis, (42) non mencientes set pocius veritatem dicentes et veniatis {pa}cifice manifestantes quod cupimus coniu{rat}i per nomen eterni, vivi et veri Dei, 97."

---

75 This word is not in H, but can be found in SSM L.3.f.37, BoO p. 196, and Bodleian MS Rawl. D252.

76 SSM L.3.f.37: "Genealogia, chyde, ministri tartarei sedis primachye, principes prepotentes sedis apolloice, potestates, maonanierye." S3: "Geuolia chide..." GH, following only Sl. 3854 here, reads "{.}eneolia, chide." Compare also H "genii, Liachidae."

(35) not hurting or roaring or raging against either me or my associates or frightening any creatures, offending nobody, but rather [obeying] my petitions and diligently fulfilling my orders."

(36) Then standing on his feet, he should strike the whistle[277] seven-times, and then circumambulate once around the circle, saying "Bethala" etc. up to "come together." (37) Then standing in the middle of the circle with the open hand over the air, he should show the sign to them, saying: "May those who are called, come to the Seal of Solomon, and may they give true answers to me."

(38) Here begins the placating of the spirits.

"**Geneolia, Chide,** ministers of the Tartarean seat of Primachia, mighty princes of the seat of Apologia, powers of Maonamiria, (39) I invoke you and by invoking you I conjure and protected by the strength of the heavenly majesty, I potently command you through Him who spoke, and it was done, whom all creatures obey, and through this ineffable name 'Tetragrammaton:' **IOHT, HE, VAU, DALETH**,[278] (40) through which all the ages were formed, which heard, all celestial, terrestrial, and infernal hosts tremble at worship (41) that you cease all pretexts and come quickly and without delay, from all parts of the world, responding rationally to everything which I will ask, not harming me nor my associates, (42) not speaking deceptively, but rather truthfully and may you come peacefully, revealing what we wish, being conjured with the eternal name of the living and true God, 97."[279]

---

277 See below, chap. CXL.2-5.

278 Note on the form "ioht, he, uau, *deleth*" see introduction. SSM reads: Ioth, he, vau, he.

279 Name 97 is "Elyorem." This whole passage has a parallel in H, pp. 120-122: "Beralanensis, Baldachiensis, Paumachiæ & Apologiæ sedes, per Reges potestatesque magnanimas, ac principes præpotentes, Genio Liachidæ, ministri Tartareæ sedis: Primac, hic princeps sedis Apologiæ, nona cohorte: Ego vos inuoco, & inuocando vos coniuro, atque supernæ Maiestatis munitus virtute, potenter impero, per eum qui dixit, & factum est, & cui obediunt omnes creaturæ: & per hoc nomen ineffabile, Tetragrammaton IHVH Iehouah, in quo est plasmatum omne seculum, quo audito Elementa corruunt, aër concutitur, mare retrogradatur, ignis extinguitur, Terra tremit, omnesque exercitus Cælestium, terrestrium, & infernorum tremunt, turbantur & corruunt: quatenus cito, & sine mora, & omni occasione remota, ab vniuersis Mundi partibus, veniatis: & rationabiliter de omnibus quæcunq; interrogauero, respondeatis vos, & veniatis pacificè,

(43) Quo facto statim apparebunt visiones infinite et illusiones sicut choros, organa, cithare et omnia instrumenta dulcissima, ut possint socios ad exitum provocare, quia supra magistrum nichil possunt. (44) Illis vero transactis venient exercitus militum et ballivorum, ut debeant pro timore de circulo fugere. (45) Post hec venient sagittarii cum omnium ferarum genere, ac si eos crederent devorare. Set operans providus loquatur sociis dicens: (46) "Nolite timere. Ecce signum Domini, creatoris nostri. Convertimini ad eum, quia potens est vos eripere de ore malignancium."

(47) Tunc dicat magister spiritibus manu clausa: "Fugiat hinc iniquitas vestra virtute vexilli Dei," et tunc aperiat,[77] ut obedire cogantur, et statim nichil socii videbunt. (48) Tunc confortando eos dic: "Sicio. Potemus. Quid vobis videtur? Nolite timere. Sperantes autem in Domino misericordia circumdabit. Letamini igitur in Domino et gloriamini," et scias, quod de cetero non timebunt. (49) Tunc dicat eis, quod de cetero non loquantur, et tunc in medio circuli conversus teneat manum dextram in aere dicens: (50) "Ecce opus sacratissimum. Ecce mirabilis descripcio. Ecce capita[78] vestra prefigurata sanctissimis Dei nominibus exornata. (51) Ecce [signum][79] Salomonis cum suis literis, karacteribus et figuris, quod ante vestram adduxi presenciam. (52) Ecce personam exorcizatoris in medio exorcismi,

---

77 D adds: "signum dei."
78 D: "Ecce opus sacratissimum est signum dei, et est mirabilis descripcio. Id est tota quasi accidentalis dei potencia. Ecce capita...."
79 So D and SSM. A is missing the word. GH inserts: "<sigillum>." H reads "pentaculum."

(43) With that done, immediately infinite visions and illusions will appear, such as choirs, organs, lutes, and all the sorts of the sweetest instruments, in order to provoke the associates to flee, because they are able to exert no such influence over the master. (44) After this armies of soldiers and bailiffs will come, in order to frighten them to flee from the circle. (45) After these archers with all types of wild beasts will come, and act as if they intended to devour them. But he should speak with caring to the associates saying, (46) "Have no fear. Behold the sign of the Lord, our creator. Turn back to him, because he has the power to snatch you away from the jaws of the wicked."

(47) Then the master, with closed hands,[280] says as follows to the spirits: "Flee hence with your iniquities, by virtue of the banner of God." And then he should uncover [the Seal of God], to compel them to obey, and immediately the associates will see them no more. (48) Then encourage them, saying, "I am thirsty. We may drink. What does it seem like to you? Don't be afraid, but put your hope in the mercy of the Lord. Therefore rejoice in the Lord." And know that they will fear no more. (49) Then tell them that they should not speak any more, and then, in the middle of the circle, he should hold his right hand in the air, saying, (50) "Behold the most sacred work. Behold this wonderful depiction. Behold your divisions prefigured, embellished with the most holy names of God. (51) Behold the [sign] of Solomon with its letters, characters, and figures, which I have brought before your presence. (52) Behold the per-

---

visibiles, & affabiles: & nunc sine mora, manifestantes quod cupimus: coniurati per nomen æterni, viui & veri Dei **Heliorem**." Compare also Byzantine exorcism in Delatte 1957 p. 43: "'ξορκίζω τοίνυν ὑμας, πνεύματα Βεραλάνευσις, Βαλδακιόνσης, Πανμαχία καί Ἀπολογίου καθέδραι, διὰ τῶν μεγαλοφύχων βασιλέων καί δυνάμεων καί ἀρχῶν ἰσχυροτάτων, Γενιολιακίδαι, δοῦλοι τῆς ταρταρέας καθέδρας, Πριμάκ ὁ πρῶτος τῆς ἀπωλείας καθέδρας ἐκ τοῦ ἐννάτου τάγματος ἐγώ ὑμᾶς ἐξορκίζω ἐνδυναμωθεῖς τῆ θεία ἰσχύϊ διὰ τοῦ μεγάλου Θεοῦ ον τὰ πάντα ὑπόκεινται καί ὑπείκουσι καί διὰ τοῦ Τετραγραμμάτον Γεχοβά ἀκούοντα τὰ στοιχεῖα ταράσσονται, ὁ ἀήρ κινεῖται, ἡ θάλασσα στρίφει εἰς τὰ ὀπίσω, τὸ πῦρ σβέννυται, ἡ γῆ σείεται καί τρέμει καί πᾶν τάγμα ἐπουρανίων καί ἐπιγείων καί καταχθονίων τρέμει καί φοβεῖται." In view of Petrus's reading "nona cohorte," and the Greek "τοῦ ἐννάτου τάγματος" ("ninth battalion"), "maonamirie" should probably read "Nona Moera," ("the Ninth Part"). According to Ioannis Marathakis (personal communication), "in Petrus's version, all the words 'Beralanensis, Baldachiensis, Paumachiae et Apologiae' are in my opinion attributes of the word 'sedes': Apologiae is obvious from Honorius; Paumachiae is another corruption of Primariae; Baldachiensis probably means a throne with a 'Baldacchino' (a canopy of state)."

280 H: adhibens manum pentaculo ("holding out his hand to the pentacle") ... tenens manum prope pentaculum ("holding his hand near the pentacle").

qui est optime a Deo munitus, intrepidus, providus viribus, qui potenter vos exorcizando vocavit et vocat. (53) Venite igitur cum omni festinacione, o Aye, Samye, ne differatis venire. Per nomina eterna vivi et veri Dei, 98, 99, et per hoc presens sacratissimum opus et per sanctum sigillum, (54) quod super vos potenter imperat, et per virtutem celestium spirituum et per personam exorcizatoris coniurati festinate venire et obedire preceptori vestro, qui vocatur 'Occinnomos.'"

(55) Hic sibilet undique semel et statim videbit motus et signa propria, set non nocebunt de cetero. Et tunc dicat sicut homo ferens imperium divine maiestatis et quasi eos in infimo suppeditans: (56) "Quid tardatis? Que est ista mora, quam facitis? Properate vos et obedite preceptori vestro, Bachac super Abrac ruens, Abeor super Aberor." (57) Et statim venient in forma propria, si illis venientibus, dum fuerint circa circulum, dicat magister ostendens eis sigillum: "Ecce coniuracionem vestram. Nolite inobedientes fieri." (58) Et statim videbit eos in forma pulcherrima et pacifica dicentes: "Pete quod vis. Nunc parati sumus quicquid preceperis adimplere, quia nos Dominus subiugavit." Tunc pete quod vis, et tibi fiet vel aliis, pro quibus volueris operari.

(Quartum opus vel tractatus)

CXXXIV Capitula 4^i tractatus de terreis angelis

De incarceratis habendis; De carceribus reserandis; De thesauris et metallis et lapidibus preciosis et omnibus rebus absconditis habendis; (2) De apparencia corporum mortuorum quod loquantur et resuscitata apparea[n]t; De apparencia creacionis animalium de terra. (3) Set ista duo subtraximus, quia erant contra Domini voluntatem, scilicet mortuum apparenter suscitare et animalia de terra apparenter creare. Finiunt capitula 4i tractatus.

son of the exorcist in the midst of the exorcism, who has been well fortified by God, undaunted, prepared with powers, who has powerfully called you, and calls you with exorcising. (53) Come therefore with all haste, O **Aye, Samye**, come without delay. Through the eternal names of the living and true God, 98, 99, and by this most holy work, and by the Holy Seal, (54) which commands power over you, and by the virtue of the heavenly spirits, and by the person of the exorcist who is conjuring you, hasten to come and obey your master, who is called '**Occinnomos**.'"

(55) Here he should whistle once on each side, and immediately he will see movements and relevant signs, but they will not harm anything. And then he should speak like one bearing the command of divine majesty, and as if they are humbly satisfying your needs: (56) "Why are you not yet here? What is the reason for your delay? Hurry and obey the commands of your master, Bachac rushing upon Abrac, Abeor over Aberor." (57) And they will come immediately in their proper forms, and while they are gathering around the circle, the master showing to them the seal, should say: "Behold your conjuration,[281] if you become disobedient." (58) And immediately he will see them in a most beautiful form, and peaceful, saying "Ask what you wish; we are now prepared to fulfill whatever you order, because the Lord has subjugated us." Then ask what you wish, and it will be done for you, or for others, on behalf of whom you wished to work.

(Fourth Book or Treatise.)

CXXXIV. Topics of the Fourth Treatise, concerning the Spirits of the Earth.

To extract someone from prison; to unlock prisons; to have treasures and metals and precious stones and all hidden things; (2) that dead bodies appear, which seem to rise again and speak; that animals appear to be created from the land. (3) But we have removed those two, because they were against the Lord's will, namely, to raise up the dead, and to appear to create living creatures from the earth. The end of the topics of the fourth treatise.

---

281 The parallel text in H reads "ecce conclusionem vestram" ("behold your conclusion" or perhaps better "behold your confinement").

CXXXV Incipit modus operandi in eis.

Eodem enim modo, quo in precedenti opere continetur, potes operari de istis spiritibus terreis, si suffumigium et nomina mutarentur, circulus et sigilla. (2) De quibus spiritibus breviter hic dicamus, qui sunt turpissimi et omni pravitate pleni. (3) Eorum natura est radices arborum et segetum exstirpare, thesauros occultos in terra custodire et conservare, terremotus facere, fundamenta civitatum vel castrorum destruere, (4) homines in cisternis deprimere et cavernis, incarceratos temptare, homines destruere, lapides preciosos in terra occultos adlibitum dare et nocere cuicumque.

(5) Corpora eorum sunt ita grossa sicut et alta, magna et terribilia, quorum pedes sunt quilibet 10 digitorum, in quibus sunt ungues ad modum serpentum, et habent 5 vultus in capite; (6) unus est bufonis, alter leonis, tercius serpentis, quartus hominis mortui lugentis et plangentis, quintus hominis incomprehensibilis. (7) Duos tigrides gerunt in cauda. Tenent in manibus duos dracones. Color[um] eorum nigerrimus omni nigredine inestimabili.

(8) Sunt autem 5. Corniger rex meridionalis, et habet 4 ministros in 4 mundi partibus, Trocornifer in oriente, Malafer in occidente, Euiraber in meridie, Mulcifer in septemtrione. (9) Et quilibet habet legiones centum, et in qualibet sunt demones 4500, qui omnes istis 4 obediunt et subduntur, et isti 4 sunt, qui possunt omnes alios spiritus a thesauris absconditis fugare, ligare et constringere, et sunt ministri infernales.

(10) Princeps eorum est Labadau. Eius coadiutor est Asmodeus, qui dat thesaurum indestructibilem cuiuslibet monete. (11) Motus eorum est castrorum ruina, segetum et plantarum exstirpacio. Signum est, quod totus mundus videbitur destrui invocanti. (12) Suffumigium eorum est sulphur, circulus eorum concavus et rotundus et distet a circulo magistri per 9 pedes.

CXXXV. *The beginning of the way of operating with them.*

You can work with the terrestrial spirits using the same method described in the preceding work, if the suffumigations and the names are altered, as well as the circle and the seals. (2) We will speak about these spirits briefly here. They are most ugly and full of all kinds of wickedness. (3) Their nature is to root out the roots of trees and crops, to guard and preserve treasures hidden in the earth, to cause earthquakes, to destroy the foundations of cities or castles, (4) to drag down people into pits or caves, to tempt those who are imprisoned, to destroy people, to give precious stones hidden in the earth as desired, and to harm anything.

(5) Their bodies are as big as they are high, large and frightening; their feet each have ten toes, which have claws like those of reptiles, and they have five faces on their heads; (6) One is of a toad, another of a lion, the third of a serpent, the fourth of a dead man mourning and striking, the fifth of an incomprehensible man. (7) Two tigers carry them upon their tails. They hold two dragons in their hands. Their color is blacker than the deepest black imaginable.

(8) But they are five. Corniger ("horn-bearing") is king of the south, and he has four attendants in the four parts of the world: Trocornifer in the East, Malafer in the West, Euiraber in the South, Mulcifer[282] in the North. (9) And each of them has a hundred legions, and in each legion is 4500 daemons, who all obey and are subject to these four, and these four are able to drive away all other spirits from hidden treasures, to bind and constrain, and they are the ministers of Hell.

(10) Their prince is Labadau. His assistant is Asmodeus, who gives indestructible treasure of whatever type of coin.[283] (11) Their movement causes the ruin of castles, rooting up crops and plants. The sign that they have appeared, is that the whole world will seem to be destroyed when they have been invoked. (12) Their suffumigation is sulfur; their circle is hollow and round, and set apart from the circle of the master by feet nine.

---

282 *Corniger*: "having horns" Compare SSM L.5.f.64: Corniger, Corcornifer, Furcaber, Mulcifer, Labadan, Admodeus [sic]. SSM L.5.f.58 ff (*cap 4: de oficiis particularibus spirituum*) lists offices for a long list of daemons, including Corniger, Mulciber, and Malafar, with short descriptions of their offices, for example: *Mulciber, facit fluctuare montaneas velut mare* ("Mulciber makes mountains rise up like waves at sea.").

283 In Leipzig Cod. Mag. 16 p. 162-163 their names read: Corniger, <u>Cornifer</u>, Malafer, Furcuber, Lucifer, Acadan, and Asmodaÿ.

(13) Sigillum terre

"{H}oreaua. recolia. narex. axo et abdia. laadia. cauethlegia. byaron. eleymath. thetanyra. cadulaua.[80] (14) Mathia. nysmaria. pergaria. perelyn. pernigyn. perlabudyn. perkedusyn. perbatusyn. pergalmegue. garaneu, ut tartari cogerentur."[81]

(15) Coaccio eorum sive coniuracio

"Invoco vos, terree potestates, et invocando coniuro" et cetera, ut supra in precedenti opere. Tunc, cum dixerint "Quid vis?," pete quod vis, et fiet.

(16) Set melius est scribere peticionem in tegula nova vel tegul[is][82] cum carbonibus et in eorum ponere circulo, et sic eos non audies nec videbis, et tum quicquid petitum fuerit facient in instanti. (17) Et de istis nunquam vel raro Christianus se intromittit, nec eorum consilia sunt credenda.

(18) Circulus, in quo apparent spiritus.[83]

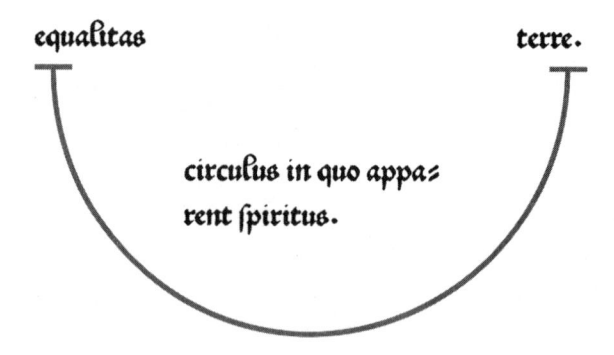

equalitas   terre.

circulus in quo apparent spiritus.

---

80 The c is barely legible, but supported by SSM and Leipzig cod. Mag. 16 p. 166. GH reads "adulaua."
81 SSM L.1.f.23, line 42-L.1.f.24, line 3: <u>Horeana</u>. recholya. <u>nathexaxo</u>. et abdya. laadya. <u>Kauecleya</u>. [L.1.f.24] byaron. eleymath. thetanyra. cadulana. mathya. nysmarya. pergarya. per elyn. <u>per iugyn</u>. <u>per kabudyn</u>. per kedussyn. per batussyn. <u>per gualmegue</u>. <u>per guaranen</u>, ut tartari cogerentur.; L.3.f.59 lines 13-16: Horeana. <u>recolya</u>. nathexaxo. et abdya. laad<u>d</u>ya....
82 GH misreads as "vel tegula" and marked as an accretion to be deleted, but it is clear the plural was intended, since it speaks of placing *them* in the circle.
83 Sloane 3854. f. 137r.

(13) Seal of the earth.

"{H}oreaua, Recolia, Narex, Axo and Abdia, Laadia, Cauethlegia, Byaron, Eleymath, Thetanyra, Cadulaua, (14) Mathia, Nysmaria, Pergaria, Perelyn, Pernigyn, Perlabudyn, Perkedusyn, Perbatusyn, Pergalmegue, Garaneu, that the infernal ones assemble."

(15) Calling them forth, or the conjuration.

"I call upon you, O powers of the earth, and I invoke and conjure you..." and so on, as given in the preceding work. Then, when they have said "what do you wish?", ask what you wish, and it will happen.

(16) But it is better to write the petition on a new tile (or tiles) with charcoal, and put them in the circle, and thus you will neither hear them nor see them, and then whatever you wish they will make happen in an instant. (17) And concerning these, a Christian should seldom or never let himself enter into dealings with them, nor should their advice be believed.

(18) Circle in which the spirits appear.[284]

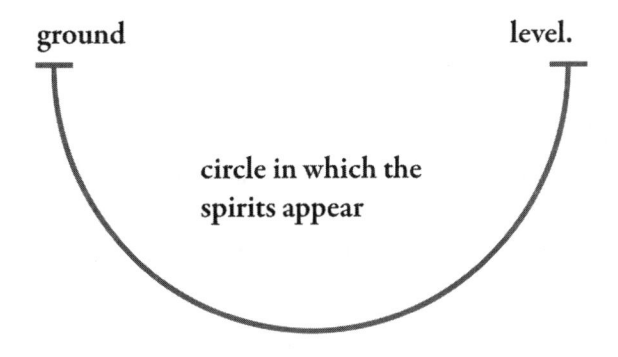

ground   **level.**

circle in which the spirits appear

---

284 Figure of a pit, with label "equalitas terre" ("ground level").

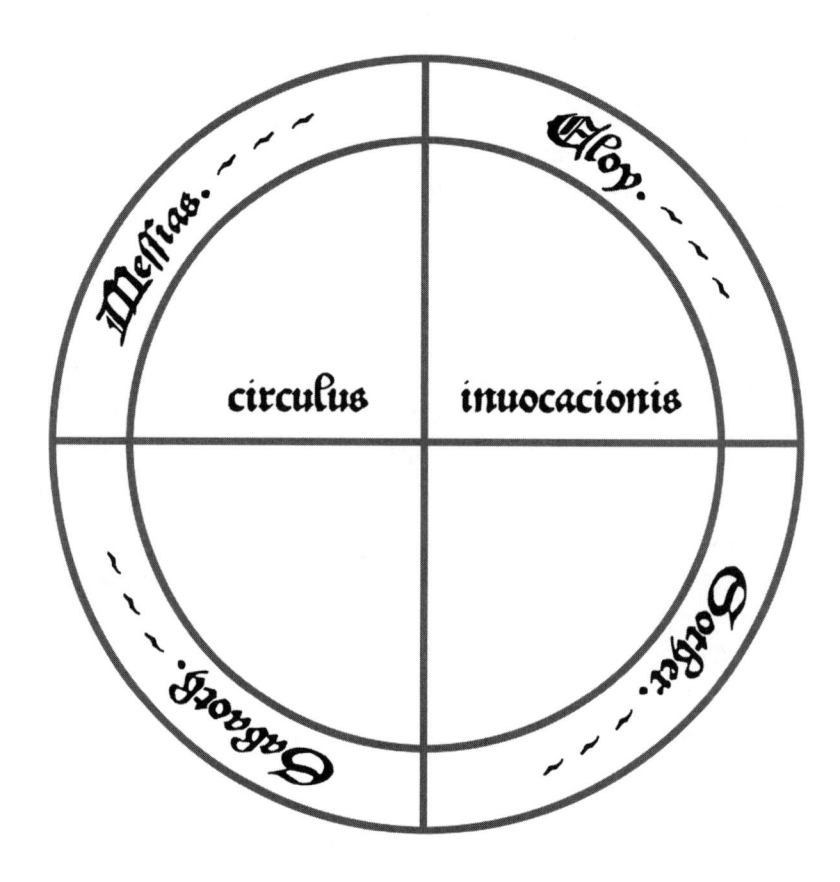

[Circular diagram with four quadrants: upper-left labeled "Messias", upper-right labeled "Eloy", lower-left labeled "Sabaoth", lower-right labeled "Other"; inner left half labeled "circulus" and inner right half labeled "inuocacionis"]

In hac operacione sed[84] de angelis terreis duo isti circuli necessarii; (19) iste primus, qui est concavus, est in quo veniunt advocati, set iste secundus est planus, in quo invocans stare debet, et debet distare a primo per 9 pedes. (20) Et de hiis maxime operantur pagani et rarissime Christiani.

CXXXVI Incipit quintus liber.

(Primum capitulum quinti tractatus)

Incipit 5us et ultimus tractatus de exposicione predictorum in generali in 4 primis tractatibus, quia in libro Honorii sunt 5 tractatus, (2) primus de

---

84 GH: "4."

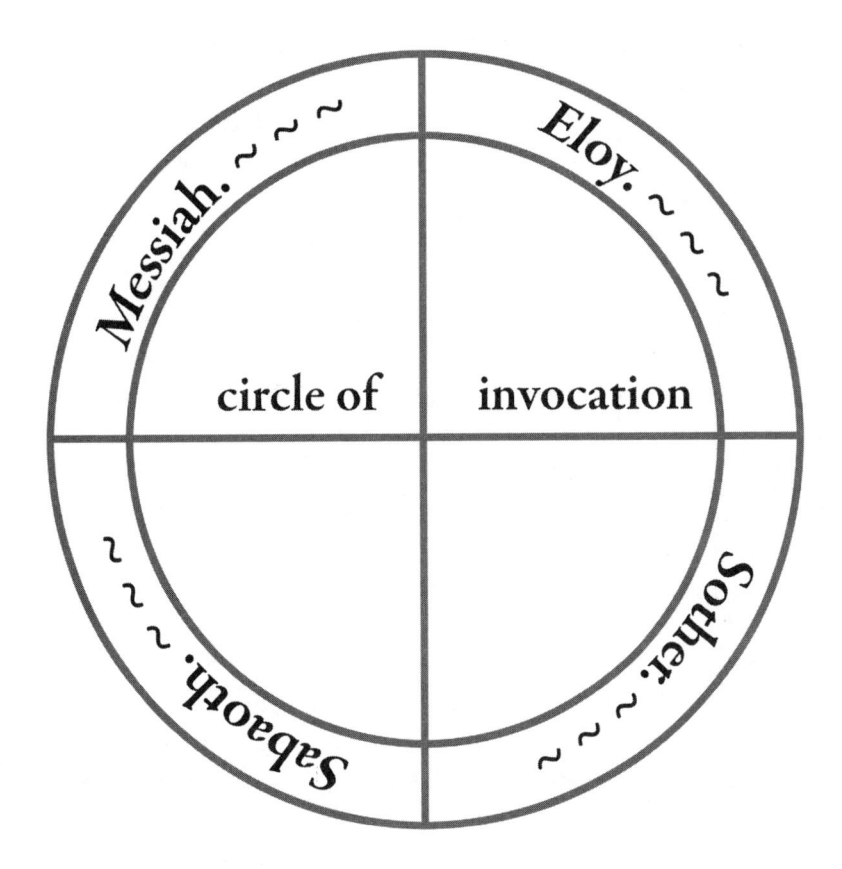

Diagram: A circle divided into quadrants labeled "circle of invocation" inside, with four names around the border: Messiah, Eloy, Sother, Sabaoth.

In this operation, namely regarding the angels of the earth, two circles are necessary: (19) The first one is hollow; it is where the ones summoned come, but the second should be level, in which the one calling-upon them should stand, and it should stand nine feet apart from the first. (20) And it is especially the pagans who operate with these, and very rarely should Christians.[285]

CXXXVI. Here Begins Book Five.

(First chapter of the fifth treatise)

Beginning of the fifth and final treatise, concerning the general exposition of the preceding in the first four treatises, because in the book of Honorius

---

285 From Sloane 3854, f. 137r. Inside is the label "the circle of invocation, and around the border are four names of God: Eloy, Sother, Sabaoth, Messias."

visione divina, secundus de angelis bonis, tercius de aereis, quartus de terreis, quintus de exposicione horum.

(3) De visione divina; De cognicione potestatis divine; De absolucione peccatorum; Ne homo incidat in peccatum mortale; De redempcione trium animarum a purgatorio.

(4) Omnium autem horum 5 operum precedencium ordo iacet suo modo verissimo situatus. De primo enim iam patet peticio explanata. (5) De secundo autem taliter postulabis: "... ut abluto corpore me vivente mea possit anima cum tua incomprehensibili potencia a te cognita cum tuis sanctis angelis tuam cognoscere potestatem." (6) De 3° taliter postulabis: "... ut abluto corpore te cum tuis novem angelorum ordinibus me vivente mea possit anima collaudare, et meorum concedas veniam peccatorum." (7) Quarto taliter est dicendum: "... ut abluto corpore dehinc nullam possim committere maculam peccatorum, set meo vivente corpore puro corde, mente et opere te cum tuis novem angelorum ordinibus mea possit anima collaudare" et cetera. (8) Quinta peticio taliter situetur: "... ut meo abluto corpore te <te>cum tuis" et cetera, "... ex tua gracia N, N, N tales a penis purgatorii eripias et suorum veniam tribuas peccatorum, (9) ut ipsi iam defuncti tuam possint agnoscere, laudare et glorificare maiestatem." Istud opus potes novies facere sine ira Dei et qualibet vice, secundum quod predixi, tres animas impetrabis. (10) Et scias, quod, de omnibus aliis si eodem modo petieris, optinebis. <Vel sic. Ut abluto corpore celestes. igneas. aereas. aquaticas et terreas efficaciter possim cognoscere potestates.>[85]

---

85 GH has this marked defective, but see SSM for sixth variant of the petition.

there are five treatises, (2) the first concerning the divine vision, the second concerning the good angels, the third concerning the aerial (spirits), the fourth concerning the terrestrial (spirits), the fifth concerning the exposition of these.

(3) Concerning the divine vision; concerning knowledge of divine power; concerning the absolution of sins; lest one falls into mortal sin; concerning the redemption of three souls from Purgatory.

(4) Moreover, of these five preceding works, their order is set down in the most correct manner.[286] Concerning the first, the petition is as plainly shown. (5) But you should ask for the second in this manner: "... that with my body being washed, my soul will be able to understand your incomprehensible power, known from you, with your holy angels, while I live." (6) The third should be asked for in this manner: "... that with my body being washed, my soul will be able to praise you, side by side with your nine orders of angels, while I live, and may you grant a pardon for my sins." (7) The fourth should be said in this manner: "... that with my body being washed, hereafter I will not be able to commit the stain of sin, but pure in heart, in mind, and in deed, my soul will be able to praise you, side by side with your nine orders of the angels, while my body lives" and so forth. (8) The fifth petition should be phrased thus: "... that, with my body being washed, side by side with your ..." and so forth, "... by your grace, save N., N., and N., from the pains of purgatory, and pardon their sins, (9) in order that they being released may be able to acknowledge, praise, and glorify your majesty." You will be able to do this work nine times without the wrath of God, and each time you will secure three souls by following what I have said above. (10) And you should know that, concerning all others you will obtain them if you alter the petition in the same manner. <Or thus, "that with my body being washed, I may be able to learn the heavenly, fiery, airy, aquatic, and earthly powers effectually.">

---

286 Compare CII.1-3.

CXXXVII 2ᵐ capitulum quinti tractatus de consecracione hincausti[86] sigilli Dei eterni, vivi et veri operantis

'{D}eus invisibilis, Deus inestimabilis, Deus ineffabilis, Deus incommutabilis, (2) Deus incoruptibilis, Deus piissime, Deus dulcissime, Deus excelse, Deus gloriose, Deus inmense, Deus tocius misericordie, ego, licet indignus—vel: plenus iniquitate, dolo et malicia—, (3) suplex ad tuam venio misericordiam orans ac deprecans, ut non respicias ad universa et innumerabilia peccata mea set, sicut consuevisti peccatorum misereri et preces humilium exaudire, (4) ita me, famulum tuum N, licet indignum, exaudire digneris clamantem ad te pro hac benediccione huius creature sanguinis, ut ipse aptus et dignus efficiatur pro hincausto sigilli tui sacri et preciosi et nominis tui "Semenphoras", (5) ita ut aptitudinem, quam optinere debet, optineat per sanctissimum nomen tuum, quod 4 literis scribitur, ioht, he, vau, deleth—Agla, Eloy, Yaym, Theos, Deus—quo audito celestia, terrestria et infernalia tremunt et colunt. (6) Et per hec sanctissima nomina: On, Alpha et Ω, principium et finis, El, Ely, Eloe, Eloy, Elion, Sother, Emanuel, Sabaoth, Adonay, Egge, Ya, Ya, Ye, Ye, (7) benedicatur hec cruoris creatura et preparetur et aptetur pro hincausto sacri sigilli tui et sanctissimi nominis "Semenphoras" tui, quod est benedictum per infinita secula seculorum. Amen'.

(8) Oracio

'Domine Iesu Christe, per ineffabilem misericordiam tuam parce michi et miserere mei et exaudi me nunc per invocacionem nominis trinitatis, Patris et Filii et Spiritus sancti, (9) ut acceptas habeas, et tibi placeant, oraciones et verba oris mei, per invocacionem tuorum sanctorum 100 nominum,

---

86 i.e. encausti.

CXXXVII. Second Chapter of the Fifth Treatise, concerning the consecration of the ink[287] used for the Seal of the Eternal, Living, and True God.[288]

"O invisible God, O inestimable God, O ineffable God, O unchangeable God, (2) O incorruptible God, O pious God, O sweetest God, O exalted God, O glorious God, O immeasurable God, O God of all mercy, I, although unworthy—or, full of iniquity, deceit, and wickedness—(3) I come seeking your mercy, beseeching and entreating, that you not look back on all my countless faults, but even as you are accustomed to have mercy on sinners, and hear the prayers of the humble, (4) so too deign to hear me, your servant N., although unworthy, beseeching you for the blessing of this creature of blood, that it may be made suitable and worthy for the ink of your sacred and precious seal, and precious and of your name "Shem Ha-Meforash," (5) that it may possess the properties it must maintain, through your most holy name, which is written with four letters, IOHT, HE, VAU, DALETH[289]—Agla, Eloy, Yaym, Theos, God—which heard, all that inhabit Heaven, Earth, and Hell do tremble. (6) And through these most holy names: On, Alpha and Omega, the Beginning and the End, El, Ely, Eloe, Eloy, Elion, Sother, Emanuel, Sabaoth, Adonay, Egge, Ya, Ya, Ye, Ye, (7) may this creature of blood be blessed and may it be prepared and may it be suitable for ink for your sacred seal and your most holy name "Shem Ha-Meforash," which is blessed forever and ever Amen."

(8) Prayer.[290]

"O Lord Jesus Christ,[291] through your ineffable mercy spare me and pity me, and hear me now, through the invocation of the name of the Trinity, of the Father, and of the Son, and of the Holy Spirit, (9) in order that the prayers and words from my mouth are acceptable and pleasing to you, through the invo-

---

287 *Lat.* Hincausti, i.e. encausti: ink; traditionally a purple-red ink.
288 In R, CXXXVII.20-22, 1-19 are found before VII.
289 This unusual variation of the Tetragrammaton is also found in CXXXIII.38. See introduction.
290 Compare Young 2015, p. 13
291 Compare R 27v.

scilicet Agla, Monhon' et cetera 'humiliter et fideliter deprecans, (10) licet ego indignus, tamen in te confidens, ut sanctifices et benedicas cruorem istum per sanctissima nomina tua predicta et per nomen "Semenphoras" 72 literarum, (11) quatinus per virtutem et sanctitatem et potestatem eorundem nominum et per virtutem et potestatem tuam divinam sit cruor iste consecratus ☥, benedictus ☥, confirmatus ☥ per virtutem sacratissimi corporis et sanguinis tui, (12) ut virtutem, quam optinere debet, et aptitudinem optineat et efficaciter sine aliqua fallacia veraciter valeat ad scribendum sigillum tuum sanctum, (13) ut sanctam virtutem optineat et potestatem habeat, ad quam est institutum, prestante Domino, qui sedet in altissimis, cui sit laus, honor et gloria per infinita secula seculorum. Amen'.

(14) Oracio benediccionis

'Benedicat te Pater ☥, benedicat te Filius ☥, benedicat te Spiritus sanctus ☥. (15) Sancta mater Domini nostri Iesu Christi te benedicat et sanctificet, ut virtutem sacramenti in sigillo Dei ex te scribendo, o cruor, optineas, quam optinere debes. (16) Benedicant te omnes sancte virgines, benedicant te hodie et in omni tempore omnes sancti et electi Dei. Omnes virtutes celestes te benedicant et confirment. (17) Angeli omnes et archangeli, virtutes, principatus, potestates, troni, dominaciones, cherubyn et seraphin ex auctoritate et licencia Dei te benedicant. (18) Per merita et oraciones omnium sanctorum tuorum, Domine Iesu Christe, benedicas ☥ et sanctifices ☥ et consecres ☥ cruorem istum sigilli Dei et confirmes per omnipotenciam tuam, (19) et virtutem et potestatem optineat sigillum tuum de eo scribendum, quam debet, et ad quam est institutum et confirmatum, prestante Domino nostro Iesu Christo, cuius regnum et imperium sine fine manet in secula seculorum. Amen'.

(20) Antequam iste 3 oraciones supra cruorem dicantur procedenter versus Ierusalem, dicatur supra eum exorcismus salis, quod ponitur in aqua, ter, nisi quod nomina sic debent mutari: (21) "Exorcizo te, creatura cruoris" loco de '... creatura salis' et 'qui per Salomonem te in sigillum Dei mitti iussit' loco de 'qui per Heliseum te in aqua mitti iussit' et sic de aliis.

cation of your one hundred holy names, namely Agla, Monhon"and so on,[292] "humbly and faithfully begging you, (10) I although unworthy, yet trusting in you, that you would sanctify and bless this blood by your most sacred names aforesaid, and by the name "Shem Ha-Meforash" of seventy-two letters, (11) that by the virtue, sanctity, and power of the same names, and by your divine virtue and power, this same blood may be consecrated ✠ blessed ✠ strengthened ✠ through the virtue of your most holy body and blood, (12) that it may obtain the virtue and ability which it must possess, and effectually without any deceit, for correctly writing your sacred seal, (13) in order that it maintains the sacred virtue and have the power, for which it has been prepared, with the Lord providing, who sits in the highest place, to whom be praise, honor and glory forever and ever. Amen."

(14) Prayer of benediction

"May the Father bless you ✠; may the Son bless you ✠; may the Holy Spirit bless you. ✠ (15) May the holy mother of our Lord Jesus Christ bless and sanctify you, O blood, that you may have the sacramental power for writing the Seal of God, that you may possess the properties you must maintain. (16) May all the holy virgins bless you; may all the saints and elect of God bless you and strengthen you today and for all times. (17) May all Angels and Archangels, Virtues, Principalities, Powers, Thrones, Dominations, Cherubim, and Seraphim bless you, by the authority and permission of God. (18) Through the merits and prayers of all your saints, O Lord Jesus Christ, may you bless ✠ and sanctify ✠ and consecrate ✠ this blood for this Seal of God, and may you strengthen it through your omnipotence, (19) and that through its writing, your seal may maintain the virtue and power which it should have, and for which it has been instituted and confirmed, with our Lord Jesus Christ providing, who lives and reigns forever, world without end. Amen."

(20) Before that, three prayers should be said over the blood, while facing towards Jerusalem: The exorcism of the salt should be said over it three times, which is placed in the water, except the words should be changed thus: (21) Say "I exorcise you, O creature of blood" instead of "I exorcise you O creature of salt" and say "which God, through Solomon, commanded to be put into the seal of God" in place of "which God, through Elisha, commanded be put

---

292 CI.2

(22) Illo autem exorcismo sic ter dicto cum stola in collo dic ter oraciones tres precedentes. Quo facto sigilli Domini cruor erit benedictus.

CXXXVIII Tercium capitulum quinti tractatus de exposicione precepti missarum dati in primo tractatu et subintellecti in quolibet tractatuum premissorum

(2) Prima dies

In prima die secunde mundacionis dicet sacerdos missam alicuius diei Dominice extra ieiunium vel alicuius secundum maiorem effectum, quem habet ad illam. (3) In loco prefacionis dicat hanc oracionem: ' ... nos tibi semper et ubique gracias agere, Domine, sancte Pater, omnipotens eterne Deus, per Christum Dominum nostrum, (4) per quem maiestatem tuam laudant angeli, adorant dominaciones, tremunt potestates, celi celorumque virtutes ac beata seraphin socia exultacione concelebrant, cum quibus et nostras voces' et cetera.[87]

(5) Secunda dies

In secunda die hanc loco prefacionis cum missa apostolorum: '... Te, Domine,[88] suppliciter exorare, ut gregem tuum, pastor eterne, non desera<n>s set per beatos apostolos tuos' et cetera.

(6) 3ª dies

In 3ª die missam ieiunii vel quadragesime et hanc oracionem: "... nos tibi semper et ubique gracias agere, Domine, sancte Pater, omnipotens eterne Deus, qui corporali ieiunio vicia' et cetera.[89]

(7) 4ª dies

---

[87] The preface starts "Vere dignum et iustum est, aequum et salutare, nos tibi ..." and concludes as follows: "... et nostras voces, ut admitti iubeas deprecamur, supplici confessione dicentes:."

[88] "Vere dignum et iustum est, aequum et salutare te Domine...."

[89] "... vitia comprimis, mentem elevas, virtutem largiris et praemia: per Christum Dominum nostrum. Per quem maiestatem tuam laudant Angeli, adorant Dominationes, tremunt Potestates. Coeli, coelorumque Virtutes, ac beata Seraphim, socia exsultatione concelebrant. Cum quibus et nostras voces, ut admitti iubeas deprecamur, supplici confessione dicentes: "

into the water" and similarly for the rest, (22) Then having said this exorcism three times, with the stole around your neck, then say the other three prayers preceding, likewise three times. When this has been done, the consecration of the blood for the Seal of the Lord will be complete.

CXXXVIII. *The third chapter of the Fifth Treatise, concerning the exposition of teachings of the Masses given in the first treatise, and a little more explanation of the treatises set before.*

(2) The first day

On the first day of the second purification the priest should say Mass of any Sunday outside of fasting or othewise for the greater effect which it has towards that. (3) In place of the preface, he should say this prayer: "[It is truly right and just, and for our salvation] that we should give thanks to you, always and everywhere, O Lord, O holy Father, almighty eternal God, through Christ our Lord, (4) through whom the Angels praise your greatness, the Dominations adore it, the Powers tremble in awe, the heavens and the heavenly Virtues and the blessed Seraphim share in triumphant chorus to celebrate it. Together with these ... our voices also" and so forth.[293]

(5) The second day

On the second day, say this in place of the preface, along with a mass of the Apostles: "[It is truly right and just, and for our salvation] O Lord, to humbly beseech you, that you not abandon your flock, O eternal shepherd, but through your blessed Apostles" and so on.[294]

(6) The third day

On the third day, say a mass of fasting, or the fortieth, and this prayer: "[It is truly right and just, and for our salvation] that we should give thanks to you, always and everywhere, O Lord, O holy Father, almighty eternal God, who by this bodily fasting curbs our vices" etc.[295]

(7) The fourth day

---

293 "... together with these we beg you, that you may bid our voices also to be admitted while we say with humble praise." GH p. 35: In ch cxxxviii additional information is given about the saying of masses during the second purification: We are told which mass should be said and what its preface should be on each day ...
294 This seems to be simply the traditional Preface of the Apostles. I see no alteration.
295 "... lifts up our minds and bestows on us strength and rewards; through Christ our Lord. Through whom the Angels praise your greatness" etc. as above.

In 4ᵃ die missam de nativitate imperatricis angelorum [et] " ... Et te in nativitate beate Marie" et cetera.

(8) 5ᵃ dies

In 5ᵃ die missam annunciacionis eiusdem [et] " ... Et te in annunciacione" et cetera.

(9) 6ᵃ dies.

In 6ᵃ die missam nativitatis Christi, et ista sit prefacio: '... Quia per incarnati verbi misterium nova' et cetera.⁹⁰

(10) 7ᵃ dies

In 7ᵃ die missam epiphanie, et prefacio: '... Quia, cum unigenitus tuus in substancia nostre' et cetera.⁹¹

(11) 8ᵃ dies

In 8ᵃ die missam purificacionis, et prefacio: " ... Et te in purificacione beate Marie ...."

(12) 9ᵃ dies.

In nona die missam resurreccionis, et prefacio: '... <Et> te quidem, Domine, omni tempore set in hac potissimum nocte'—vel 'die'—'gloriosius predicare, cum pascha nostrum" et cetera.⁹²

(13) 10ᵃ dies

In 10ᵃ die missam ascencionis, et prefacio: ' ... Qui post resurreccionem suam omnibus discipulis suis manifestus apparuit' et cetera.

(14) XIᵃ dies

In XIᵃ die missam assumpcionis beate Marie, et prefacio sit: " ... Et te in assumpcione" et cetera.

---

90 "... nova mentis nostrae oculis lux tuae claritatis infulsit: ut, dum visibiliter Deum cognoscimus, per hunc in invisibilum amorem rapiamur. Et ideo cum Angelis et Archangelis, cum Thronis et Dominationibus, cumque omni militai coelestis exercitus, hymnum gloriae tuae canimus sine fine dicentes."

91 "Vere dignum et iustum est, aequum et salutare, nos tibi semper, et ubique gratias agere: Domine sancte, Pater omnipotens, aeterne Deus: Quia cum Unigenitus tuus in substantia nostrae mortalitatis apparuit, nova nos immortalitatis suae luce reparavit. Et ideo cum Angelis et Archangelis, cum Thronis et Dominationibus, cumque omni militia coelestis exercitus, hymnum gloriae tuae canimus, sine fine dicentes."

92 "Vere dignum et iustum est, aequum et salutare, te quidem, Domine, omni tempore, sed [in hac potissimum nocte vel die, vel] in hoc potissimum gloriosius praedicare, cum Pascha nostrum immolatus est Christus. Ipse enim verus est Agnus, qui abstulit peccata mundi. Qui mortem nostram moriendo destruxit, et vitam resurgendo reparavit. Et ideo" etc.

On the fourth day, a mass of the nativity of the queen of the angels, [and] "... and you in the birth of the blessed Mary" and so on.

(8) The fifth day

On the fifth day, another Mass of the Annunciation, [and] "... and you in the annunciation" and so on.

(9) The sixth day

On the sixth day, a Mass of the Nativity of Christ, and its preface should be: "... because by the mystery of the incarnate Word, the new" and so on.[296]

(10) The seventh day

On the seventh day, a Mass of the Epiphany, and the preface "... because, when your only-begotten Son appeared in the substance of our" and so on.[297]

(11) The eighth day

On the eighth day, a Mass of Purification, and the preface "... and you, in the purification, O blessed Mary...."

(12) The ninth day

On the ninth day, a Mass of the Resurrection, and the preface: "[It is truly right and just, and to salvation] to praise you, O Lord, at all times, but especially on this night"—or "day"—"when our Passover" and so on.[298]

(13) The tenth day

On the tenth day, a Mass of the Ascension, and the preface: "... who, after his resurrection, appeared visibly to all his disciples" and so on.

(14) The eleventh day

On the eleventh day, a Mass of the Assumption of blessed Mary, and the preface: "... and you, in the assumption" and so on.

---

296 "... a new light of your glory has shone upon the eyes of our mind, so that while we acknowledge God in visible form, we may be drawn by him to the love of invisible things. And therefore with the Angels and Archangels, with the Thrones and Dominations, and with all the hosts of the heavenly army, we sing the hymn of your glory, forever saying."

297 "It it truly right and just, and for our salvation, that we should at all times, and in all places, give thanks to you, O holy Lord, Father almighty, everlasting God; because when your only-begotten Son appeared in the substance of our mortal flesh, with the new light of his own immortality, he restored us. And therefore with Angels and Archangels, with Throne and Dominations, and with all the heavenly hosts, we sing the hymn of your glory forever, saying."

298 "... when our Passover was sacrificed for us. For he is the true lamb who has taken away the sins of the world, who by dying destroyed our death, and by rising again restored our life. And so" etc.

(15) 12ª dies

In 12ª die missam omnium sanctorum, et prefacio apostolorum sit, nisi quod vox apostolorum in vocem omnium sanctorum commutetur.

(16) 13ª dies

In 13ª die missam angelorum, et prefacio apostolorum, nisi quod beati apostoli in beatos angelos transmutentur.

(17) 14ª dies

In 14ª die missam Spiritus sancti, et prefacio sit: '... Qui ascendens super omnes celos' et cetera.

(18) 15ª dies

In quintadecima die missam sancte crucis, et prefacio sit: " ... Qui salutem humani generis in ligno" et cetera.

(19) 16ª dies

In 16ª die missam trinitatis, et prefacio sit: " ... Qui cum unigenito filio tuo et Spiritu sancto unus es<t> Deus" et cetera.

CXXXIX *Quartum capitulum quinti tractatus de inicio aggrediendi opus invocacionis*

Excitacio ventorum est principium operandi in illa XIª hora diei operis sacri et debet fieri extra domum, longe a circulo ad duo stadia vel tria.

(2) Et debet prius esse bene preparatus de necessariis suis, de optimo vino, de 7 ensibus, de sibilo, de virgula coruli, de sigillis, de signo Dei, de thure, de thuribulo, de candela virginea et sic de aliis, ut prius patet.

(3) Et scias, quod in illa pelle, ubi est sigillum Domini, debent esse tria sigilla predicta sub signo ita, quod pendeant de manu. (4) Sigillum angelorum sit immediate sub signo Dei et sub illo sigillum aereorum et sub illo terreorum.

(15) The twelfth day

On the twelfth day, a Mass of All Saints, and the preface of the Apostles, except the wording "the voice of the Apostles" should be altered to "in the voice of all the saints."

(16) The thirteenth day

On the thirteenth day, a Mass of the Angels, and preface of the Apostles, except wording "the Apostles" should be altered to "the blessed angels."

(17) The fourteenth day

On the fourteenth day, a Mass of the Holy Spirit, and the preface "... who ascends over all the heavens" etc.

(18) The fifteenth day

On the fifteenth day, a Mass of the Holy Cross, and the preface "... who placed the salvation of the human race in the wood of the cross" etc.

(19) The sixteenth day

On the sixteenth day, as Mass of the Trinity, and the preface "... who with your only-begotten son and the Holy Spirit are one God" etc.

CXXXIX. *The fourth chapter of the Fifth Treatise. Concerning the beginning of undertaking the work of invocation.*

The raising up of the winds is the first part of the operation in the eleventh hour of the day of the sacred work, and it must be done outside the house, away from the circle by two or even three stadia.[299]

(2) And previously you should have properly prepared all the requisites, namely the finest wine, seven swords, the whistle, the hazel wand, the seals, the Sign of God, incense, the censer, the virgin candle, and the rest, as revealed earlier.

(3) And you should know, that on that skin, where the Seal of the Lord is, the three preceding seals must be under the Seal in such a way that they should hang from the hand. (4) The seal of the angels should be immediately under the seal of God, and under that the seal of the air, and under that of the earth.

---

299 Stade: 125 paces. Two or three stadia would be approximately one quarter to a third of a mile (or .2 KM).

(5) Et quando cognoscentur motus eorum appropinquare, oportet ire ad circulum et delere 7 nomina creatoris et tunc item ut prius extra iuxta circulum excitare, et cum videbitis motus eorum, intrare circulum et facere ut est predictum.

(6) Virga autem sit quadrata, et in uno latere scribatur in summitate "Adonay," in secundo latere "Sabaoth," in 3° "Hiskiros," in 4° "Emanuel." (7) In medio virge fiat pentagonus Salomonis et ubi virga tenetur crux, et sic erit parata operi sacro et miro.

CXL *Quintum capitulum quinti tractatus de composicione sibili et exposicione cuiusdam dicti in 3° tractatu*

(2) Fac sibilum de ere albo vel de argento vel de auro vel avellana, et sit eptagonum, id est septem latera habens, sit grossum ad placitum, sit longum ad longitudinem trium digitorum.

(3) Tunc in summitate eius sculpatur hoc nomen: "**On**," et inferius in alia summitate "**Beel**," et in latere primo, ubi est forus sibili, scribatur nomen regis orientalis, scilicet "**Barthan**," in secundo latere a dextris nomen regis consol, scilicet "**Formione**," (4) in 3° regis meridiei, scilicet "**Yammax**," in 4° regis nogahelis, scilicet "**Sarabocres**," in 5° latere regis occidentalis, scilicet "**Harthan**," in 6° regis frigicapicis, "**Abaa**," (5) in 7° regis septemtrionalis, "**Maymon**," et postea benedic eum sicut cruorem, nisi quod mutabis nomen, et ubi dicebatur "in sigillum Dei te mitti iussit" nunc dices "in clamatum spirituum te clangere iussit."

(6) Et scias, quod quando vocantur angeli boni, non debet habere sibilum neque virgam neque enses, et tu debes stare extra circulum, et ipsi

(5) And when you recognize their approaching movements, you should go to the circle and erase the seven names of the Creator, and then likewise as before, to raise them up, from outside but near the circle, and when you see their movements, to enter the circle and to do as aforesaid.

(6) But the wand should have four sides. On one side should be written "Adonay;" on the second side "Sabaoth;" on the third, "Hiskiros;"[300] on the fourth "Emanuel." (7) On the middle of the wand make the pentagonal figure of Solomon, and where the wand is held, a cross, and thus it will be prepared for sacred and wonderful works.

CXL. *The fifth chapter of the fifth Treatise, concerning the composition of the whistle, and an explanation of certain sayings in the third Treatise.*

(2) Make a whistle from white copper,[301] or from silver, or from gold, or even hazel, and it should be heptagonal, i.e. having seven sides. It may be as large as you please, and its length should be as long as three fingers.[302]

(3) Then, on the top should be engraved this name: "**On**;" and below, on the other end, "**Beel**[303];" and on the first side, where the finger holes are, the name of the eastern king should be written, namely "**Barthan**," and on the side to the right, the name of the king of Consol, namely "**Formione**." (4) On the third, that of the king of the South, namely "**Yammax**," on the fourth, the king of Nogahel [sic], namely "**Sarabocres**," on the fifth side, that of the western king, namely "**Harthan**," on the sixth, that of the king of Frigicap, (5) "**Abaa**," and on the seventh side, the name of the northern king, "**Maymon**."

And afterwards, bless it as you did the blood, except that you should change the wording, and instead of saying "commanded to be put into the Seal of God" now you should say "command you to clang in proclaiming the spirits."

(6) And know, that whenever good angels are called, you must not have the whistle, wand, nor the swords, and you must stand outside the circle, and

---

300 Hiskiros: *Greek* ισχυρος, Iskhiros (Mighty One).
301 A copper/nickel/(zinc) alloy.
302 As a measure of length, *digitus* generally means the breadth of a finger, or about ¾ to 7/8 of an inch.
303 B 25v reads "bael," with "beel" written in the margin. It is not certain whether the spirit Boel/Bohel is intended, or if this is an otherwise unattested name of God.

debent apparere infra circulum, qui debet esse altus tribus pedibus et semis.

(7) Set in aliis aereis et terreis oportet predicta habere. Set differt inter illos, quia illi aerei apparent extra circulum in aere homine existente infra circulum, (8) qui debet esse totus planus sicut +epiparet+,[93] set in terreis sic est, quod ipsi apparent infra circulum concavum, profundum et rotundum homine existente infra alium circulum ab illis circulis predictis, (9) qui tamen similiter debet esse planus et equus, et circa eum scripta solum 4 nomina Dei, prout patet.

(10) Angeli hore sunt qui regnant in hora operis, angeli diei qui in die operis, angeli mensis angeli Lune vel principii mensis, angeli faciei qui regnant facie, ubi est eorum dominium, ascendente, temporis omnes insimul, (11) et principes eorum omnium sunt 7, ut patuit supra: Casziel, Satquiel et cetera. Adhuc sunt 7 superiores, scilicet Barachiel, Uriel et cetera.

CXLI.

Explicit liber de vita anime racionalis, qui liber sacer vel liber angelorum vel liber iuratus nuncupatur, quem fecit Honorius, magister Thebarum. (2) Hic est liber, quo Deus in hac vita facialiter quit videri. Hic est liber, quo quilibet potest salvari et in vitam eternam procul dubio deduci. Hic est liber, quo infernus et purgatorium queunt sine morte videri. (3) Hic est liber, quo omnis creatura exceptis novem ordinibus angelorum possunt subiugari. Hic est liber, quo omnes s[c]iencie possunt haberi. (4) Hic est liber, quo substancia imbecillissima potest substancias robustissimas et devincere et subiugare. Hic est liber, quem nulla lex habet nisi Christiana, et si habet, nil sibi prodest. (5) Hic est liber, qui est maius iocale

---

93 Reading equiparet. GH: sicut eriperet *in marg. Ext. B; an* sic, ut equiparet (sc. terrae) *vel fort.* sicut et prius patet *(cfr LI.15 et CXXXIX.2) scribendum sit?"*

they themselves will appear within[304] the circle, which must be three and a half feet high.

(7) But you must have those instruments when dealing with aerial or terrestrial spirits. But it differs between them, because those of the air appear above the circle in the air, while you are within the other circle, (8) which must be completely level and equalized, but those of the earth are such that they will appear within the hollow circle, deep and round, while you are within the other circle, which is apart from those preceding circles, (9) yet it must similarly be flat and level, and around it written only four names of God, as shown.

(10) The angels of the hour are those who rule in the hour of the work; the angels of the day, those who rule on the day which you work; the angels of the month, those angels ruling the Moon or beginning of the month; the angels of the aspect (or face),[305] those who rule the face where their dominion is, with the ascendant, all at the same time, (11) and there are seven leaders of all of them, as shown above: Casziel, Satquiel, and so on.

Furthermore, there are seven superiors, namely Barachiel, Uriel, and the rest.

CXLI.

Here ends the book concerning the life of the rational soul, which is called the Sacred Book, or the Book of the Angels, or the Sworn Book, which was made by Honorius, the master of Thebes. (2) This is the book, with which one is able to see God face to face, while still alive. This is the book, with which anyone is able to be saved and without doubt led into eternal life. This is the book, with which Hell and Purgatory can be seen without dying. (3) This is the book, whereby all creatures are able to be subjugated, except for the nine orders of angels. This is the book, whereby all knowledge can be obtained. (4) This is the book, whereby one with the weakest substance is able to subdue and subjugate those with the strongest substances. This is the book, which no religion possesses except the Christian, and those of other faiths will find nothing useful for themselves in it. (5) This is the book, which is the greatest

---

304 This seems to be the meaning here, as in IV.2, although "below" or "under" would be the more common meaning. Mesler 2012 p. 114 similarly reads "within" in her translation of CXV.35 (mistakenly identified as LXV).
305 Face: i.e. decan.

a Domino datum omni alio iocali exclusis sacramentis. Hic est liber, quo natura corporalis et visibilis cum incorporali et invisibili alloqui, racionari et instrui potest. (6) Hic est liber, quo innumerabiles thesauri haberi possunt. Et multa alia per hunc fieri queunt, que narrare dispendium esset. Ideo merito sacer nuncupatur.

Scriptus fuit liber iste et completus
Die martis hora 10^a que est ho

jewel of all the jewels given by the Lord, other than the sacraments. This is the book, whereby one of corporeal and visible nature is able speak to, reason with, and be instructed by those with incorporeal and invisible natures. (6) This is the book, whereby innumerable treasures can be obtained. And many other things can be done through this, more than can be told. Therefore it is rightly called sacred.

The writing of this book has been completed on the tenth hour of this day, Tuesday, which is ho....[306]

---

306 The manuscript breaks off right in the middle of this colophon.

Appendix I.
Corrections and Addenda
to Hedegård 2002

p. 67 line 21: "Casziel" should read "Cafziel"

p. 96 line 1: "*peritus*" should read "penitus" per Sl. 3854 123r, R 50r, and Ars Not.

p. 113 line 7: "aquisicione" should read "acquisitione". See Sl. 3854 128r col. 2.

p. 119 "volusiti" should read "voluisti" per Sl. 3853 131r & Sl. 3854 130r.

p. 139 line 4: "per nominatos" should read "pernominatos." See Sl. 3854 135v, Sl. 3853 156r, and SSH L.3.f.35.

p. 139 line 16: "con[v]icto" should read "concito". So Sl. 3854 136r, Sl. 3853 157r. SSM: "excito."

p. 141, line 4: "{.}eneolia, Chide" should read "{G}eneolia, Chide." Compare Sl. 3853: "Geuolia chide"; Heptameron: "genii, Liachidae."

p. 143 line 16: "adulaua" should read "cadulaua." The c is barely legible, but supported by SSM.

p. 143 line 21 "[vel tegula]" should read "vel tegulis" per Sl. 3854 137r.

p. 144: "In hac operacione 4" should read "In hac operacione sed"

p. 206 line 14: "11" add "virtute virtute": Sl. 3853 155r omits second "virtute"; SSM: "cum omnium suorum fulgencium spirituum [in marg: collegio] potenciam et [erased word], virtute huius celestis ...."

Appendix II.
Variants of Some of the figures

Seal of God, reconstructed per Sloane 313, fol. 4r

Appendix II: Variants of Some of the Figures 305

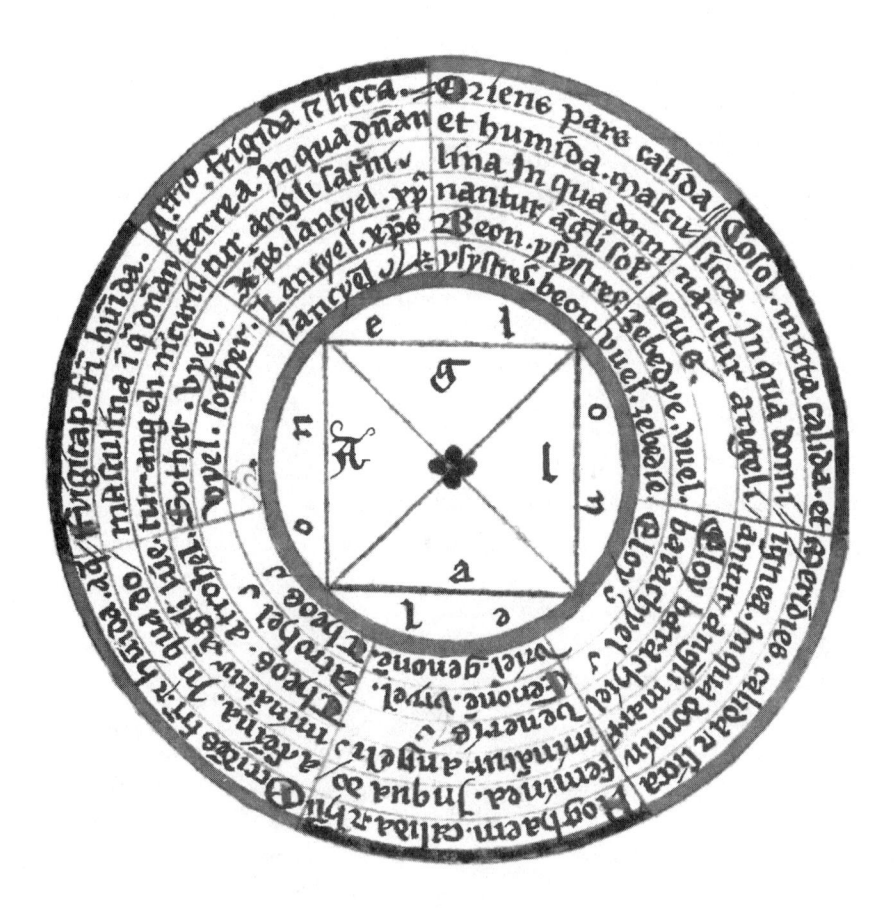

Magic circle per SSM, L.4.f.22

Bibliography

Manuscripts, primary sources

The *Sworn Book* is represented in the following manuscripts:

London, British Library:

Sloane 3854 (mid-14th century) Folios 112r-139r. "Honorii Magistri Thebarum liber cui titulus 'Juratus.'" or "Liber Juratus, vel liber de vita Animæ rationalis Qui Liber Sacer, vel Liber Angelorum nuncupatur quem fecit Honorius Magister Thebarum, " etc. This is the oldest and best quality manuscript, and formed the main basis for this transcription, as well as that of GH and Boudet. Carefully written and legible, with rubricated initials, although many initials were never supplied.
Sloane 313 (second half of 14th century). 27 folios. Missing 3 folios between 24 and 25. The title in the catalog reads simply "Tract on Magic, " or "Salomonis opus sacrum ab Honorio ordinatum, tractatus de arte magica." It is an important independent witness to most of the text, belonging to another family than Sl. 3854. This manuscript is known to have been in the collection of dramatist Ben Jonson (1572-1637). It was later owned by John Dee, and contains marginal notes in his handwriting.[1]
Sloane 3885 (The watermark has been dated to 1588) Folios 58-96. "Liber sacer Salomonis, " "Tractatus de re magica ab Honorio filio Euclidis magistro Thebarum ex septem voluminibus artis magicae compilatus, et intitulatus Liber sacer, sive juratus, " or "Opera Salomonis ab Honorio ordinata" (cursive script). Contains only the first three treatises. The Honorius material is bound with unrelated texts, including the *Practica Nigromanciae* (i.e. *Thesaurus Spirituum*) of pseudo-Bacon.
Royal 17Axlii (Latin and English, dated mid-sixteenth century because of borrowing from Agrippa not found in the older manuscripts). 82 folios. Does not include all of the text, but breaks off just after the beginning of chapter CXV, namely just short of the actual instructions for invoking the angels. The title in the catalog reads "The Sworne Booke of Honoryus." Illuminated with drawings of angels and their seals, as well as marginal flourishes and ornaments, usually colored, sometimes in gold; chapter headings in red, blue, or green. On the fly-leaf (f. 1) are some late 16th cent. pen-drawings with the initials R. T. Sophie Page 2004 includes some wonderful color photos from this manuscript. Waite 1898 correctly identified this manuscript as sixteenth century, even though he omitted to give

---

1 Roberts, R. J., Andrew G. Watson, and John Dee. *John Dee's Library Catalogue.* London: Bibliographical Society, 1990, pp. 57, 168.

the catalog identification. According to Jean-Patrice Boudet, this is a presentation copy on vellum, probably created for some noble.[2]

Sloane 3853 (Mid-16th century): This manuscript contains large portions of the *Sworn Book*, along with excerpts from Agrippa (with citations) and many other texts. English and Latin. Although belonging to the same family of manuscripts as Sl. 3854 and Sl. 3885 (see above), it was not used by GH, but is an important witness to portions of the text, including the drawing of the magic circle, and shows some independence. Contains 127v-137v ("fol 163f"): Catalogued as 'The Divine Seal of Solomon,' 127v variation of Sigillum Dei Aemeth; 128r-v: English version of IV.49-65; 129r-130v: XXVII-XXX, LXXVII-LXXIX, LXX; 130v-134v: CII-CXV.48; 134v-135v: LXXIII, XCIII; 135v-137v: CXXXV.8-17, CXXXVII.1-19, CI.2-8. 149r-174v: CXXVII ff.

Sloane 3849 (dated 1577) Article 7, folios 30-38 contains excerpts from LIH.

Germany

SSM: Halle, Universitätsbibliothek Kassel - Landesbibliothek und Murhardsche Bibliothek der Stadt Kassel, Ms. 4° astron. 3. Latin, 15th ce. A beautiful and unique manuscript of Ganell's *Summa sacre magice*. (written circa 1346). Available online at http://orka.bibliothek.uni-kassel.de/viewer/image/1343812736802/1/. This text quotes extensively from *Liber Iuratus*, as well as other texts. John Dee owned and annotated this manuscript at one time.

SSMG: Berlin, Staatsbibliothek Preußischer Kulturbesitz, Ms. Germ. Fol. 903. German translation of Ganell's *Summa Sacre Magice* (SSM). Circe 1580's.[3]

Leipzig Cod. Mag. 16: (pp. 1-176), titled *Die alleredelste und allerhöchste Kunst und Wissenschaft, das ist: Magia universalis divina angelica ac diabolica* ("The noblest and highest art and science, namely the universal divine angelic and demonic magic"). German, ca 1750. PART 1: To behold the face of the Deity (the 100 names of God pp. 25 ff); PART 2 (pp 55 ff): Knowledge of the angels (e.g. Saturn: Boel, Cassiel, Micraton, Saterquiel); PART 3 (pp 94 ff): Knowledge of the spirits of the air, their binding and which spirits are under them (Hartan, Bileth, etc); PART 4 (pp 160 ff): Knowledge of the spirits of the earth; PART 5 (pp. 170 ff): Knowledge of the great name of God, in Hebrew *Shem ha-Meforash* (and construction of the Seal of God).[4] Includes names of spirits of the planets (pp. 57 ff and 99 ff); the magic circle (p. 98, p. 112), spirits of the earth (CXXXIV ff, pp. 160 ff)... circle for invoking spirits of the earth (p. 165) sigillum dei (p. 175, called "das sigillum salomonis").

---

2 Boudet 2002 p. 852.
3 Gilly 2002 p. 290.
4 The manuscript continues with a version of *Thesaurus Spirituum*.

Manuscripts, secondary sources

Florence: Bibliotheca Medicea Laurenzian, Plut. 89 sup. 38, art. XX fol. 259-259v and 260v. The colophon shows that it was partially copied at Rome in 1494. Treatise titled *Magisterium eumatice artis, sive scientie magicalis*, repeatedly cites *Liber Iuratus* of the "blessed" Honorius. http://teca.bmlonline.it/ImageViewer/servlet/ImageViewer?idr=TECA0001046610#page/1/mode/1up (accessed Sep 24, 2015)
London, British Library: Additional MS. 36674
Oxford, Bodleian Library: Aubrey 24, Michael 276.

Printed sources, primary

Boudet, Jean-Patrice, "Magie théurgique, angélologie et vision béatifique dans le Liber sacratus sive juratus attribué à Honorius de Thèbes " *Mélanges de l'Ecole française de Rome:* Moyen âge, Volume 114, Issue 2, L'Ecole, 2002. Includes a critical edition of much of the Latin text.

Gollancz, Hermann. *Mafteah shelomoh Clavicula Salomonis: a Hebrew manuscript.* Frankfurt a.M.: J. Kauffmann. 1903.

———. *Sepher Maphteah Shelomo (book of the Key of Solomon) An exact facsimile of an original book of magic in Hebrew. With illustrations now produced for the first time by Hermann Gollancz.* London: Oxford University Press, H. Milford, 1914. Several sections of this eclectic manuscript appear to be a translation (into Hebrew) of portions of the *Sworn Book*, including "On the composition of the Divine Seal" (fol. 3b-5b), 26 prayers (from Ars Not.) parallel those in Honorius chapters LIII ff (AGLA... MONHON... TETRAGRAMMATON. It is apparent that these were taken from Honorius and not directly from *Ars Notoria* because of the divine names prepended, as well as the fact that other Honorius elements are included in the manuscript. It is interesting that these prayers lead off the manuscript, followed by the composition of the divine seal. *Maphteah* calls the material that parallels *Heptameron* the "Book of Light." (35a). Concerning the spirits of the air that rule during the seven days: 36a-37b; names and seals of angels from Rasiel 40b-41b; names of angels that minister before Boal (Boel) 49b; general conjuration 52b (?); seal of terrestrial spirits 64b (?); construction of the whistle 64b-65a. Apparently some versions of Raziel/Rasiel included seals of the angels.

Hedegård, Gösta. *Liber iuratus Honorii: a critical edition of the Latin version of the Sworn Book of Honorius.* Stockholm: Almqvist & Wiksell International, 2002.

Printed sources, secondary

Agrippa, Heinrich, *De occulta philosophia Libri Tres,* [Köln,] 1533. Critical edition V. Perrone Compagni. Leiden. Leiden and London: Brill, 1992. English translation: *Three Books of Occult Philosophy*, translated by J[ohn] F[rench], London, 1641.

Agrippa von Nettesheim, Heinrich Cornelius (pseud.), Andreas Kolbe, and Petrus de Abano, *Liber quartus de occulta philosophia, seu de Cerimoniis magicis: cui accesserunt elementa magica Petri de Abano.* Marpurgi: [Andreas Kolbe], 1559.

Alfonso X El Sabo, King of Castile and Leon, and Alfonso D'Agostino. *Astromagia: ms. Reg. lat. 1283a.* Napoli: Liguori, 1992.

Betz, Hans Dieter. *The Greek Magical Papyri in Translation, Including the Demotic Spells.* Chicago: University of Chicago Press, 1986

Bohak, Gideon. *Ancient Jewish Magic: A History.* Cambridge, UK: Cambridge University Press, 2008.

Boudet, Jean-Patrice, "Magie théurgique, angélologie et vision béatifique dans le Liber sacratus sive juratus attribué à Honorius de Thèbes" *Mélanges de l'Ecole française de Rome:* Moyen âge, Volume 114, Issue 2, L'Ecole, 2002.

___, *Entre science et nigromance: astrologie, divination et magie dans l'occident médiéval, XIIe-XVe siècle.* Paris: Publications de la Sorbonne, 2006.

Bremmer, Jan N., and Jan R. Veenstra. *The Metamorphosis of Magic from Late Antiquity to the Early Modern Period.* Leuven: Peeters, 2002.

Buhlman, Jan, "Notice of the Liber juratus in Early Fourteenth-century France, Societas Magica Newsletter, Fall 2005, Issue 14. http://www.societasmagica.org/userfiles/files/Newsletters/docs/SMN_Fall_2005_Issue_14.pdf accessed September 24, 2015.

Casanowicz, Immanuel Moses. *Jewish Amulets in the United States National Museum.* Washington, D.C.: U.S. National Museum, 1976.

Chardonnens, László, and Jan R. Veenstra. "Carved in Lead and Concealed in Stone: A Late Medieval Sigillum Dei at Doornenburg Castle, " in *Magic, Ritual, and Witchcraft*, Volume 9, Number 2, Winter 2014.

Charlesworth, James H. *The Old Testament Pseudepigrapha.* Vol. I. New York, NY: Doubleday, 1983.

Dan, Joseph, Rachel Elior, and Peter Schäfer. *Creation and re-creation in Jewish thought: festschrift in honor of Joseph Dan on the occasion of his seventieth birthday.* Tübingen: Mohr Siebeck, 2005.

Davies, Owen. *Grimoires: A History of Magic Books.* Oxford: Oxford University Press, 2009.

Delatte, Louis, *Un office byzantin d'exorcisme.* [Bruxelles]: [Palais des académies], 1957.

Driscoll, Daniel J., *The Sworn Book of Honourius the Magician,* Gillette, New Jersey: Heptangle Books, 1977. Reprinted in 1983 by the same publisher.

Fanger, Claire. *Conjuring spirits: texts and traditions of medieval ritual magic.* University Park, Pa: Pennsylvania State University Press, 1998.

___. *Esoterica,* Volume VIII, Michigan State University: East Lansing, MI, 2006, pp. 180-183. http://www.esoteric.msu.edu/VolumeVIII/EsotericaVIII.pdf, accessed Sep 24, 2015.

___. *Invoking Angels: Theurgic Ideas and Practices, Thirteenth to Sixteenth Centuries.* University Park, PA: Pennsylvania State University Press, 2012.

Fludd, Robert. *Medicina catholica: seu, mysticum artis medicandi sacrarium; in tomos divisum 2, in quibus metaphysica et physica tam sanitatis tuendae, quam morborum propulsandorum ratio pertractantur. 1. 1.* Francofurti: Fitzer, 1629. https://play.google.com/store/books/details?id=GV9DAAAAcAAJ&rdid=book-GV9DAAAAcAAJ&rdot=1, retrieved 10/11/2015.

Gehr, Damaris Aschera. *La Summa magice di Berengario Ganello*: tesi di dottorato. (masch.) Venedig 2007.

___. "Luxus und Luxusdiskurse in der gelehrten lateinischen Magie des 12. bis 14. Jahrhunderts" in Jutta Eming/ Gaby Pailer /Franziska Schössler / Johannes Traulsen (eds.), Fremde - Luxus - Räume. *Konzeptionen von Luxus in Vormoderne und Moderne,* Frank & Timme, Berlin 2015, pp. 147-165.

Gilly, Carlos. "Between Paracelsus, Pelagius and Ganellus: Hermetism in John Dee, " in *Magia, alchimia, scienza dal '400 al '700; L'influsso di Ermete Trismegisto / Magic, Alchemy and Science, 15th-18th Centuries,* edited by Carlos Gilly and Cis van Heertum (Florence: Centro Di, 2002) Vol I: 286-94.

Greenfield, Richard P. H. *Traditions of Belief in Late Byzantine Demonology.* Amsterdam: Adolf M. Hakkert, 1988.

___. "Contribution to the Study of Palaeologan Magic" in Maguire 1995, pp. 117-153.

Greer, John Michael, and Christopher Warnock. *Picatrix: The Classic Medieval Handbook of Astrological Magic.* [Iowa City, IA]: Adocentyn Press, 2011.

Harms, Daniel, James R. Clark, and Joseph H. Peterson. *The Book of Oberon: A Sourcebook of Elizabethan Magic.* Woodbury, MN: Llewellyn, 2015.

Honorius III, Pope, pseud. *Grimoire du pape Honorius: avec un recueil des plus rares secrets.* Rome: [publisher not identified], 1760.

Honorius of Thebes. See Hedegård.

Idel, Moshe, "The Kabbaleh in Byzantium: Preliminary Remarks" in Bonfil, Robert. *Jews in Byzantium: Dialects of Minority and Majority Cultures.* Leiden: Brill, 2012

Iroé-Grego. *La véritable magie noire, ou, Le secret des secrets: manuscrit trouvé à Jérusalem, dans le sépulcre de Salomon : contenant 1.° Quarante-cinq talismans avec leurs gravures, ainsi que la manière de s'en servir, et leurs merveilleuses propriétés ; 2.° Tous les caractères magiques connus jusqu'à ce jour.* A Rome [i.e. France], 1750.

Kieckhefer, Richard. *Magic in the Middle Ages.* Cambridge: Cambridge University Press, 1989.

___, *Forbidden Rites: A Necromancer's Manual of the Fifteenth Century*. University Park, Pa: Pennsylvania State University Press, 1998.

___, "The Devil's Contemplatives" in Fanger 1998, pp. 250-265.

Kircher, Athanasius. *Oedipus Aegyptiacus, I-II*, Rome, 1652-54.

Klaassen, Frank. "English Manuscripts of Magic, 1300-1500: A Preliminary Survey," in Fanger, 1998, pp. 3-31.

Lawrence-Mathers, Anne, and Carolina Escobar-Vargas. *Magic and Medieval Society*, London; New York: Routledge, 2014.

Lidaka, Juris. "The Book of Angels, Rings, Characters and Images of the Planets: Attributed to Osbern Bokenham," in Fanger, 1998, pp. 32-75.

___. "REVIEWS – Liber Iuratus Honorii: A Critical Edition of the Latin Version of the Sworn Book of Honorius," in *Speculum. A Journal Medieval Studies*, 2004; 79 (1).

Maguire, Henry. *Byzantine Magic*. Washington, D.C.: Dumbarton Oaks Research Library and Collection, 1995.

Marathakis, Ioannis. *The Magical Treatise of Solomon, or Hygromanteia: Also Called the Apotelesmatikē Pragmateia, Epistle to Rehoboam, Solomōnikē*, Singapore: Golden Hoard Press, 2011.

Marrone, Steven P. *A History of Science, Magic and Belief: From Medieval to Early Modern Europe*. Basingstoke: Palgrave Macmillan, 2015.

Mathiesen. "A Thirteenth-Century Ritual to Attain the Beatific Vision from the Sworn Book of Honorius of Thebes," in Fanger, 1998, pp. 143-162.

McCartney, Eugene S., *Greek and Roman Weather Lore of Winds*. New York: Published by the Classical Association of the Atlantic States, 1930. <http://www.st-andrews.ac.uk/library/specialcollections/collections/rarebooks/projects/lightingthepast/>.

McGraw, Matthew. "The Supernatural and the Limits of Materiality in Medieval Histories, Travelogues, and Romances From William of Malmesbury to Geoffrey Chaucer", PhD dissertation, UC Riverside, 2013. http://escholarship.org/uc/item/9ck303t5 retrieved August 2, 2015.

Mesler, Katelyn. "The *Liber iuratus Honorii* and the Christian Reception of Angel Magic" in Fanger 2012.

Page, Sophie. *Magic in Medieval Manuscripts*. Toronto: University of Toronto Press, 2004.

___. *Magic in the Cloister: Pious Motives, Illicit Interests, and Occult Approaches to the Medieval Universe*. University Park, Pennsylvania: The Pennsylvania State University Press, 2013.

Peterson, Joseph H. *John Dee's Five Books of Mystery Original Sourcebook of Enochian Magic*. Newburyport: Red Wheel Weiser, 2002.

___. *The Sixth and Seventh Books of Moses, or, Moses, Magical Spirits-Art: Known As the Wonderful Arts of the Old Wise Hebrews, Taken from the Mosaic Books of the*

Cabala and the Talmud, for the Good of Mankind. Lake Worth, Fla: Ibis Press, 2008.

___, see also Harms, Clark, and Peterson

Petrus de Abano. *Heptameron, seu elementa magica* : 1565, in Karl Anton Nowotny. *De occulta philosophia.* Graz: Akademische Druck u. Verlagsanstalt, 1967.

Postles, David. *Social Geographies in England (1200-1640).* Washington, DC: New Academia Pub, 2007.

Ptolemy, and Frank Egleston Robbins. *Tetrabiblos.* Cambridge, Mass: Harvard University Press, 1980.

Scholem, "Some Sources of Jewish Arabic Demonology," in *Journal of Jewish Studies*, Volume 16, Issue 1-2, London: 1965.

Schwartz, Dov. 2003. "Conceptions of Astral Magic Within Jewish Rationalism in the Byzantine Empire". *Aleph: Historical Studies in Science and Judaism.* 3: 165-211.

Schwartz, Michael D. "Mystical Texts" in Safrai, Shemuel, *The Literature of the Sages, Second Part.* Assen, Netherlands: Fortress Press, 2006, pp. 393-420.

Skemer, Don C. *Binding Words: Textual Amulets in the Middle Ages.* University Park, Pa: Pennsylvania State University Press, 2006.

Thorndike, Lynn. *A History of Magic and Experimental Science, volume II,* New York: Macmillan Co, 1923.

Veenstra, Jan R, *Magic and divination at the courts of Burgundy and France: text and context of Laurens Pignon's Contre les devineurs (1411).* Leiden: Brill, 1998.

___. "Honorius and the Sigil of God: The *Liber iuratus* in Berengario Ganell's *Summa sacre magice*" in Fanger 2012, p. 151 ff.

___. See also Bremmer and Veenstra.

Véronèse, Julien. *L'Ars notoria au Moyen Âge: introduction et édition critique.* Firenze: SISMEL edizioni del Galluzzo, 2007.

___. *L'Almandal et l'Almadel latins au Moyen Âge: introduction et éditions critiques.* Firenze: SISMEL edizioni del Galluzzo, 2012.

Waite, Arthur Edward, *The Book of Black Magic and of Pacts,* privately printed: 1898; enlarged and revised as *The Secret Tradition in Goëtia. The Book of Ceremonial Magic Including the Rites and Mysteries of Goëtic Theurgy, Sorcery and Infernal Necromancy.* London: W. Rider & Son, 1911. Reprint New Hyde Park, N.Y.: University Books, 1961.

Wilkinson, Robert J. *Tetragrammaton: Western Christians and the Hebrew Name of God: from the Beginnings to the Seventeenth Century.* 2015.

Index of Spirit Names

Abaa (Haaba, Habaa, Ἀβά. SSM: Abaah; H diverges), king of the spirits of the air of Mercury, governing between the West and the North, i.e. the region knows as frigicap; said to be neither fully for good nor fully evil. Said to be "most wise." 19, 237, 251, 253, 255, 257, 259, 261, 263, 265, 297

Abalidoth (Ἀβαλιδώθ), 19

Abdala (Abdalaa), 20

Abouzaba (Abuzaha, Abuzampa, Ἀβουζαβα), 20

Abucaba (Abuchaba, Habucaba. SSM: Abucaba, Aabucaba). daemon of the air subordinate to the Moon and its wind, which is called Zephyr. Considered good. Same as Habuchaba? Minister to Harthan, **205**, 231, 245-253, 257, 265

Abunalich (Abumalith, Aboumaleth, Ἀβουμαλήθ), 19. Compare Albunalich.

Abuzoba, 18

Acadan, 279n

Acythael, 213n

Admodeus [sic], 279n

Albunalich (SSM: Albunalic; H: Abumalith; D: Ἀβουμαλήθ), spirit or daemon of the air, governing in the North, minister to king Maymon, subordinate to the planet Saturn and its wind; said to be evil, arrogant, and wild. **201, 233**, 251, 253, 255, 265

Alchibany (Alcibany, Alcybany. SSM: Altybany), name of one of the southwest winds, and spirit of the air of the north rising up from the southwest, associated with Saturn, and calling up its wind, which is called "Africus" (the east wind), said to be evil, arrogant, and wild. **201**, 233, 245, 247, 249

Alflas (SSM: Alphlas), name of one of the southwest winds, and spirit of the air of the north rising up from the southwest, subordinate to the planet Saturn, and calling up its wind, which is called "Africus" (the east wind), said to be evil, arrogant, and wild. **201, 233**, 245-249

Almutab, 18

Amabiel (Amabihel, **Amabiel, Annabyl,** Ἀμαβιήλ; SSM: Annabyl), planetary spirit associated with Mars and the south. 19, 271, **209, 213, 221**

Amaymon, 24, 26

Amocap (Amochap. SSM: Amocab), spirit of the air, governing in the West, subordinate to the Moon and its wind, which is called Zephyr. Considered good. **205, 231**, 245, 247, 249

Anael (Hanael, Hanahel, Haniel, ἀναήλ; SSM: Anael), prince of angels associated with the planet Venus and the southwest. The name of this angel is found on the Seal of God. 19, 67, 71, **213, 221**

Andas (Adas, Ἀδάς), 19

Arcan (Ἀρκαν), 20. See also Harcan

Asassaiel (Asasayel, Asassayel, Asasiel, Ἀσασιήλ; SSM: Asassayel), planetary spirit associated with Jupiter and the southeast. 19, 201, 271

Asmoday, 279n

Asmodeus, terrestrial spirit, assistant of prince Labadau. This demon is the best well known of all spirits listed by Honorius, including from the *Book of Tobit* and the *Testament of Solomon*. The name is believed to be

313

Zoroastrian in origin, in the Avestan language *Aeshma-daeva* ("demon of wrath."). 34, 279

Assaibi (Assaiby, Asaibi, Hassaybi, ᾽Ασαϊβί; SSM: Aassayby; H: Assaibi, Hassayby), spirit or daemon of the air, governing in the North, minister to king Maymon, subordinate to the planet Saturn and its wind, which is called "Africus" (the "southwest wind"), said to be evil, arrogant, and wild. 19, **201, 233,** 251, 253, 255, 265

Assassayel (Asassaiel), 209, 213, 221

Athitael (Athithael, Atithael; SSM: Acytael), planetary spirit associated with the Moon. **20, 205, 209, 213, 221,** 271

Atraurbiabilis (Attraurbiabilis; SSM: Atrahurbyabylys, Hatraurbyabylys), name of one of the eastern winds, associated with Mars. Spirit of the air, governing in the South, subordinate to the planet Mars, and calling up its wind, which is called "Subsolanus" (the east wind), said to be evil, arrogant, and wild. **203, 231,** 245, 247, 249

Aybalidech: See Haibalidech

Aycolaytoum, 19

Bael, 297n

Baldakionsis, 21

Balidet (Βαλιδέτ), 19

Barachiel (Baruchiel, Barakiel, Baraqiel), one of seven superior angels (along with Uriel). 22, 299

Barthan (Barcan, Barchan, Barkan, Βαρκαν; SSM: Barchan, Barthan), king of daemons associated with the Sun and the north winds; ruling in the East.. 19, 21, **203, 229,** 251-255, 259-271, 297

Bassal, 20

Baxhatau (Baxhathau, Baxatau; SSM: Baxahathau), spirit of the air, governing in the East, subordinate to the Sun and its wind, which is called the North wind. Considered good, and most powerful; name of one of the north winds, associated with the Sun, minister of King Barthan. 229, 245, 247, 249

Baylul, 20

Baysul, 20

Beel, 297

Beelzebub (Belzebub), prince of daemons of the air. 254n, 271

Belzebut, 247, 261

Beralanysis, 21

Bileth (Bilar, Bilet, Βιλέθ; SSM: Byleth), daemon of the air associated with the Moon and the west winds, minister of king Harthan. 20, 34, **205, 231,** 251, 253, 257, 265

Bohel (Beel, Boel. SSM: Boel), planetary spirit associated with Saturn and the North. **19, 33n, 201, 209, 213, 219, 221,** 271, 297n

Boon, 29

Bylol (Bibol), 18

Caffaa, 20

Cafhael (Caphael; SSM: Caphael), planetary spirit associated with the Sun and the east. **19, 203, 209, 213, 221,** 271

Cafziel (Caphciel, Caphzyel; SSM: Cafzyel), planetary angel or spirit, associated with Saturn and the North. The name of this angel is found on the Seal of God. 19, **33n, 201, 209, 213, 219, 221,** 271

Cahala, 20

Calta, 20

Cambores (SSM: Cambores), name of one of the winds of the east (subsolanus) and west (zephyr), associated with Venus. Spirit of the air, governing between the South

Index of Spirit Names

and the West, subordinate to the planet Venus and calling up its winds, which are called "Subsolar" (Easterly) and "Zephyr" (Westerly), said to be neither fully for good nor fully evil. **205**, 237, 245-249

Cana, 20

Carmeal (Carmehal. SSM: Carmeal), name of one of the eastern winds, associated with Mars. Spirit of the air, governing in the South, subordinate to the planet Mars, and calling up its wind, which is called "Subsolanus" (the east wind), said to be evil, arrogant, and wild. **203**, 231, 245, 247, 249

Carmox (Carmax, Καρμάξ ; SSM: Carmos; H: Carmax), daemon associated with Mars and the south. Spirit of the air, governing in the South, minister to King Iammax, subordinate to the planet Mars and its wind, which is called "Subsolanus" (the east wind), said to be evil, arrogant, and wild. 19, **203**, 231, 251-255, 265

Casfeel, 19

Cassael, 19

Cassiel (Kasiel, Κασιήλ), 19

Castiel (Kastiel, Καστιήλ), 19

Casziel, 22, 67, 69, 299

Caualasyel, 19

Caudas (Caudes; SSM: Caaudas, Candones), daemon or spirit of the air, associated with the East, minister of king Barthan; name of one of the north winds, associated with the Sun, minister of King Barthan. Considered good. Confused with Chaudas (?). 19, **203**, 229, 245-251, 253, 255, 265

Chatas, 19

Corcornifer, 279n

Cornifer, 279n

Corniger ("horned one"), southern king of terrestrial spirits. 16, 279

Cricios, 19

Cynabal (Cunabal (Κυναβάλ), 19

Cynassa (Cinassa; SSM: Synassa; H diverges), daemon associated with Venus and the eastern and western winds (zephyr). Spirit of the air, governing between the South and the West, minister to King Sarabocres, subordinate to the planet Venus and its winds, which are called "Subsolar" (Easterly) and "Zephyr" (Westerly), said to be neither fully for good nor fully evil. 19, **205**, 235, 251-257, 265

Daniel, 19

Dardaci (aka Daniel), 19

Dardiel (Dardihel, Dardyel, Δαρδιήλ; SSM: Dardyel), planetary spirit associated with the Sun and the east. **19, 203, 209, 213, 221,** 271

Darial, 20

devil, the, 159

Drohas (SSM: Drohas), name of one of the west and southwest winds, associated with the planet Mercury. Spirit of the air, governing between the West and the North, subordinate to the planet Mercury and calling up its winds, which are called "Zephyr" (Westerly) and "Africus" (the east wind), said to be neither fully for good nor fully evil. **205**, 237, 245-249

Ebuzoba (cp Abouzaba), 20

Egyn, 24

Eladeb (SSM: Eladeb; H diverges), daemon associated with the west and southwest winds. Spirit or daemon of the air, governing between the West and the North, minister of King Abaa, subordinate to the planet Mercury and its winds, which are called "Zephyr" (Westerly) and

"Africus" (the east wind), said to be neither fully for good nor fully evil. 20, **205, 237**, 251-257, 265

Esmahel, 20

Euiraber, terrestrial spirit, attendant of King Corniger, in the South. 279

Faccas, 19-20

Flaef (Phlaeph, Φλαέ), 19

Formione (SSM: Formione; H: Suth [sic]), king of spirits of the air, governing between the East and the South, subordinate to the planet Jupiter and its winds, which are called Borean (Northerly") and Subsolar ("Easterly"), said to be neither fully for good nor fully evil. Said to be "most beautiful." 19, **201**, 235, 251-255, 259-265, 269, 297

Furcaber, Furcuber, 279n

Gabriel (Γαβριήλ ; SSM: Gabryel), planetary spirit associated with the Moon; name of one of four archangel (along with Michael, Raphael, and Uriel). Name of this angel is found on the Seal of God. 18, 20, 22n, 67, 71, 101, 179, 189, **205, 209, 213, 221**, 271

Gahathus (Gaatus, Gahatus. SSM: Gaatus), name of one of the north winds, associated with the Sun, minister of King Barthan. Spirit of the air, governing in the East, subordinate to the Sun and its wind, which is called the North wind. Considered good. 229, 245, 247, 249

Guth (SSM: Guth; missing from H), spirit or daemon of the air, governing between the East and the South, minister to King Formione, subordinate to the planet Jupiter and its winds, which are called Borean (Northerly") and Subsolar ("Easterly"), said to be neither fully for good nor fully evil. 19, **201, 235**, 251-255, 265

Guthryn (Guthrin, Guthryn, Gutrhyn. SSM: Gutryn; H: Gutrix), spirit or daemon of the air, governing between the East and the South, minister to King Formione, subordinate to the planet Jupiter and its winds, which are called Borean (Northerly") and Subsolar ("Easterly"), said to be neither fully for good nor fully evil. 19, 201, 235, 251, 253, 255, 255, 265

Gutriz (Goutriz, Γουτρίζ), 19

Habaa (cp Abaa), 20, **205**

Habuchaba (Abucaba, **Abuchaba**; SSM: Abucaba), daemon associated with the West, minister of king Harthan. **231**

Haibalidech (Haybalidech, Aybalidech; SSM: Alybalydech; H: Balidet; D: Βαλιδέτ), spirit or daemon of the air, governing in the North, minister to king Maymon, subordinate to the planet Saturn and its wind, which is called "Africus" (the "southwest wind"), said to be evil, arrogant, and wild. 19, 201, 233, 251, 253, 255, 265

Halmitab (Almutab), 18

Hanael (Hanahel, Anael), 19, 203, 209, 221, 271. See Anael

Harit (Harith; SSM: Haryx), spirit of the air, governing between the East and the South, subordinate to the planet Jupiter, and calling up its winds, which are called Borean (Northerly") and Subsolar ("Easterly"), said to be neither fully for good nor fully evil. 201, 235, 245, 247, 249

Harith (SSM: Gutryn), name of one of the northeast winds, associated with Jupiter

Harmanel (Harnariel), 19

Index of Spirit Names

Harthan (cp Arcan; SSM: Arthan), king of the daemons associated with the Moon and the west winds, said to be most mild (or gentle). 20, 205, 231, 251-265, 297

Hebetel (**Hebethel; SSM: Hebethel**), name of one of the west winds, associated with the Moon. Spirit of the air, governing in the West, subordinate to the Moon and its wind, which is called Zephyr. Considered good. 18, 205, 231, 245, 247, 249

Heyeyl, 20

Hocroel (Hocrohel), 29, 51, 241, 243

Hurathapel (Hurathaphel, Khourataphel, Χουραταφήλ; **SSM: Huracaphel**), planetary spirit associated with the Sun and the east. **19, 203, 209, 221,** 271

Hyachonaababur (Yaconaababur; SSM: yaconaababur), name of one of the eastern winds, associated with Mars. **203**

Hycandas, 19

Hyici (Hyyci. SSM: Hyeycy; H diverges), daemon associated with the planet Mercury and the west and southwest winds. Spirit of the air, governing between the West and the North, minister of King Abaa, subordinate to the planet Mercury and its winds, which are called "Zephyr" (Westerly) and "Africus" (the east wind), said to be neither fully for good nor fully evil. **20, 205, 237,** 251, 253, 255, 257, 265

Iaconaababur (Yaconaababur; SSM: Yaconablabur), spirit of the air, governing in the South, subordinate to the planet Mars, and calling up its wind, which is called "Subsolanus" (the east wind), said to be evil, arrogant, and wild. See also Hyachonaababur. 231, 245-249

Ialchal (Yalcal; SSM: Yarabal?), daemon associated with the Sun and the north winds, minister of King Barthan. 19, **203**

Iammax (Yammax. SSM: Yammax; H: Samax), king of daemons associated with Mars and the south. King of spirits of the air, governing in the South, subordinate to the planet Mars and its wind, which is called "Subsolanus" (the east wind), said to be evil, arrogant, and wild. Also said to be "most mighty." 19, 203, 231, 251, 253, 255, 259, 261, 263, 265, 269, 297

Iarabal (Yarabal; SSM: Yarabal), spirit of the air, governing in the East, subordinate to the Sun and its wind, which is called the North wind. Considered good Name of one of the north winds, associated with the Sun, minister of King Barthan. Confused with Ialchal (?). 229, 245-249

Ichanol (Ycanohl, Ycanol; SSM:Ytanol; H: Ismoli), spirit of the air, governing in the South, minister to King Iammax, subordinate to the planet Mars and its wind, which is called "Subsolanus" (the east wind), said to be evil, arrogant, and wild. 19, 203, 231, 251, 253, 255, 265

Ienomei, 241, 243

Iesse (SSM: Yesse), name of one of the northeast winds, associated with Jupiter. Spirit of the air, governing between the East and the South, subordinate to the planet Jupiter, and calling up its winds, which are called Borean (Northerly") and Subsolar ("Easterly"), said to be neither fully for good nor fully evil. **201, 235,** 245, 247, 249

Ilamos, 20
Innial (Innyal, **Innyhal**; SSM: Iunyal), spirit of the air, governing in the South, subordinate to the planet Mars, and calling up its wind, which is called "Subsolanus" (the east wind), said to be evil, arrogant, and wild. Name of one of the eastern winds. **231**, 203
Iobial, 19
Ismoli (Ἰσμολί), 19
Ituraiel, 271
Iucuciel, 19
Jegudiel, 22n
Karathiel, 29, 241, 243
Karmal, 19
Labadau (Labadan, 279n), prince of terrestrial spirits. 279
Lanael, 29
Lanciel, 241, 243
Lucifer, 279n
Machatan (Machotan, Μαχωτάν), 19
Maguth (Magouth, Μαγούθ; SSM: Maguth; H: Maguth), spirit of the air, governing between the East and the South, minister to King Formione, subordinate to the planet Jupiter and its winds, which are called Borean (Northerly") and Subsolar ("Easterly"), said to be neither fully for good nor fully evil. 19, **201**, 235, 251-255, 265
Malafer (Malafar), terrestrial spirit, attendant of King Corniger, in the West. 279
Marastac, 19
Maxtarcop, 19
Maylalu, 20
Maymon (Maimon; SSM: Maaymon; H: Maymon; D: Μαϋμον), king of spirits or daemons of the air, governing in the North, subordinate to the planet Saturn and its wind, which is called "Africus" (the "southwest wind"), said to be evil, arrogant, and wild. Also said to be most harsh (or severe). 19, 201, 233, 251-255, 259-265, 297
Mayrion, 19
Mextyura (SSM: Mextyura), name of one of the southwest winds, and spirit of the air of the north rising up from the southwest, associated with Saturn, and calling up its wind, which is called "Africus" (the east wind), said to be evil, arrogant, and wild. **201**, 233, 245, 247, 249
Michael (Mychael, Μιχαήλ), planetary spirit associated with the Moon. Name of one of four archangel (along with Gabriel, Uriel, and Raphael). Name of this angel is found on the Seal of God. 18-20, 22n, 67, 69, 101, 179, **205**, 209, 213, 221
Michathon, 209, 221
Micrathon (Michrathon, Mycraton; SSM: Mycrathon), planetary spirit associated with Saturn and the North. 19, **33n**, 201, 213, 271
Miel (Myel, Myhel, Μιήλ; SSM: Myel), planetary spirit associated with the planet Mercury and the northwest. 20, 33n, 205, **209**, 213, 221, 271
Milalu (Mylalu; SSM: Mylaluh), daemon associated with the Moon and the west winds; daemon associated with the West, minister of king Harthan. 18, **205**, 231, 251, 253, 257, 265
Milau (Mylau; SSM: Mylalu), name of one of the west winds, associated with the Moon; spirit of the air, governing in the West, subordinate to the Moon and its wind, which is called Zephyr. Considered good. 205, 231, 245, 247, 249
Miriel, 20
Misabou (Missabu, Μισσαβού), 20

Index of Spirit Names

Modiat (Modiath, Mediath, Μοδιαθ or Μεδιάθ), 20
Mulciber (cp Mulcifer), 279n
Mulcifer, terrestrial spirit, attendant of King Corniger, in the North. 279
Mychael (cp Michael; SSM: Michael), planetary spirit associated with the planet Mercury and the northwest. 20, **33n, 205**, 271
Mychial, 213n
Mycraton: See Micrathon
Myel, Myhel: See Miel
Mylalu: See Milalu
Mylau: See Milau
Naadob (SSM: Naadobp), name of one of the northeast winds, associated with Jupiter. Spirit of the air, governing between the East and the South, subordinate to the planet Jupiter, and calling up its winds, which are called Borean (Northerly") and Subsolar ("Easterly"), said to be neither fully for good nor fully evil. **201, 235,** 245-249
Naasa (**Naassa**; SSM: Naassah), name of one of the winds of the east (subsolanus) and west (zephyr), associated with Venus. Spirit of the air, governing between the South and the West, subordinate to the planet Venus and calling up its winds, which are called "Subsolar" (Easterly) and "Zephyr" (Westerly), said to be neither fully for good nor fully evil. **205, 237,** 245-249
Nacha, 20
Namoz, 20
Nassar (SSM: Naassar; H diverges), spirit of the air, governing between the South and the West, minister to King Sarabocres, subordinate to the planet Venus and its winds, which are called "Subsolar" (Easterly) and "Zephyr" (Westerly), said to be neither fully for good nor fully evil. Daemon associated with Venus and the eastern and western winds (zephyr). **19, 205, 235, 237,** 245-253, 257, 265
Nesaph (SSM: Nesaph), name of one of the northeast winds, associated with Jupiter. Spirit of the air, governing between the East and the South, subordinate to the planet Jupiter, and calling up its winds, which are called Borean (Northerly") and Subsolar ("Easterly"), said to be neither fully for good nor fully evil. **201, 235,** 245-249
Oilol (Oylol; SSM: Oylol), spirit of the air (?), governing in the West, subordinate to the Moon and its wind, which is called Zephyr. Considered good. 205, **231,** 245-249
Oriens (Orienens), 24
Ourouel (Οὐρουήλ), 19
Pahamcociel (Pahamcocihel, **Paamchociel, Paamcociel**; SSM: Paamtotyel), planetary spirit associated with Jupiter and the southeast. **19, 201, 209, 213, 221,** 271
Palas (same in SSM), name of one of the west and southwest winds, associated with the planet Mercury. Spirit of the air, governing between the West and the North, subordinate to the planet Mercury and calling up its winds, which are called "Zephyr" (Westerly) and "Africus" (the east wind), said to be neither fully for good nor fully evil. **205, 237,** 245-249
Panmachia, 21
Pasfran (Paffran, Pafran, Παφράν; SSM: Pasfran), daemons associated with Mars and the south. Pasfrau (SSM: Pasfrau; H: Paffran), spirit of the air, governing in the South, minister to

King Iammax, subordinate to the planet Mars and its wind, which is called "Subsolanus" (the east wind), said to be evil, arrogant, and wild. 19, 203, 231, 251, 253, 255, 265

Paymon, 24

Primak, 21

Proathophas (Prohathophas; SSM: Prohatofas, Proathofas), spirit of the air, governing in the South, subordinate to the planet Mars, and calling up its wind, which is called "Subsolanus" (the east wind), said to be evil, arrogant, and wild. **203, 231**, 245-249

Quyron (Quiron; SSM: Quyron; H diverges), spirit of the air, governing between the West and the North, minister of King Abaa, subordinate to the planet Mercury and its winds, which are called "Zephyr" (Westerly) and "Africus" (the east wind), said to be neither fully for good nor fully evil. Daemon associated with the planet Mercury and the west and southwest winds. 20, 205, 237, 251-257, 265

Rachiel (Rakhiel, ῥαχιήλ), 19

Raphael (ῥαφαήλ; SSM: Raphael), planetary spirit associated with the Sun and the east. Name of one of four archangel (along with Michael, Gabriel, and Uriel); (SSM: Raphyel), planetary spirit associated with Jupiter and the southeast. The name of this angel is found on the Seal of God. 18-20, 22n, 67, 69, 101, 179, **201, 203, 209, 213, 221**, 271

Raquiel (cp Rachiel; SSM: Raquyel), planetary spirit associated with Venus and the southwest. 19, **203, 209, 213, 221**, 271

Rion (Ryon; SSM: Ryon), name of one of the northeast winds, associated

with Jupiter. Spirit of the air, governing between the East and the South, subordinate to the planet Jupiter, and calling up its winds, which are called Borean (Northerly") and Subsolar ("Easterly"), said to be neither fully for good nor fully evil. 201, 235, 245, 247, 249

Rubeus Pugnator ("Red Fighter"), 19

Sachiel (Sakiel, Sakhiel, Σαχιήλ), 19

Salathiel, 22n

Salguiel (Salguyel; SSM: Salquyel), planetary spirit associated with Venus and the southwest. **19, 203, 209, 221**, 271

Saliciel (Salatiel), 19

Sallales (Σαλλάλες), 20

Samael (Samahel, Samäel, Σαμαήλ; SSM: Samael), planetary spirit associated with Mars and the south. Name of this angel is found on the Seal of God. 18-20, 67, 69, 75, **209, 213, 221**, 271

Samax (Σαμάξ), 19

Samayel (cp Samyel, Samael), 20

Sambas (Zambas; SSM: Sambas), name of one of the west and southwest winds, associated with the planet Mercury. 205, 245-249

Samiel (Samyel. SSM: Samyel. Compare Samael), planetary spirit associated with the Moon. 18, 20, **205, 209, 213, 221**, 271

Sarabocres (Σαραβότρες; SSM: Sarabotres; H: Sarabrotres, later misspelled Sarabotes), king of daemons or spirits of the air, governing between the South and the West, subordinate to the planet Venus and its winds, which are called "Subsolar" (Easterly) and "Zephyr" (Westerly), said to be neither fully for good nor fully evil. Said to be "most noble." 19, **205**, 235, 251-265, 297

Sarapiel (Saraphiel, Σαραφιήλ ; SSM: Sarypyel), planetary spirit associated with the planet Mercury and the northwest. 20, **205, 213, 221**, 271

Sariel, 19, 20

Saripiel (Sarypyel), **33n, 209**

Satan, 49

Saterquiel (Satryquiel; SSM: Satryquyel), planetary spirit associated with Saturn and the North. **19, 33n, 201,** 213, 221

Sathquyel, 209

Satiel (**Sathiel,** Satihel, Satael, Σαταήλ; SSM: Sathyel), planetary spirit associated with Mars and the south. **19, 209, 213, 221,** 271

Satquiel (SSM: Satquyel), planetary spirit associated with Jupiter and the southeast. Name of this angel is found on the Seal of God. 19, 22, **67, 69, 201, 213, 221,** 271, 299

Selaphiel, 22n

Seraquiel, 213n

Stanalcon, 19

Staus, 19

Suquinos (Soukinos, Σουκίνος), 20

Suth (South, Σούθ), 19

Szamahel, 20

Talanasiel (Caualasyel), 19

Taxael, 19

Thaadas (**Taadas;** SSM:Thaadas), daemon associated with the East, minister of king Barthan. Daemon associated with the Sun and the north winds, minister of King Barthan. 19, **203,** 229, 251-255, 265

Tous: See Tus.

Trachatat (Tracatath, Trachathath. SSM: Trachatat), spirit of the air, governing between the South and the West, subordinate to the planet Venus and calling up its winds, which are called "Subsolar" (Easterly) and "Zephyr" (Westerly), said to be neither fully for good nor fully evil. 205, 237, 245-249

Trocornifer, terrestrial spirit, attendant of King Corniger, in the East. 279

Tus (Tous, Τούς), 19, 21

Uriel (SSM: Vuel), name of one of four archangel (along with Michael, Gabriel, and Raphael); one of seven higher angels (along with Barachiel). 22, 29, 179, **241, 243,** 299

Varcan (cp. Barthan), 19

Vihel, 29, 241, 243

Vriel, 19. See also Uriel

Yaciatal, 19

Yaconaababur: See Iaconaababur

Yalcal (SSM: Yarabal), daemon associated with the East, minister of king Barthan. **229,** 251, 253, 255, 265

Yammax: *see* Iammax.

Yarabal: See Iarabal

Yasfla (SSM: Yasfla; missing from H), spirit or daemon of the air, governing in the North, minister to king Maymon, subordinate to the planet Saturn and its wind, which is called "Africus" (the "southwest wind"), said to be evil, arrogant, and wild. 19, 201, **233,** 251-255, 265

Ycaachel, 19

Ycanohl: See Ichanol

Yfasue, 19

Ynial (Ynnyal), 245, 247, 249

Ysicres, 241, 243

Yturahihel (**Yturaihel,** Yturaiel; SSM: Yturayel), planetary spirit associated with Mars and the south. 19, **209, 213, 221**

Zach (SSM: Zach; H diverges), daemon associated with the planet Mercury and the west and southwest winds. Spirit of the air, governing between the West and the North, minister of King Abaa, subordinate to the

planet Mercury and its winds, which are called "Zephyr" (Westerly) and "Africus" (the east wind), said to be neither fully for good nor fully evil. 20, **205**, **237**, 251-257, 265

Zambas (Sambas; SSM: Sambas), spirit of the air, governing between the West and the North, subordinate to the planet Mercury and calling up its winds, which are called "Zephyr" (Westerly) and "Africus" (the east wind), said to be neither fully for good nor fully evil. 237, 247, 249

Zobha (SSM: Zobha), name of one of the west and southwest winds, associated with the planet Mercury. Spirit of the air, governing between the West and the North, subordinate to the planet Mercury and calling up its winds, which are called "Zephyr" (Westerly) and "Africus" (the east wind), said to be neither fully for good nor fully evil. **205**, **237**, 245, 247, 249

Zombar, 20

Index of Divine Names

The one hundred names of God are from Honorius chapter CI.2; those which compose the 72-letter name are from Ganell, SSM (L.2.f.25 ll 5-26)

Abbadia (Abbadya, Abdia), CI.2.29
Abdon, CI.2.65
Abracalabrah, SSM.45
Abracaleus, SSM.55
Abracio, CI.2.63
Abryon, SSM.65
Achionadabir (Hachionadabir), CI.2.53
Admyhel, CI.2.17
Adon, SSM.11
Adonay, Hebrew. Also on Seal of God, CI.2.52
AGLA, Hebrew (acronym). Also in 72 names, as well as Seal of God, CI.2.1; SSM.9
Alla, SSM.51
Alpha et Ω, Latin ("The First and the Last"), from Revelations., CI.2.30
Alpha ω, SSM.7
Amphynethon, CI.2.6
Anephenethon, CI.2.64
Anethy, CI.2.22
Araton, SSM.29
Archima, CI.2.99
Asmamyas, SSM.43
Athedyon, SSM.22
Athyonodabazar, SSM.19
Ay, SSM.59
Baruch, CI.2.69; SSM.8
Capkyb, SSM.32
Christus, Greek ("Christ"), also on Seal of God, CI.2.93
Cirrhos, CI.2.86
Delectycon, SSM.58
Ecthothas, CI.2.62
Egyrion, CI.2.37
El SSM.3
Elgybor, SSM.41
Eloon, SSM.53
Elscha, CI.2.28
Ely Deus, Latin, CI.2.4
Ely, SSM.33
Elyorem, CI.2.97
Elzephares, CI.2.36
Emanuel, Hebrew ("God with us"), CI.2.15
Epafgricus, SSM.47
Eryhona, CI.2.23
Eryon, CI.2.42
Eye assereye, SSM.69
Eye, SSM.57
Flemoyon, SSM.37
Fothon, CI.2.49
Gelemoht, CI.2.59
Gelon, CI.2.78
Genouem, CI.2.71
Geuer, SSM.21
Gofgamel, SSM.50
Gofgameli, CI.2.14
Gofgar, CI.2.95
Ha; SSM.0
Hel, CI.2.79
Heloy, Also on Seal of God, CI.2.98
Hely, Hebrew, CI.2.10
Hofbor, CI.2.34
Hofga, CI.2.55
Hofob, CI.2.20
Hombonar, CI.2.39
Honzmorb, CI.2.18
Horha, CI.2.92
Horlon, CI.2.11; *See also* Orlon
Hospesk, CI.2.94
Ianemyer, CI.2.8
Ihelur, CI.2.13
Ioht, CI.2.19
Ioth, SSM.12
Iuestre, CI.2.24

Jeremon, CI.2.33
Karex, CI.2.83
Kyrios, Greek ("Lord"), CI.2.77;
  Kyryos, SSM.34
Lamyara, CI.2.7
Lauagelaguyn, SSM.28
Lauaquyryn, SSM.20
Lauazyryn, SSM.54
Layafalasyn, SSM.68
Leiste, CI.2.31
Letamynyn, SSM.10
Letellethe, CI.2.50
Leyndra, CI.2.56
Maloht, CI.2.26
Maney, SSM.42
Maniyas [JV: Mamyas], SSM.40
Melthe, CI.2.66
Merkerpon, CI.2.35
Mesamarathon, CI.2.21
Messias, Hebrew ("savior"), CI.2.72
Monon (Monhon), CI.2.2
Narach, SSM.48
Nathanathay, CI.2.45; Nathanathoy,
  SSM.44
Nomygon, CI.2.88; SSM.62
Nomyx, SSM.24
Nosulaceps, CI.2.57; Nosulaseps,
  SSM.64
Nothi, CI.2.81
Noymos, CI.2.43
Occynnomos, CI.2.96
Occynomeryon, SSM.61;
  Occynoneryon, CI.2.61
Ocleiste, CI.2.5; Ocleyste, SSM.71
Omytheon, CI.2.54
On, Greek: "being", also used repeatedly
  on the Seal of God, CI.2.16; SSM.5
Onay, SSM.2
Onella, SSM.39
Onoytheon, SSM.23
Opiron, CI.2.87
Orihel, CI.2.89
Orion, CI.2.41
Oristion, CI.2.32; Oristyon, SSM.25

Orlon, SSM.66. *See also* Horlon
Oryona, SSM.63
Pantheon, CI.2.73; SSM.36
Paraclitus, Greek ("one who consoles
  or uplifts"), CI.2.60
Pep [*Pele?], CI.2.44
Pheta, CI.2.38
Porho, CI.2.48
Porrenthimon, CI.2.12
Quyesteron, SSM.13
Rabarmas, CI.2.75
Rabur, CI.2.100; SSM.52
Raby, SSM.6
Radix, SSM.30
Romolyon, SSM.46
Sabaoth, Hebrew ("of Hosts"),
  CI.2.84
Saday, Hebrew, Shaddai. Also on the
  Seal of God, CI.2.25
Sadyon, CI.2.9
Sampsoyny, SSM.17
Sanathyel, SSM.26
Sechce, CI.2.27
Sellah, CI.2.85
Sother, Greek ("savior"). Also on Seal
  of God, CI.2.67
Sporgongo, CI.2.70
Stimulamathon, CI.2.40
Suparyas, SSM.35
Tantalatysten, SSM.56
Techel, CI.2.80
Tetragramaton, Greek ("four
  lettered"), CI.2.3
Theon, Greek, CI.2.46
Theos, Greek ("God"), CI.2.90;
  SSM.1
Thetebar, SSM.18
Tucheon (JV: Tutheon), SSM.72.
  Compare Tutheon
Tunayon, SSM.14, SSM.60
Tutheon, CI.2.58. *Compare* Tucheon
Usirion, CI.2.68
Va, CI.2.91
Vabalganarytyn, SSM.27

Vagalnarytyn, SSM.49
Xρs [=Christus], SSM.4
Yalgal, SSM.15
Yaua, SSM.31
Ydardycon, SSM.70
Ye, SSM.67
Ymeynlethon, CI.2.82

Yschiros, Greek ("Strong"), CI.2.76
Ysiston, CI.2.47
Ysmas, CI.2.51
Ysyston, SSM.16
Yuestre, SSM.38
Zabuather, CI.2.74

General Index

Aaron (biblical prophet), 155n, 181, 221
Abraham, 155, 157, 165, 181
absolution of sins, 53, 195
abstinence, 16, 36, 183
Abulafia, 15
Adam (first man), 63, 105, 157, 161, 181
adamant stone, 59, 225
address to the angels, 223
adjuration of spirits, 267
Aemeth (*Heb.* Truth), 27
agreement, causing, 59, 225
Agrippa, Heinrich, 13, 35, 79n, 138n, 213n, 219n, 306, 307
Agrippa, Pseudo-, 231n-235n
air (element), 29; nature of the element, 227; purifying or causing pollution, 225
Alfonso X "El Sabio" of Castile, 18, 20-21
alms, 36, 125
altar, 131
amulets, 27, 28
anemoi (Greek wind gods), 34
angels of Jupiter, 213n; Saturn, 213n; of the hour, 209, 299; conjuration of, 217-219; placating, 219; good, 285; planetary, 213, 221; types of, 61; vision of, 61, and *passim*
anger, causing, 183, 201
animals, 55, 59, 61; gathering, 225; making them appear to be created, 277; to know, 199
answers from angels, 215
Apologias cathedrai, 21
Apostles Creed, 17
apostles, 135, 179, 185
appeasing people, 77
Aquilo (wind), 34
Aquinas, Thomas, 195n

Arabic, 21, 29n, 221, 251n; Arabic magic, 30n, 34
Arabs, 7
Arians, 63n
armies, illusion of, 275
Ars Almadel, 16
Ars Notoria, 12, 16, 24, 42-43, 91 ff, and *passim*
ashes, 39, 183
aspect (decan), 209, 211, 239
associates, 249, 257, 259, 265, 273, 275
Astromagia, 18
Athanasian Creed, 17
Athens, 13, 51
Augustinian friars of York, 8
Bacon, Pseudo-, 306
banquets, magical, 42
baptism, 49
bathing, 185, 187, 211
beasts, wild, 59; make appear, 225
beatific vision (devequt), 14-15, 23, 25, 53, 61, 77, 85, 87-195, 285
bed, 39, 183, 187n
beliefs, bending someone's, 205
Benedictine Order (Order of Saint Benedict), 17
Betz, Hans Dieter, 27n
binding of angels, 215-217; of spirits, 57, 61, 77, 183, 237
birds, 59; gathering, 225
blessing of the blood, 75; of the place, 209, 239
blood, 42, 73, 75, 287, 289; blessing, 297
bodies of angels, 199
body, fortification, 191
Bohak, Gideon, 22n
bonds of spirits, 269
Book of Angels (Liber de angelis) of Pseudo-Messahala, 18-20
Book of Life, 107

Book of Oberon, 32n, 79n, 85n, 171n, 177n, 264n, 269n
book, the physical *Sworn Book*, 51; consecration, 55
Boudet, Jean-Patrice, 7, 8n, 10-12, 17, 18n, 27n, 40, 43-44, 133n, 306-307
Bredin, Mark, 22n
Bremmer, Jan N., 27n
Bruno, Giordano, 8, 10n
buildings, seals from walls of, 28
burning, make appear, 225; causing, 231
Butler, E. M., 10
Byzantine, 15, 17-18, 21-22, 25; exorcism, 275n; magic, 32
candles, 36, 249, 295
Cardanus, 21
cardinal directions, 22, 29
Casanowicz, Immanuel Moses, 22n
Catholic Church, 12, *17*, 49, 51, 87, 89; faith, 189
celebacy, 145
censer, 36, 209, 245, 259, 263, 295
Chaldean, 125
chalk, 37
charcoal, 36-37, 209, 245, 259
Chardonnens, László, 8n, 10, 28, 31n
Charlesworth, 22n
chastity, 125, 129, 131, 183
choir, 187
Christ, 25, 37, 63, 81, 87
Christianity, 15-6; Western, 16; Christians, 63, 65, 283
church, 131, 209, 239, 249
circles, magic, 14-15, 22, 29-30, 33, 37, 39, 42, 215, 217n, 221, 239-245, 249, 257-259, 263-279, 295-299, 305; for invoking spirits of the earth, 283; for the spirit to appear in, 279, 281; constucting, 207
Clavicula Salomonis, 16; see also *Key of Solomon*
clay, 37-38, 207
cleanliness, 125, 129, 131, 173, 193, 223

colors for the Seal of God, 73
confession, 36, 123
confining spirits, 57, 223
conjuration of angels, 217-219
consecrating the book, 55, 95, 199, 223; of blood/ink, 291; of the Seal of God, 73-77
Consol (Cosol, i.e. Southeastern region), 29, 35, 235, 241, 243
constraining spirits, 223
corruption, 57; of the air, 225
council of masters, 51
Creed, *17*, 87
cross, 37, 297; sign of the, 221
crucifixion, 191
d'Astarac, Jean, 8
Dan, Joseph, 34n
dancing, 59n
danger, avoiding, 59, 77, 129, 183, 225
Daniel, biblical prophet, 63n, 181
date of text, 11-12
David, biblical prophet, 179, 183, 185, 193, 195
Davies, Owen, 7, 8n, 40n
day into night, changing, 223
De novem candariis, 16, 23n
De officiis spirituum, 16
De quattuor annulis, 16
dead bodies, 61; making them appear to rise and speak, 277
Dead Sea Scrolls, 34
death, 49-55; causing, 203, 231; contemplating death prohibited, 195; death, to know the hour, 197; of the soul, 133
decan, 209n, 211n, 239, 299
Dee, John, 8, 10, 22, 27, 40, 45, 219n, 306
Delatte, Louis, 17, 18n, 19-20
desire, arousing, 203, 225, 237
destruction, 57; causing, 203; mirror of, 225
dew, 57; causing or removing, 201, 203, 225

diet, 36, 125, 131, 173, 251
dignities, procure, 237
discord, causing, 59, 225, 233
divination, mirror or glass, 57
dogs, 59
Domican Order, 25
Dowd, Marr, 29n
dragons, 59; make appear, 225
dreams, 16, 36, 39, 125, 193
drinking, 259, 275
Driscoll, Daniel, 10, 43
Duling, 27
Dutch seal, 28
earth (element), 29; (soil), 37-38, 207
earthquakes, cause, 279
East (direction), 29-30, 203, 241, 243
eating, 185, 275
Egypt, 13, 181
elemental spirits, 285
elements, 55, 199; four, 29
Elijah, 181
Elisha, 289
enemies, destroying, 225; overcoming, 165; reconciling with, 235-237
English, 221
Enoch, 181
Enochian magic, 40
Escobar-Vargas, 12
eucharist, 133, 173, 175, 207, 209, 239
Euclid, father of Honorius, 13, 51
exorcism, 17, 21, 275n, 289, 291
exorcist, 277
Eymerich, 8
faith, 63, 111
Fanger, Claire, 7, 43, 63n
fasting, 36, 39, 75, 123, 125, 129, 131, 173, 175n, 183, 239, 291
favor, causing, 225; gaining, 59, 77; granting, 201
fear, 259
fire, 29, 249; protection from, 129; spirits of, 33, 55, 197
fish, 59; gathering, 225
Fitzer, G., 27n

flowers, 57; producing or removing, 201, 203, 225
Fludd, Robert, 35-36
form, imposing on spirits, 223
fortresses, 57, 59; magically creating, 225
friendship and favor of women, 235
frightening, 273, 275
Frigicap (Northwestern direction), 29, 35-36, 241, 245
frost, 57; causing, 225
fruit, 57; producing, 203, 225
future, reveal, 55, 65, 197, 205, 237
Galle, Griet, 223n
Ganell, Berengar, 11-12, 21, 23-28, 31n, 32, 34, 38-40, 45, 269n, 307. See also *Summa Sacre Magice*
gardens, 59; make appear, 225
garments, 22, 37, 79; black, 187; hemp, 211
Gehr, Damaris, 11, 20n, 36n
German manuscript (Leip. Cod. Mag. 16), 23, 30, 235n, 241n, 279n, 280n, 307
Germany, 17
Gertrude of Helfta, 17, 25
ghosts, 28
gift for spirits, 211, 215, 219, 221
Gilly, Carlos, 11n, 28, 45, 307n
girls, 59; make appear, 225
gladness, causing, 201, 235
glass, divination, 57
gloves, 22, 37, 77
gold, procuring, 229
Gollancz, Hermann, 133n
good will of people, procuring, 225, 229
Gospel, 63
Gower, John, 8
grace, 95, 133, 149, 159-169
Grand Grimoire, 40
gratitude, causing, 203, 229
Greece, 13, 15
greed, causing, 233
Greek, 15, 17, 21, 30, 34, 41, 65, 125,

221; language, 13; Greeks, 29n
Greek Magical Papyri (PGM), 27
Greenbaum, Dorian Gieseler, 29n
Greenfield, Richard, 22n, 32n
Greer, John Michael, 30n
Gregory the Great, 17, 195n
griffins, 59; make appear, 225
Grimoire of Pope Honorius, 40, 269n
Grimorium Verum, 27n
Grosseteste, 29n
Guerrero, Francisco, 83n
hair, 36, 211
hair shirt (sackcloth, cilice), 16, 187, 217
harm, cause, 279
hatred, causing, 233
hay, 183
hazel, 38-39
health, 77, 155, 183; bringing, 231, 235; guarding, 203
Hebrew, 15-16, 23, 30-31, 35, 37n, 65, 125, 211n, 215n, 217n
Hedegård, Gösta, 10-12, 14n, 17, 41, 42, 44, 67n, 91n, 95n, 127n, 138n, 142n, 144n, 163n, 177n, 216n, 218n, 221n, 249n, 254n, 260n, 264n, 266n, 269n, 271n, 272n, 274n, 280n, 282n, 284n, 291n, 298n, 306, 307
Hekalot Rabbati, 15
Hekaloth, 16
hell, 55, 191, 279, 299; vision of, 199
hemp, 37
Heptameron, 17, 19-21, 25n, 213n, 217n, 239n, 271n, 272n, 273n, 274n, 275n, 277n
herbs, 55; producing or removing, 201, 203; to know, 199
Herod, 189
hierarchy of angels, 17, 33, 55, 61, 65, 145, 175, 193, 197, 199, 271, 285, 289, 291, 299
honors, acquiring, 229
horses, 42, 57; making them fast, 225, 231

hostility of people and other beings, dissolving, 229
hours, 22
house, 295
human nature, 55; to know, 199
humility, 221
humors, 29
hunters, 59; make appear, 225
hyssop, 185
ice, causing, 201
Idel, Moshe, 15n
idols, 63
illness, cure or cause, 59, 183, 237
illusions, 49, 275
implements, ritual, 24, 36. See also, candles, incense, knife, sword, wand, whistle, etc.
imprisonment, hinder, 237; releasing from, 59
incense, 22, 36-37, 39, 75, 131, 209, 213, 245, 249, 259, 263, 279, 295
incitement, 57; inciting people against rulers, 225
influencing people, 201
ink, 15, 42; consecration, 287, 289
insanity, risk of, 195
invisibility, 57, 225
invocation of planetary angels, 213; of spirits, 265
Iroé-Grego, 9n
Isaac, 157
Islam, 63n
Jacob, 157, 165
Jerome, 79n
Jerusalem, 167, 189; facing, 289; heavenly, 155
jesters, make appear, 59, 225
jewels, procuring, 229
Jews, 7, 31, 63; magic, 30
John the Baptist, 185, 189
John the Evangelist, 191
John XXII, pope, 12
John, apostle, 141
Johnston, Sarah Iles, 27n

Jonah, 183
Jonson, Ben, 40n, 306
Joseph, 189
journeys, speeding, 205, 233
joy, causing, 201, 235
Judaism, 15-16, 22, 24
judge, favor of, 77, 129, 131, 237
Jupiter, 29, 201, 213n, 235
Kabbalah, 16, 24
Kappadokes, 32
Kassel, 45
Kelly, Edward, 22, 40
Key of Solomon, 8, 27n, 28, 173n. See also *Clavicula Salomonis*
Kieckhefer, Richard, 10-12, 16, 18, 21n, 26n, 42, 57n, 79n
killing, 59, 225, 233
Kircher, Athanasius, 28
Klaassen, Frank, 8n, 10, 22, 42n, 133n
kneeling, 213, 259, 271
knife, 37, 211
knowledge, 49, 95, 129, 131, 223, 237; of past, present, and future, 55, 65, 205; of the angels, 55; of the Heavens, 55; recover lost, 237; to obtain, 197
Latin (language), 15, 30, 221
laughter, causing, 203
laurel wood, 38
Lawrence-Mathers, 12
lawsuits, settle, 235
Lazarus, 191
lead (metal), procuring, 233
Leipzig University, 45
Levi, 9n
Liber Semiphoras, 16, 21
Liber Trium Animarum (LTA), 24
Lidaka, Juris, 18n, 43
lightning, 57; causing, 223; sign of spirits' presence, 231
limbs, maiming, 233
lime, 207
liturgical hours, 16
locks, opening, 59, 225, 237

Lord's Prayer, 91n
love, causing, 201, 203, 237
lust, causing, 203
luxury, causing, 237
Magi (three "kings"), 189
magus, meaning of the word, 65
Marathakis, Ioannis, 22n, 45, 275n
marriage, 237
Mars, 29, 33, 203, 231
Mary Magdalen, 165, 171, 189, 191
Mary, mother of James and Salome, 191
Mary, mother of Jesus, 81, 83, 85, 133, 171, 179, 189, 267
masses, 39, 61n, 91n, 125, 131, 133, 239, 291-295
Mathiesen, Robert, 7, 8n, 10-11, 17, 25
McCartney, 34n
McGraw, 34n
Medicine, 36
memory, 95, 107, 157, 205
Menuisier, Jean Michel, 8
Mercury, 29, 205, 237
Merkabah, 16, 24
Mesler, Katelyn, 10, 23, 24n, 39n, 42n, 63n, 79n, 299n
metals, precious, 59; procure, 237
Mézèieres, 8
miracles, 191; water into wine, 189
mirror of destruction, 57, 225; divination, 57
Moon, 29, 253, 271, 299
mortar, 38, 207
Moses, 65, 155, 181, 219
Munich handbook of necromancy (CLM 849), 18, 21n, 26, 42, 57n, 79n, 171n
murder, provoking, 203, 231
Museum of Witchcraft (Boscastle), 10
musical instruments, 275
nails of the cross, 65, 83
names of God, erasing, 245, 257, 297
names of Mary, 85-87
names of saints, 33

Naples, 13, 51
necromancy (nigromancy), 18, 49, 133n
Netherlands, 28
night into day, changing, 197
Noah, 181
Nogahel (Nogahem), 29, 35, 235, 241, 243
North (direction), 30, 201, 241, 245; Northeast (direction), 29; Northwest region, 205
notae, 141n
oath, 51
offices of angels, 197, 199
Orthodox Christianity, 17, 22
pagans, 63, 283
Page, Sophie, 306
palace, heavenly, 16, 173, 189, 193
paper, 37-38, 243
Paradise, 85, 181
parchment, 15, 37, 73, 295
Paul, apostle, 141, 165, 191
pearls, 209
penance, 149, 173
pentagram (pentalpha), 27
Pépin, Olivier, 7
Peter of Auvergne, 223n
Peterson, Joseph, 21n, 22n, 27n, 40n, 43, 211n, 219n
petition or question, 211, 285; altering, 195
Petrus de Abano, 13, 17, 18n, 21, 23n, 30, 213n, 223n, 275n
phantasms, 28
Picatrix, 18, 30n
pit, 299
placating of spirits, 219, 273; the Divine Majesty, 175
place, preparation of the, 243
plague, causing, 231; biblical, 65
planets, classical ("wandering stars"), 29-30, 55, 201 ff, 213, 243; to know, 197; planetary correspondences, 16; divinities, 34

plants, 55; to know, 199
pleasures, 59; make appear, 225
pollution of the air, 225
pope, 12, 49, 193n
Postles, 215n
poverty, 36, 38, 183, 207; cause, 237
Practica Nigromanciae, 306
prayer, 36, 39 and *passim*
Preface of the Apostles, 291
prelates, 49
priests, 17, 37, 39, 131, 133, 239, 291; priesthood, 177n
prison, freeing someone from, 277; unlocking, 59
prophets, 63
protection, 129, 131; from evil, 77
psalter, 175, 187
Pseudo-Dionysius, 17, 25, 33
Ptolomy, 30
Purgatory, 17, 53, 55, 195, 285, 299; vision of, 199
purification, 57, 111, 153, 165, 239; first, 127-133; second, 173; prayers of, 223; of the air, 225
purity, 36, 75, 145
quarrels, settle, 235
questions put to angels, 215
rain, 57; causing, 205, 225
raising up winds, 245
Raziel, 16, 18, 20, 32, 42, 211n
redaction, 254n
redemption of mankind, 189; of souls from Purgatory, 195, 285
repentance, 123
resurrection, 191
Rituale Romanum (Roman Ritual), 79n
river, 57; producing, 225
Robbins, Frank Egleston, 30n
Roberts, Julian, 40n, 306n
Royal manuscript, 21, 287n
rulers (royalty), 57
sacraments, 65, 77, 145, 153, 173, 239, 301
sadness, causing, 201

saints, 33, 77, 131, 135, 157, 171
salt, blessing of, 17; exorcism of, 289
salvation, 77, 89, 151
sand, 207
Saturn, 29, 201, 213n, 233
Scholem, 19n, 34, 251n
Schwartz, Dov, 15n
Schwartz, Michael D., 15n, 25n
Scotus, Michael, 21
Seal of God (Seal of Solomon, *Signum Dei, Sigillum Dei*), 8-9, 16n, 23, 27, 32, 37, 39-40, 61, 65-75, 183n, 201n, 213, 217, 221, 243, 251, 259, 263, 267, 271, 275-291, 295, 297, 304
seals, magic, 14, 25-26, 37, 57, 197, 259; of angels, 41, 55; of archangels, 17-18; of daemons/spirits, 199; of spirits, 24, 223, 257, 295; of spirits (spoken), 215, 269; of the air (physical), 295; of the earth (physical), 295; of the earth (spoken), 281; of Solomon, 15, 42, 273
seat of Apologia, of, Primachia, and of Samaym, 39. *See also* throne
seclusion, 187
secrecy, 7
secret, revealing, 205, 231, 271
seeing spirits, 129
Shamayim (Heb. Heaven), 16, 211n, 215n
shaving, 36, 211
Shem ha-Meforash, 16, 23, 31, 53, 65, 287, 289
ships, 59; detaining, 225
shirt, hair (cilice), 37
Sibylline Oracles, 22
sickness, 77; causing, 231, 235; curing or causing, 225, 237
sign of the cross, 221
signs that the spirits are present, 34, 229, 231, 233, 235, 237, 239, 277, 279, 297
Sigo of St. Florent de Saumur, Abbott, 221n

silver, procuring, 231, 237
Simeon, 189
Simon of Faversham, 223n
Sixth and Seventh Books of Moses, 16n
Skemer, 31n
sleep, 125, 193; sleep visions, 39
snow, 57; causing, 201, 225
Sodom and Gomorrah, 181
soldiers, 57, 59; fighting, make appear, 225; magically producing, 225, 231
Solomon, King, 15, 27, 38, 41-42, 53, 61, 75, 77, 79, 141, 173, 189, 211n, 213, 217, 227, 271-275, 289; pentagonal figure of, 297
Solomonic magic, 16, 27, 30, 41-42
souls, knowledge of, 199
South (direction), 29, 33, 203, 241, 243; southeast (region), 201; southwest (region), 201, 205
Spain, 28
spheres of the planets, 217-221
spirits, 33-34 and *passim*; adjuration, 267; of the air, 23, 223 ff, 227 ff, 285; appearance, 279; aquatic, 55, 199; Consol, 235; of the earth, 23, 55, 277 ff, 285; East, 229; elemental, 33, 285; Frigicap, 237; infernal, 55; Jupiter, 201, 251; Mars, 203; Mercury, 205; Moon, 205; Nogahem, 235; Northern, 229, 233; Northwest, 237; placating, 273; Saturn, 201; seeing and conversing with, 129; Southern, 229, 231; Southeast, 235; Southwest, 235; Sun, 203, 229, 251, 255; Venus, 203, 205; West, 231
staff of Aaron, 181
staff of Joseph, 189
staff, magic, 38, 259n
standing, 273
star, 27; stars, 55, 199; to know, 197
Stephen, Saint, 191
stole (garment), 37, 291
stolen goods, recovering, 225
stones, 37-38, 207; precious, 27, 59

stools, 38, 257
storms, 183; controlling, 59, 225
students, 51, 53
subjugating earthly and infernal creatures, 219
suffering, 175n, 193
suffumigation, 15, 57, 209, 213, 245, 249, 259, 279. See also incense
sulfur, 279
Summa Sacre Magice, 11, 23, 27n, 28, 30, 31n, 32n, 34, 37n, 39, 40, 63n, 74-75, 131n, 175n, 177n, 178n, 183n, 186n, 187n, 191n, 193n, 201n, 203n, 207n, 209n, 211n, 213n, 214n, 215n, 216n, 217n, 218n, 219n, 221n, 225n, 235n, 241n, 242n, 243n, 244n, 245n, 247n, 251n, 254n, 257n, 259n, 260n, 261n, 262n, 263n, 266n, 268n, 269n, 270n, 271n, 272n, 273n, 274n, 279n, 280n, 307
Sun, 29-30, 203, 251
Susanna, 183
swords, magic, 33, 35, 38, 42, 249, 257-263, 269, 271, 295, 297
Synaxis icon, 22n
tables, for constraining spirits, 57, 223
tablets of Moses, 65
Talmud, 34
Tartar cathedra, 21
temple of Solomon, 189
temptation of Jesus, 189
termini, eight, 115-123, 197
Testament of Solomon, 27, 34
Theban alphabet, 13-14
Thebes, 11, 13, 40, 51, 299
theft, causing, 233-235
Theodoric of Freiberg, 25
Thesaurus Spirituum, 32, 42, 306, 307n
thieves, 57
Thomas, apostle, 191
Thorndike, Lynn, 10, 18n, 133n
thoughts, evil, causing, 233
throne, seat of Samaym, 211, 215, 219, 221; spirit, 39, 42

thunder, 57; causing, 223; sign of spirits' presence, 231
tiles, 38, 207; for petitions, 281
times, 197
tin, procuring, 237
Tobit, 34
Toledo, 13, 51
topics, 195, 197
Tot Grecus (Toz Grecus), 31n
transfiguration, 57, 225; cause, 237
transmutation of elements, 199
transmute bodies, 237
transporting, 57; absent person, 225; goods, 225, 231
treasons, causing, 231
treasure, 59, 277, 279
Trithemius, Johannes, 8, 13
Tzerentzes, 32
University of Paris, 8
Veenstra, Jan, 8n, 10, 12, 14n, 16n, 23, 25n, 27n, 28, 31n, 39n, 63n, 131n, 177n, 211n
Velimirovic, Nikolai, 22n
Venus, 29, 203, 205, 237, 253
Véritable magie noire, La, 9, 28
Véronèse, Julien, 8n, 43-44
victory, cause, 237
Vinculum Salomonis, 23
virtue, causing, 203
visions, 275
Waite, A.E., 9-10, 306
wand (laurel or hazel), 14, 33, 38, 42, 259-263, 297
war, causing, 203, 231; war, inciting between people, birds, fish, or animals, 225
Warnock, Christopher, 30n
water, 29, 185, 187; spirits of, to know, 199
Watson, Andrew G., 40n, 306n
wax, 36
weaknesses, granting or taking away, 229

wealth, 36, 77; causing, 203, 225; gaining, 59, 229, 237
West (direction), 29-30, 205, 241, 243
whistle, magic, 33, 38, 42, 273, 277, 295, 297
Wicca, 14
Wilkinson, Robert J., 221n
will, bending someone's, 205
William of Auvergne, 7, 11-12
winds, 29, 34-36, 41, 201-205, 227-237, 249, 251, 265, 267; st, 205; raising up, 245, 257, 295
wine, 39, 249, 251, 295
witchcraft (modern), 14
women, 51; causing desire in, 225; friendship and favor of, 235; gaining desire of, 59; inciting love in, 203; isolation from, 77
words, magic, 57
Young, 287n
youth, recover, 237
Zebedee, 211, 217, 219
zephyr, 34

IBIS PRESS
Titles of Related Interest by Joseph Peterson

The Clavis or Key to the Magic of Solomon
From an Original Talismanic Grimoire in Full Color
by Ebenezer Sibley and Frederick Hockley
With Extensive Commentary by Joseph Peterson

ISBN: 978-089254-159-1
400 Pages, 7.5" x 9". Hardcover
$95.00.

The Sixth and Seventh Books of Moses
Joseph Peterson
Includes 8 pages of color seals!

ISBN: 978-0-89254-130-0
368 Pages, 7" x 10". Hardcover
$55.00.

Arbatel: Concerning the Magic of the Ancients
Original Sourcebook of Angel Magic
Newly translated from the original Latin
edited & annotated by Joseph Peterson

ISBN: 978-0-89254-152-2
128 Pages, 6" x 9". Paperback.
$35.00